MICROSOFT® CERTIFIED SOLUTION DEVELOPER

MCSD Analyzing Requirements and Defining .NET Solution Architectures Study Guide

(Exam 70-300)

Scott Duffy
David Waddleton

McGraw-Hill/Osborne

New York Chicago San Francisco Lisbon London Madrid
Mexico City Milan New Delhi San Juan Seoul Singapore Sydney Toronto

The McGraw·Hill Companies

McGraw-Hill/Osborne
2100 Powell Street, 10th Floor
Emeryville, California 94608
U.S.A.

To arrange bulk purchase discounts for sales promotions, premiums, or fund-raisers, please contact **McGraw-Hill**/Osborne at the above address. For information on translations or book distributors outside the U.S.A., please see the International Contact Information page immediately following the index of this book.

MCSD Analyzing Requirements and Defining .NET Solution Architectures Study Guide (Exam 70-300)

1234567890 FGR FGR 019876543

Book p/n 0-07-212584-5 and CD p/n 0-07-212585-3
parts of ISBN 0-07-212586-1

Publisher Brandon A. Nordin	**Acquisitions Coordinator** Jessica Wilson	**Indexer** Valerie Robbins
Vice President **& Associate Publisher** Scott Rogers	**Technical Editor** Kenneth Lind	**Computer Designers** Carie Abrew, Tara A. Davis
	Copy Editor Emily Rader	**Illustrators** Kathleen Fay Edwards, Melinda
Acquisitions Editor Nancy Maragioglio		Moore Lytle, Lyssa Wald
	Proofreader Robin Small	
Project Editor Patty Mon		**Series Design** Roberta Steele

This book was composed with Corel VENTURA™ Publisher.

DEDICATION

My wife, Liez'l. You inspire me to do greater things.

My parents. You set me on the right course in life, for which I am eternally grateful.

—Scott Duffy

This book is dedicated to my wife, Vicki, and my children, Ashley, Bethany, and Samuel. Thanks for allowing me to take this time away from you to write this book and fulfill a dream. I would like to thank my grandparents, Joe and Evelyn Waddleton, who set the standards for the rest of us to follow.

—David Waddleton

ABOUT THE CONTRIBUTORS

About the Authors

Scott Duffy has been providing IT consulting services to medium- and large-sized organizations for more than six years. His 12 years of professional experience covers a wide range of platforms and technologies, including programming in mainframe, client-server, and web-based application environments. He is actively involved in every stage of the software development process, including leading the development efforts. When he's not designing software applications for clients, Scott keeps himself busy with his writing projects.

To contact Scott to discuss your organization's business needs, or about any other matter, please e-mail him at scott.duffy@mydemos.com or visit his web site at http://www.mydemos.com.

David Waddleton began his career as a software developer at a small consulting company after receiving a degree in B.S. in Computer Science at Ouachita Baptist University. He has written software ranging from automating machinery to complex e-commerce sites. He has been developing software for the last 11 years. He currently works as an independent contractor and is the owner of Daviton Technologies, Inc. (http://www.we-learn.net), a small consulting company providing consulting and training services. He has obtained the following certifications: Visual Studio 6 Microsoft Certified Solutions Developer (MCSD), Microsoft Certified Professional (MCP), and Microsoft Certified Trainer (MCT). He spends his free time with his wife and kids. He can be reached as DavidWaddleton@hotmail.com.

About the Technical Editor

Kenneth S. Lind, MCSD, MCAD, MCSE+I, MCSE, MCP+SB, MCT, and CTT+, is an independent training consultant and author working out of Toronto, Ontario. Kenneth has over 20 years experience in software development and has developed applications using C, FORTRAN, C++, Java, VB, C#, and assembler. Kenneth left his native Sweden after receiving an engineering degree in telecommunication, a move he never regretted. Kenneth has specialized in object-oriented (OO) development and its use in Java and C++. His most recent project has been coauthorship of a certification study guide for C# .NET published by McGraw-Hill/Osborne. Kenneth can be reached at KennethSLind@hotmail.com.

About LearnKey

LearnKey provides self-paced learning content and multimedia delivery solutions to enhance personal skills and business productivity. LearnKey claims the largest library of rich streaming-media training content that engages learners in dynamic media-rich instruction complete with video clips, audio, full motion graphics, and animated illustrations. LearnKey can be found on the Web at www.LearnKey.com.

CONTENTS AT A GLANCE

CONTENTS

Part II
Designing the Solution 209

6 Conceptual Design **249**

7 Logical Design **285**

ACKNOWLEDGMENTS

If at first you don't succeed, try, try, again. Then quit.
No use being a damn fool about it.

—W. C. Fields

I very much appreciate the efforts of everyone who was involved in getting this book published. I owe a great debt of gratitude to many people:

- Nancy Maragioglio, Patty Mon, Jessica Wilson, and all the fine people at McGraw-Hill/Osborne. This book really would not exist in any usable form without their expertise.
- David Waddleton, my coauthor. Thanks David.
- Ken Lind, my technical editor. Thanks for all your efforts.
- Emily Rader, my copy editor. You did an excellent job turning my gibberish into actual English sentences.
- Jawahara Saidullah, my agent at Waterside Productions.
- And last but not least, my wife Liez'l. Thank you sweetheart, for your patience and perseverance while I was sequestered in my office writing this. I owe you so much.

—Scott Duffy

For me this book would not have been possible without the support of my wife, Vicki. Thank you for your time and patience, and for waking me up from my study sessions. I would like to also thank my children Ashley, Bethany, and Samuel for being patient and understanding. My appreciation goes out to Nancy and Jessica for their guidance and direction during the editing process. I would especially like to thank my parents, Dr Donald and Irma Waddleton, for giving me the encouragement needed to reach for my goals and persevere in order to achieve them.

—David Waddleton

Τhis book was written to assist you in preparing for and passing the Analyzing and Defining Microsoft® .NET Solution Architecture exam (Exam 70-300). The text and exercises were created to help familiarize you with the topics you will be tested on during the actual exam.

In This Book

While this book is designed to be a focused exam preparation tool, in it you will also find discussion of the theory and methodologies behind working with the .NET Framework. The hands-on exercises were designed to give you additional experience with the .NET Framework while reinforcing your understanding of the concepts.

In Every Chapter

The Study Guide series contains a number of chapter elements that were designed to help you identify important items, to reinforce key points, and to offer expert tips for taking the exam. Each chapter contains the following:

- **Certification Objectives** Each chapter begins with a listing of the exam objectives that will be covered in the chapter.

- **Exam Watch** These are tips designed to help you focus your studies on areas that will be important for the exam.

- **Practice Exercises** Hands-on experience is a key factor to success on exam day, and these practice exercises are designed to help you reinforce your skills. It's important that you work through these exercises rather than simply reading them, so that you increase your exposure to and familiarity with the .NET Framework.

- **On the Job** Designed to let you benefit from our experience, this element provides insights into the practical application of the theories presented in the text.

■ **Scenarios & Solutions**   This element introduces you to common real-life situations that you may encounter on the job and provides you with a quick solution.

SCENARIO & SOLUTION

To store a small amount of noncritical user data in an ASP.NET application,…	Use browser cookies.
To store data that rarely changes in memory so that all sessions in an ASP.NET application can have quicker access to it,…	Use a Cache object.
To handle more than just a few concurrent users in your ASP.NET application,…	Do *not* use the Session object.
To store data that rarely changes in memory so that all applications running on the server in ASP.NET can have quicker access to it,…	Use the Application object.

■ **The Certification Summary**   This is a general review of the material that was presented in the chapter. These summaries provide a quick-review option prior to taking the exam.

■ **The Two-Minute Drill**   At the end of every chapter, you will find a listing of the key objective points from the chapter. These are great as a final review study tool.

■ **The Self Test**   Our self-assessment section presents questions similar to those you'll find on the actual exam; it is designed to help you identify those areas in which you may need additional study. Complete answers with explanations are located at the end of each chapter.

On the CD-ROM

This book includes a CD-ROM with simulation assessment software containing practice test questions that are found *only* on the CD-ROM.

PDF versions of the chapters from the book are also available on the CD-ROM. Please be aware, though, that the PDFs are not always the final versions of the chapters and that slight differences may appear between the PDF and printed versions.

For more information about the CD-ROM, please see Appendix A.

Welcome to *MCSD Analyzing Requirements and Defining .NET Solution Architectures Study Guide (Exam 70-300)*. The authors have written this book to help prepare you for the Analyzing and Defining Microsoft® .NET Solution Architectures exam. As you're preparing for your MCSD, this book will guide you through the key points of each of the exam objectives.

The MCSD Program

Candidates for the MCSD certification are typically lead developers who design and develop leading-edge enterprise solutions with Microsoft development tools, technologies, platforms, and the Microsoft .NET Framework. Microsoft recommends that the MCSD candidate have at least two years of experience in developing and maintaining applications before attempting the certification.

MCSD Certification Requirements

Achieving the MCSD certification requires passing four core exams and one elective exam. The core exams are listed in the following box.

MCSD CORE EXAMS
Solution Architecture Exam (Required) Exam 70-300: Analyzing Requirements and Defining .NET Solution Architectures
Web Application Development Exams (One Required) Exam 70-305: Developing and Implementing Web Applications with Microsoft Visual Basic .NET and Microsoft Visual Studio .NET Or Exam 70-315: Developing and Implementing Web Applications with Microsoft Visual C# .NET and Microsoft Visual Studio .NET

MCSD CORE EXAMS
Windows Application Development Exams (One Required) **Exam 70-306:** Developing and Implementing Windows-based Applications with Microsoft Visual Basic .NET and Microsoft Visual Studio .NET Or **Exam 70-316:** Developing and Implementing Windows-based Applications with Microsoft Visual C# .NET and Microsoft Visual Studio .NET
Web Services and Server Components Exams (One Required) **Exam 70-310:** Developing XML Web Services and Server Components with Microsoft Visual Basic .NET and the Microsoft .NET Framework Or **Exam 70-320:** Developing XML Web Services and Server Components with Microsoft Visual C# and the Microsoft .NET Framework

In addition to the core exams, you must pass one of the following elective exams:

- **Exam 70-229:** Designing and Implementing Databases with Microsoft SQL Server 2000, Enterprise Edition

- **Exam 70-230:** Designing and Implementing Solutions with Microsoft BizTalk Server 2000 Enterprise Edition

- **Exam 70-234:** Designing and Implementing Solutions with Microsoft Commerce Server 2000

exam
ⓦatch

For the latest information on available exams, visit www.microsoft.com/traincert. Exams are subject to change without notice, so be sure to check this site frequently as you prepare for your exam.

Exam Credit

When you pass Exam 70-300, you immediately achieve the status of Microsoft Certified Professional (MCP) and earn core credit toward your MCSD certification.

Skills Being Measured

You can view the complete set of skills being measured at the MCSD web site, at www.microsoft.com/traincert/mcp/mcsd/requirements.asp. According to Microsoft, the following is a quick summary of what you'll be faced with on the exam.

Performance-Based vs. Knowledge-Based Questions

The exam questions fall into two broad categories, knowledge-based and performance-based. Knowledge-based questions are designed to test your knowledge of specific facts. Performance-based questions are designed to measure your ability to perform on the job by presenting examples of situations and scenarios that a developer might encounter in the real world.

- **Free response items** Traditional multiple-choice items, these questions are designed to test your basic knowledge of facts.
- **Case study–based items** Designed to simulate what situations developers actually encounter on the job, these questions test your ability to analyze information and make decisions.

You should take advantage of the sample questions available for download from the Exam and Testing Procedures Web page at www.microsoft.com/traincert/mcpexams/faq/procedures.asp.

Signing Up

To schedule your exam, call any Sylvan Prometric or VUE center. Online registration is also available through the Register for an Exam web page at www.microsoft.com/traincert/mcpexams/register. This site gives you information about the registration process and provides locations for testing centers near you.

Part I

Determining a Solution

MCSD
MICROSOFT® CERTIFIED SOLUTION DEVELOPER

1

Understanding the .NET Framework

W hen you get right down to the most basic level of development, the primary goal of software design is quite simple. When you think about it, the only thing that *really* matters is that the software you're developing does what the user needs it to do. If a hospital needs a program that can store and retrieve patient information, then that's all you need to worry about. Every other design consideration is secondary to fulfilling the business requirements.

Unfortunately, it is not that simple. There are many other things the software designer needs to worry about. For instance, have the client's requirements been understood correctly? What about other considerations, such as application performance, security, and availability? What type of computer hardware does the client have or need? What else is the client likely to want to do with the data in the future?

Analyzing the business requirements and designing the proper solution is perhaps the most important task in software development. A good design will make a program easier to support and enhance as requirements change. It will allow the program to grow as the business grows, almost without limit. A bad design will make a program impossible to support and maintain, and will place severe limits on the application's usefulness as a business gets larger.

As programming has evolved, so, too, have software design practices. Each new programming methodology has created a paradigm shift in how software designers are required to design programs. There are four major programming methodologies:

- **Unstructured**   A program that is executed sequentially
- **Procedural**   A program that uses functions to perform certain tasks
- **Modular**   A program that is split across multiple files to group related functionality together
- **Object-oriented**   A program that uses classes and objects to group related data and functionality together

Not surprisingly, good software design is much more important for programs that are developed using an object-oriented methodology than for programs developed using an unstructured one. Unstructured programming requires the least forethought and planning, while object-oriented programming requires the most.

The Microsoft MCSD 70-300 exam *Analyzing Requirements and Defining .NET Solution Architectures* covers several important software design skills that are used when developing programs for the .NET environment:

- Envisioning the solution
- Gathering and analyzing business requirements
- Developing specifications
- Creating the conceptual design
- Creating the logical design
- Creating the physical design
- Creating standards and processes

These skills represent the basis of good software design in an object-oriented environment. Even software designers who work in programming environments other than .NET will benefit from learning them, although some of the required skills for the exam are specific to the challenges and advantages of working in the .NET environment.

The rest of this chapter is an introduction to Microsoft .NET and the .NET Framework. It is important for software designers to have a good understanding of .NET before they can begin thinking about the proper conceptual and logical design for a program. The knowledge acquired in this chapter will provide a solid foundation on which the rest of the book will be based.

OBJECTIVE 1.01

Introducing .NET

Microsoft .NET is Microsoft's set of next-generation software technologies that allow people, computer systems, and devices to communicate with one another in ways never before possible. In many ways, .NET is more of a revolution than an evolution. In one giant step, Microsoft has changed the way software development teams think about how software applications are supposed to work.

Microsoft formally released the .NET platform in January 2002, primarily as a way to develop applications that can easily communicate over the Internet. In particular, .NET was designed to make it easier to develop a new type of application called web services.

author's note *Microsoft maintains an extensive collection of .NET-related resources and articles on its web site at http://www.microsoft.com/net. The site contains links to both business and technical resources. Microsoft also maintains a site for the .NET developer community at http://www.gotdotnet.com.*

The .NET platform is made up of a collection of new and enhanced Microsoft technologies:

- **Visual Studio .NET** An integrated development environment (IDE) for creating .NET applications
- **.NET Framework and .NET Compact Framework** The runtime environments for building, deploying, and running .NET applications
- **.NET Enterprise Servers** The Windows family of server operating systems and server products such as Exchange and SQL Server
- **Smart clients** A range of devices that can consume web services and run .NET applications such as Windows XP or CE

In this section, we will examine why designing applications for .NET is different than designing applications under the Win32 API and COM programming models, and how XML web services represents a new way of designing distributed applications.

The .NET Paradigm

The dictionary defines a *paradigm* as a set of concepts, assumptions, and practices that constitutes a way of viewing a particular topic. Before the introduction of .NET, the common paradigm for developing Windows applications involved using technologies such as Component Object Model (COM) for software components, Distributed COM (DCOM) for distributed applications, Microsoft Transaction Server/COM+ (MTS/COM+) for managing transactions, Active Server Pages (ASP) for web-based applications, and ActiveX Data Objects (ADO) for database access.

This old paradigm for developing distributed applications was called the Windows DNA (Distributed Internet Applications Architecture). The Windows DNA was originally introduced as a scalable architecture for developing distributed web and *n*-tier applications. However, over the years, the needs of distributed applications have passed the limits of the original DCOM model defined more than five years ago.

The new paradigm for developing applications involves class libraries for software components, web services and .NET remoting for distributed applications, COM+ for managing transactions, ASP.NET for web-based applications, and ADO .NET for database access. (.NET remoting is a powerful set of .NET framework classes that allows developers to access remote applications through a variety of different methods. .NET remoting is briefly discussed in this chapter's "From the Classroom" section.) Some of the technology may sound the same, but developers will see significant changes in the way these technologies are used.

on the
job

Over the past seven or eight years, billions of dollars have been invested worldwide in developing applications for the old Windows DNA infrastructure (COM and MTS). .NET has been available in beta form since late 2000 and as a final product since early 2002, but conversion to .NET has been understandably slow. This is primarily due to the amount of work and cost involved in upgrading existing systems and applications for hard-to-describe immediate benefits. In fact, many companies are still developing new applications under the old model because their .NET infrastructure is not yet in place.

The .NET platform solves many of the problems software developers face every day and should make developing software easier and more enjoyable. Figure 1-1 shows how applications connect to the operating system (and to each other) through the .NET platform.

You will still find traces of the old DNA paradigm in .NET. In fact, .NET applications have the ability to connect and interact with COM components, which make transitioning to .NET easier. But the fact remains that the COM/DCOM model of programming has definitely been replaced in the .NET world.

What Was Wrong with COM/DCOM?

The old paradigm was based on using Microsoft's COM object model for interprocess communication. There was nothing inherently wrong with using COM objects to create distributable components. In fact, they were quite easy to create using a language that did most of the work for you, such as Visual Basic—let's not talk about C++, though. They were also quite easy to use.

Of course, there were some circumstances where COM was not particularly well suited. For instance, calling an object that resided on a different server across a network was not easy to set up. And if the network was slow and unreliable (such as the Internet), it was impossible.

FIGURE 1-1

.NET acts as a middleware component between the application and Windows.

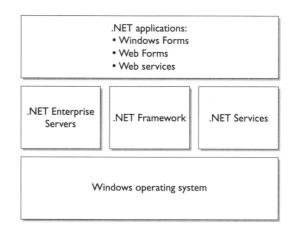

Also, despite COM's popularity, it remained a Microsoft-only technology. An attempt to port DCOM to Unix did not go very far. Because more than 70 percent of the web servers on the Internet use operating systems other than Windows (such as Unix), this meant another solution had to be found.

Why Is .NET Better than COM/DCOM?

In some ways, comparing the Windows DNA architecture to .NET is like comparing apples to apple trees. Microsoft has spent considerable time and effort attempting to improve the good things about the old platform and fix some of the fundamental problems. For example, developers working in .NET can still develop COM components, but they are not limited to COM. That allows you to choose better ways of developing components, such as class libraries and web services, depending on the circumstances.

One of the biggest problems with the DCOM method for distributed application development is that the client computer needs to be specially configured to connect to the server component. This involves setting up proxies, stubs, and registry settings on the client machine. This configuration is not just necessary for the first remote component, it is required for each remote component. In short, the complex deployment model for DCOM applications is this method's biggest weakness.

Using an XML web service, on the other hand, requires no special client configuration. Since web services are generally accessed over the Internet using standard technologies like Hypertext Transfer Protocol (HTTP), Extensible Markup

Language (XML), and Simple Object Access Protocol (SOAP), most clients already have all that is required to connect to a web service; and adding additional web services requires no additional configuration on the client side.

There is also the problem of security and firewalls when trying to develop an application over a public network such as the Internet. Most systems administrators allow open access to only a few ports through the company firewall. All other ports are generally blocked for security purposes, which means applications that use these nonstandard ports will not operate from behind the firewall.

Employees of large corporations experience the effects of this when they attempt to use applications such as MSN Messenger and ICQ. These applications have trouble making it past secure firewalls. However, if those applications were instead designed to access the network using XML and SOAP over HTTP, they would generally have no trouble accessing the Internet.

COM components have some other shortcomings as well. For instance, it is very difficult to implement versioning in COM. *Versioning* is a technique that is used to allow more than one version of a particular software component to be installed on a computer at the same time.

In COM, trying to provide an upgrade to a widely used component will likely cause many applications that rely on that component to break. It is often better to create a completely new component, with a new name, than attempt to upgrade an existing one. Even Microsoft was prone to this versioning headache, as evidenced by the many versions of ADO it has created over the years—1.0, 1.5, 2.0, 2.1, and 2.5. The mixture of system files required to support this many versions on the same machine is evidence of the problem that versioning created in the past.

.NET provides a much better way to implement versioning. The two key features that support this in .NET are application isolation and side-by-side execution. *Application isolation* is the idea that installing a new application on your machine should not affect an existing application. For example, with application isolation, if a new application installs version 2.0 of some important component, other applications that rely on version 1.0 of that component will not be affected.

Side-by-side execution is the concept that those two versions of the same component can be installed and functioning on the same machine. If you want to upgrade your existing applications to use a new version of a component, you must manually configure them to do so. Otherwise, the default behavior is to continue to use the old version.

What New Features and Benefits Does .NET Provide?

We have already seen how .NET compares with the old Windows DNA way of designing and developing applications. In addition to the improvements in that area, .NET also provides developers with several important new benefits and features:

- A fully object-oriented programming environment, including the mandatory use of .NET Framework

- A Common Type System (CTS) instead of language-specific data types

- An environment where memory and other system resources are managed by the system and not by the application

- An environment where all the programming languages can interoperate seamlessly

- An environment where all programming languages have similar runtime performance

- With Windows Server 2003, the ability to turn existing COM components into web services without having to recompile them

- The ability to add .NET Framework components to a COM+ application to take advantage of transactions, object pooling, queued components, and events

- Application partitions, which allow you to have two or more copies of the same application to run on the same computer with different configurations

- An escape from "DLL hell," allowing different versions of the same dynamic link library (DLL) to run on the same machine

Of course, there is no application environment that can be all things to all people. There will always be developers who feel more comfortable working in a C++ environment, just as there are developers today who still write programs directly in machine code. Any programming language or environment that makes things easier for developers also often restricts them a bit. For example, a C++ application that runs directly on the operating system is generally responsible for allocating memory its own data storage area in memory. When it has finished using the memory, the application is supposed to release the data storage area for other applications to use. Sometimes an application mistakenly forgets to release memory it no longer needs, a condition known as a *memory leak*.

When a .NET application attempts to use a component for the first time, the .NET Framework allocates and assigns memory for that component. When the application has exited or indicates that it no longer needs the component, the .NET Framework knows that it can release the memory used by that component. This process runs automatically in the background and is called *garbage collection.*

Garbage collection happens automatically behind the scenes and cannot be called directly by .NET applications. If you are creating and destroying objects rapidly—thousands of times per second—your application could consume an enormous amount of computer memory before the garbage collection kicks in. There is no way to avoid this with managed code.

There will be some developers who still prefer to allocate and deallocate their own memory, not wanting to rely on the system to handle those functions. Such developers can continue to create unmanaged code (such as traditional COM components) that can interoperate with .NET applications, marrying the old technology with the new.

COM and .NET Compatibility

Despite the obvious shift from creating applications in the old Windows DNA environment to creating applications in the new .NET environment, Microsoft realizes that many companies have large investments in COM components and applications. As we will see, COM components and .NET assemblies are fundamentally different technologies, but there is a way to make the old and new technologies work together.

.NET applications can call COM components as long as those components have been converted using a runtime callable wrapper (RCW). As its name implies, an RCW allows the .NET runtime—the Common Language Runtime (CLR)—to call the COM object inside the wrapper. The COM object will still run outside the .NET environment as unmanaged code, but the .NET application will treat it like any other .NET-compatible component.

In addition, 32-bit Windows applications can call .NET components, as long as these components have been converted into COM objects by using a COM callable wrapper (CCW). The CCW allows .NET components to be hosted inside a COM-compatible environment, such as Visual Basic 6.0 or MTS/COM+.

Things to Be Aware of when Choosing .NET

Choosing to convert an existing application to .NET is not a trivial task. First, you cannot expect to be able to create a .NET application using the same programming language you used to create the old application. More than likely, the syntax of the language you were using has changed quite a bit due to the new .NET way of doing things. For instance, it is often said that Visual Basic .NET (or just VB .NET, for short) is almost a totally different language than its Visual Basic 6.0 predecessor. Choosing to upgrade an existing application to .NET is not just a matter of recompiling—code changes will definitely be required.

Second, applications need to be modified to use .NET Framework classes to perform certain tasks. For instance, instead of using the Microsoft XML parser (MSXML) COM component, applications will instead use the classes provided by the System.XML namespace. In order to use text boxes and push buttons, the application will need to use the Windows controls provided by the System.Drawing namespace. In many cases, this means a lot of code needs to be rewritten.

Third, support for some of the older Windows development technologies has been dropped or drastically reduced in .NET. Dynamic Data Exchange (DDE), Data Access Objects (DAO) and Remote Data Objects (RDO) data binding to controls, Visual Basic 5.0 controls, ActiveX documents, user controls, and web classes are not supported in .NET. Applications that rely on add-ins or third-party components will need a significant amount of rework, as will applications that call the Win32 API functions directly.

Because applications are likely to require some rework under the new .NET architecture, it may be wise to examine the design of the application as a whole and see if changes need to be made at that level. For instance, you may find that an application that was originally created as one large executable might be significantly better if broken into two pieces—one that runs on a client PC and one that runs on a server.

on the
Job

Microsoft provides a conversion tool to help Visual Basic developers convert to .NET, but it only takes you part of the way. You are almost better off developing programs in .NET from scratch instead of trying to convert them.

Of course, this section was not meant to scare you away from converting to .NET. On the contrary, the platform simplifies application development and improves the performance, reliability, and security of applications that run inside its environment. But anyone embarking on a .NET conversion project should be aware that the gap between the current programming methodologies and the new .NET methodology is wider than gaps created when previous new technologies were introduced.

Introduction to Web Services

Companies have been developing applications over the Internet since the mid-1990s. In the early days, applications were quite limited in what they could do. Back then, web applications used the Common Gateway Interface (CGI). CGI applications, as they were called, were written in server-side languages, such as Perl or C, which ran directly on the operating system with no restrictions. These applications had no help, in that developers had to code their own way to communicate with the web browser, store user data, and handle user sessions.

A short time later, web application environments such as ASP were developed that provided developers some standard ways to communicate with the browser (for example, the Request and Response ASP objects) and handle user sessions and data (for example, the ASP Session and Application objects). When these ASP applications were integrated with other technologies such as ADO, MTS/COM+, and even custom-designed COM components, developers could create some powerful and dynamic web applications.

Figure 1-2 shows the way a typical ASP/COM web application is structured. The ASP application uses COM components that provide essential services, such as data access to the application.

These types of applications worked well for users who used web browsers to access them. For example, let's assume a web-based e-mail client exists at http:// www.example.com/mailreader. Users can use their browsers to log in to that application and read their e-mail. The problem is that you can't easily use Microsoft Outlook, or any other 32-bit Windows application, to read e-mail from that location. The Hypertext Markup Language (HTML) application is a great delivery system to deliver e-mail to browsers but terrible for delivering e-mail to other pieces of software.

One of the solutions for this problem that has been developed in recent years is the concept of web services. The term *XML web services* describes an industry

FIGURE 1-2

A typical three-tier web application without .NET

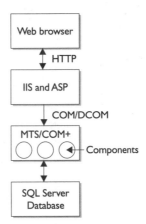

standard way of integrating applications using XML, SOAP, Web Services Description Language (WSDL), and Universal Description, Discovery, and Integration (UDDI) over the Internet. Practically speaking, a web service is an application that is accessible over the Internet using XML. This makes it easy for other applications to use that service in their own applications.

on the **Job** *XML, SOAP, and WSDL are all standards created and maintained by the World Wide Web Consortium (W3C). You can read the official specifications on its web site at http://www.w3.org/. UDDI is a standard maintained by OASIS, at http://www.uddi.org/.*

Figure 1-3 shows how the typical web service application is structured. The web service can interface with many different applications and systems.

There are many web services already available on the Internet today, such as the following:

- Obtaining stock quotes
- Searching the Amazon.com product database
- Searching the Google web index database
- Feeding topic-specific news headlines

Developers can integrate these web services into their own applications and web sites. And since XML web services is an industry standard, it doesn't matter what operating system or platform you use to either develop or consume these services.

on the **Job** *Applications that use web services are said to consume them.*

FIGURE 1-3

Web services can accept SOAP messages from almost any platform.

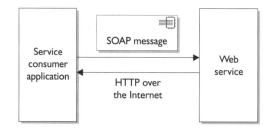

The following industry standards are often associated with web services:

- **XML (Extensible Markup Language)** A flexible and powerful new way of formatting data using markup tags
- **SOAP (Simple Object Access Protocol)** An XML-compatible way of sending and receiving messages across the Internet
- **WSDL (Web Services Description Language)** An XML-based language used to describe a web service
- **UDDI (Universal Description, Discovery, and Integration)** A registry that lists business and web services on the Internet using WSDL

Web services hosted in an ASP.NET environment can easily be tested using a web browser. Figure 1-4 shows an example of a web service being manually tested. Of course, this is not the way the web service itself will be used by the users, but being able to easily test the application using a simple web browser is a convenient tool for developers.

FIGURE 1-4

The ASP.NET testing interface for web services

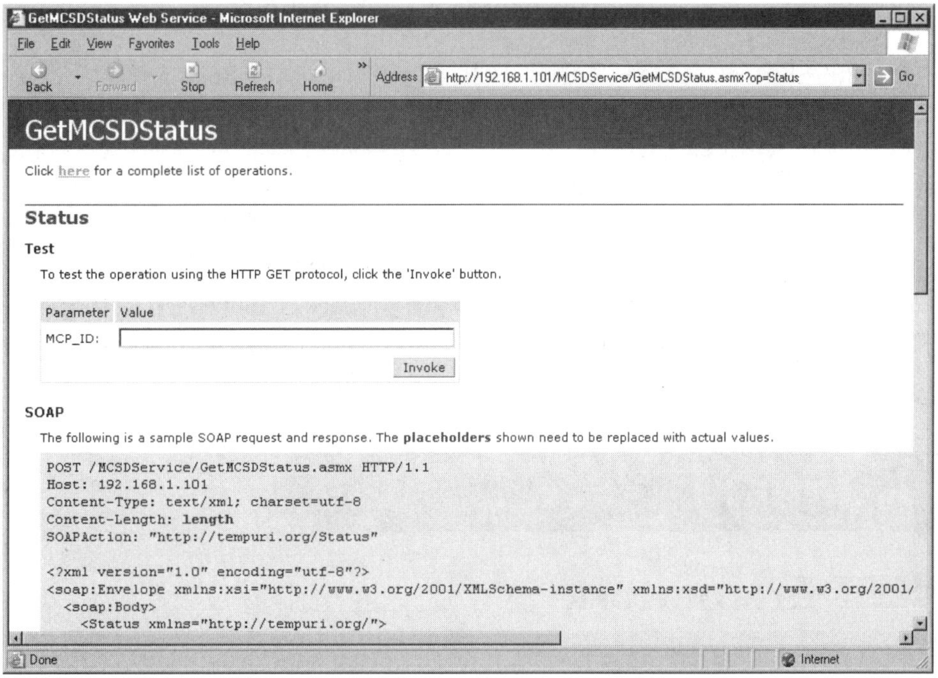

FROM THE CLASSROOM

.NET Remoting

.NET remoting can be used to enable different applications to communicate with each other, regardless of whether they reside on the same machine or on different machines across a network. Remoting even allows applications running on different operating systems to communicate with each other, which is what gives .NET an advantage over Distributed COM (DCOM).

Remoting is a very flexible mechanism for application communication, since it can be configured to use binary encoding for when performance is critical or XML encoding for interoperability among different systems. Remoting has security features and can be transmitted over different channels. Objects that can be serialized can be accessed by .NET remoting, which overcomes many of the performance problems introduced by object marshalling. Marshalling is the process by which an object's code and data is packed together, transmitted over a communication channel, and unpacked at the other end into a format that the receiving system understands. Excessive marshalling of objects can be a serious application bottleneck that slows down application performance.

The .NET Framework handles most of the work related to remoting by providing framework classes for channels and formatters. In order for an application on one computer to access a component stored on another computer, all it has to do is create a new instance of the remote component. .NET will create a proxy object on the client computer for your application to use. When you access a method of the local proxy object, .NET will send the call over the channel for the server to process. All of the communication aspects are hidden from the application, as if the object existed on the local machine all along.

—Scott Duffy, MCSD, MCP+SB, SCJP, IBMCD-XML

OBJECTIVE 1.02

.NET Framework

The .NET Framework is the key technology that defines .NET. It is an application environment for building, deploying, and running .NET applications. The .NET Framework consists of the following two components:

- **Common Language Runtime (CLR)** The environment that manages the code during runtime
- **Base Class Library (BCL)** A huge collection of managed code classes that provide essential services to applications developed in .NET

In this section, we will examine the services provided by the .NET Framework more closely.

Understanding the .NET Framework

The .NET Framework is an extensive collection of classes that is accessible by all .NET programming languages. In fact, .NET ships with over 3,000 classes in the framework. These classes, known collectively as the Base Class Library (BCL), provide a core set of data types, events, exceptions, interfaces, and attributes to applications, as well as components that provide a database, a user interface, a file system, a network, a remote application, and security services.

Framework classes are organized into related groups called namespaces. In order for an application to be able to access a class, it has to first access the related namespace. In this manner, two classes can have the same name as long as they exist in different namespaces. Namespaces can themselves be organized into hierarchies that can be several levels deep.

Only two top-level namespaces ship natively with .NET—Microsoft and System. The Microsoft namespace provides application compilation and code generation services for three of the Microsoft programming languages: Visual C#, Visual Basic, and JScript. It also provides access to Windows-specific components, such as events and the system registry.

The System namespace contains the fundamental classes to support .NET. Dozens of classes exist directly under the System namespace (such as Object and String), while thousands more exist in the namespaces beneath the System namespace.

There are about twenty built-in data types in .NET. Since the BCL defines this standard set of types, components written in one language that wish to define a string can easily pass that string to components written in other languages that are expecting a string. Because there are so many ways of creating strings in an unmanaged environment, programs often have to perform some conversion routines on the string before passing it to a component written in another programming language.

The BCL also defines a number of web classes collectively known as ASP.NET. These classes live in the System.Web namespace. ASP.NET classes allow developers to create web-based applications, which are accessed primarily using a web browser. With ASP.NET, developers can create web applications in any .NET programming language of their choice, with better performance due to just-in-time (JIT) compiling and a new server-side control model that provides a clean separation of content and behavior. Whereas old ASP applications often intermixed HTML and ASP code, ASP.NET code is often completely separate from the HTML web pages it acts on.

The BCL provides a core set of data access classes known as ADO .NET. These classes live in the System.Data namespace. ADO .NET provides efficient, object-oriented access to databases similar to the way ADO COM objects did under the Windows DNA programming model. However, ADO .NET classes focus on disconnected recordsets (called datasets in the .NET paradigm), which means that applications do not have to keep connections open to the database while they are analyzing and modifying data.

There are also .NET Framework classes for handling XML that lives in the System.XML namespace. The BCL includes an XML parser and support for other XML technologies such as Extensible Stylesheet Language Transformation (XSLT).

Assemblies

Applications or components written in one of the .NET programming languages are compiled into assemblies. An *assembly* is a binary file formatted in Microsoft Intermediate Language (MSIL). Theoretically, once a program has been compiled from source code into an assembly, it should be impossible to determine what the original programming language was. Identical programs written in different programming languages should compile to almost the same assembly code.

on the
() o b

MSIL is an abstract language that is not closely related to any particular brand of operating system or CPU. This means that .NET assemblies do not contain code specific to Microsoft Windows or the Intel Pentium processor.

Assemblies contain both the MSIL code and some related metadata. *Metadata* is "data about data," and the assembly metadata lists the names of the external components the code relies on, as well as the exposed property and method names. COM components also contained some metadata (called a *type library*), but the assembly metadata is much more complete. Programmers can even add their own metadata to provide other applications more information on how and when to use the component.

The metadata also enables the improved versioning capabilities discussed earlier in this chapter (see "Why is .NET Better Than COM/DCOM?"). .NET ensures that applications are linked to components with the correct version number and that a new version of a component can be installed on a system without interfering with an older version of the same component.

The Common Language Runtime (CLR)

The Common Language Runtime (CLR) is a runtime environment for executing .NET applications. That means that the CLR sits between the .NET program code and the operating system, managing the interaction between the two. That is why .NET applications are often called *managed code*. Code that executes outside the .NET environment is often called *unmanaged code*.

The CLR loads the .NET assemblies into memory and compiles them into binary executables specific to the local CPU. This process is called just-in-time (JIT) compiling. This distinguishes the CLR from the Java Virtual Machine (JVM) in that the JVM is a bytecode interpreter. Compiled languages are generally faster than interpreted ones.

The CLR provides two great benefits to .NET developers:

- All .NET languages are fairly equal in terms of performance, so the choice of programming language becomes one of developer preference rather than suitability to task.

- Applications written in one language can seamlessly use components created in another, which is sometimes called *language interoperability*.

The one exception to the performance rule is Visual C++ .NET with Managed Extensions (Managed C++). Managed C++ allows managed and unmanaged code to exist in the same application. You can use the unmanaged code for low-level, performance-critical code and the managed code to access .NET framework classes and components. Examples of performance-critical code would be things like video games, movie-editing software, and other CPU-intensive tasks.

Because the .NET-managed environment adds a small amount of processing overhead and a few restrictions on direct access to certain system resources, software programs that require a lot of processing power or direct access to certain resources will probably continue to be created outside the .NET environment.

on the **Job**

Although Microsoft claims that the CLR enables applications written in any .NET language to have similar performance, there are still some performance considerations. For instance, when Microsoft converted DirectX to Visual C# .NET, it noticed a 40 percent drop in overall performance. But when that same application was converted to Visual C++ .NET, the performance was nearly equal to the original. This is because Visual C++ applications can directly access the operating system, unlike other programming languages in the .NET environment.

Choosing a .NET Project Template

Microsoft .NET supports several different application types. There are Windows Forms applications, which run directly on a PC running Windows. There are also Web Forms applications, which run inside a web browser over a network. And then there are web services, which are accessible using other applications over a network. Each of these applications is slightly different than the others in .NET. They each use a different set of .NET Framework class libraries and require a different set of support files within Visual Studio. In the case of web-based applications, they require a .NET-compatible server, such as Internet Information Server (IIS), to develop and deploy the applications.

In all, there are eight project templates available in Visual Studio .NET to assist developers with creating new projects:

- Windows Application
- ASP.NET Web Application
- ASP.NET Web Service
- Console Application
- Windows Service
- Class Library
- Windows Control Library
- Web Control Library

These templates, along with two or three empty project templates, can be created using either Visual Basic or Visual C# in the Visual Studio .NET environment. Each language has its own unique set of project templates, and some of those templates may not be available in other languages. For instance, developers who code in Visual C++ .NET have the opportunity to create Microsoft Foundation Class (MFC), Active Template Library (ATL), and Managed C++ projects. (Don't throw away those MFC books just yet.)

- A *Windows application* is your basic type of application. This application is designed to have a user interface and runs directly in the Windows environment as a stand-alone application. Windows applications can also access database services, consume web services, and communicate with remote applications across a network.

- An *ASP.NET web application* is your traditional web-based application that runs on a web server and is accessible through a browser. Since this web application communicates using the HTML standard over the Internet, it is generally accessible using any browser.

- An *ASP.NET web service* is a new type of web-based application that communicates through the XML and SOAP standards. This application provides a service that is accessible by other applications, such as providing currency exchange rates or stock quotes.

- A *console application* is a command-line application that is designed to run inside a Windows command prompt (sometimes also called a *DOS box*). This application is restricted by the command prompt's text-based user interface. Console applications communicate with the user using text only—there are no dialog boxes, menus, or buttons. The command prompt can be accessed in Windows XP by selecting Run from the Windows Start menu, typing **cmd**, and clicking the OK button.

- A *Windows service* is a Windows application that does not have a user interface. This type of application typically performs behind-the-scenes tasks and is the most hidden from the user of any type of application. Services can be designed to start automatically, every time the operating system starts up, and they typically stay running until the computer is shut down. For instance, antivirus software usually installs itself as a Windows service and runs invisibly in the background while you're working. Sometimes a service creates an icon in the system tray, but usually it does not.

■ A *class library* is a reusable class or component that can be shared with other .NET applications. For instance, the .NET Framework contains thousands of class libraries that are accessible by any application that runs in the .NET environment.

■ The *Windows Control Library* and *Web Control Library* projects allow developers to create custom controls (buttons, text boxes, and so on) that can be used in Windows or web applications, respectively.

Each of the preceding eight project templates helps you by initializing the development environment with some standard files, code, and project configuration settings. For instance, if you use the ASP.NET Web Service project template, you will start off with a number of default files with which to begin creating your web service.

In addition to the programming language–related templates, there are a few project design, testing, and deployment-related templates in Visual Studio .NET. These templates may or may not be available in your copy of Visual Studio because their availability depends on the edition of Visual Studio you are using and the options that were selected when it was installed:

■ **Setup Project**   A Windows Installer project, making application deployment via CD or the web easier

■ **Database Project**   A project allowing direct manipulation of database objects and data

■ **Enterprise Templates**   A set of complex project templates for large enterprise applications

■ **Visual Studio Analyzer Project**   A project that helps with performance tuning

■ **Visual Studio .NET Add-Ins**   Build add-in tools for the Visual Studio environment

■ **Application Center Test (ACT) Project**   A project designed to stress-test web servers and analyze performance bottlenecks

As you can see, Visual Studio .NET is a rich and expandable environment for developing both simple and complex projects within the .NET environment. There are many project templates, and as companies begin to standardize on their own architecture they will develop custom templates of their own.

SCENARIO & SOLUTION

What applications are designed to run inside a Windows GUI?	Windows Forms applications
What applications are designed to run inside a web browser?	Web Forms applications
What applications use XML and SOAP to communicate with other applications?	Web services applications
What applications are designed to run inside a Windows command prompt?	Console applications

OBJECTIVE 1.03

Visual Studio .NET Software Design Tools

Visual Studio .NET provides application developers a powerful set of development and design tools. Along with the integrated development environment (IDE), Visual Studio ships with a number of other software applications to help developers with application design, testing, and monitoring in the .NET environment.

The Visual Studio .NET Development Environment

The core of the Visual Studio developer tools is, of course, the actual development environment. Microsoft has packed more features into this version of the IDE than any previous version. Not only does the environment provide a rich set of tools for editing multiple programming languages (such as Visual Basic, Visual C#, and Visual C++), it provides tools for other file types as well, such as XML and HTML.

on the
job

Although Microsoft provides compilers for four languages with its Visual Studio .NET product, only three of them can be edited and compiled within the graphical development environment—Visual Basic, Visual C#, and Visual C++. JScript .NET is created using a simple text editor (such as Windows Notepad) and compiled using a command-line compiler.

Developers will find the integrated Microsoft Developer Network (MSDN) help useful because it is a comprehensive help system built right into the tool rather than a separate application, as it was in the past. And a number of advanced "smart features" such as IntelliSense will make developers more productive than ever.

on the job
Visual Studio .NET runs on Windows NT 4.0, Windows XP, and Windows 2000 operating systems. It does not run on Windows 98, Windows ME, or Windows NT 4.0 Terminal Server.

The screen shot in Figure 1-5 shows the Visual Studio .NET environment in action. This screen shows a project that contains a combination of Visual Basic .NET classes, an XML file, and a Visual Basic .NET COM component. As you can see, Microsoft's IntelliSense is helping me remember the correct property and method names of the System.Windows.Forms.Label class. While these files are being edited, another Visual Studio tab contains MSDN help.

Microsoft Visual Studio .NET currently comes in the following four editions:

- **Professional**   The Visual Studio IDE, five .NET programming languages, and the .NET Framework classes
- **Academic**   The Professional Edition plus a few instructional features
- **Enterprise Developer**   The Professional Edition, plus SQL Server 2000, Visual SourceSafe, and enterprise templates
- **Enterprise Architect**   The Enterprise Developer Edition, plus Microsoft Visio's database and UML modeling solutions

Additional .NET language compilers are available from either Microsoft or various third parties for the following programming languages:

- A Programming Language (APL)
- Visual C++, shipped with Visual Studio .NET
- Visual C# (pronounced "C sharp"), shipped with Visual Studio .NET
- COBOL
- Component Pascal
- Eiffel
- Forth
- Fortran

- Haskell
- JScript, shipped with Visual Studio .NET
- Mercury
- Mondrian
- Oberon
- Pascal
- Perl
- Python
- Report Program Generator (RPG)
- Scheme
- S#
- Standard Meta Language (Standard ML)
- Visual Basic, shipped with Visual Studio .NET

FIGURE 1-5

Code being edited within the Visual Studio environment

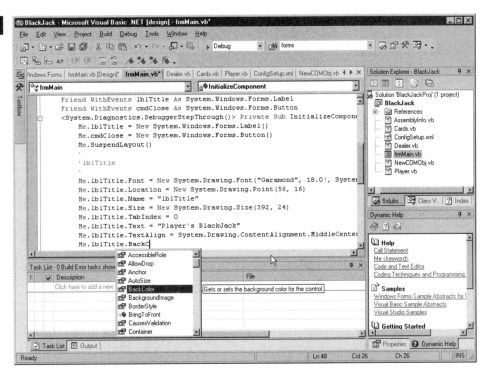

These compilers produce code that is compatible with the .NET runtime environment. Using .NET's multilanguage capability, developers can easily create applications that use one or more of those languages together.

I should mention at this point that, because of the .NET Framework classes and the limitations imposed by intermediate language (IL) assemblies, the syntax of .NET-compatible programming languages may be radically different from existing compilers. For instance, many people say that VB .NET bears very little resemblance to Visual Basic 6.0—it's almost like learning a new programming language. This is something to keep in mind when estimating the amount of learning involved in moving to .NET.

Visio for Enterprise Architects

Microsoft purchased Visio Corp. in September 1999. At the time, Visio was the leading enterprise-wide business diagramming and technical drawing software maker. Visio was the software that companies preferred to use when it came to creating organizational charts, drawing network diagrams, and developing graphical representations of how things worked. Visio was a convenient piece of software to have loaded on your machine because you could very easily and quickly put a small diagram together with boxes, lines, arrows, and other small icons. This matched very well the way people describe how things work using a whiteboard or the back of a cocktail napkin.

Over time, Visio has been enhanced to provide software design templates. Software designers can sit down and draw classes, identify relationships, design a database schema, and do other software design tasks. For instance, Visio 2000 included a set of Unified Modeling Language (UML) templates so that designers could create UML diagrams quickly and easily. Not all UML types were represented, but you could create some of the basic diagrams such as use cases and class diagrams.

The Enterprise Architect edition of Visual Studio .NET includes a product named Visio for Enterprise Architects. This tool contains all the features of Visio Professional 2002 and includes full-feature database and software modeling solutions. Visio has the ability to automatically reverse-engineer existing Visual Studio projects to generate UML class diagrams. It can also generate code skeletons for VB .NET, Visual C++, and Visual C# based on UML class diagrams. This means that when the software design phase is complete, code files in the development language of choice will be set up and ready to go. All you have to do is supply the business logic.

On the database side, Visio can automatically generate Structured Query Language (SQL) Data Description Language (DDL) scripts for the creation of databases based on an application's conceptual and logical designs. Visio supports the Object Role Modeling (ORM) notation for database conceptual design. ORM is discussed at length in Chapter 5. Visio also is able to import and export files based on Computer Associate's popular ERwin database-modeling tool.

Figure 1-6 shows a screen shot of Visio for Enterprise Architects.

Other Enterprise Tools

As with prior versions of Visual Studio, the .NET version ships with a number of other software components that aim to make life easier for developers. Of course, with such a rich editing environment, many of these tools are built right in to the main development interface.

For instance, Visual Studio .NET for Enterprise Architects ships with the following additional tools:

- ISAPI Web Debug Tool
- MFC-ATL Trace Tool
- Spy++

FIGURE 1-6

Using Visio to create the conceptual and logical designs of an application

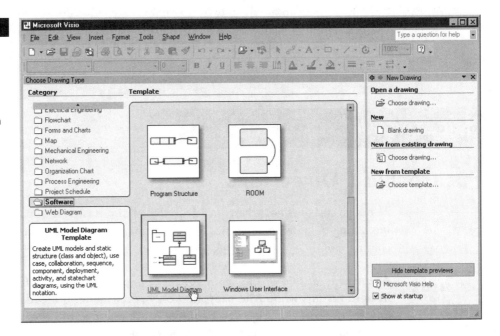

SCENARIO & SOLUTION	
What benefits does the CLR provide?	The ability to run applications on several different platforms and operating systems without recompiling
What benefits does the .NET Framework provide?	A standardized set of functionality available across all .NET platforms
What benefits does the .NET Compact Framework provide?	A standardized set of functionality available for mobile devices
What benefits does Visual Studio .NET provide?	A single IDE for developing Visual Basic, Visual C#, Visual C++, XML, and XSL files
What benefits does the MSIL provide?	The ability for code developed using different programming languages to interoperate seamlessly

- Visual C++ Error Lookup
- Visual C++ Remote Debugger

Many of these tools will only be useful for Visual C++ developers, because Visual C++ programs can be developed to run outside the .NET environment as unmanaged code. Visual Studio .NET contains a very capable debugger built right into it for developers to use on managed .NET applications.

OBJECTIVE 1.04

Future .NET Directions

Although this does not relate directly to the Solutions Architecture exam, it may be interesting to know some of the changes coming to the .NET platform over the coming months.

on the
job

At the time of this writing, some of these improvements to .NET were already in Beta testing, while Microsoft had only recently announced others. Of course, the one thing we can't control is the passage of time, so by the time you read this, this might have become old news.

.NET Platform Enhancements

Microsoft is currently testing a new version of the .NET Framework and Visual Studio .NET, and it is continuing to roll out new versions of its enterprise applications that include tighter integration with .NET.

- *Visual Studio .NET 2003* offers developers a tighter integration with the new Windows Server 2003. It also offers support for the new .NET Compact Framework for small and mobile devices as well as improved application performance.

- *.NET Framework 1.1* will include support for developing mobile web applications. In additional, .NET will be able to support side-by-side execution of multiple versions of an application or component on the same computer through versioning. For example, this will allow two versions of the .NET Framework itself to exist on one machine (version 1.0 and version 1.1, for example), so that an application can run in the environment it was designed for. There are other features in that release, including enhancements to scalability and performance of .NET applications as well as support for IPv6, the new protocol for IP addressing.

- *SQL Server code-named "Yukon"* will extend the CLR environment inside of SQL Server. That means developers will be able to write SQL-stored procedures using familiar languages like Visual Basic .NET and Visual C#.

Cross-Platform .NET Including Mono and Apache

ECMA International, formerly known as the European Computer Manufacturers Association, has standardized the Common Language Infrastructure (CLI) and the C# programming language. The CLI (ECMA standard 335) is a standard that describes executable code and the environment in which that code runs. In fact, the CLI describes MSIL and CLR. The C# specification (ECMA standard 334) describes the syntax and constraints of the C# programming language.

on the **job** *ECMA standards can be downloaded from the organization's web site at http://www.ecma-international.org/.*

What this means to you and me is that we do not have to rely on Microsoft to provide a .NET runtime environment and programming language. We may choose to use the Microsoft set of tools because of quality and performance, but we are not tied to them.

Already there are a number of projects under way to create .NET-compatible environments on other operating systems. The most well-known effort is the Mono project (http://www.go-mono.com/). Mono is an open-source implementation of the Microsoft .NET development platform. Already there are downloadable versions of this environment for several flavors of Linux—RedHat, SuSE, and Mandrake. You can download a C# compiler as well.

There are three main advantages to this open-source approach:

■ It's free.

■ .NET applications are supported on a platform other than Windows.

■ Developers have full access to the source code, so they can fix bugs and make changes.

There are two big disadvantages, however. First, because the package is still in development, it is not complete. Only a handful of base classes have been developed compared with the 3,000 that the .NET framework provides. Second, developers lose the productivity provided by the Visual Studio IDE; nevertheless, if you don't mind working in a command-line environment and can wait for all the classes to be developed, open source .NET is a great benefit for all developers.

Surprisingly, the Mono project also provides support for ASP.NET. That is, you can run an ASP.NET web server on Linux right now. As the base classes get developed, the number of features will rival Microsoft's own product.

Another interesting project that provides cross-platform .NET is Covalent's Enterprise Ready Server (ERS) Apache. Apache is perhaps the most widely used web server in the world. Covalent provides an enterprise-level version of Apache 2.0, which, among other features, supports ASP.NET.

These open-source and cross-platform initiatives serve to reinforce the notion that the .NET platform is trying hard to overcome the deficiencies of past architectures. Pretty soon, you will be able to configure a .NET-compatible machine that does not contain any Microsoft software, or you will be able to do your development within the user-friendly confines of Visual Studio .NET running on a Windows platform and move the .NET assemblies over to a Unix box for production rollout. Those are the directions in which Microsoft .NET appears to be heading.

In the next chapter, we will begin to explore the purpose of developing an enterprise architecture. We will then move on to the details of analyzing the feasibility and scope of a project—two tasks that usually occur before beginning to gather requirements and design a solution.

SUMMARY

Microsoft .NET was designed to make it easier to create applications that are distributed across a heterogeneous network such as the Internet. .NET alters the Windows programming model, in that applications run inside the .NET environment rather than directly on top of the operating system. This .NET environment is called the Common Language Runtime (CLR).

.NET provides developers with a rich collection of classes called the Base Class Library (BCL). The BCL is part of the .NET Framework, which provides a core set of services to .NET applications, including classes for the Windows user interface (called Windows Forms), a database (called ADO .NET), a web user interface (called Web Forms), an XML parser, XML web services, and security components, just to name a few.

XML web services solve many problems associated with distributed applications. Web services use industry standards like XML and SOAP for communication, can communicate over the HTTP protocol to avoid problems with firewalls, and can make it easier for applications developed separately (by different developers) to communicate with each other. Web services are offered by *providers* and used by *consumers*.

Visual Studio .NET is a powerful tool for software development. It supports a large set of file and project types, and it has MSDN development help built in to the application. Design tools such as Visio for Enterprise Architects make software design easier by tying together the design and development processes.

TWO-MINUTE DRILL

Introducing .NET

❑ .NET Framework acts as a middleware component, running between applications and the operating system.

❑ .NET makes it easier to develop web services applications, which are specifically designed to work over the Internet.

❑ Web services use Internet standards such as XML, SOAP, WSDL, and UDDI.

❑ Web services allow applications developed using different tools to use each others services.

❑ .NET applications can still use COM objects, which allows organizations to introduce .NET gradually into their enterprise architectures.

.NET Framework

❑ The .NET Framework is an environment for building, deploying, and running .NET applications.

❑ The Common Language Runtime (CLR) is the execution environment for .NET.

❑ CLR loads, manages, and runs your code, as well as provides a number of essential support services.

❑ .NET applications are not compiled into machine code; they are compiled into assemblies that contain a mixture of Microsoft Intermediate Language (MSIL) and metadata.

❑ The .NET Framework provides the CLR thousands of base classes and type libraries for use during program execution.

Visual Studio .NET Software Design Tools

❑ Visual Studio .NET ships with four supported languages: Visual C#, Visual C++, Visual Basic, and JScript.

❑ Over 20 languages are currently available or are in development for the CLR.

❑ Some versions of Visual Studio .NET ship with SQL Server, Visual SourceSafe, and Microsoft Visio.

Future .NET Directions

❑ Microsoft is continuing to improve the .NET platform by integrating it more tightly with the operating system and SQL Server.

❑ Third-party developers are working on versions of .NET for Unix systems using the Mono Project.

SELF TEST

The following questions will help you measure your understanding of the material presented in this chapter. Read all the choices carefully because there might be more than one correct answer. Choose all correct answers for each question.

Introducing .NET

1. What is the primary goal of software design?

   A. Create an application that is secure

   B. Create an application that is easy to maintain in the future

   C. Adhere to the Microsoft Solution Framework

   D. Create an application that fulfills business requirements

2. How can managed .NET applications call COM components?

   A. .NET applications are designed to be compatible with COM technology.

   B. COM components can be called using the Assembly-COM Interface Layer (ACIL).

   C. COM components can be called through a COM callable wrapper (CCW).

   D. COM components can be called through a runtime callable wrapper (RCW).

3. How can COM components call .NET components?

   A. .NET applications are designed to be compatible with COM technology.

   B. They can't; the two technologies are incompatible.

   C. .NET components can be called through a COM callable wrapper (CCW).

   D. .NET components can be called through a runtime callable wrapper (RCW).

4. Which of the following industry-standard technologies is generally associated with web services? (Choose all that apply.)

   A. XML

   B. HTML

   C. SOAP

   D. COM/DCOM

   E. XSLT

   F. WSDL/UDDI

5. You are designing an order entry application that will be used by your company's sales force. They have indicated that they would like to be able to enter orders remotely (from customer's offices) using their Apple PowerBook notebooks or their Windows CE devices over the Internet. There is also a 1-800 call center that enters orders through desktop PCs. Assuming this is being developed in a .NET environment, which of the following remote application types is the best solution?

    A. A client application that connects using Distributed COM

    B. A client application that connects using XML web services

    C. A simple web browser client that connects to an ASP.NET application

    D. A two-tier client application that connects directly to the database using ODBC

.NET Framework

6. Which of the following essential system services does the .NET Framework provide to managed applications? (Choose all that apply.)

    A. Database access

    B. File system access

    C. Access to remote applications

    D. Type library (TLB) to MSIL assembly conversion

7. The company you work for has decided to use the .NET platform for any new applications that will be developed. There are a large number of existing applications and components running inside a COM+ environment running on Windows 2000 server. Although many of the applications also will be converted to .NET over the coming months, there are a handful of legacy applications—applications that are still required but are no longer in active development. Which of the following options is the best method for integrating the legacy components with the new .NET environment?

    A. Since COM components are unmanaged code, they cannot be called by .NET applications.

    B. As long as the COM components and .NET applications are running on the same server, it will work as is.

    C. .NET applications can call COM components as long as they are in a COM callable wrapper (CCW).

    D. .NET applications can call COM components as long as they are in a runtime callable wrapper (RCW).

8. What is the internal format of .NET assemblies?

   A. Microsoft Intermediate Language (MSIL) only

   B. CPU-specific executables

   C. A combination of metadata and intermediate language code

   D. XML

9. You are a developer working with two components: Cat and Dog. The Cat component was written in Visual C#, while the Dog component was written in JScript .NET. Which of the following would be valid reasons to want to rewrite the Dog component in Visual C#? (Choose all that apply.)

   A. JScript components cannot be edited within the Visual Studio IDE.

   B. JScript components cannot be used by Visual C# applications.

   C. Components written in other languages cannot be used as base classes.

   D. JScript components run slower than Visual C# components.

10. There are five classes in the .NET Base Class Library named ControlCollection. What is the name of the mechanism in .NET that allows multiple classes with the same class name to coexist?

    A. Class overriding

    B. Class overloading

    C. Inheritance

    D. Namespaces

Visual Studio .NET Software Design Tools

11. Which of the following programming languages can be compiled using the Visual Studio .NET development environment? (Choose all that apply.)

    A. Visual C#

    B. Mono

    C. JScript

    D. Visual C++

12. Joe is a Microsoft Certified Developer who has over five years experience working in the Visual Basic programming language. Joe is the primary developer on a programming team responsible for developing business accounting software. Joe's boss read an article on .NET and has decided it would be a good idea for the next version of the company's accounting package to be written in

Visual Basic .NET. Why is Visual Basic .NET so different from previous versions of Visual Basic? (Choose all that apply.)

A. VB .NET is fully object oriented, while previous versions were not.

B. VB .NET is an interpreted language, while VB6 was compiled.

C. VB .NET calls base classes to perform most common tasks instead of using external COM objects like ADO and MSXML.

D. Since .NET is a managed environment, VB .NET does not support COM+ features like transactions and object pooling.

13. What are the primary advantages of using Visio for Enterprise Architects when coding in a Visual Studio .NET environment? (Choose all that apply.)

A. Developers can write applications in Visio without having to learn another programming language.

B. Visio includes many software design templates for UML and ORM.

C. UML class diagrams can be converted into skeleton classes for Visual C#, Visual C++, and Visual Basic .NET.

D. Visio can reverse-engineer .NET projects to create UML class diagrams.

Future .NET Directions

14. Microsoft has announced that the new version of SQL Server, code named Yukon, will include tighter integration between SQL Server and .NET. How will this integration benefit developers?

A. A full version of SQL Server will ship with Visual Studio .NET.

B. Instead of using ADO .NET, applications will be able to access SQL Server using a special web service.

C. SQL Server Enterprise Manager will be one of the project templates available in Visual Studio.

D. Developers will be able to write stored procedures using Visual C#, Visual C++, or Visual Basic .NET instead of SQL.

15. Which of the following .NET technologies developed by Microsoft are available as an open standard? (Choose all that apply.)

A. Visual Basic

B. C#

C. Common Language Infrastructure (CLI)

D. Java

LAB QUESTION

ABC Corporation has a wide variety of servers—using many different machines and operating systems—to run its internal applications. It would like to standardize on a single architecture one day, but for now it uses a wide variety of systems to run its operations. The company has an IBM mainframe to handle its centralized data services, a dozen Microsoft Windows 2000 servers to handle its internal and external web sites and applications, and a handful of Sun Unix machines to manage its extensive end-to-end order processing and distribution systems.

The IT department has recently decided to move the data services off the mainframe and onto a small cluster of PCs. Your group is in charge of designing the best solution for this large-scale project.

You've already decided that a move this size will have to be done gradually. Given the number of applications involved and the critical importance of most of those systems, trying to migrate the data store from the mainframe to the server cluster all at once will be way too risky.

Given what you know about the migration plan, availability, and performance requirements, what are the benefits of using custom .NET components as a middle layer between the applications and the database?

SELF TEST ANSWERS

Introducing .NET

1. ☑ **D.** The goal of software design is to fulfill user requirements.
   ☒ **A** and **B** are incorrect because they are secondary requirements. Creating an application that is secure and can be easily maintained means nothing if the application cannot do the basic tasks required of it. **C** is incorrect because the Microsoft Solution Framework is only one way to achieve the goal of good software design and is not the goal itself.

2. ☑ **D.** .NET applications can call COM components through a runtime callable wrapper (RCW). Using a conversion tool shipped with the .NET Framework, COM components can be imported into any .NET application without recompiling the component. In addition, Visual Basic .NET applications have the special ability to use COM components without having to manually convert them.
   ☒ **A** is incorrect because COM components and .NET assemblies do not have inherent compatibility. **B** is incorrect because there is no such thing as the Assembly-COM Interface Layer. **C** is incorrect because COM callable wrappers (CCW) allow COM-compatible environments to use a .NET component but not the other way around.

3. ☑ **C.** COM-compatible environments can access .NET components by creating a COM callable wrapper (CCW) for the component. Although this is not as easy as having .NET applications call COM components, unmanaged Windows applications can call .NET components if they are configured properly.
   ☒ **A** is incorrect because COM components and .NET assemblies do not have inherent compatibility. **B** is incorrect because unmanaged Windows applications such as COM objects can indeed call .NET components if they are properly set up. **D** is incorrect because runtime callable wrappers (RCW) allow .NET applications to use COM components but not the other way around.

4. ☑ **A, C,** and **F.** The four technologies most closely associated with web services on that list are XML, SOAP, WSDL, and UDDI. SOAP is the XML-based message format used for service providers and consumers to communicate across the Internet. WSDL is an XML-based data format for describing web services, and UDDI is an industry-standard method for locating businesses and web services across the Internet.
   ☒ **B** is incorrect because HTML deals primarily with human-readable web pages. **D** is incorrect because although COM and DCOM often allow applications to be distributed across a network, those applications are based on COM and not XML. **E** is incorrect because XSLT

concerns itself with translating XML documents into other XML-related formats. Although XSLT may be used for formatting SOAP messages, it is an XML technology and not a web service technology.

5. ☑ **C.** An ASP.NET web site would be the best overall solution for this scenario. All three platforms (Windows desktop, Mac notebook, and Windows CE device) come with full-featured web browsers that support rich functionality.

   ☒ **A** is incorrect because not all platforms support COM/DCOM (such as the Mac OS). DCOM applications are also difficult to implement across a slow and unreliable network such as the Internet. **B** is incorrect because XML web services require a separate client to be developed for each of the three OS platforms. Security would also have to be implemented manually. **D** is incorrect because clients would have to be developed for each of the three OS platforms, and not all platforms support ODBC (such as Mac OS). Also, security would have to be implemented manually in this scenario.

.NET Framework

6. ☑ **A, B,** and **C.** The .NET Framework provides a core set of essential services to .NET applications, including components that provide access to databases, file systems, and remote applications.

   ☒ **D** is incorrect because .NET can only interact with COM components that have already been converted to assemblies. Usually a developer performs conversion manually before integrating COM components into .NET application development.

7. ☑ **D.** COM components must be wrapped in a runtime callable wrapper (RCW). As the name suggests, these wrappers give the CLR access to unmanaged code inside.

   ☒ **A** is incorrect because, with the right configuration, .NET and COM can call each other's objects. **B** is incorrect because .NET applications can access both local and remote COM objects as long as they are properly configured. **C** is incorrect because COM callable wrappers (CCW) allow COM objects to call managed code inside .NET.

8. ☑ **C.** Assemblies contain a detailed type library in the form of metadata, along with intermediate language (IL) code.

   ☒ **A** is incorrect because assemblies contain a lot of information besides the compiled IL code. Metadata provides other applications with details on the name and type of properties and methods within the object. Developers can also insert their own metadata into the file. **B** is incorrect because assemblies are not CPU specific. The process of just-in-time compiling is what turns an assembly into machine-specific code. **D** is incorrect because assemblies are a binary format and not XML.

9. ☑ **A.** JScript .NET programs are created and modified using a simple text editor and turned into an assembly using a command-line compiler.
☒ **B** is incorrect because all .NET languages are compiled to intermediate language, and they are all able to interoperate equally well with each other. **C** is incorrect for the same reason. In any .NET language, you can inherit from classes written in other languages. **D** is incorrect because, in general, no programming language can gain a significant performance advantage over any other programming language—with the possible exception of Visual C++, which has the ability to use unmanaged code for performance-critical operations.

10. ☑ **D.** Multiple classes can exist with the same name as long as they are in separate namespaces.
☒ **A** and **B** are incorrect because overriding and overloading are actions performed on methods and not classes. **C** is incorrect because inheritance allows one class to extend the members of another and has nothing to do with how those classes are named.

Visual Studio .NET Software Design Tools

11. ☑ **A** and **D.** Three programming languages can be edited and compiled using the development tool: VB .NET, C#, and Visual C++.
☒ **B** is incorrect because Mono is not a programming language; it is an open-source, cross-platform version of the .NET platform. **C** is incorrect because JScript is compiled using a command-line tool and is not part of the development environment.

12. ☑ **A** and **C.** VB .NET is an object-oriented programming language that supports many object-oriented features such as polymorphism, inheritance, and encapsulation. In addition, the language uses .NET Framework classes for everything from GUI form controls to data types.
☒ **B** is incorrect because VB .NET is indeed compiled. .NET applications are compiled into assemblies and compiled again using JIT compiling before runtime. **D** is incorrect because VB .NET components can be imported as COM callable wrappers into COM+ for services such as transactions and object pooling.

13. ☑ **B, C,** and **D.** Visio for Enterprise Architects includes many UML and ORM templates to aid in software design. Those templates can then be turned into skeleton code when programming is ready to begin. Existing projects can also be turned into UML classes to make documentation easier.
☒ **A** is incorrect because Visio only allows you to design software. Programming will still have to be done using a traditional programming language such as Visual Basic .NET, Visual C#, or Visual C++.

Future .NET Directions

14. ☑ **D.** The next version of SQL Server is expected to include support for the CLR, which will allow developers to write stored procedures in any .NET language.

    ☒ **A** and **C** are incorrect because Microsoft has not announced these features. In any event, given the fundamentally different purposes of SQL Server and Visual Studio .NET, it would not make sense for this to happen. **B** is incorrect because providing database access through a web service would be slower and less flexible.

15. ☑ **B** and **C.** ECMA International has standardized C# and the CLI.

    ☒ **A** is incorrect because Visual Basic is a proprietary Microsoft technology. **D** is incorrect because Java belongs to Sun Microsystems and is not related to Microsoft's .NET platform.

LAB ANSWER

Using .NET components as a middle tier between applications and the database can provide several benefits. First, the components can serve as an additional layer of security. The components can block applications and users from gaining access to data they are not supposed to see. The components can also provide security through an extensive audit trail and real-time notification of events.

Second, components can implement data caching for frequently called static data, saving execution time. Programmers can include complex intelligence in the component to know how frequently a cache needs to be refreshed and what data should never be cached.

Third, data components can perform complex processing that spans several database transactions, ensuring data integrity. For instance, for a bill payment at a bank, a component can be used to ensure that the money is both withdrawn from the client's account and paid into the correct payee's account.

Fourth, components can perform additional business processing work, reducing the amount of data transmitted over a network. For instance, instead of an application retrieving 100,000 rows of data in order to perform a complex mean and medium calculation on them, the server component can do that calculation without having to transmit so much data to the client requesting the information.

The fact that .NET components can be easily wrapped inside an XML web service allows applications developed on different operating systems such as Unix to access the data. It also provides a solid basis for standardization of the enterprise architecture in the future.

2

Visualizing
the Solution

Some software architects believe that software is constructed, not developed. The difference may not seem obvious at first, but by definition the word "construction" implies a completely different approach than the word "development." The verb "develop" is defined as the process by which something grows or improves gradually over time. For instance, you can develop your muscles through weightlifting or develop impressive piano skills through regular practice. Building software is similar to building an office tower; you start with a *vision*, draw up a detailed plan, and strictly follow that plan until the project is complete.

I expect it will take quite some time to convince people to stop using the term "software development." As much as I believe good software requires a lot more planning than the word "development" implies, too many people, including Microsoft, use that term to refer to this process. So who am I to try to change their minds?

In this chapter, we will start with an introductory look at the Microsoft Solutions Framework. The bulk of this chapter examines the first phase of that model, known as the *envisioning phase*. In order to understand the systems and business operating environment we will be deploying our application in, we must have some understanding of our organization's enterprise architecture—we will discuss what that is (and why it's important) later in the chapter. The final sections of the chapter deal with the process of the envisioning phase: creating a solution concept, assessing feasibility, defining scope, and identifying key project risks.

The Microsoft Solutions Framework

The Microsoft Solutions Framework (MSF) is a framework developed by Microsoft to help guide project teams involved in creating software. It is important to understand from the outset that the MSF does not attempt to be a step-by-step approach to developing software. A step-by-step approach, where the development process would be broken down into a series of checklists, would not be flexible enough for the vast majority of project teams to use effectively. When you consider that some software development projects are made up of only two or three people, while others have dozens or even hundreds of team members, you can understand the problem. It would be virtually impossible to create a single step-by-step procedure that would be able to meet the needs of both very small and very large teams at the same time. While all teams have the same basic goal of developing the best solution for the business problem, the method of accomplishing that goal depends on other factors such as team size, budget, and schedule.

author's note

A framework is a collection of layered or otherwise related components.

Instead of a comprehensive approach, Microsoft has developed a framework for the development process. This framework sets the rules related to building teams and embarking on solution design and development. Following the MSF path is analogous to following a well-worn footpath across the mountains. Such a path exists because it is the best path available to navigate across a treacherous terrain. You are not obliged to follow the path, and you can even take shortcuts if you find them necessary along the way. The footpath makes the journey easier and helps you avoid getting lost, but it doesn't eliminate the effort required.

The MSF has been divided into five major components—two *models* and three *disciplines*. The two MSF models are the team model and the process model; the *team model* describes the process used to build a successful project team, while the *process model* describes the process used to build a successful computer application.

The three MSF disciplines are the project management discipline, the risk management discipline, and the readiness management discipline. The *project management discipline* describes Microsoft's distributed approach to project management, the *risk management discipline* describes methods to manage risk and uncertainty in a project, and the *readiness management discipline* describes an approach to knowledge and skills management within the team.

MSF Team Model

The *MSF team model* is designed to assist with the structuring of successful project teams. This model defines several project roles, although not every project team will contain someone for every role. It also specifies, in a general way, the tasks that fall within each role. Following are the six main roles in the MSF team model:

Team Model Roles

- **Product management**   Acts as a client advocate and manages the customer
- **Program management**   Ensures the project is developed on schedule
- **Development**   Designs and constructs the solution

- **Test**   Develops a test strategy and conducts tests
- **User experience**   Acts as a user advocate and designs the user interface
- **Release management**   Acts as an operations advocate and manages the rollout of the product

Of course, the fact that there are six roles defined by the team model does not imply that a minimum of six people are required in order to adequately staff a project team. In reality, smaller projects usually have one person filling more than one role. Several of the roles above have some overlap, such as product management and program management. Likewise, the fact that six roles are defined by the team model is not meant to imply that a team is limited to only six people, as some larger projects might require dozens of people in the developer role.

Just as software code is delivered during the developing phase, design documents are delivered during the envisioning and planning phases. Once the makeup of the project team has been decided, the product manager should create a "project structure" document. This document is one of the three deliverables that are produced during the envisioning phase of the MSF process model. The other two documents deal with vision/scope and risk assessment, and will be discussed later in this chapter.

Team Model Concepts

Besides the definition of roles, the team model also covers the fundamentals of building a good team. Table 2-1 lists the six key concepts of building good teams according to the team model approach.

TABLE 2-1   The Six Key Concepts of the MSF Team Model

Key Concept	Description
Team of peers	Each role has equal value in decision making.
Customer-focused mindset	A satisfied customer is always the first priority.
Product mindset	Always consider the results of your labor, no matter what it is, as a "product."
Zero-defect mindset	Every member of the team should be committed to delivering a quality product.
Willingness to learn	Be open to new ways of solving old problems.
Motivated teams	Motivated teams create better products.

MSF Process Model

While the team model defines an approach to creating successful project teams, the *MSF process model* covers Microsoft's recommended approach to successful application development. This model breaks the entire software development process into five distinct phases. The phases should be completed in the proper sequence (from Phase 1 through Phase 5). However, each phase cannot begin until the phase before it has ended. Each phase represents the next logical step required to design and build quality software.

Process Model Phases

The five phases of the MSF process model are

- **Phase 1: Envisioning**   Defining the project vision and scope
- **Phase 2: Planning**   Developing project plans and specifications
- **Phase 3: Developing**   Building code and documentation
- **Phase 4: Stabilizing**   Performing testing and bug fixing
- **Phase 5: Deploying**   Implementing the solution in the customer environment

After the deploying phase is complete, we go back to the envisioning phase again to start the process over for the next set of features. This is known as the *iterative approach*. The purpose of the iterative approach is to break a large software project up into multiple versions. For instance, instead of spending more than a year developing the first version of an application, the iterative approach recommends that the project be developed and deployed in stages—perhaps three releases six months apart in this example. Each new version of the application goes through the entire MSF process from envisioning to deployment, and hopefully each new release improves on the last.

exam
ⓦatch

You will not encounter any specific questions about the MSF on the exam, but it is important to understand its phases and the order in which tasks should be performed.

MSF Disciplines

Continuing with our look at the MSF, the next component is called the *project management discipline*. This discipline introduces a distributed team approach to project management. You may have noticed that the MSF team model lacks a role called project management. The MSF approach advocates the distribution of traditional project manager tasks to the various team leaders of the other roles, with a program manager to coordinate them and provide support.

The *risk management discipline* defines a proactive approach to dealing with uncertainty in a project's life cycle. Some risks can be avoided, while others just need to be accepted as potential liabilities. This discipline outlines a framework for evaluating and managing project risks from the start to the end of a project's life.

The third discipline of the MSF is the *readiness management discipline.* Microsoft defines readiness as a measurement of the current state of knowledge, skills, and abilities of the individuals within an organization, compared to the desired state. The readiness management discipline is a process to help you define how the current skills of each individual on a project team compare with what they will need for their project role.

Revisions to the MSF

Microsoft occasionally makes revisions (sometimes major and sometimes minor) to the MSF. As of this writing, the current release of the framework is version 3.1. So even if you were once familiar with the MSF approach to software development, it might be worth going back over it to see what has changed. For example, the previous version of the process model had only four phases—the deployment phase was added in version 3.0. Also, Microsoft now recommends the iterative approach to development instead of the old milestone-driven approach.

More information on the Microsoft Solutions Framework can be found on the official MSF web site, which is located at http://www.microsoft.com/msf.

SCENARIO & SOLUTION	
Which MSF model is used to help construct a project team?	Team model
Which MSF model is used to help design and develop an application?	Process model
According to the MSF, which project role is responsible for managing the overall project schedule?	Program management
According to the MSF, which project role is responsible for managing user requirements definition?	User experience

FROM THE CLASSROOM

Iterative Development Defined

The iterative approach, which is at the heart of the Microsoft Solutions Framework process model, is an ideal way to develop object-oriented software applications. It allows you to design, develop and implement software applications in a more focused manner than if a project did not use such a model. Developing software in smaller, more manageable chunks can actually improve the overall quality of the product in the end.

There are four big benefits to iterative development. First, customers get their hands on working software much sooner and can provide feedback to the development team to be incorporated in the next release. Second, developers can see what works and what doesn't work earlier on in the process, allowing them to make the appropriate adjustments. Third, the project team can stay motivated because it sees regular visible success. Fourth, the project is more manageable—a massive three-year project can be turned into six smaller but more manageable projects, each of them six months in duration.

The MSF development model is not the only development model to recommend the iterative approach. Iterative programming is a core concept of the Unified Process (UP) and its cousin, the Rational Unified Process (RUP). It is also a central idea of the popular Extreme Programming (XP) methodology used by many open-source software projects such as Mozilla and Linux.

—*Scott Duffy, MCSD, MCP+SB, SCJP, IBMCD-XML*

Developing an Enterprise Architecture

Even with the MSF model at our disposal, we're still lacking an important ingredient before we can jump into software design. We are lacking the proper context in which the software we are going to create exists. We are lacking an understanding of how the organization views technology and how technology is currently being used. We are lacking an understanding of the enterprise architecture.

Enterprise architecture (EA) means different things to different people—it really depends on who you ask. Some might say it's a business document that describes the nature of a business and its relationship with itself, its customers, and its vendors. Others might portray it as more of a technical document describing the systems and applications used inside an organization and explaining how data travels from one system to another. In reality, both views are correct. The EA document, also called an *EA model,* should contain both a business view of an enterprise and a technology view of an enterprise. The purpose of creating an EA model is to align these two views.

The first step when creating an EA model is to define the current business and technical architecture. This is called the *baseline,* and it serves as a way to document the way things actually operate within a business. Creating even this baseline model can be a bit of a challenge, as it involves an honest assessment of the way things really are—no matter how improper or dysfunctional it may seem.

The next step in creating an EA model is to perform an analysis of the baseline model to identify any improvements that can be made in the business or technical architecture. This can be the toughest step of the entire process because it requires you to put aside personal biases and not worry about the political implications of certain changes. Some processes are unnecessarily complex and need to be simplified. By all means, simplify!

The third step is to take this analysis of the baseline and use it to design a future architecture model to which the enterprise can slowly transition. This is called the *target architecture,* and it aims to solve many of the process problems identified during the analysis stage. The target architecture should answer the question, "How will this organization look in five years?" Of course, the target environment might be radically different from one defined in the baseline unless you're lucky or just happen to be in a slow-growth industry, in which case the two models may be very similar.

The final step is to identify how the organization will be transformed from the baseline to the target architecture. What changes will be implemented? How quickly will the corporate structure be reformed to meet the challenges of the future business environment? Crafting this transformation is a delicate process because these changes will undoubtedly affect the day-to-day lives of some of the employees of a company. If departments are merged, will there be layoffs? If technology is shifted, what type of training will be provided? A target architecture that is well thought out is very useful, but one that is not can cause more problems than it solves. As someone once said, "if you fail to plan, you plan to fail."

Enterprise architecture plays a key role in application development because it is important to understand how the solution concept, which we will learn about later in this chapter, fits in to the "big picture." If the organization is moving toward one technology standard, such as XML web services, that should be taken into consideration when designing the solution.

Defining the Baseline Architecture

The baseline architecture is the definition of the current architecture of an organization. This model contains both a business and a technical view of the company. The business view describes the operational elements of an organization and how they interrelate. Someone should be able to read the business view section of the baseline architecture and completely understand how an organization operates.

The technical view describes the computer systems and applications within an organization and how they interrelate. There will be some overlap (hopefully) between the business and technical views in that the elements of the organization that interact on an operational level (customers, salespeople, orders, invoices, and so on) should also have some relationship at the technical level.

Defining the Business View

In a large company, you are unlikely to find a single person that understands both the business and technical architectures to such a degree that you can construct the entire EA model based solely on their knowledge. This means that you will need to work with people from almost all departments within the company. Only someone from the sales department can accurately explain how people in the sales department interact with people and systems inside and outside the company. Likewise, only the accounting department will be able to explain things from the point of view of the accounting department. It is the collection of all these points of view that goes into building the business model of the enterprise.

The business view of the EA model should take into consideration the following list of operational elements:

- **People**   The human resources of an enterprise
- **Strategy**   The enterprise vision and focus
- **Functions**   The processes and tasks of day-to-day operations
- **Information**   The knowledge and data that feeds the processes
- **Infrastructure**   The equipment, machinery, and other IT resources that exist inside the organization
- **Organizational structure**   The hierarchical and geographical structure of a company

These six elements are combined to define the overall structure of the enterprise. The purpose of creating the business view is to document these elements, including the relationships between them.

We can take advantage of a number of popular modeling methodologies when creating the EA model, including use case, activity, and state diagrams. These three diagrams are created using the Unified Modeling Language (UML), a popular methodology for designing object-oriented systems and applications. The interactions between components of an organization can be modeled graphically, similar to graphic modeling in an object-oriented application.

e x a m
ⓦatch

UML is a graphical language for visualizing object-oriented systems. For more information, visit the official UML web site at http://www.uml.org.

Figure 2-1 shows an example of a UML state diagram. This state diagram reflects the changes of an object within the system over time. This example shows how the state of an order changes between the time that a warehouse receives it and the time that the order is shipped.

FIGURE 2-1

A UML state diagram can be used to define a business process.

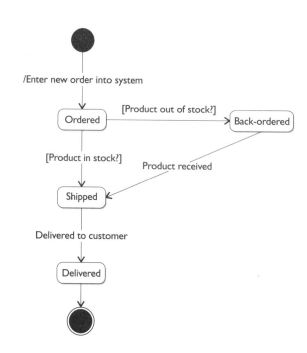

EXERCISE 2-1

Create a UML State Diagram Using Visio for Enterprise Architects

A UML state diagram is a useful tool for describing the behavior of a system. Visio for Enterprise Architects makes it extremely simple to create a diagram that can be used inside an EA model. In this exercise, we will create a UML state diagram that models all of the valid states of a food order at a fast-food restaurant.

1. Choose Start | All Programs and choose Microsoft Visio to start the application.

2. Choose File | New | Software and select UML Model Diagram to create a blank UML model.

3. Choose UML Statechart from the list of templates on the left.

4. Drag the Initial State icon from the template onto the blank page and place it near the top of the page. The Initial State icon looks like a large dot.

5. To add the first state to the diagram, drag the State icon from the template onto the blank page just underneath the Initial State icon. The State icon looks like a rectangle with rounded corners.

6. Name this state "Awaiting Payment" by right-clicking on the State icon, selecting Properties, and typing **Awaiting Payment** in the Name field of the UML State Properties dialog box, as shown in the following illustration. Click OK when finished.

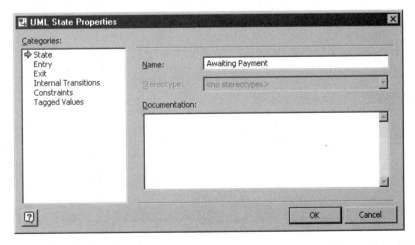

7. Using the same method, add two more states: "Paid" and "Completed."

8. Drag the Transition arrow from the template onto the diagram, connecting the Initial State icon with the first state, Awaiting Payment.

9. Identify an action with this transition by right-clicking on the Transition icon and selecting Properties.

10. Choose the Actions category.

11. Select the New button and choose Create Action. Name this action **Enter order**, as shown in the following illustration.

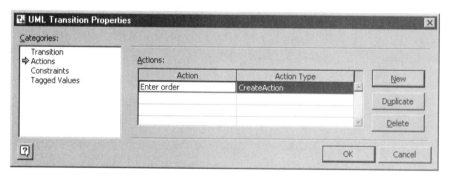

12. Add transitions for the other states. Name them **Accept payment** and **Deliver food**.

13. Add a Final State icon to the diagram from the templates and place it underneath the three states. Connect it to the Completed state using a transition arrow. The Final State icon looks like a large dot with a circle around it.

14. The UML state diagram will look something like the illustration shown next:

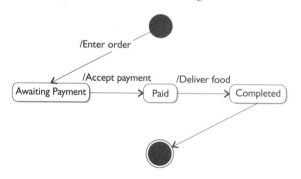

Defining the Technical View

The technical model is, of course, a different story and needs to be treated separately from the business model. The technical processes might be in some ways easier to construct than the business processes, because the existence and structure of systems, networks, and applications are more absolute and usually better documented.

Typically, the EA technical view is subdivided into five smaller architectures:

- **Infrastructure architecture**   Describes the physical network
- **Information architecture (IA)**   Describes the information and data collected
- **Enterprisewide technical architecture (EWTA)**   Describes the core systems and tools
- **Application architecture**   Describes the software development approach
- **Integration architecture**   Describes how new systems will integrate with existing ones

Figure 2-2 shows how the five architecture types fit within the EA model.

Infrastructure architecture is the network hardware and wiring that connects everything together. The big topics to consider are required capacity, security, and monitoring methods.

Information architecture (IA) is concerned with the data collected by an organization. The IA is usually examined from both a logical and a physical point of view. At the logical level, the IA documents the relationship between the various business entities involved, such as employees, customers, orders, and vendors. At a physical level, the IA documents what data is stored, where it is stored, and how applications within the organization access that data.

FIGURE 2-2

The enterprise technical architecture consists of five architecture types.

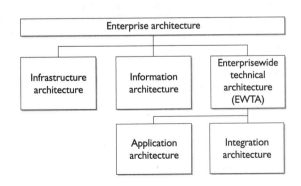

Enterprisewide technical architecture (EWTA) describes the set of technologies upon which third-party or custom-developed applications are built. These technologies include operating systems, programming languages, database systems, application servers, and web servers. EWTA also describes other tools used within the organization such as e-mail, reporting tools, and knowledge management.

Application architecture describes the approach a project should take when a company is developing new applications. For instance, this is where a company would choose the .NET platform as the corporate standard technology for creating new applications. The application architecture document can go even further and suggest a web services model or recommend continuing to develop applications in COM+ using the appropriate .NET wrappers, as discussed in the last chapter.

Integration architecture is the final piece of EA model. It describes how an organization will manage the transition from the current baseline architecture to the new target architecture. Are systems going to run in parallel, or will they be switched over to the new architecture all at once? Can some systems be transitioned seamlessly over to the new architecture without affecting any of the existing systems? The integration architecture should be able to answer that.

We have already said that, in some ways, the technical architecture will correlate well with the business architecture. This has to be true to some degree, or else the business wouldn't be able to function at all. If there were no correlation, information from the order system would not make its way to the distribution systems for processing. The business-technical integration may not be ideal (the ideal scenario will be considered during the target architecture phase), but there has to be a fair bit of correlation already.

SCENARIO & SOLUTION

Which EA component documents the LAN, WAN, and other corporate networks?	Infrastructure architecture
Which EA component documents the type of data collected by an organization?	Information architecture
Which EA component documents the technical approach that should be taken when designing a new application?	Application architecture
Which EA component documents how the organization will transition to the target architecture?	Integration architecture

Analyzing the Business Environment

Once the EA model is complete, it still may not be entirely clear what problems need solving within an organization. Things may seem to be working as they should, and you may be tempted to stop the process right there since nothing appears to need to be fixed.

Of course, questions still need to be asked about the existing business processes. Are the business processes unnecessarily complex? Are there tasks being performed manually that can be automated? Have we identified the processes in the organization that are not working effectively and efficiently, where the stated goal of the process is not really being achieved? It really does require an honest analysis, without regard to personalities or politics. Sure, you don't want to offend the executives of your company (your ultimate bosses) by saying that senior managers are making decisions without having proper or timely access to information. However, if that is an area that needs improvement, it should be pointed out.

Besides an analysis of how things are (or are not) currently working, you also need to consider the future needs of the organization. What aspects of the industry you operate in are expected to change over the next few years? Are there any business avenues that aren't being explored, and will the company be able to react when new opportunities do arise? The answers to all of these questions will help you understand some of the potential improvements that need to be made with the current architecture.

Aligning the Business and Technical Architectures

Once we have completed the analysis of the business view, we will need to analyze the current technical architecture of the organization. The chances are good that there are technical issues that will need fixing, as technology continues to change and improve over time. Perhaps there is too much variety in the hardware and software composition of the organization—a seemingly random mixture of server types, operating systems, networks, and application software—or perhaps the underlying systems are already struggling to meet the current needs of the business and will surely buckle under the weight of future needs.

The technical architecture needs to be able to support the stated business goals of the company. If the organization will double in size in five years, a plan needs to be designed today that will support that growth. If the organization will expand into new lines of business, its technical architecture must be flexible enough to support that expansion as well.

Once the analysis has been performed on the business and technical components of the architecture, it is time to create the target architecture. This part of the process is critical because you are articulating the future vision that was identified in the last two steps of the process.

Making a Commitment to Architecture

Spending a lot of time and money developing an EA model would be worthless if the business did not intend to follow it. The EA model is like a road map. It will show you where you are, where you want to be, and even how to get there.

Developing and sticking to EA model takes commitment from all levels of an organization—from the executive offices all the way down to the leaders of the smallest project teams. What makes the EA model so important is that it answers the question, "What can this company do to improve itself over the next few years?" If only the top executives of a company can answer that question, then everyone in the company may not be working together.

Of particular importance to software designers is the fact that the EA model has a direct impact on how software is designed within the organization. In fact, the EA model will define the playing field in which the designer and developers have to work. If the company plans to spend lots of time, energy, and money building a companywide .NET infrastructure, you will find it hard to suggest a Java 2 Platform, Enterprise Edition (J2EE) solution for a particular business problem. Likewise, if the company has invested heavily in making all its applications web based for cross-platform accessibility on the client side, you would need a really good reason to pursue a Windows-only application as a possible solution to another business problem.

It's important to understand the enterprise architecture of the organization, at least in a general way, before embarking on developing solutions for business problems. Not very many companies take the time to create a proper plan such as this, although those companies usually provide a set of technical standards related to database management software, operating systems, and application server software to guide designers in their decision making.

CERTIFICATION OBJECTIVE 2.01

Developing a Solution Concept

A *solution concept* outlines the solution approach at a high level. It should also be detailed enough so that the planning phase can begin. You should consider the following aspects of the solution when coming up with a solution concept:

- Hardware requirements
- Software requirements
- Integration with existing systems
- Performance requirements

Of course, at this early stage of the project, the solution concept should not be too detailed. We will be gathering more exact business and technical requirements in the planning phase of development before designing a proper solution. For now, we are concentrating on generalities.

Even at the earliest stage of the project, you should have a pretty good idea of what business problem you are trying to solve and what approach you will take to solve it. After all, projects do not start without a predefined purpose. Usually, a project begins with a basic goal. From that goal, one or more solution concepts can be derived and the best course of action decided on.

For example, let's say your boss has asked you to develop an application to track the amount of time employees spend on a per-project basis. Before you jump in and develop detailed specifications for the project, it is a good idea to draw up a couple of good concepts. Your early solution concept for this application might be a web-based solution developed using ASP.NET. The solution concept could also include the ability to link to the human resources database in order to retrieve updated employee information regularly and even the ability to link to the billing system to update customer invoices. There also might be a need for an administrator's web site to manage the application and run various reports. This is an example of a solution concept.

exam
Ⓦatch

Remember, the envisioning phase deals only in concepts. This phase establishes the overall vision for the project and sets the stage for more detailed design in the planning phase.

The construction phase of the project might not be able to create the entire application described by the solution concept in the first release, and that is fine. As we learned at the beginning of the chapter, the MSF process model suggests that the project be broken up into smaller pieces to make them more manageable. As we will see later in the chapter, the project scope uses solution concept to set the tasks to be implemented in the first version of the application.

Let's look at a case study for an example of how a solution concept is developed.

Case Study: Developing a Solution Concept for the RPM System

Jack is a systems analyst for Bottled Water, Inc. (BWI). Occasionally, BWI offers coupons to consumers that they can use to get a discount on BWI water from their local retailer. Each retailer then turns the coupons in to BWI for a credit on its next invoice.

Currently, BWI uses a manual process to credit retailers for the coupons they submit. A data entry clerk hand-counts the coupons received from each retailer and goes into the accounts receivable (AR) system to apply a credit to the retailer's account. This makes it very difficult for management to track how many coupons have been used or to perform any sophisticated analysis on coupon usage. The BWI sales and marketing department would also like to embark on other types of promotions involving the retailers, but that would create even more manual work for the data entry clerks. Some type of automated system for managing retailer promotions needs to be developed.

The BWI Solution Concept

Jack is responsible for designing a solution for this problem. Jack decides he will propose a solution concept first, and if his boss likes that idea, Jack can turn it into a formal design. Based on what he knows about BWI's business requirements, Jack understands that the sales department needs some sort of promotion management system. In his solution concept, he calls this system the Retailer Promotion Management (RPM) system. This system will

- Allow clerks to enter more detail about the number and type of coupons received from each retailer

- Allow sales managers to enable two or three other predefined types of promotions for individual retailers

- Allow sales managers to set limits on the size of the discount individual retailers can earn using promotions
- Automatically link to the AR system to manage monthly credits owed to retailers as a result of these promotions

There may be other requirements, but those will be taken into account during the design phase. Jack believes this system can be run using existing PC and server hardware within the company. BWI will, however, need to develop a custom application for this promotion management system. The application will also need its own database to store its data.

Jack is a good friend of one of the AR system programmers, so he calls her up to ask about integration issues. She assures him that the AR system is already able to receive a nightly feed from any authorized system, so it would not be difficult for the AR system to accept retailer discounts in this manner. She agrees to send Jack the batch interface documentation related to this nightly feed. Jack takes a quick look at the documents and does not see anything that alarms him. The RPM system should be able to send all the data that the AR system requires without difficulty.

Jack also mentions in his solution concept that the RPM system will need to access a database of existing retailers from somewhere. At the current time, he hasn't determined which database will provide the information, although he's sure that it won't pose a problem. Other applications within the company access this information without a problem, so this question can be answered during the design phase.

Lastly, Jack's solution concept touches on performance issues. Because all of the potential users are connected to the company's internal LAN, Jack believes network performance won't be an issue. This application will handle only 50 or so transactions per day, so network or server traffic will have little or no impact on the existing infrastructure.

That is the extent of Jack's solution concept. He still hasn't finished the envisioning phase, but he has a good start to what the solution will eventually look like.

on the job

The envisioning phase is complete when the solution concept has been developed and the project feasibility, scope, and risks have been analyzed.

CERTIFICATION OBJECTIVE 2.02

Analyzing the Feasibility of a Solution

Once you have developed a solution concept, it is time for a reality check: is the project feasible? Feasibility is the "go or no go" decision part of the envisioning phase. There are many factors that enter into the equation when discussing feasibility, such as

- Business feasibility
- Technical feasibility
- Availability of skills and resources

Business feasibility is simply an honest analysis of whether the solution concept meets the needs of the business. Does this solution make things easier or harder for the business? Does it increase profits (by increasing sales or decreasing expenses), or will it cost the business money? By analyzing the business feasibility, we will determine whether it is worth it to proceed from the point of view of the business. Will the benefit outweigh the investment of time, money, and effort?

Technical feasibility is an analysis of whether the solution concept is technically wise and possible. Can the solution scale to meet the growing needs of the business? Are there any performance or security issues that need to be addressed? If there are any technical reasons why this solution can't or shouldn't be implemented, this is the first place to bring them up.

Another important aspect of feasibility, of course, is the *availability of resources.* It's fine to propose a system that will follow the XML web services model running in a .NET environment, but if no one in your organization has .NET skills, this could be a problem that needs to be addressed before the project can continue. Furthermore, if your project will need the full-time involvement of three developers and no one on your project team has any spare time, that also needs to be addressed before the project can go any further.

on the job

The MSF team model is a helpful guide when forming teams for development projects. The team model states that there are six main roles in any team-based development effort; however, those roles do not necessarily directly correlate directly to job titles or individuals.

Case Study: Analyzing Feasibility for the RPM System

Now that Jack has designed a solution concept for the Retailer Promotion Management system, he can begin to analyze the feasibility of his solution. To facilitate the process, he decides to analyze business feasibility, technical feasibility, and resource availability separately.

To help himself come to a conclusion about business feasibility, Jack decides to develop a few screen shots of the application. How will the data entry clerk use the application? How will the sales manager use the application? Jack uses a graphical design program to create a few screens. After he is able to see for himself that the user interface could be quite simple, Jack comes to the conclusion that the RPM system really would make things easier for the business.

The overall goal for the coupon-entry user interface is simplicity. Jack calculates that it will take only ten seconds to enter the coupon information for each retailer, as opposed to the two minutes it takes using the current accounting system. The amount of time saved will greatly reduce the workload of the data entry clerks. In addition, the system will provide additional flexibility for creating and managing promotions in a way that does not currently exist within BWI, and this potentially could lead to increased sales. After analyzing the various possibilities, Jack is able to make a convincing case that this application is feasible from a business perspective.

Regarding technical feasibility, Jack believes that the application will not be a burden on technical resources. The application will be able to scale easily as the business grows, since it will be able to handle multiple users and a large pool of retailers. Because the application will not be exposed to the Internet and only a handful of people within the company will have access, an appropriate security system will be fairly simple to implement. Jack concludes that the project is technically feasible and sound.

On the subject of organizational skills and technical resources, Jack's boss assures him that, when the time comes, the proper team with all the necessary skill sets will be able to be formed. Product and program managers will be assigned, and the team will have appropriate developer and tester resources available to it. Given the size and scope of the project, Jack is confident that getting the appropriate resources and skills together on a project team will not be a problem.

Jack is able to conclude that the project is feasible from business, technical, and resource perspectives. The decision is made that the project should proceed.

Analyzing and Refining the Scope of the Solution Project

Defining the scope of a solution involves an understanding of the various constraints that will be imposed on a project. Whereas the project vision is drafted without consideration for time and expense, the project scope must take the dreams and downsize them to fit within reality.

In the MSF envisioning phase, the project scope defines the functionality that will be developed and released in a single version of the project. Whereas an application might eventually encompass 15 or 20 separate business functions, the scope of the project consists of the initial 4 or 5 functions to be deployed after the first cycle during the iterative development process. Each iteration in the development process requires its own scope, even though the solution concept might change very little during that time.

The project scope is important because it provides a good start for the design phase of the project. Based on what features are included in the scope, a project leader will be able to define a rough schedule and begin thinking about the types of resources required to design and develop the solution. When the client wants one or more new features added to the project after the design phase has ended, this is known as *scope creep.* Scope creep is not necessarily a bad thing, but your project has to have a change management process in place to handle such occurrences.

Of course, there is a limit to the number of new features that can be added to an application before it starts to affect the delivery schedule or the project budget. That is when you have to put a stop to scope creep and say, "It will have to wait until the next release." Of course, if the client insists that the new features be in this release, the project schedule, the budget, or both, will have to be redone, which might mean having to revise the design specifications. These disturbances to the development process should be avoided if at all possible.

As you are creating the solution concept and setting the scope for the project, document your decisions in a "vision/scope document". This document is one of the three deliverables that are produced during the envisioning phase. The other two documents deal with risk assessment and project structure, and have been discussed elsewhere in this chapter.

e x a m
ⓦ a t c h *In the MSF process model, the project vision is an unbounded view of the solution to the business problem at hand. The project scope identifies the part of the vision that can be realistically accomplished in this release.*

Case Study: Defining the Scope for the RPM System

Jack decides it is important to follow the MSF process model and develop the RPM system in small, manageable parts. He decides that the system should be developed in three phases:

- **Phase one**   Create a data entry application for existing coupons that links nightly to the accounting system.

- **Phase two**   Add reporting functions to the application to better track and manage the coupon programs, and add the ability to create monthly limits to the number of coupons a retailer can send in.

- **Phase three**   Add a few more promotion types and modify the data entry and reporting functions to support them.

The scope for the first phase is to develop a simple data entry application using Microsoft VB .NET that links to a SQL Server 2000 database. Using the application, data entry clerks will be able to add, update, search, and delete coupons that are associated to retailers. All transactional activity will then be passed on to the accounting system so that credits can be applied to a retailer's monthly invoice. The RPM application must have basic security and auditing features.

Now that the project scope has been defined, Jack can move on to the final step of the envisioning phase: identifying project risks.

CERTIFICATION OBJECTIVE 2.04

Identifying Key Project Risks

Any event that can have an adverse affect on a project is a risk. It might seem odd to start off a project by thinking about all the things that can go wrong. After all, the whole purpose of following a proper design and development methodology is to ensure that nothing goes wrong. However, things can and will go wrong on any project. If you follow a proper design process, you will have predicted in advance everything that could negatively impact the project, and you will have worked toward minimizing the probability or impact of these events. The goal of this step of the envisioning phase is to identify the most likely or serious risks to the project. Once those risks have been identified, you can figure out how to avoid them during the planning phase of the project.

The results of this initial risk assessment should be saved in a "risk assessment document." This document is the third of the three deliverables that are produced during the envisioning phase. The other two documents deal with project structure and vision/scope, and were discussed earlier in this chapter.

When you think about it, there are many things that can have an adverse affect on a project. For example:

- A key team member could leave the company or suddenly be transferred to another project (a people risk).

- The development phase may take longer than planned because of the number of new skills the developers will have to learn (a people risk).

- The product might have several bugs due to an overly aggressive schedule (a process risk).

- Government regulations for this product could change between now and the delivery date (an environmental risk).

All of these examples are considered risks to the project. Of course, not all of these risks are considered equal, as we will see later in this section.

The MSF risk management discipline lists over 20 potential sources of risk, broken into four major categories. This list should stimulate a project team's planning when thinking about risk. Consider each category carefully and identify any risks (whether they are likely or not) that could affect the project. Table 2-2 lists what Microsoft suggests are the potential sources of risk in a project.

It is often a good project team exercise to try to list as many potential risks to the project as you can. This can be during a brainstorming session where the project team sits in a room and all risks are listed on a whiteboard. All potential risks should be considered. At this stage, be very careful when dismissing risks that have not yet been assessed.

TABLE 2-2	Risk Category	Risk Source
Categories and Potential Sources of Risk	People	Customers End users Sponsors Stakeholders Personnel Organization Skills Politics Morale
	Process	Mission and goals Decision making Project characteristics Budget, cost, and schedule Requirements Design Building Testing
	Technology	Security Development and test environments Tools Deployment Support Operational environment Availability
	Environmental	Legal Regulatory Competition Economic Technology Business

The next step is to assign probability and impact values to each of the risks that have been identified. The probability of each risk occurring is listed either as a percentage or as a numerical value from one to ten. An impact value also needs to be assigned, and it represents how serious the potential effect on the project will be if the risk occurs. Impact is listed either as a value from one to ten or simply as "low," "medium," or "high."

A project risk is anything that can negatively impact the project.

At this point in the process, we have identified the project risks and assessed the probability and impact of each risk on the project. Table 2-3 provides an example of such an assessment.

Of course, most projects have many more potential risks. Large and complex projects potentially can have dozens of risks; and any time one project is dependent on another for information or resources, there is the potential for even more risks.

You may feel as though you are going overboard with the number of risks you are considering, but that's okay because you have to evaluate the potential for catastrophic events to occur, such as a server hardware failure or a key vendor going bankrupt. From experience, I would suggest that some risks could be grouped together if they are closely related. For instance, you do not have to consider the failure of the web server and the database server separately—they can both go under the general risk of "server failure." Some sense of reasonableness should exist in the list of risks, however. Some risks, such as the destruction of the planet Earth, are too catastrophic to consider. If that happens, we will have bigger problems to worry about than missing the delivery schedule for our infinitesimally unimportant little project.

Of course, there is a way to distinguish between unlikely but severe risks and those that are more likely but will cause only mild impact. There are many ways to do this, but I usually add a third column to my table that multiplies the probability and impact values together to come up with a measurement of total risk. Table 2-4 shows how the preceding example (see Table 2-3) looks with the inclusion of the total risk calculation. I have resorted the table, placing the risks in order of severity from top to bottom.

As you can see, an overly aggressive project schedule is the most serious risk this project faces. There is also a serious risk that the development phase will take longer than normal due to a steep learning curve for some developers. These risks are

TABLE 2-3	Risk	Probability (1–10)	Impact (1–10)
	Lead developer suddenly leaving the team	3	7
Project Risks Example	Long development phase due to learning curve on new skills	7	5
	Overly aggressive schedule	7	7
	Change in government regulations	3	3

TABLE 2-4	Risk	Probability (1–10)	Impact (1–10)	Total Risk (P × I)
	Overly aggressive schedule	7	7	49
Project Risks Example Including Total Risk Calculation	Long development phase due to learning curve on new skills	7	5	35
	Lead developer suddenly leaving the team	3	7	21
	Change in government regulations	3	3	9

related, but the project schedule could still be considered aggressive even with experienced developers working on the project, so solving one risk does not solve the other. This type of risk assessment gives the project team leaders a useful "heads up" to potential problems down the road.

exam

Ⓦatch

The three documents that get created during the envisioning phase in the MSF process model are the vision/scope document, the risk assessment document, and the project structure document.

Case Study: Identifying Key Project Risks for the RPM System

In Chapter 3, you will learn about gathering and analyzing business and user requirements. As you will learn in that chapter, the business requirements document is a definitive list of what operating tasks the user expects the system to perform. Having an intimate understanding of this document is crucial for the success of the project; however, there are other important factors in order for a project to be able to succeed.

Oftentimes, mitigating the possible events that could cause serious harm to the project—the project risks—are not explicitly listed as a business requirement, although protecting the project from those risks is one of the important tasks of the project team. For the RPM system, Jack can identify three project risks.

First, the project team has not been identified, which could delay the start of the planning phase of the project. Jack's boss assures him that this will be taken care of, but it is still a risk. Jack assigns a probability of 2 out of 10 to this risk, but the impact would be a 7, so the total risk is be 2 × 7, or 14.

Second, the new promotion types have not been identified, which could necessitate changes to application design in a later release. Since the new promotion types are not needed until a later version of the application (the first version will handle only

<table>
<tr><td colspan="2" align="center">**SCENARIO & SOLUTION**</td></tr>
<tr><td>What is the high-level outline of a solution called?</td><td>Solution concept</td></tr>
<tr><td>What type of feasibility examines the skills of the project team?</td><td>Availability of resources</td></tr>
<tr><td>What milestone of the envisioning phase applies time and budget realities to the project vision?</td><td>Scope</td></tr>
</table>

coupons), it won't have a big impact now. Jack assigns this a probability of 5, but an impact of only 1, so the total risk (5 × 1) is only a 5.

Third, since the application is being developed in .NET, Jack worries that the developers might need to be sent to a training course before project development can begin. In part, this relates to the first risk in that the development team hasn't been identified. He thinks this should be listed separately, however, because even if the project team members are identified tomorrow, they still might need to be trained. Jack assigns this a probability of 6 and an impact of 3, for a total risk (6 × 3) of 18.

Those are the only risks Jack is able to come up with for this project. Of course, as the project progresses, other risks may be identified and need to be addressed. All of the risks seem manageable to him, and he's confident the project will be a success.

In the next chapter, we will complete the envisioning phase of the project and begin the planning phase. We will see how analyzing the business, user, and operational requirements is key to proper application design.

CERTIFICATION SUMMARY

An enterprise architecture (EA) model documents an organization's business and technical structure. It analyzes the various entities that belong to the company (for example, its people, strategy, and information) and the relationships between them. EA models often use common diagramming methods (for example, UML use case, activity, and state diagrams) to illustrate the architecture more clearly. The EA model also analyzes the technical assets of the company (for example, servers, networks, and data) to see how well the technical and business architectures support each other.

Based on this analysis, a target architecture is developed as a map to show how a company needs to transform itself over the next few years.

A solution concept outlines the solution approach at a high level. The solution concept needs to be detailed enough so that the planning phase can begin. The solution concept generally states in a paragraph or two what the project team's approach will be to solving the problem at hand.

Analyzing business and technical feasibility is the next step in the process. This step results in a "go or no go" decision being made about the project. The solution concept must be examined from both a business and a technical perspective to decide if the proposed solution is feasible. This is also where questions about the availability of certain technical skills within the organization will be considered.

Project scope incorporates a bit more reality into the project vision and solution concept. The purpose of the project scope is to outline specifically what application functionality will be delivered in the initial release and what is planned for future releases. The scope feeds directly into the planning phase of the project.

Finally, identifying key project risks is the last step of the envisioning phase. A risk is any event that could have a negative impact on a project's costs, functionality, or schedule. If your project is relying on outside help, either from a vendor or from another project team within your organization, that should be mentioned here as a possible risk. Each identified risk is assigned a probability score and an impact score, and these can be combined to indicate the level of importance, or overall risk. Risks identified here will be mitigated in future phases of the project.

TWO-MINUTE DRILL

The Microsoft Solutions Framework

❑ The Microsoft Solutions Framework (MSF) is made up of two models and three disciplines: the process model, the team model, the project management discipline, the risk management discipline, and the readiness management discipline.

❑ The process model outlines a method for developing software solutions in which a large project is split into several smaller projects—a process called iterative development—and each of these smaller projects is split into five phases: envisioning, designing, developing, stabilizing, and deploying.

❑ The team model outlines a method for building a project team that centers around six key areas of responsibility: product management, program management, development, test, user experience, and release management.

Developing an Enterprise Architecture

❑ The enterprise architecture (EA) model is a document that outlines the business and technical structure of an organization.

❑ The EA model is used for transforming a business from its current architecture, called a baseline architecture, to its future architecture, called a target architecture.

❑ Understanding the EA model allows project architects to design solutions that meet the stated future needs and vision of an organization.

Developing a Solution Concept

❑ A solution concept is a high-level outline of a proposed solution.

❑ It states the overall vision for how the project will meet the requirements of the business.

Analyzing the Feasibility of a Solution

❑ There are three aspects to assessing the feasibility of a project: business feasibility, technical feasibility, and the feasibility based on the availability of resources.

❑ This is the "go or no go" decision of the envisioning phase.

Analyzing and Refining the Scope of the Solution Project

❑ The project scope incorporates the reality of time and budget into the solution concept.

❑ It describes what a project is able to deliver in its first release, which feeds into the planning phase of the project.

Identifying Key Project Risks

❑ A risk is any event that could potentially have a negative impact on the project's schedule, cost, or functionality.

❑ Each risk is analyzed to determine its probability and impact.

SELF TEST

The following questions will help you measure your understanding of the material presented in this chapter. Read all the choices carefully because there might be more than one correct answer. Choose all correct answers for each question.

The Microsoft Solutions Framework

1. Which of the following models are parts of the Microsoft Solutions Framework? (Choose all that apply.)

   A. Program model

   B. Process model

   C. Team model

   D. Project model

2. Which of the following is the Microsoft Solutions Framework designed to provide:

   A. A step-by-step process for developing software

   B. A series of templates that can be used in Visual Studio .NET to create software quickly

   C. A way to develop software in half the time of traditional methods

   D. A set of rules related to building teams and embarking on solution design and development

Developing an Enterprise Architecture

3. What is the purpose of creating an enterprise architecture model?

   A. Ensure that the business view of the enterprise is aligned with the technical view and that the best overall business and technical structure exists

   B. Map geographically where all the servers and networks are installed throughout an organization

   C. Define the roles and responsibilities of each individual in an organization

   D. Identify the systems and applications used throughout an organization

4. Which of the following components belong inside the technical view of an enterprise architecture model? (Choose all that apply.)

   A. Infrastructure architecture

   B. Information architecture

    C. Integration architecture

    D. Organization architecture

Developing a Solution Concept

5. Which of the following details are likely to be part of a solution concept? (Choose all that apply.)

    A. A high-level description of the approach

    B. Results of performance tests between two vendor solutions

    C. A proof-of-concept application that proves a solution is viable

    D. Consideration of existing systems

6. Which one of the following statements would you most likely see in a solution concept?

    A. The Employee class is a parent of the Manager class.

    B. The project will require two full-time developer resources—one will develop the data entry application, and the other will develop the database and stored procedures.

    C. The customer will be able to access the application over the Internet using any web browser.

    D. The project should take six weeks to develop, including QA testing.

Analyzing the Feasibility of a Solution

7. Tony, a solutions architect at Acme Corporation, is trying to assess the feasibility of adding online ordering to the company's existing web site. He expects that the project will require new web server hardware that will cost $100,000, plus the purchase of an off-the-shelf e-commerce application that will cost $25,000. The three months it will take a developer to integrate the solution into the company's web site will cost $40,000. Based on a survey of a handful of existing customers and taking into account the current level of traffic to the company's web site, Tony expects approximately $40,000 a year in sales from the new web site. Based on these facts, which of the following statements best describes the project feasibility?

    A. The project is feasible because the project will pay for itself in only four years.

    B. The project is not technically feasible because there are other costs that need to be taken into account.

    C. The project is not feasible from a business point of view because it is likely that the hardware and e-commerce software will need to be upgraded again by the time the project pays for itself in four years.

    D. The project is not feasible from an availability of resources point of view because the developer does not have sufficient experience with the e-commerce software.

8. What would the best course of action be if it were decided that a solution concept was not feasible during the envisioning phase?

    A. Continue to develop solution concepts until an appropriate solution can be found.

    B. Stop work on the project because the business problem cannot be solved.

    C. Continue on to the design phase because you cannot really tell if a project will be feasible this early in the process.

    D. Hire more development resources in order to overcome the feasibility issues.

9. What are some of the valid reasons a project might not be feasible? (Choose all that apply.)

    A. The solution would take too long to develop.

    B. Several key project risks have been identified.

    C. The technical architecture does not exist to support the solution, and no money is available in the budget to build such an architecture.

    D. The project looks like it will require 30 hours a week of your time over the next two months, but you have another high-priority project that needs to be completed during that time as well.

Analyzing and Refining the Scope of the Solution Project

10. Which one of the following statements would you be most likely to see in a project scope?

    A. The first screen will have the words "Private Water Testing System" in the title bar, along with minimize and maximize control buttons.

    B. When the user attempts to log in, the system will authenticate their user ID and password against the SQL Server database located on DBO2.

    C. The first phase of the project will implement the data entry portion of the application, while the second phase will introduce some basic reporting.

    D. Use Case 12.1 documents how the customer will make an online purchase using the application's web interface.

11. Margaret is developing the next release of her company's point-of-sale system. She has begun the developing phase of the project, and she has been asked to add some new functionality to

the application that was not specified in the project scope. What is the industry term used to describe this event?

A. Scope instrumentation

B. Reenvisioning

C. Scope development

D. Scope creep

12. Margaret has been asked to include new features late in the project development phase. She has asked the client to hold off until the next release, but the client absolutely insists that the new features be included in this release. What is the term used to describe the incorporation of changes into a project after the design phase has ended?

A. Application redesign

B. Client management

C. Change management

D. Rearchitecting

Identifying Key Project Risks

13. Which of the following would be considered a project risk? (Choose all that apply.)

A. The lead programmer might get hit by a bus.

B. The client might request modifications halfway through the project that would require major changes to the application.

C. Programmers may have overestimated the amount of time required to develop the program, and as a result it might be delivered early.

D. Programmers may have underestimated the amount of time required to develop the program, and as a result it might be delivered late.

14. Which of the following risk estimates need to be generated during the envisioning phase of the project?

A. Probability

B. Probability and impact

C. Probability, impact, and project budget

D. Probability, impact, and cost-benefit analysis

15. Margaret is developing the next release of her company's PC-based point-of-sale system. The major improvement in this release is that the system can provide regular (but not real-time) sales updates to the central reporting server throughout the day, instead of only a single update done overnight. A number of project risks have been identified. Which of the following risks would have the most serious impact on the project?

    A. The application will require more computer memory and hard disk space, so there is a risk that customers might have to upgrade their computer hardware to install the new version.

    B. Half of the developers are new to the project, so development might take two weeks longer than planned.

    C. The application will be more difficult to test, so all software flaws might not be fixed before release.

    D. The business requirements might change, so there is a risk of project delays and rework.

LAB QUESTION

You have been asked to design a PC-based point-of-sale (POS) terminal for a movie theater. Systems already exist for scheduling movies, and recording sales. The POS system will have to support only the action of purchasing tickets. A theater employee will be using the system to sell tickets to the customers as they walk in the front door. During the ticket-purchasing activity, the POS system will verify that there are enough available seats, calculate the cost of the tickets, accept payment, and send the tickets to be printed.

Define the solution concept, feasibility, and scope for this project and identify and evaluate the key project risks.

SELF TEST ANSWERS

The Microsoft Solutions Framework

1. ☑ **B and C.** The process and team models are the two models contained in the solutions framework.
   ☒ **A and D** are incorrect because they are not models within the MSF.

2. ☑ **D.** The goal of the MSF is to share the vast experience of Microsoft and some of its partners in designing software and building project teams.
   ☒ **A** is incorrect because the framework is not a step-by-step process for developing software. **B** is incorrect because there are no MSF templates for Visual Studio. **C** is incorrect because, although you may save some time designing software, using the MSF is not specifically designed to develop software in half the time. Its purpose is to help you develop the best solution possible with regard to the needs of the business.

Developing an Enterprise Architecture

3. ☑ **A.** An EA model defines the current processes and procedures of an organization, as well as the structure of its technology. It concerns itself with aligning the business and technical views of the company.
   ☒ **B** is incorrect because geographical mapping is not a core task in EA modeling. **C** is incorrect because it is a feature of the MSF team model and not EA modeling. **D** is incorrect because the identification of the systems and applications in the organization is only a small part of the overall purpose of the EA model. It is much more important to understand how those systems interconnect and how data flows throughout the organization.

4. ☑ **A, B, and C.** Infrastructure, information, and integration architectures are three of the five components of the EA technical view. The other two are enterprisewide technical architecture and application architecture.
   ☒ **D** is incorrect because there is no architecture within the EA model called organization architecture.

Developing a Solution Concept

5. ☑ **A and D.** Solution concepts are high-level approaches to solving business problems. A solution concept should take into consideration existing systems in order to be considered the best possible solution.

☒   **B** is incorrect because the solution concept is not concerned with low-level details such as performance test results. **C** is incorrect because proof-of-concepts involve feasibility, belong in the design phase, and should not be part of the solution concept, which is concerned with developing high-level concepts.

6.   ☑   **C.** A solution concept should propose a specific, high-level solution to the business problem at hand, without getting into too much detail.
     ☒   **A** is incorrect because solution concepts do not deal with objects or classes. **B** is incorrect because even if the resources have been identified in advance, it is also too early to talk about specific assignments for these resources. **D** is incorrect because, although a rough schedule may be set in advance, the solution concept is concerned only with the approach to solving a business problem and not other planning or coordination tasks.

Analyzing the Feasibility of a Solution

7.   ☑   **C.** From the business point of view, this project will cost way too much for the expected benefit. By the time the deployment costs have been recouped, the server hardware and application software will likely need to be upgraded.
     ☒   **A** is incorrect because the project is clearly not feasible from a business point of view—the costs far exceed the benefits. **B** is incorrect because cost is not a technical feasibility consideration. **D** is incorrect because, with proper documentation and vendor support, a smart developer should be able to install and configure application software.

8.   ☑   **A.** The purpose of developing a solution concept and analyzing it for feasibility before committing time and resources to a proper design is to determine if a project is infeasible at the beginning of the process. Just because one solution is infeasible does not mean another simpler solution would not be more feasible but still adequate for the user's requirements.
     ☒   **B** is incorrect because the infeasibility of one solution concept does not mean a solution to a business problem cannot be found. **C** is incorrect because it is not wise to invest time and money in a project that appears infeasible during the envisioning phase. **D** is incorrect because some feasibility issues, such as business feasibility and technical feasibility problems, cannot be overcome by hiring more resources.

9.   ☑   **A, C,** and **D.** These three reasons fall into the categories of business feasibility, technical feasibility, and availability of resources, respectively. All are reasons that are difficult or impossible to overcome and therefore need to be flagged as issues of feasibility.
     ☒   **B** is incorrect because it is not impossible to overcome key project risks. Project risks can usually be managed. Simply having several key project risks is not enough to become a feasibility issue.

Analyzing and Refining the Scope of the Solution Project

10. ☑ **C.** A project scope provides the details of each version of a project and identifies, in general terms, what each version will deliver to the client.
☒ **A** is incorrect because this type of statement is too specific, and belongs in the design phase. **B** is incorrect because these statements specify too much technical information and are part of physical design. **D** is incorrect because use cases are also design phase artifacts.

11. ☑ **D.** Scope creep occurs when new requirements are added to the scope after the design phase is complete.
☒ **A, B,** and **C** are incorrect because they are not industry-standard terms.

12. ☑ **C.** Change management is the name of the process used to manage requested changes to the application requirements. These changes can be accepted, rejected, or deferred to a future release.
☒ **A, B,** and **D** are incorrect because they are not industry-standard terms.

Identifying Key Project Risks

13. ☑ **A, B,** and **D.** Project risks are events that may or may not occur and would negatively impact the project.
☒ **C** is incorrect because finishing a project early would not have a negative effect.

14. ☑ **B.** Estimates of probability and impact should be attached to key project risks to help assess how serious they are. You can even combine these two values into a single value to estimate total project risk.
☒ **A** is incorrect because impact also needs to be estimated for an accurate reflection of the true level of risk. **C** and **D** are incorrect because total project budget and cost-benefit analysis are not a function of risk.

15. ☑ **A.** Developing an application that would negatively impact the customer's ability to upgrade from an older release would be the most serious risk.
☒ **B** is incorrect because two extra weeks of development time on a big project is not considered serious. **C** is incorrect because testing will be performed, regardless of its difficulty. **D** is incorrect because changing business requirements can be easily managed through a change management process.

LAB ANSWER

The solution concept you visualized might, of course, be different from the one outlined here. You should be able to justify (in your own mind) any differences between your solution and this one. Keep in mind that the solution concept needs to be a high-level concept but detailed enough to be able to begin the design phase.

The solution concept for the movie ticket point-of-sale (POS) system is a custom Windows application that will be developed with a very simple user interface. The system will be developed to work with a touch-screen monitor, if possible, to eliminate the need for a keyboard and mouse at the cashier's window. The POS system will need its own database to store the movie schedules that have been downloaded from the scheduling system and keep track of ticket sales by individual theater.

The system will be able to print tickets on an appropriate printer, as well as communicate with the sales and scheduling systems.

The application appears feasible from business, technical, and availability of resources perspectives. It should not be too costly to develop, and it does provide a benefit to the business. None of the technology envisioned in the solution should pose a problem. The application will not be a burden to computers or networks, and security will not be an issue. For the sake of this example, we will assume that suitable programming resources have already been identified so that will not be an issue either.

It does not make sense to break up the deployment of this application into multiple versions, so the scope of this release is to deliver the entire solution concept. The application will allow cashiers to sell tickets to customers and cause those tickets to print on the ticket printer. The application will integrate with back-end systems to download movie schedules and record sales information.

The key project risks are usually specific to an individual project or organization and are difficult to gather just from the user requirements. On this small project, if the application developer leaves before the project is finished, it will have a serious impact on the schedule. If it is not possible to get a touch-screen interface, it will have a slight impact on the quality of the POS system from the cashier's point of view. Another risk is that if the application crashes in production, it will have a serious impact on the business in that it will not be able to sell tickets. Following a risk management strategy can reduce the negative impact of these risks on the project.

3

Gathering and Analyzing Business and User Requirements

The gathering of business requirements is the process of defining and summarizing user workflow, processes, and rules into a written non-technical format. A requirement describes a condition or capability to which a system must conform. This can be either derived directly from user needs, or stated in a contract, standard, specification, or other formally imposed document. We take the information that was provided from the vision statement and use it to create a more detailed solution. The vision statement gives a general guideline to what the problem is that needs to be solved. Next, we have to figure out the details of the problem and create documents that can be used to determine how to solve the problem. During the envisioning phase, business requirements or high-level requirements are identified and analyzed. The planning phase will take those requirements and refine them further. The result is a functional specifications document. This document is the culmination of the business requirements for the solution. Requirements fall into four main categories: business requirements, user requirements, operational requirements, and system requirements. All of these requirements are covered in this chapter.

CERTIFICATION OBJECTIVE 3.01

Gathering and Analyzing Business Requirements

The first step to analyzing business and user requirements is to assess the current business perspective. This includes examination of the business processes, organizational structure, and social/political environmental factors. By examining this first, we can form a basic understanding of the common business context, rules, and organizational information.

This information is critical to understand before proceeding to the next step, which is gathering the business requirements. Gathering requirements is the discovery and processing of information related to the vision of the project. Finally, this information is applied to models and use cases to identify features and dependencies.

Scenario 3.1: RecruitmentService.net Case Study

RecruitmentService.net is a fictional online employment agency dedicated to serving employers and job seekers. RecruitmentService.net maintains information on 50,000 jobs and over 75,000 resumes globally, and has a monthly subscription client base. It is headquartered in Chicago and has 150 employees. The year 2001 resulted in annual revenues of $5 million. RecruitmentService.net is undertaking a major renovation of their system, and it has hired you as a consultant as it considers the merits of using Windows 2003 and the .NET framework for the next version of their system. It is interested in using .NET technologies in implementing the new solution. RecruitmentService.net is interested in examining the benefits of web services. Their top competitor attracts some 41 million unique visits each month with more than 800,000 U.S. job listings and more than 17 million. It also operates sites in 20 other countries in Asia, Australia, Europe, and North America. In 2001, this competitor also recognized annual revenues of $536 million.

The purpose of the renovation is to create an application that is easier to maintain and that will support multiple types of devices for viewing. The current solution does not support multiple languages, but will adapt to the needed changes.

The Existing IT Environment

RecruitmentService.net has ten web servers, all of which run Windows 2000 Server. The web servers are built on Pentium III 500 MHz servers with 512 MB of memory, which use IIS 5.0. The data tier consists of a two-node cluster of dual-processor servers running Windows 2000 Advanced Server and SQL Server 7.0. The RecruitmentService.net application was developed using Visual Basic 6, ASP, and SQL. Some of the business functionality is encapsulated into COM objects.

Business Process

RecruitmentService.net is completely dependent on its web servers. To maintain a competitive advantage, continuous availability of the entire site is required. Download speed of the HTML and ASP pages is critical to the business. Employers input their job postings to the web site, and the web development content approval team verifies the posting information.

The web development team then generates a job seekers database. Job seekers have read-only access to the database data. Network administrators maintain the SQL server. RecruitmentService.net would like to both simplify and improve the method by which information is exchanged with employers and job seekers. For example, they would like to make it easier for employers with multiple job openings to submit those listings in a batch, instead of requiring that they fill out a job posting form for each opening. They would also like to allow job seekers to read job postings and check on the status of applications via web-enabled cell phones and other wireless devices.

Interviews with Key Personnel

The following notes are from key stakeholders and clients for the application.

CEO Interview Notes

As the web site grows, so must the increase in performance to meet the needs of today's user. We must also maintain 100 percent uptime. Though we have clients and users all over the world, up to now we have primarily served the English-speaking world. We are ready to begin expanding into other cultures, and we would like to test a Spanish version of our site within the next six months. This will be followed by a German version, and then a French version shortly thereafter.

Chief Technology Officer Interview Notes

The system must support scalability. Anticipating significant growth, RecruitmentService .net must be able to add new machines into its racks with minimal cost and no system downtime. The system needs to handle a peak of 1,000 new records of incoming data per hour. We had some requests from large clients, especially those who use non-Windows systems such as Unix and IBM mainframes, to improve the way data can be exchanged between systems. We recently had a large international client who posted 125 job descriptions, and because of incompatibilities in our system, we had to enter each job listing manually. We suspect XML may be a good solution to this kind of problem. Whatever solution we choose, we would like a database to be able to create data directly in a format we could share with our clients.

The following products will be implemented: Windows 2000 Server for the web tier, and Windows 2000 Advanced Server for the infrastructure and data tier. The web servers will continue to run IIS 5.0. We are open to whatever software and hardware we may need to add, if the switch to .NET makes sense and supports all of our intended functionality.

Three times a week, the IT department at RecruitmentService.net runs a stored procedure that attempts to locate the redundant accounts, deletes accounts that have been inactive for more that a year, and creates a list of users to receive certain targeted e-mails. This procedure may affect several thousand records in a space of a few minutes.

exam
Watch

The exam will have scenarios like this one containing information that will have to be deciphered to answer multiple choice questions and create diagrams.

Analyzing the Current Business State

Examination of the current and future business perspectives is the beginning phase of gathering information. It is necessary to understand the current perspective in order to create a solution that fits and solves all the needs of that particular business.

Analyze Business Processes

The processes of a business are defined as a number of different use cases, each of which represents a specific workflow in the business. A use case defines what should happen in a business process when work is performed. It describes the performance of a sequence of steps that produces a valuable result to a particular business actor. A business process should generate value for the business. Keywords that are essential to understanding what a use case is include:

- **Actor**   A representation of a role played by an outside object. This actor can represent multiple physical objects.

- **Use case**   A representation of a set of events that occurs when an actor uses a system to complete a process. A use case is generally a large process, not an individual step or transaction.

- **System boundary**   Represents the extent of responsibilities of the system being used. The use case should only represent the interactions of a single system.

There are several standard relationships among use cases or between actors and use cases. These are:

- **Constraint**   A specification for conditions and propositions that must be maintained as true in order for the system to be valid.

- **Extends**   Indicates an instance of use case B, and can derive functionality from use case A. An example would be a Recruiter class that extends specific behavior from the Accounts object.

- **Package**   A grouping of model elements, represented by a symbol that looks like a manila file folder.

- **Communication**   Defines how an actor participates in a use case. An actor can only use the Communication object to link to other objects in the diagram.

- **Interface**   Specifies the externally visible operations of a class, component, package, or other elements without specifying internal structure.

- **Note**   Diagram comment that has no semantic influence on the model elements.

EXERCISE 3-1

Create a Use Case Diagram

This exercise illustrates a use case diagram that shows the actions of a job seeker.

1. To open Microsoft Visio, click Start | All Programs | Microsoft Visio. Visio comes in three versions: Standard, Professional, and Enterprise. The Professional version comes with the Architect Version of Visual Studio.NET. The following image illustrates this process.

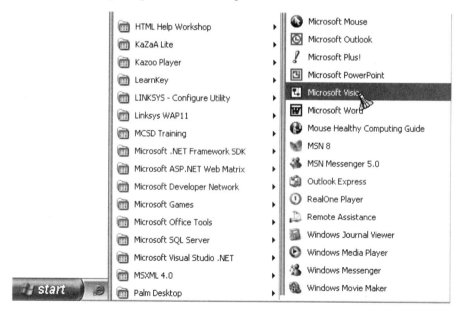

2. Select BasisUseCaseStart.vsd. from the Chapter 3 CD-ROM code directory.

3. When the file opens, you will see a boundary defined as the web site. There is one actor, which will be named in the exercise. There are four defined use case objects inside the boundary. The following illustration displays how the screen should look.

■ *Accounts* defines the master list of accounts to the system.

■ *Account* defines a type of view of the accounts to the specified actor.

■ Job Postings

■ Resumes

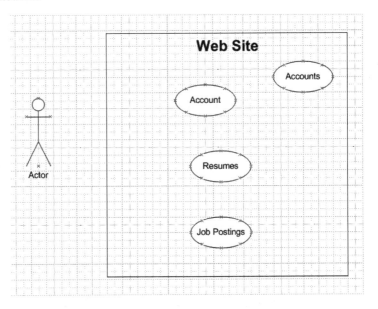

4. To name the actor, double-click the Actor on the workspace. The following illustration shows the property window that displays. Change the Name property to Job Seeker.

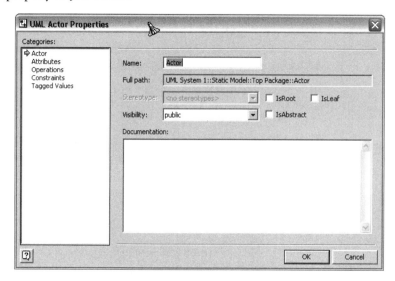

5. To add communication links between the actor and use case, drag and drop a Communication object to the workspace. The Communication object and others that will be used in the exercise are located on the left side of the screen under the Shapes window, just above the Model Explorer. The following illustration shown on the left displays the workspace where the objects we are going to use in this exercise are contained. Take the left end of the Communication object and drag it to the Actor. When the Actor turns red, drop the end. The following image shown on the right illustrates this process. Next take the right end of the Communication object and do the same for Account.

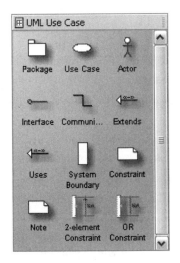

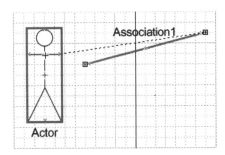

6. While the line is still selected, double-click or right-click on the line and select Properties. A dialog box is displayed that allows the setting of options for the type of communication. The following illustration shows this window. In the Name property, type **Create Account**.

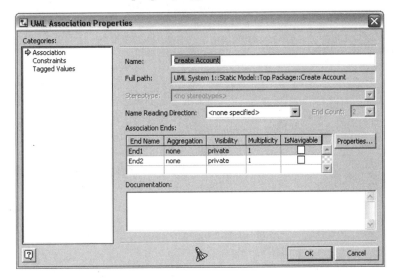

7. Drag and drop two more Communication objects. Connect the Actor to the Resumes and Job Postings use cases. The communication link to Resumes should be named Create Resumes. The communication link to Job Postings should be named View Job Postings.

8. Drag and drop an Extends object to the workspace. Connect the arrow end to the Account use case and the other end to the Accounts use case. The Account use case is actually an extension of the Accounts use case. The Accounts use case represents the master list of accounts for the system.

9. To change what gets displayed on the diagram, the Connection objects might not be showing the names. To correct this, right-click on a Connection object and select Shape Display Options from the context menu. The following dialog box appears, which shows options to display or suppress specific values of a UML element view, such as showing or hiding attributes on a Class shape. Select the options that you want to display.

10. If you chose the options shown in the previous illustration, the result should look like this:

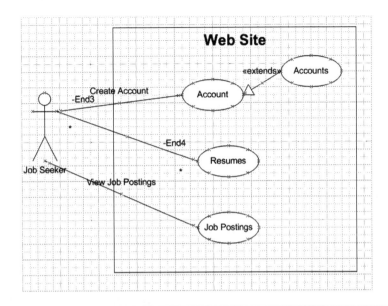

Building a Use Case Process

Some characteristics of a good business use case are to make sure that the description is clear and easy to understand for everyone. Each use case is complete from an outside (actor's) point of view. Each use case is normally involved with at least one actor. Use cases are initiated by actors, interact with actors to perform the activities, and deliver results.

Let's use a sample business use case to demonstrate these elements.

An example of a process is that of creating a new job seeker account. This process would entail the creation of a unique account name and password plus submission information for the online resume. The user could optionally create saved job searches for future examination.

exam
ⓦatch

You will need to be able to identify business processes and accurately determine the order of the steps.

Business processes fall into several categories:

■ **Common processes** These would include tasks involved with accounting systems or human resource systems, for example. These are processes that exist in all businesses.

- **Industry-specific processes**   These are processes that only exist in a specific line of business. Reservation systems are a common industry-specific process in the airline and hotel industries.

- **Competitive processes**   These processes define how a business is unique compared to its competitors and customers. For example, RecruitmentService.net supports a single login process and competitor B does not support any quick login processes.

- **Support processes**   These processes assist with daily and maintenance operations. For example, RecruitmentService.net runs a process that cleans up account information three times a week.

Prioritizing Business Processes

After a list of business processes has been created and defined, they need to be prioritized. This will determine the order and construction of later requirements and development processes. Priorities will vary business by business, but there are some standard process review issues that should be considered and prioritized based on individual project needs. The following questions address the issues of revenue, costs, customer contact, business goals, and change:

- Does implementing this process significantly increase or decrease our revenue?

- Is there significant cost involved?

- Does this process involve contact with customers?

- Does it fit with our business model?

- What is the impact of change on this process and does it have to change?

- Does this process interact with or depend on other processes?

- Does this process fall within the problem domain?

These questions will help define your core processes so you can determine if other processes are missing or need to be changed. A good business process description can be written by following these guidelines:

- Describe the workflow, not just the purpose of the business use case.

- Describe all possible processes in the business use case.

- Describe only those processes that are inside the business.
- Describe only relevant processes, not those that do not intersect.

You should be able to create a list of processes and activities that focus on high priority and high value. By prioritizing the processes, you can select the most critical processes in need of change. This also helps constrain the boundary and define the processes so there is no ambiguity.

Analyzing Personnel and Training Needs

Users are the individuals who will use the business solution in their daily work or who are affected by the business solution. There are three types of users: direct, indirect, and hidden. Direct users are individuals who will use the solution. Indirect users are people who do not directly use the application but are affected by it. Hidden users work with the solution, but they might not be easily identified. Because users fall into multiple categories, we want to create user profiles to help us determine the various impacts of the solutions being proposed. This includes end users who would use the solutions as well as people who are receiving information based on the solution, or who need to interact indirectly with the solution. For example, this could include managers who get reports from the solutions or third-party users.

Creating user profiles allows the requirements process to examine the needs of the various users, because it is very common that business goals are written in terms of customer expectations and needs. Users also have expectations and needs that need to be addressed. If these are ignored, the solution may fit the business goals and objectives, but fail because the users do not accept the solution. The organizational structure determines how user profiles are created. This allows the generation of an organization chart that can be used to determine user responsibilities and interactions. Examining the organizational structure helps determine which parts of the organization will be affected by the project. An example of information that would go into a user profile includes:

- Definition of user (title or role)
- User goals
- Responsibilities
- Likes and dislikes

- Education level
- Expectations and change requests
- Computer experience
- Knowledge of business applications and processes

From examining the case study, we can identify a few user profiles. There are the following actors: Administrators, Job Seekers, Hiring Companies, Sales, and Support Staff.

After creating profiles, we can then create a training assessment to determine which users need training and what type of training is needed. For example, the solution is to be developed with .NET technologies, so the developers will need skill assessments completed to determine the level of training needed to develop the new solution. This also helps the training group to determine staffing needs for performing training later.

Analyze the Organizational Structure, Both Current and Projected

While examining the business processes, another important factor is assessing the impact of the solution on users. To determine the impact, there are several artifacts that can aid in the examination of the current view: mission statement, organization charts, and marketing materials. Artifacts can be defined as documents or files that could consist of reports, screen captures, and user or technical documentation. After gathering this information, we can examine the organizational structure. For example, it is very common to have individuals responsible for performing actions that span several organization positions. By examining an organization chart alone, key information could be missed about the roles and responsibilities of such individuals.

exam
Ⓦatⓒh

Organizational information is generally used to resolve conflicting information that can be presented in the case studies.

Analyze Vertical Market Position and Industry Position

To assess the vertical market position, a market analysis must be performed. This documents the marketplace in which the business organization currently competes and plans to compete. An examination for each marketplace would include documenting the business organization's competitors and their competing applications. This includes an examination of:

- Market needs
- The size of markets
- Market saturation
- Market segments for each market segment identifying:
  - Profile
  - Demographics
  - Market channels
  - Market expectations
  - Market trends
  - Major competitors

When examining the competing businesses, much of this information is probably public and can be gathered from information at your local library or Chamber of Commerce. You will want to include a brief analysis of the business and a description of target markets and services. The next step is to examine the competitor's product and service and detail their strengths and weaknesses. This gives you a view of your market.

From the case study, we can gather further information. RecruitmentService.net had a good year last year, but it must continue to expand and meet its customers' ever changing needs in order to remain competitive. You can also gather that RecruitmentService.net is relatively small compared to its main competitor. The main competitor is in more markets and has a larger volume of resumes and job postings. Expansion of services a nd the market share will be imperative if RecruitmentService.net wants to remain competitive. This can only be accomplished with careful planning.

Analyze the Organizational Political Climate

Assessing the business political environment is another important feature of examining the organizational structure. The assessment is done to determine the key stakeholders in both the business processes and for the project. From the case study, there isn't much information about the political climate. The examination of the political climate can also be helpful in identifying individuals who can help provide a positive influence for those who are more hesitant to accept the change. Assessing the political climate also requires looking at the historical perspective of the company and industry. This also helps with understanding how decisions are made within the organization.

Stakeholders are individuals or groups who have an interest at stake in the outcome of the project. Their goals or priorities are not always identical to those of the customer. Each stakeholder will have requirements or features that are important to them. Many of the project documents and processes involved informing stakeholders with the progress of the project and identifying features. Stakeholders can include:

- Department managers of users who will be using the system
- Department managers affected by the new system
- Support staff affected by the system

Analyze Business Reach or Scope

The examination of the current reach and scope is an internal analysis. This analysis is the examination of the lines of business, target market segments, and products. This also includes taking the core business services and determining the key feature sets, target user groups, strengths, and weaknesses. This view in combination with the competitive market analysis gives a comprehensive overview of the business and its environment.

Analyze Current and Future Regulatory Requirements

Another factor in evaluating the business market is examining current and future regulatory requirements. Legal and regulatory requirements are defined by governmental law or regulation and must not be violated by the business. The business may face regulations at many levels. For example, the solution may need to comply with the Americans with Disabilities Act, making sure that users with disabilities can access information. An example of industry standards would be guidelines published by the World Wide Web Consortium (W3C). It defines standards that detail how the Web should work in different browsers and guidelines for compliance with creating accessible applications.

Preparing the Vision/Scope Document

At this point, we have gathered enough information to complete the vision/scope document. This started with the examination of the business process to identify key flows of the business. User profiles were created to determine the types of users and the level of training that will probably be needed to educate them. Competitive analysis was done to determine the key features of the competition and the position of the business in the market. Stakeholders have been identified, as well as regulatory requirements.

The approval of the vision/scope document is the ending milestone of the envisioning phase and begins the planning phase. The requirements gathered during the envisioning phase are high-level requirements and will be further defined in the planning phase. The vision/scope document approval means that the customer and the project team have agreed upon the direction of the project and features that the solution will include. A general timeline is also established. This is a living document; it will get revised and updated as the process continues.

The deliverables for the envisioning phase are as follows:

- Vision/scope document
- Risk assessment document
- Project structure document

Analyzing Business Requirements for the Solution

The next phase is the planning phase. During this phase the project team works through the design process, creates work plans, develops cost estimates, and schedules for various deliverables. The planning phase is comprised of three levels of design: conceptual, logical, and physical. Each of these levels will be described in later chapters in more detail; in this chapter we will focus on preparation for these stages. This phase culminates with the completion of the functional specifications.

The initial phase of requirements gathering is to generate high-level requirements. These are created from the examination of the business and by obtaining input from key stakeholders. This level of requirements presents a 10,000-foot view of the solution.

Requirements break down into three types: business, functional, and nonfunctional. Business requirements can be considered *why requirements*. These requirements capture the highest level of answers to the question "Why are we doing this?" and should capture the fundamental reason for the project's existence.

Functional requirements can be considered *what requirements*. For example: What is necessary for this process to work properly? These requirements capture the functionality that must be built into the system to satisfy the business requirements.

Nonfunctional requirements can be considered *how or how well requirements*. For example: How does is the specific process work? These are the technology-specific requirements. This includes items like capability, usability, performance, reliability, and so on.

All of these requirements also have the following general characteristics:

- A formal statement of purpose that defines the scope of the task to be performed.

- Validation criteria to determine if the task has been performed correctly. For example, this could be a screen that appears when the task is completed, or an external action that can no longer be performed.

- Requirements may have extra characteristics that are needed to give a more complete description. Examples of these attributes are:

  - **Requirement identification**   This can be used to trace the requirement when creating further documents.

  - **Categorization**   What type of requirement is this? Examples include data requirement, functional requirement, nonfunctional requirement, or constraint.

  - **Criticality to customer**   Could be high, medium, or low.

  - **Criticality to user**   Could be high, medium, or low.

  - **Frequency of execution**   For example, daily, weekly, monthly, or yearly, if applicable.

  - **Implementation status**   Is this requirement not implemented, implemented, or preexisting?

  - **Source**   How was this requirement discovered?

  - **Volatility**   How often does this requirement change?

Scenario 3.2: RecruitmentService.net Case Study Requirements

Using Scenario 3.1 as a basis of information, identify the key requirement features.

Requirement 1.1 states that job seekers are able to create up to five saved job searches, which can be viewed or e-mailed at specified intervals. The preferred method is to e-mail results or the results can be viewed from the web site. This requirement is defined as a functional requirement. To determine the validity, a status check is done to determine if the requirement has been performed at the appropriate time. Since this is the most common way that the users will be receiving job listings, it is determined to have a criticality of high. The only preexisting condition is that the saved search must be properly formed to return results.

Requirement Identification	Requirement 1.1
Purpose	Create job searches
Validation criteria	Status check to determine is the job has been performed at the appropriate time
Categorization	Functional requirement
Customer criticality	High, because this the main way customers will receive information
Frequency of execution	User defined
Preexisting conditions	Property formatted saved search that returns results
Dependencies	Exchange servers Valid search criteria

In Scenario 3.2, you can see an example of how a requirement from Scenario 3.1 would be defined. It gives a general description and specific information that gives further clarity about the requirement. Since there are different types of requirements that will need to be defined, the attributes or extra characteristics can change.

Identifying Business Requirements

The process of identifying business requirements starts with collecting information about your requirements. Applying these techniques requires the examination of the circumstances and type of requirements that need to be gathered. There are six information-gathering techniques that can be used: shadowing, interviewing, focus groups, surveys, user instruction, and prototyping.

Shadowing is the act of observing users. While observing a user's daily routine and tasks, you can interview the user during their normal processes to gain information that could be overlooked in a more formal interview. This gives the user an opportunity to explain how and why their processes function. This provides two main benefits: gaining information from the user's perspective and uncovering hidden information. Questions to keep in mind during this process are: What are the required tasks? What can be done to improve the system? What are the characteristics of the users? What activities are not performed daily? Who performs the tasks? Why are the tasks being performed? When are the tasks started and completed?

Interviewing is the act of asking a series of questions. Interviewing is a great way to get started in the requirements-gathering process. This is an opportunity to have one-on-one contact and helps generate information. This process does depend upon the skill of the interviewer and interviewee, and there can be potential problems with this method. For example, the wrong people could be interviewed. Another problem might be poorly planned questions that therefore result in answers that fail to provide the necessary information.

Focus groups are sessions with a representative group of users with similar user profiles. This is a valuable way to gather information because each user has their own perspective on their processes. In a focus group, you bring together from six to nine users to discuss issues and concerns about the features of a user interface. The session typically lasts about two hours and is run by a moderator who maintains the group's focus. The group can provide more information about their activities and give a unique perspective on business processes. Early releases of the solution can be viewed by this type of group to allow feedback from a controlled collection of users.

Surveys are a way to gather information about specific subjects from a large group of people. This process allows users to anonymously contribute information that may not come to light via other techniques, such as user frustrations with policies and practices. A downside to this technique is that it can be very labor intensive to develop and administer.

User instruction is the technique of allowing the user to teach you about their processes. Some users may be uncomfortable teaching others and therefore may not like this technique. Identifying the experts in business activities can help you develop models for new processes, however, and this is a good way to examine user interfaces, artifacts, and user profiling.

Prototyping is the creation of a simple version of a solution. This helps users have a visual reference for processes that don't yet exist or are difficult to explain. Prototyping is a good way to shadow a user in a controlled environment to help with the gathering of requirements. This technique is useful for verifying workflow processes and testing the integration of technologies.

Identify Dependencies, Both Inside and Outside the Company

Assessing internal and external dependencies can be done while using the requirements-gathering techniques described previously. Dependencies are determined by crossover of data from different systems and processes. Internal dependencies would be required information or processes that exist within the business. External dependencies, which are dependencies that exist outside of the system, can require extensive planning and integration. This could be a critical unknown that affects many internal processes.

By examining the case study, we can see that RecruitmentService.net will have dependencies on the types of ways that job submissions are generated from different customer systems. For example, Customer A has a human resource system that is hosted on a Unix mainframe. The customer's human resource system can generate XML files that RecruitmentService.net can use to import multiple job listings using their listing specifications. The project team creates and notes requirements to fulfill these dependencies. They also notice that they have an internal dependency to their internal human resource system to track user account status and payments.

Identifying Features of the Solution

After starting the information-gathering process, two types of requirements will appear: features and extensibility requirements. Features define the functionality that the solution must deliver to be complete. These requirements are based on the business process needed, and how that process will interact with the user. Features are created by taking the initial business requirements and evolving them into functional and nonfunctional requirements. These requirements are grouped together to create features for the solution. An example of a feature from the case study would be security login, which is more specific than the security process.

Define Design Goals

Design goals are a list of categories or attributes of the solution that the team hopes to accomplish with design. The goals need to be stated specifically so they can be agreed upon by all team members in the planning stages. This list of design goals helps determine what features and requirements are important and helps resolve conflict between requirements. An example of a design goal is *extensibility* requirements, which specify the degree to which an application or component will be able to be enhanced in the future to meet changing requirements or goals. Design goals are used in conjunction with features. Using our case study to illustrate, an example of a feature would be that the proposed system will generate job search results. An example of the design goal of an extensibility requirement would be that the job search results can be sent to media other than e-mail, such as personal digital assistants and cell phones. See Table 3-1 for additional examples of design goals.

An example of scalability for RecruitmentService.net is that their web site will be displayed in different languages in the future. An integration requirement from the RecruitmentService.net Case Study would define a set of standards for interfacing with external systems for exchanging data.

Define Data Requirements, Types, and Flows

Up to this point, we have looked at requirements for business processes, features, and dependencies. Now we need to examine data requirements. Data requirements specify a mandatory data type for an application, application domain, or component. The application domain is defined as a group of applications that work together to accomplish a specific purpose. The objective of data requirements is to specify data in terms of objects, context in terms of attributes, and relationships in terms of other data types. From our requirements discovery process, the team should have gathered a list and samples of reports, screen prints of entry screens, file outputs, or other similar data. This information is known as the artifacts of the project and, when combined with the understanding of the business processes, gives the team enough information to chart the definition and flow of data. Sometimes there is no

TABLE 3-1		
	Security	Extensibility
Examples of Design Goals	Maintainability	Reusability
	Scalability	Manageability
	Performance	Reliability
	Availability	Integration with existing systems
	Ease of development and deployment	

data to use for requirements, but enough information can be gathered from the requirements that are defined. The case study indicates several data requirements. For example, with a new application, there is no preexisting data to use to determine requirements. You may gather requirements from artifacts like screen prints, drawings, or marketing materials.

Data types specify mandatory data about a business object. This is the beginning stage of looking at a data model of information. Typically your data types are defined by attributes, constraints or default values, and relationship to other objects. An example of this would be the customer.

A customer has the following attributes (among others): first name, last name, contact information, and payment method.

A *data flow diagram* is primarily for data discovery. The data flow diagrams can be used to convey information to help users, team members, and developers understand the various states that the data goes into. These states typically follow the business processes closely.

Data flow is sometimes the only diagram used to determine the business processes.

Create Data Flow Diagrams

To understand how to create a data flow diagram, we need to define a few data flow diagram notation objects:

- *Processes* transform data flow into outgoing data flow.
- *Data stores* are repositories of data in the system. They are sometimes referred to as files.
- *Data flows* are pipelines through which packets of information flow.
- *External entities or interfaces* are objects outside the system, with which the system communicates. External entities are sources and destinations of the system's inputs and outputs.

Using Visio, the default data flow modeling objects use the Gane-Sarson model. The other popular type of data flow modeling is DeMarco & Yourdon. Before using the Gane-Sarson model, there are some rules to understand, as follows:

- All shapes on each detail page must be interconnected with data flows.
- A process can't originate data. It must be receiving data from an interface or a data store.

- Names of elements must be unique between each type of object—that is, Data Store, Data Flow, Process, and Interface.

- If more than one data flow exists with the same source and target, these data flows must have different names. For example, if you have two data flows going between a data store and a process, the data flows must have different names. The following illustration shows this.

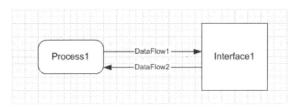

- Data flows must be connected to a process at start or end.

- Data flows must be connected at both ends.

- Data flows can't be connected to the same object at both ends to create a loop.

These rules ensure that the model is valid. The nice thing about Microsoft Visio is that it will do this validation for you. Data flow diagramming is an important piece of the project because the project team and user can all share a common understanding of how the business processes function. Based on the Gane-Sarson model, we have the following diagram objects.

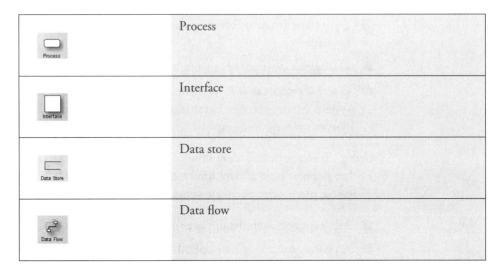

Create a Data Flow Diagram

The data flow diagram that we are going to create displays the data flow for a job submission.

1. Open Visio and select File | New | Software | Data Flow Model Diagram.

You will notice that your Visio application is divided into two parts. The section to the left is your stencils. This is where your selection of objects that can be drawn to the screen is stored for easy access. You should see the four data flow objects: Process, Data Flow, Data Store, and Interface. The section on the right is the workspace. This is where all of the objects that you select are drawn and displayed on the screen.

2. You will now create the Recruiter interface object. To add this object, select the Interface object in the stencil area and drag and drop it to the workspace. Double-click it to enter edit mode for the object, then type **Recruiter** to name this object. You can use the formatting options to style your text.

exam
ⓌatchÂ

To add an object, select the object from the list of stencils and then drag and drop it onto the workspace where you want it.

3. We are going to use the Model Explorer to create the rest of the objects. The following illustration shows what the Model Explorer looks like. If for some reason the Model Explorer window is not visible, click DFD in the menu, then click View | Model Explorer. You are working with objects under the title "DFD System 1" in the Model Explorer. To add an item (either Top Process, Data Stores, or Interfaces in the Model Explorer), right-click on the selected section and it will create a new object. To rename the new item, right-click on the appropriate item and select Rename, then type in the new name. The following table details the list of objects to be created and the name for each.

Type	Name
Process	Customer
Process	File Import
Process	Search Process
Data Store	Saved Search
Data Store	Job Submission

4. Drag and drop the items from the Model Explorer to the workspace. Arrange the items, first by row and then left to right:

- Row 1: Saved Search in top middle of workspace
- Row 2: Customer, Search Process, Saved Search
- Row 3: Recruiter, File Import, Job Submission

5. To attach the objects together, we need to use Data Flow objects. A Data Flow object is basically a line with an arrow to show the direction. To attach objects, the ends are dragged and dropped on the appropriate objects. The object to be dropped on will turn red to show that it is the receiving object. The following table shows how the rest of the diagram will be connected.

Name	Originating Point	Destination Point
Submission	Recruiter	File Import
Save Submission	File Import	Job Submission
Request Data	Job Submission	Search Process
Request Search	Customer	Search Process
Return Request	Search Process	Saved Search
View Search	Saved Search	Customer

You are now finished. The diagram should look something like this:

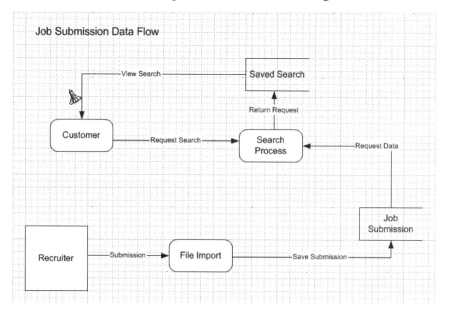

In this example, we demonstrate in a data flow diagram how job submissions reach a job seeker. The submission goes into a file import process to a job submission data store where it waits for a job seeker to request information. The job seeker or the customer in the diagram can then query against available jobs to determine which to view. This process is now complete. To view the submission would be another data flow diagram to show how that process works.

Using the combination of high-level requirements and data flow diagrams, the project team is now able to start defining in more detail functional and nonfunctional requirements that affect the users directly.

exam
ⓦatch

In creating flow diagrams, you will need to be able to accurately determine the type of users so they can be associated with the right tasks.

Assessing User Requirements

Start this assessment by breaking down the processes into fine details and creating use cases. Use cases describe the process steps that an actor performs and the system responses in order to complete a specific business goal. Actors are defined as users or other systems that interact in the process.

Identity Use Cases

A properly created use case tightly displays the user/system interactions required to perform business processes, ensuring the system will follow the business needs. They also help provide traceability from business processes to business requirements to the implemented system. The case study use case would show several actors. Job seekers, recruiters, administrators, and managers would be surrounding an object representing the web site. When creating use cases, it is helpful to examine each actor and identify all tasks in the system with which the actor would be involved. For each actor, what information is necessary to perform the task? What use cases will support and maintain the system? What information must be modified or created in the system? The use cases define the responsibilities that an organization or individual completes on a specific process from start to finish. Use cases have some general elements in common:

- ■ **Identifier** Each use case should have an identifier to make it unique from other use cases.
- ■ **Name** Name the use case to identify what process is being described.
- ■ **Overview description** To quickly summarize the information.
- ■ **List of actors** The users or systems that participate in the process steps of a use case. This also is helpful for providing a quick view of responsibilities of an actor.
- ■ **Triggers** Define what event happened to cause the use case to start.
- ■ **Required conditions** Define what information must be available and/or state what the system should be set to.
- ■ **Event steps** Define the flow of the process and include the actor's actions. The event steps should identify if steps are optional or conditional.

■ **Expected outcome** Identifies what the final result of this process should produce or accomplish.

As the team processes the information they have gathered, these elements can be gathered from the requirements.

There are several types of use case diagrams and documents that can be created:

■ The workflow process model displays how people communicate and coordinate together.

■ The system use case demonstrates how a particular system can be used.

■ The user use case model displays what a user can do, from a user profile perspective.

Another tool that is available are usage scenarios. Every use case must have at least one usage scenario. Usage scenarios bring clarity and completeness to the process. They are used as the main documentation for deriving test harnesses. Test harnesses are a mechanism in testing to create unit tests to make sure that all requirements are met and to prevent bugs in the software. There are two types of usage scenarios that are documented. *Current-state* usage scenarios document how users currently interact with business processes to successfully accomplish business tasks. This document helps identify the business processes needed to accomplish this task. This is a repeatable series of steps that can be discussed with the user to give a clearer focus.

The *future-state* use cases and scenarios need to be created to show how the finished solution will appear. When finished, you have two sets of diagrams to show the current state today and how it will look in the future. The creation of these types of diagrams helps define the requirements further and iterate through the processes to make sure that dependencies were not missed. It also gives the project team a clear way to validate the requirements and processes of the solution.

Examining user requirements involves more than looking at how the user will perform actions in the system. Another aspect is the examination of where the application will be used. Other requirements are necessary if the solution will be used in other countries and/or by users of other nationalities. This process is called *internationalization.* Internationalization is the process of writing applications in a way that makes localizing the application to a particular region as easy as possible. Internationalization aims to remove the burden of re-engineering an application when writing for multiple countries or regions. Locale is the definition of a language and a culture, geographical, and political region. In computer terms, the locale determines the culture settings that your system operates in.

Identifying Localization Requirements

Localization is the process of translating local specific application elements to a particular locale. These elements include textual elements, visual elements, and content. This also affects how money is handled unless the currency is universal, like the Euro for Europe. For applications it affects, localization resources need to be created during the development process. An example from our case study would be that it must be able to be viewed in English and Spanish. This locale setting is determined by the user's browser.

Identifying Globalization Requirements

Globalization encompasses both internationalization and localization. This refers to the entire solution process from design through implementation and localization. Globalization requirements define how specific process should handle locale information. These requirements help identify which processes and other requirements need this further customization to allow for globalization. Depending on the level of globalization, the requirements process takes the base set of requirements and extends them.

There are some key assumptions that must be examined. For example, language and the various dialects are the most obvious and the easiest to overlook. It is very possible to have words with different meanings in the same dialect of a language. Cultural differences are the most subtle, but there is generally high awareness of the potential issue. For example, images or colors that may be perfectly acceptable in one country may be considered inappropriate in that same usage in another culture. Another example is how address and date fields in other countries use non-U.S. formats for information.

Business practices and processes differences could be obvious or subtle. As an example, Japan does not round taxes, where other countries use the standard "bank rounding." Differences in computing environment are challenging because of specialized technical skills required to recognize and address them. In Japan and other Asian countries, for example, it is possible to have different types of encoding methods for different systems and data. Recognizing these factors helps with the gathering process when looking for differences and issues. An example of a globalization requirement could be to provide a library of locale-aware formatting and parsing functions for numbers, dates, and currencies.

From the case study, examples of localization, internationalization, and globalization would be the ability for the web site to support English, Spanish, German, and French. Each language would require specific types of routines to display appropriate types of currency and date information. Another requirement would be the fact that the application would have to use .NET's features of localization resource files to hold language-specific information.

Identify Accessibility Requirements

Accessibility requirements specifies the degree to which the user interface of an application or component shall be usable by users with common disabilities, whether they are auditory, visual, physical, or cognitive. There are published standards for the minimum requirements for accessibility requirements for web applications at http://www.w3.org/WAI/. The primary goal of these guidelines is to promote accessibility.

Scenario 3.3: Accessibility for Web Sites

Mr. Lee is in the market for some new clothes, appliances, and music. As he frequently does, he is spending a weeknight evening shopping online. He has one of the most common visual disabilities for men, *color blindness,* which in his case means an inability to distinguish between green and red.

He has difficulty reading the text on many web sites. When he first started using the Web, he had thought that a lot of sites used poor color contrast, since to him many sites seemed to use similar shades of brown. He eventually realized that many sites were using color combinations that were indistinguishable to him because of his red/green color blindness.

After additional experimentation, Mr. Lee discovered that on some sites, the colors were controlled by style sheets and that he could override these with his own style sheets in his browser. But other sites did not use style sheets and sometimes he could not override those. As he continued to experiment with turning style sheets on or off, he realized that on some sites the sale prices were indicated in red text, which only became visible for him when he turned off the sites' style sheets—when possible—and used his own.

After a half hour of browsing, Mr. Lee makes a number of online purchases. Because of increased readability, he buys mainly from web sites where he can use his own style sheets.

Example requirements:

RecruitmentService.net will use cascading style sheets (CSS) to control the color scheme for the system.

Here is a quick reference on how to make accessible web sites:

Element	Description
Images and animations	Use the alt attribute to describe the function of each visual.
Image maps	Use the client-side map and text for hot spots.
Multimedia	Provide captioning and transcripts of audio, and descriptions of video.
Hypertext links	Use text that makes sense when read out of context. For example, avoid "click here."
Page organization	Use headings, lists, and consistent structure. Use CSS for layout and style where possible.
Graphs and charts	Summarize or use the longdesc attribute.
Scripts, applets, and plug-ins	Provide alternative content in case active features are inaccessible or unsupported.
Frames	Use the noframes element and meaningful titles.
Tables	Make line-by-line reading sensible. Summarize.
To check your work	Validate. Find tools, checklist, and guidelines at http://www.w3.org/TR/WCAG.

FROM THE CLASSROOM

Web Accessibility Design

Increasing discovery, access, and usability of your web site for all visitors is a major benefit from applying many of the WCAG 1.0 checkpoints. The proportion of people with disabilities can range up to 20 percent in some populations. A significant portion of those people with disabilities—in some countries as many as 8 to 10 percent of the overall population—can benefit from web sites conforming with WCAG 1.0.

—David Waddleton, MCSD, MCT, MCP

Following these guidelines will also make web content more available to all users, whatever user agent they are using (desktop browser, voice browser, mobile phone, automobile-based personal computer, and so on) or whatever constraints they may be operating under (noisy surroundings, under- or over-illuminated rooms, a hands-free environment, and so on). An example of this for RecruitmentService.net would be to allow customers to access information from personal digital assistants (PDA) and receive notifications from other types of handheld devices.

Gathering and Analyzing Operational Requirements

Identify Maintainability Requirements

Maintainability requirements are a measure of the ease with which a software system can be maintained. It is defined as the ease with which a software system or component can be modified to correct faults, improve performance, or adapt to a changed environment. Maintainability requirements help minimize maintenance costs and organizational staffing needs. This is made possible by ensuring that minor defects in an application or component are easy to correct or enhance. An example of a maintainability requirement would be how long it takes to fix a severe, average, or minor bug or error. Maintainability should include updating the associated documentation and types of testing necessary for validation. It is also helpful to specify a specific maximum time to complete the task.

Identify Scalability Requirements

A scalability requirement is a developer-oriented functional requirement that specifies the degree to which the specified system shall be able to modify its existing capacities. Scalability requirements may specify the future ability to handle more simultaneous users or interactions, or to store more information in its databases. They can be specified as individual textual requirements or tables of related requirements. Scalability requirements are not the same as scalability mechanisms such as increasing the amount of hardware components, scaling of components, and performance tuning.

Identify Availability Requirements

An availability requirement specifies the proportion of the time that the solution should function properly. These requirements are defined in terms of the minimum average percent of time that the solution must operate without scheduled or unscheduled downtime. Because some aspects of a solution are more critical than others, the availability requirements are normally restricted to critical capabilities. Availability is directly related to other quality factors such as reliability, maintainability, and security. This requirement is not the same as an availability mechanism like redundancy, which eliminates single points of failure, software failure monitoring, software upgrades, and regular hardware maintenance.

Identify Reliability Requirements

A reliability requirement specifies the maximum permitted frequency of the failure. This provides assurance to the user that the solution will function properly for long periods of time and minimize user disruptions. Reliability requirements should specify the conditions to which they apply. Reliability is related to availability— if the reliability is high, the availability is also high, and there is a very short time-to-fix period.

Identify Deployment Requirements

Deployment requirements specify the ease with which a solution shall be able to be successfully installed in its production environment. A typical objective is to ensure that time and money are not wasted during the installation process. This ensures that the solutions have a clearly defined path for deployment. An example of a deployment requirement would be how long it takes for the support staff to install the required components on production equipment and time for users to perform the client installation. Deployment requirements can be validated during later stages by observing the performance of the solution and defining a reasonable limit on the average installation time. Deployment requirements are especially important when dealing with untrained users and customers. These requirements also affect your support staff when users and/or customers have to perform any of the installations.

exam
Watch

You will need to be able to identify all possible ways to deploy applications.

Identify Security Requirements

A security requirement specifies the degree to which a business shall protect itself and its sensitive data and communications from accidental, malicious, or unauthorized access, or destruction. The following list identifies objectives of the security requirements:

- Identify users and clients
- Properly verify identities
- Ensure that users and client applications can only access data and services for which they have been authorized
- Detect intrusion attempts by unauthorized users
- Ensure that communications and data are not intentionally corrupted
- Ensure that confidential communications are kept secure and private
- Enable auditing of status and usage of security mechanisms
- Enable solution to handle attacks
- Ensure that system maintenance does not disrupt security mechanisms

Security requirements depend on the correctness of the solution, because implementing defects are often bugs that produce security vulnerabilities. The team must keep in mind that it is impossible to create a 100 percent secure solution. Security requirements create other type of use cases, defined as *abuse cases*. Abuse cases show user interactions that attempt to violate the security of the solution. This also helps create a set of validations that require testing to determine the level of success. These validations can be additional work flows and testing scenarios.

Some sub-requirements that can also be defined under the security requirements are: identification, authentication, authorization, immunity, integrity, intrusion detection, nonrepudiation, privacy, security auditing, survivability, physical protection, and system maintenance security.

exam
ⓦatch

You will define security requirements as a general category, but you will need to be able to identify them to perform the proper actions.

Identification requirements specify the extent to which a solution shall identify its users and external applications before interacting with them. Identification is the process that the solution uses to recognize users. Basically, all access to the system must be identified in some way. This requirement can specify that the user have a valid system-generated ID or use some other type of identification method.

Identification requirements generally are used as prerequisites for authentication requirements. Identification requirements should not be specific in terms of security architecture, such as a name or public key. A very common requirement mistake is to specify the use of user identifiers and associated passwords with design-level login use cases. This requirement will not have enough detail to implement at this time; the specifics will evolve later on in the process. Identification requirements must be consistent with privacy requirements, which may require the anonymity of users. A very common cause of public key infrastructure (PKI) failures is the lack of agreement on organization-wide identification requirements.

Authentication is the process that a business enterprise or application uses to confirm an external identity with a specified level of confidence. An *authentication requirement* specifies the extent to which the solution shall verify the identity of users and external interactions. A sample authentication requirement could be to authenticate all of its users before accepting a credit card payment by having a valid login to the system.

If identity requirements are important enough to be defined, there must be authentication requirements. Authentication requirements are typically prerequisites for authorization requirements. Authentication and identification requirements are very closely related and can be grouped together.

An access and usage privilege of authenticated users and client applications is defined as an *authorization requirement.* This is the process of authorizing specific authenticated users and client applications to access specific solutions. An example of this requirement could state that each customer should be able to obtain access to all his or her own personal account information. These types of requirements depend upon the identification and authentication requirements. Authorization is generally granted to individuals or groups of individuals. There should be a limited number of administrators with permissions to grant or change authorizations.

Immunity requirements define how the solution shall protect itself from infection by unauthorized applications like computer viruses and worms. The main objective is to protect the data and application from being destroyed. An example would be to filter out data that is inputted from an unverified source. Immunity requirements should not be specified in terms of types of software, hardware, and architecture mechanisms. These types of requirements can be optional and defined by the operations center where the application is being maintained. An example would be that network security precautions will allow access only on certain communication protocols. Another example would be to keep critical operation systems current to disallow a lapse for external access.

Integrity requirements specify the extent to which the solution shall ensure that its data and communications are not intentionally corrupted via unauthorized creation, modification, or deletion. The main objective is to prevent unauthorized individuals and programs from corrupting communications between the solutions and its external users and interfacing applications. An example could be for the solution to prevent the corruption by unauthorized individuals and applications of all e-mails that it sends to customers and other external users.

Intrusion detection requirements specify how to detect and record attempted access or modification by unauthorized individuals or programs. These requirements depend on identification, authentication, and authorization requirements. An example would be to detect and record all attempted access that fails required identification, authentication, and authorization.

Nonrepudiation requirements determine to what degree a business application shall prevent a user or system interaction from denying participation in the interaction. The purpose is to prevent future legal and liability problems that might result from someone disputing their interactions. Some examples of nonrepudiation requirements would be to save the contents of an order or invoice, data and time stamps, or the identity of the customer.

Confidentiality requirements define how to keep sensitive data and communications private from unauthorized individuals and programs. Sensitive data falls into two categories. The first is personal information, such as user address or payment information; the other is private information about the business, such as trade secrets. The main objective is to provide access to information on a "need to know" basis. Insecure data can lead to embarrassing public relations, financial losses, and legal liabilities. This requirement normally leads to the creation of privacy statements that generally appear on applications. A privacy statement is a legally binding document that describes the personal information gathering, usage, and dissemination practices of a solution.

Survivability requirements define how the solution handles certain components being intentionally damaged or destroyed. An example would be that the application will not have a single point of failure. These requirements are critical for military applications. These requirements are different from robustness requirements, which deal with unintentional failures and errors.

Physical protection requirements specify the extent to which a solution protects itself from physical assault. The main purpose is to define how an application or business is protected against physical damage, destruction, theft, or replacement of hardware, software, or personnel components due to vandalism, sabotage, or terrorism. An example would be the data center shall protect its hardware components from physical damage, destruction, theft, or surreptitious replacement. Physical protection requirements are often prerequisites for survivability requirements.

A *system maintenance security requirement* prevents authorized modifications during maintenance to prevent the security mechanisms from being defeated. An example is the application shall not violate its security requirements during the replacement of a hardware component. These requirements may conflict with other requirements that may not allow taking the application or component offline during maintenance and the repetition of security testing.

Gathering and Analyzing Requirements for Hardware, Software, and Network Infrastructure

An interim milestone during the planning stage is technology validation. The team evaluates the products or technologies that will be used to build or deploy the solution to ensure that they work according to specifications. This is the beginning of a prototype of the system that can be used to show the success of the project. Another activity that must be completed at this milestone is baselining the environment. This is an "as is" discovery or audit of the current production environment that the solution will be in. This includes server configurations, networks, desktop software, and all relevant hardware.

Identify Integration Requirements

The integration requirements involve examination of the current environment and external systems and data that the solution will cross processes with. An example of this would be integration of a warehouse inventory solution and a SAP accounting system. Each is developed by a different vendor, and they must communicate together so that the cost of inventory and the processing of orders can be maintained. In this examination, the following questions must be asked:

- What versions of the software are being used?
- Is there an update available that gives functionality that will improve the integration?
- What platforms do the solutions run on?
- How is the integration going to be performed?
- What technology is available for the integration?
- What is the format of the data (XML, binary, or proprietary)?

■ What is the mapping between the interfaces?

■ Are there APIs available?

■ Is the interface a manual or automatic process?

Business events pass data between the different solutions. Business events are exchanges of messages or tasks that occur between different systems. Part of this integration examination is examining the data flow. There are different types of data flow requirements that need to be defined:

■ **Conditional data** Information that is required to make processing decisions. This data is extracted from business events.

■ **Business rules** The processing rules that are applied to the conditional data to determine the runtime execution path or the process.

■ **Mappings** The data transformation between the business events used to input and those used as output.

■ **Business transactions** The actual exchange of data.

■ **Error handling** Defines what exceptions can occur and how they should be handled. For example, suppose an order management application sends a new order event to a shipping application for processing. Suppose also that a shipping application runs in three separate offices as three separate instances. The order management application needs to notify the appropriate application instance based on the ship-to address in the order. In addition, the order management application needs to notify the billing application of the new order.

In this scenario, the data flow requirements would be:

Section	Result
Business Events	New order event from the order management application Ship goods event to the shipping application Send invoice event to the billing application
Conditional data	The state to which the order will be shipped. This information is extracted from the billing address in the new order event.

Section	Result
Business rules	The rule used to identify the shipping application instance to receive the ship goods event, which is based on the ship-to state/province in that order and the list of state/provinces associated with each application instance.
Mappings	The data transformation mapping from New order event to the ship goods event New order event to the send invoice event
Business transaction	Both the shipping and billing applications are updated successfully, or neither is updated. Compensating action for rolling back each application in case the other fails must be defined.
Error handling	If a data error occurs, such as an order is received with an invalid state/province, the order is flagged as incomplete and the appropriate parties are notified.

e x a m
ⓦ a t c h

You need to be able to identify how different systems will need to integrate and how the integration will happen.

This examination of the data flow helps determine the requirement objectives defined above and gives a complete description and guidelines for what needs to be accomplished with the solution integration.

Analyze the IT Environment

This is the creation of a high-level inventory of application, information, and technology resources, recording their location and analyzing and prioritizing their usefulness to business processes. The inventory of an organization can be divided into three categories:

- **Applications**   The systems that make up a executable software
- **Information**   The computerized data stores containing information, often accessed though a database management system
- **Technology**   The hardware, software, and electronic networks that support applications and data stores

This inventory also includes items that are planned or under development. The steps involved in this process are analyzing, identifying, and relating to business processes.

The analyzing of information starts by identifying major applications. The following information needs to be captured: name, locations, inputs/outputs, and implementation details. Other helpful information would be to capture key functionality, dependencies, and any perceived problems with these applications.

Identifying information stores should capture information such as entity name, attributes, and relationships. Some questions to ask and things to look for include:

- What does the business need to know?

- What are the industry requirements and standards?

- What are your critical information needs?

- What are your biggest data issues?

- What are your functional data requirements?

- What are your business process data and workflow requirements?

- Are there statutory or legal constraints that affect your data and information needs?

exam
ⓦatch *You need to be able to identify existing and future hardware requirements.*

In analyzing this information you should identify the types of data and the types of information stores. There are different types of information stores, such as relational databases, indexed files, XML files, spreadsheet files, or other types of text files. The definition of information types based on applications used in the environment allows the IT organization to leverage its investment in existing technologies and products.

The identification of major technology involves collecting information such as whether it is hardware or software, name, vendor, version, location, connection type, and dependencies. This analysis takes the technology and classifies it according to use—for example, operating system, networks, servers, or workstations. It then determines the degree to which the technology is fulfilling metrics—for example, performance results compared to published metrics.

Some questions to ask and things to look for include:

- What level of technology risk can you accept?
- Do you deploy approved, standard technologies or buy ad hoc?
- Do you understand how, what, and where technology is deployed in your organization?
- Does your technology infrastructure map to your business needs?
- What are the key technology trends affecting your IT operations?
- Do you know what technical skills you need today and tomorrow?

After gathering this information, you can integrate it using the following steps. First, identify major applications used in the organization. Next, identify the major information stores. Determine which applications use which information stores. Identify the major technology components, and finally, determine which technologies support which applications and information stores.

Analyze the Impact of the Solution on the IT Environment

After analyzing the IT inventory in its current state, assessing the impact of the solution means comparing the difference between the future and current IT state. Does the solution reuse technology currently within the business? Is the solution too costly to implement or does new technology need to be purchased? Is another project going to change the current IT state? If the current state and the proposed solution are very different, it could evolve into another project just to get the current IT state to the level needed for the proposed solution.

CERTIFICATION SUMMARY

In this chapter, we discussed the gathering and analysis of business requirements. We started with the examination of the current business state. To examine the current business state, you have to start by examining business process, organization structures, and position. The examination of market position includes the assessment of the industry, competing markets, and the current reach and scope of the business.

Next, after gathering information about the business, we need to start the process of gathering requirements from the user's point of view. Some techniques that were discussed were interviewing, prototypes, and user surveys. With each of these techniques there are different advantages and drawbacks. They have to be carefully weighted into the current situation. After starting the requirement-gathering process, the identification of dependencies with other systems and outside systems is important for determining features and extensibility requirements. We next examined different types of design goals and their impact. The definition of data requirements led to the creation of data flow diagrams (DFD).

To refine the process further, use cases and usage scenarios are created. We then examined the requirements of a global application. This included the examination of what is required for creating a global application, such as localization issues and globalization requirements gathering. Along with these issues is the determination of accessibility requirements on how the application handles using different devices for handicapped individuals and mobile devices.

Lastly, we examined the role of operational requirements. The examination of operational requirements required the viewing of the current state of the technology for the business. This was the examination of maintainability, scalability, availability, reliability, deployment, and security issues at a high-level point of view. Operational requirements do not require the examination of specifics of "how" it will be implemented but the examination of why the requirements are needed and defining constraints for operations.

All of this information is gathered in preparation for the creation of the functional requirements, which will be discussed in the next chapter. This chapter should provide adequate basis for gathering and analyzing the specified requirements for your project.

✓ TWO-MINUTE DRILL

Gathering and Analyzing Business Requirements

- ❑ Use case diagrams define a sequence of actions a system performs that yields an observable result of value to a particular actor.

- ❑ High-level requirements define tasks that drive processes. The focus is on business requirements.

- ❑ The actor is an individual or group of individuals that interacts with the system.

- ❑ User profiles identify categories of users and determine tasks that are performed. This would also include expectations and skill levels.

- ❑ Market analysis is the examination of the business to determine its strengths and weaknesses in the marketplace.

- ❑ Competitive analysis is the examination of the market competition within the business's target range.

- ❑ Examine current legislature to determine if new or existing legislation rules determine constraints and processes.

- ❑ Industry regulation information defines standards and rules that define how the business operates.

- ❑ An interview is a one-on-one session with individual users.

- ❑ A user survey is a non-intrusive mechanism to get information about the system.

- ❑ A prototype creates a viewable system to convey understanding of the new system.

- ❑ User instruction is when the user instructs the interviewer on how they perform their tasks.

- ❑ Focus groups are a collaboration of different types of users discussing the solution to determine how tasks are performed and gathering information.

- ❑ Extensibility is the ability of features of an application to evolve over time.

- ❑ Security is the ability of an application to protect its resources.

- ❑ Maintainability is the ability of an application to handle small changes.

- ❑ Reusability is the ability of components of an application to be reused in other systems or within the same system.

❑ Manageability is the ability of an application to be administered.

❑ Scalability is the ability of an application to match increasing demand with an increase in resources.

❑ Availability is the ability of an application to be present and ready for use.

❑ Reliability is the ability of an application to perform in a predictable manner.

❑ Integration is the ability of two different systems to communicate in a predictable manner.

❑ Data flow diagrams describe how data flows within the system.

❑ Data types describe the types of data that are defined and used in the system.

❑ A use case is a sequence of actions a system performs that yields observable results of value to a particular actor.

❑ Use case scenarios are used to describe the flow of events during a use case.

❑ Globalization is the process of designing and developing a solution that functions in multiple cultures/locales.

❑ Localization is the process of adapting a globalized solution to a particular culture/locale.

❑ Accessibility is the ability of an application to handle users with disabilities and other types of viewing devices.

❑ Authentication is the process of discovering and verifying the identity of a principal by examining the user's credentials and validating those credentials against some authority.

❑ Denial of service means to deny service to invalid users trying to access your application.

❑ Deployment is the process by which you distribute a finished solution on other computers.

❑ Technology review is an analysis of the current hardware and software in place at the business.

❑ Requirements are created if the system needs to integrate with other systems and determine dependencies.

❑ The current and future impact of the hardware, software, and network help determine how the current state of the business technology needs to evolve to meet the solution needs.

SELF TEST

The following questions will help you measure your understanding of the material presented in this chapter. Read all the choices carefully because there might be more than one correct answer. Choose all correct answers for each question.

Gathering and Analyzing Business Requirements

1. Using Scenario 3.1, identify the appropriate main actors from the case study.

    A. Job seeker account

    B. Database administrator

    C. Network administrator

    D. Warehouse user

2. You are gathering requirements for the solution. Identify the correct items that describe use cases. (Choose all that apply.)

    A. High-level overview of processes

    B. Use case actors

    C. Defines boundaries for systems

    D. Defines a sequence of events

3. You are gathering requirements for the solution. Which of the following techniques are valid for gathering information? (Choose all that apply.)

    A. Interviewing

    B. Focus groups

    C. Online presentation

    D. Company meeting

4. You are gathering and analyzing information about the hardware, software, and network infrastructure. Identify which of the following terms are correct about the interim milestone technology validation. (Choose all that apply.)

    A. Provide input into the design process

    B. Identify issues and technical risks

    C. Identify main business processes

    D. Identify use case constraints

5. You are analyzing the current business processes. You need to analyze the market position. Which of the following is the correct definition of market position?

   A. The degree to which a business shall protect itself and its sensitive data and communications from accidental, malicious, or unauthorized access or destruction.

   B. Examination of the current environment and external systems and data that the solution will cross processes with.

   C. How the solution handles certain components being intentionally damaged or destroyed. An example would be that the application will not have a single point of failure.

   D. The marketplace in which the business organization currently competes and plans to compete.

6. You are determining the security requirements for the solution. Identify the correct definition of security requirements.

   A. Specifies the degree to which a business shall protect itself and its sensitive data and communications from accidental, malicious, or unauthorized access or destruction.

   B. Examination of the current environment and external systems and data that the solution will cross processes with.

   C. Defines how the solution handles certain components being intentionally damaged or destroyed. An example would be that the application will not have a single point of failure.

   D. Documents the marketplace in which the business organization currently competes and plans to compete.

7. You are creating integration requirements for the solution. Identify the correct definition of integration requirements.

   A. Specifies the degree to which a business shall protect itself and its sensitive data and communications from accidental, malicious, or unauthorized access or destruction.

   B. Examination of the current environment and external systems and data that the solution will cross processes with.

   C. Defines how the solution handles certain components being intentionally damaged or destroyed. An example would be that the application will not have a single point of failure.

   D. Documents the marketplace in which the business organization currently competes and plans to compete.

8. You are creating security requirements for the solution. Identify the correct definition of physical damage requirements.

    A. Specifies the degree to which a business shall protect itself and its sensitive data and communications from accidental, malicious, or unauthorized access or destruction.

    B. Examination of the current environment and external systems and data that the solution will cross processes with.

    C. Defines how the solution handles certain components being intentionally damaged or destroyed.

    D. Documents the marketplace in which the business organization currently competes and plans to compete.

9. While creating security requirements, identify the correct definition of intrusion security requirement.

    A. Specifies the extent to which a solution shall identify its users and external applications before interacting with them.

    B. Specifies the extent to which the solution shall verify the identity of users and external interactions.

    C. Determines to what degree a business application shall prevent a user or system interaction from denying participation in the interaction.

    D. Specifies how to detect and record attempted access or modification by unauthorized individuals or programs.

10. You are writing security requirements for the solution. Identify the correct definition of authentication security requirement.

    A. Specifies the extent to which a solution shall identify its users and external applications before interacting with them.

    B. Specifies the extent to which the solution shall verify the identity of users and external interactions.

    C. Determines to what degree a business application shall prevent a user or system interaction from denying participation in the interaction.

    D. Specifies how to detect and record attempted access or modification by unauthorized individuals or programs.

11. While creating security requirements, identify the correct definition of authorization security requirement.

    A. Specifies the extent to which a solution shall identify its users and external applications before interacting with them.

    B. Specifies the extent to which the solution shall verify the identity of users and external interactions.

    C. The access and usage privileges of authenticated users and client applications.

    D. Specifies how to detect and record attempted access or modification by unauthorized individuals or programs.

12. While creating security requirements, identify the correct definition of immunity security requirement.

    A. Specifies the extent to which a solution shall identify its users and external applications before interacting with them.

    B. Specifies the extent to which the solution shall verify the identity of users and external interactions.

    C. Determines to what degree a business application shall prevent a user or system interaction from denying participation in the interaction.

    D. Specifies how to detect and record attempted access or modification by unauthorized individuals or programs.

13. You are gathering requirements for the application. While examining the design goals of the solution, identify the correct example of an availability requirement.

    A. The average person-time required to fix a category 3 defect (including regression testing and documentation update) shall not exceed two person-days.

    B. The average person-time required to make a significant enhancement (including testing and documentation update) during the development of a major new version of the application shall not exceed five person-weeks.

    C. The application shall not have a single point of failure.

    D. Credit card authorizations shall have an operational availability of 99.99 percent.

14. Which of the following is the correct reliability requirement?

    A. The application shall be usable by persons with mild cognitive disabilities.

    B. The average person-time required to fix a category 3 defect (including regression testing and documentation update) shall not exceed two person-days.

    C. The application's mean time between failures shall be at least one month.

D.   The average effort required by a typical user to install the application shall not exceed 15 minutes.

15.   You are gathering requirements for the application. Identify the correct definition of maintainability requirement.

A.   The application shall not have a single point of failure.

B.   The application shall be usable by persons with mild cognitive disabilities.

C.   The average effort required by a typical user to install the application shall not exceed 15 minutes.

D.   The average person-time required to fix a category 3 defect (including regression testing and documentation update) shall not exceed two person-days.

16.   You are gathering requirements for the application. Identify the correct definition of scalability requirement.

A.   All timestamps associated with user interactions shall be accurate to the nearest second.

B.   The application shall be usable by persons with mild cognitive disabilities.

C.   The average effort required by a typical user to install the application shall not exceed 15 minutes.

D.   The application shall be able to scale as specified in the following table:

Release	Open Sales	Sales Per Year	Total Employees	Total Customers	Simultaneous Interactions
0	10	N/A	10	10	10
1	10,000	50,000	50	500,000	10,000
2	25,000	250,000	250	5,000,000	50,000
3	100,000	1,000,000	500	10,000,000	250,000

17.   You are gathering requirements for the application. Identify the correct definition of deployment requirement. (Choose all that apply.)

A.   All timestamps associated with user interactions shall be accurate to the nearest second.

B.   The average person-time required to make a significant enhancement (including testing and documentation update) during the development of a major new version of the application shall not exceed five person-weeks.

    C. The average effort required by a typical user to install the application shall not exceed 15 minutes.

    D. The user should be authenticated before using the application.

18. You are preparing to gather requirements for the solution. Which of the following interviewing techniques would be less intrusive to the users? (Choose all that apply.)

    A. Interviewing

    B. Shadowing

    C. User surveys

    D. Online chat

    E. Having users teach you

19. You are preparing to gather requirements for the solution. Which of the following interviewing techniques is the examination of artifacts? (Choose all that apply.)

    A. Interviewing

    B. User surveys

    C. Focus groups

    D. Existing documentation and diagrams

20. You are preparing to gather requirements for the solution. Which of the following techniques allows for group communication and collaboration of users? (Choose all that apply.)

    A. Interviewing

    B. Prototyping

    C. User instruction

    D. Focus groups

21. You are preparing to gather requirements for the solution. What are important attributes to consider when examining techniques for gathering information? (Choose all that apply.)

    A. Sensitivity of information

    B. Intrusion into work

    C. Injecting your opinions on how it should work

    D. Cost effectiveness

22. You are writing requirements from information gathered from customers. Which of the following attributes would be needed when creating requirements? (Choose all that apply.)

    A. Requirement identification

    B. Categorization

    C. Criticality to customer (high, medium, or low)

    D. Globalization

23. You are starting the initial phase of the project to determine the high-level requirements. What tasks are involved in gathering the high-level requirements? (Choose all that apply.)

    A. Use techniques such as interviewing, observing, and prototyping

    B. Identify category of users

    C. Identify the importance of requirements

    D. Evaluate user skill levels

24. You are interviewing users and analyzing their needs. What tasks are involved with gathering the user profiles? (Choose all that apply.)

    A. Use techniques such as interviewing, observing, and prototyping

    B. Identify category of users

    C. Identify the importance of requirements

    D. Evaluate user skill levels

25. You are processing information gathered from the users and have some reporting samples to examine. Which items are correct about data types? (Choose all that apply.)

    A. Attributes

    B. Initial default values

    C. Range (i.e., possible values)

    D. Understand the meaning of the data specified within the requirements

LAB QUESTION

RecruitmentService.net is an online employment agency dedicated to serving employers and job seekers. RecruitmentService.net maintains information on 50,000 jobs and over 75,000 resumes globally, and has a monthly subscription client base. RecruitmentService.net is headquartered in

Chicago and has 150 employees. The year 2001 resulted in annual revenues of $5 million. RecruitmentService.net is undertaking a major renovation of their system, and it has hired you as a consultant as it considers the merits of using .NET-supported technologies and the .NET framework for the next version of their system.

Existing IT Environment

RecruitmentService.net has ten web servers, all of which run Windows 2000 Server. The web sites are built on Pentium III 500 MHz servers with 512 MB of memory, which use IIS 5.0. The data tier consists of a two-node cluster of dual-processor machines running Windows 2000 Advanced Server and SQL Server 7.0. The RecruitmentService.net application was developed using Visual Basic 6, ASP, and SQL. Some of the business functionality is encapsulated into COM objects.

Business Process

RecruitmentService.net is completely dependent on the web servers. To maintain the competitive advance, continuous availability of the entire site is required. Download speed of the HTML and ASP pages is critical to the business. Employers input their job postings to the web site, and the web development content approval team verifies the posting information. The web team then generates a job seekers database. Job seekers have read-only access to the database data. Network administrators maintain the SQL server. RecruitmentService.net would like to both simplify and improve the method by which information is exchanged with employers and job seekers. For example, they would like to make it easier for employers with multiple job openings to submit those listings in a batch, instead of requiring that they fill out a job posting form for each opening. They would also like to allow job seekers to read job postings and check on the status of applications via web-enabled cell phones and other wireless devices.

Interviews

CEO

As the web site grows, so must the increase in performance to meet the needs of today's user. We must also maintain 100 percent uptime. Though we have clients and users all over the world, up to now we have primarily served the English-speaking world. We are ready to begin expanding into other cultures, and would like to test a Spanish version of our site within the next six months, to be followed soon thereafter by a German version, and then a French version.

Chief Technology Officer

The system must support scalability. With anticipated growth, RecruitmentService.net must be able to add new machines into its racks with minimal cost and no system downtime. The system needs to handle a peak of 1,000 new records of incoming data per hour. We had some requests from large clients, especially those who use non-Windows systems such as Unix and IBM mainframes, to improve the way data can be exchanged between systems. We recently had a large international client post 125 job descriptions, and because of incompatibilities in our system, we had to enter each job listing manually. We suspect XML may be a good solution to this kind of problem. Whatever solution we choose, we would like a database to be able to create data directly in a format we could share with our clients. The following products will be implemented: Windows 2000 Server for the web tier, and Windows 2000 Advanced Server for the infrastructure and data tier. The web servers will continue to run IIS 5.0. We are open to whatever software and hardware we may need to add, provided the switch to .NET makes sense and supports all of our intended functionality. Three times a week the IT department at RecruitmentService.net runs a stored procedure that attempts to locate the redundant accounts, deletes accounts that have been inactive for more that a year, and creates a list of users to receive certain targeted e-mails. This procedure may affect several thousand records in a space of a few minutes.

1. What type of requirement is the following: "RecruitmentService.net must be able to add new machines into its racks with minimal cost and no system downtime."

   A. Deployment

   B. Maintainability

   C. Security

   D. Scalability

2. By examining the case study, what type of requirement is met by allowing other means of entering data?

   A. Security

   B. Globalization

   C. Integration

   D. Localization

3. Using the case study, what is a correct example of a globalization requirement?

   A. The information should be displayed in English.

   B. It should support Spanish and French text.

   C. Translator staff is required for each language to determine the culture correctness of the information.

4. Using the case study, identify the correct example of an integration requirement.

   A. RecruitmentService.net must be able to accept data from Unix and IBM systems.

   B. The application will be web-based.

   C. The web site cannot have any downtime.

5. Upon examination of the current state of technology, what needs upgrading, assuming web services will be implemented?

   A. .NET framework added

   B. Additional server hardware

   C. Additional user workstations

   D. Not applicable to project solution

SELF TEST ANSWERS

Gathering and Analyzing Business Requirements

1. ☑ **A.** From the case study, the job seeker account is the only valid option from the list. The other options would be supporting actors.

☒ **B, C,** and **D.** Database administrator and network administrator would not be considered main actors for the system. They are not the primary users of the system. The warehouse user does not exist in this use case.

2. ☑ **A, B,** and **C.** The high-level overview of the processes, use case actors, and boundaries for systems are the essential elements of a business use case.

☒ **D.** The sequence of events is a lower-level detail that is contained in the use case scenario instead of in high-level use cases diagrams.

3. ☑ **A** and **B.** Interviewing and focus groups are valid techniques for gathering information.

☒ **C** and **D.** Online presentation is a technique of instructional teaching. A company meeting is not designed for user feedback, which is the main use of gathering information.

4. ☑ **A** and **B.** Providing input into the design process and identifying issues and technical risks are correct elements of the technology validation milestone.

☒ **C** and **D.** Identifying the main business processes and use case constraints are tasks for other milestones in the envisioning phase.

5. ☑ **D.** Determining the marketplace in which the business competes is the correct definition of market position requirement.

☒ **A, B,** and **C.** These are definitions of security, integration, and survivability requirements.

6. ☑ **A.** Security requirements specify the degree to which a business shall protect itself.

☒ **B, C,** and **D.** These are definitions of integration, survivability, and market position requirements.

7. ☑ **B.** Integration requirements examine the current environment and external systems that interact with it.

☒ **A, C,** and **D.** These answers identify security, survivability, and market position requirements.

8. ☑ **C.** Identifying how the solution handles components being intentionally damaged is the correct definition of physical damage requirement.

☒ **A, B,** and **D.** These define security, integration, and market position requirements.

9. ☑ D. Intrusion security requirements look at how to detect and record attempts and modifications from unauthorized users and programs.

   ☒ A, B, and C. A defines an identity security requirement. B is an authorization security requirement, which follows in the security process after authentication. C defines a nonrepudiation security requirement.

10. ☑ B. The identification of users and systems is an authentication requirement. This requirement starts the security process.

    ☒ A, C, and D. These answers define identity, nonrepudiation security, and intrusion security requirements.

11. ☑ C. Authorization security requirements define how to verify the users to the system. This follows after security authentication.

    ☒ A, B, and D. These answers define identity, authentication security, and intrusion security requirements.

12. ☑ D. Immunity requirements define how the solution can protect itself from computer viruses and worms.

    ☒ A, B, and C. These answers define identity, authentication security, and nonrepudiation security requirements.

13. ☑ D. Availability requirements help minimize the downtime of applications.

    ☒ A, B, and C. These are examples of maintainability and reliability requirements.

14. ☑ C. Reliability requirements specify how reliably the solution performs.

    ☒ A, B, and D. These are examples of accessibility, maintainability, and deployment requirements.

15. ☑ D. Maintainability requirements define how quickly bugs or errors are supposed to be repaired and redeployed.

    ☒ A, B, and C. These are examples of survivability, accessibility, and deployment requirements.

16. ☑ D. Scalability requirements determine how the application will scale to increase performance.

    ☒ A, B, and C. These are examples of correctness, accessibility, and deployment requirements.

17. ☑ C. Deployment requirements determine how the solution is deployed and the resource and time constraints required.

    ☒ A, B, and D. These answers define correctness, maintainability, and security requirements.

18. ☑   C. User surveys are an interviewing technique that involves minimal interaction from the user. This allows the user to perform the task during their free time and does not interrupt their daily routine.
    ☒   A, B, D, and E. Interviewing, shadowing, online chats, and having the users teach you are very intrusive gathering techniques that require more interaction from the user. These techniques require the user to make changes in their daily routines.

19. ☑   B and D. The definition of artifacts is documents that can be examined. The user surveys and existing documents are classified as artifacts.
    ☒   A and C. Interviewing and focus groups have the primary focus of examining information from multiple users' point of view.

20. ☑   D. Focus groups are the only information-gathering technique that involves group discussion.
    ☒   A, B, and C. Interviewing and user instruction are one-on-one interactions. Prototyping is used to present information if necessary to a focus group to show how a part of the system will work.

21. ☑   A, B, and D. Sensitivity of information, intrusion into work, and cost effectiveness are correct considerations when gathering requirements with users.
    ☒   C. Injecting your opinions on how the solution should work is incorrect because the interviewer or gatherer of information is supposed to be subjective.

22. ☑   A, B, and C. Requirement identification, requirement category, and criticality are very important characteristics of requirements.
    ☒   D. Globalization is actually a type of requirement, not an attribute of requirements.

23. ☑   A and C. Gathering information and prioritization of requirements are appropriate tasks for creating high-level requirements.
    ☒   B and D. The identification of users and evaluation of user skill levels are used when creating user profiles.

24. ☑   B and D. Identifying the category of users and evaluating user skill levels are descriptions of user profiles.
    ☒   A and C. Using techniques like interviewing and identifying the important requirements are tasks for gathering high-level requirements.

25. ☑   A, B, and C. Attributes, default values, and possible ranges are correct descriptions of data types. Data types are types of information the solution uses to handle information.
    ☒   D. Understanding the meaning of the data specified within the requirements is not at a detailed level that data types are defining.

LAB ANSWERS

1. ☑ **D.** Scalability is correct because it is the only requirement in the list that details how the system should act toward scaling the application.
   ☒ **A, B,** and **C.** Deployment, maintainability, and security requirements do not pertain to scaling the solution.

2. ☑ **C.** Integration requirements deal with the interchange of data between systems.
   ☒ **A, B,** and **D.** Security, globalization, and localization are incorrect types of requirements to handle this situation. They do not address how to handle the interchange of data between systems.

3. ☑ **C.** Requiring translator staff for each language to determine the culture correctness would be defined in a globalization requirement.
   ☒ **A** and **B.** Displaying information in English and supporting Spanish and French text would be defined in localization and internationalization requirements.

4. ☑ **A.** The integration requirement is the integration between different systems. Thus being able to accept data from Unix and IBM systems would be valid integration requirement examples.
   ☒ **B** and **C.** Requiring that the application will be web-based is a user requirement. Requiring that the web site cannot have any downtime is a maintainability requirement.

5. ☑ **A** and **B.** To accomplish the required goals, it is necessary to install the .NET framework and upgrade the server hardware.
   ☒ **C** and **D.** Adding user workstations may not be necessary because we do not have enough information to determine if additional internal users will be needed. D is not a valid option in this situation.

MICROSOFT® CERTIFIED SOLUTION DEVELOPER

4

Formalizing Business Requirements into Functional Specifications

CERTIFICATION OBJECTIVES

I n this chapter, you will extend the business requirements into the next phase—the creation of functional specifications. After the initial requirements have been created, functional specifications are created to determine what functionality the final solutions will have. This creation of the functional specifications allows for the further definition and restating of the requirements. Additionally, this process divides the requirements into groups of responsibility.

Next is the development of the technical specifications document. This document details the specifics about how the solution will be created. The design goals of performance, scalability, availability, deployment, security, and maintainability are addressed in this document. A development strategy is decided upon for handling auditing, error handling, integration, localization, and state management. Also in this document is the selection of how to deploy the application and the different strategies available.

After deployment, the operations strategy examines how the solution will be transitioned to the operations team and how the solution will be supported in the future. Included in this plan is how to maintain the data archiving of the information and upgrade strategies.

CERTIFICATION OBJECTIVE 4.01

Functional Specifications

The transformation of requirements into functional specifications is the shift from problem definition to solution design. The functional specifications are a repository of documents. This document defines what will be built, how it will be done, and when it will be completed. The functional specifications consist of a summary document that physically describes the functional specifications and lists artifacts that make up the specifications. These collections of documents are considered "living documents," meaning that they will change throughout the project cycle. The functional specifications document is a record of the decisions and agreements made regarding the functionality of the solution, design goals, and priorities.

Artifacts can include Unified Modeling Language (UML) models such as use case diagrams, usage scenarios, initial requirements, initial features, and various other models. The artifacts from the conceptual, logical, and physical design stages can be in electronic form or stored in formats of various tools. The manifest or summary can exist as an electronic document, such as a Microsoft Word document or Microsoft PowerPoint presentation. The functional specifications are a joint effort by the team.

The functional specifications are a virtual collection of documents.

Goals

There are four goals of the functional specifications. First is to consolidate a common understanding of the business and user requirements. The features of a solution are determined from the business and user requirements. The number of requirements will vary based upon the size of the project. The functional specifications help the customer and the project team agree on a common understanding of the requirements of the solution.

The second goal is to break down the problem and modularize the solution logically. It is important that the team identify the entire problem clearly. This is achieved by breaking the solution into distinct, unambiguous parts. The functional specifications help simplify the solution into logical parts and document them. This segmentation helps identify if design changes need to be made early in the process. Catching these errors now is less risky and less expensive than finding them later.

The third goal is to provide a framework to plan, schedule, and build the solution. The specifications provide information for the team to create tasks and cost estimates and budgets for the project. The program manager can create estimates for resources and time that the project will require. The other purpose is for the testing team to create test cases and test scenarios early in the process. The release management team uses the functional specifications for deployment and to support the development and test environments.

Lastly, the functional specifications serve as a contract between the team and the customer for what will be delivered. This is evidence of what is to be developed and delivered. In some organizations, this is written as a contract between the team and the customer. It is not necessarily a legal document, but can serve as one. This document can be used by a third-party team or groups as an addendum to a project work order.

Risks of Skipping Functional Specifications

Sometimes the team will choose to skip the functional specifications and continue to development. Budget or time constraints may interfere with creating the functional specifications. The risks associated with skipping the functional specifications are:

■ The team may develop a solution that does not completely address the customer requirements.

■ The team might be unable to clearly define customer expectations and share a common understanding with the customer. Consequently, the team might not know whether they are developing the required solution.

■ The team might not have enough detail to validate and verify that the solution meets customer expectations.

■ Estimates of budget and schedules cannot be accurately created for the project.

exam
ⓦatch

These risk factors are very important and may not be presented as risks of skipping the functional specifications.

Elements of Functional Specifications

The following table describes the possible elements of functional specifications. These elements can be separate documents.

Element	Artifacts
Conceptual design summary	Use cases, usage scenarios, context models such as screen shots
Logical design summary	Task and task sequence models, logical object and service models, conceptual models of the proposed solution, UI screen flows, logical database model
Physical design summary	Component packaging, component distribution topology, technology usage guidelines, infrastructure architecture and design, description of UI screens and physical database model
Standards and processes	Security, packaging, maintainability, supportability, stabilization, deployment

The conceptual design summary provides information on the conceptual design and provides information such as the solution overview and solution architecture. The logical design summary includes information such as users, objects, and attributes. The logical design is the next step in the evolution of the solution. The logical design takes the high-level view generated from the conceptual design and divides the information into different layers. The physical design summary provides a summary of the physical infrastructure design of the solution. The standards and processes serve as a guideline for performing various tasks for the project. In addition, this section includes details about the quality and performance metrics that will be used.

CERTIFICATION OBJECTIVE 4.02

Transforming Requirements into Functional Specifications

After gathering detailed information about business and user requirements and business processes, the team can now proceed to the analysis of the information. This is the analysis of the created documents in the envisioning phase where the initial or candidate requirements are created. There are two purposes of the analysis. The first is to review user and business processes and activities. The second purpose is to document and model the context, workflow, task sequence, and environmental relationships of the business.

The transformation is performed in the following steps:

1. Synthesizing information
2. Refining use case diagrams
3. Selecting an appropriate application architecture for the solution
4. Creating a conceptual model of the application

Synthesizing Information

The synthesizing of information is the process of assimilating gathered data and interpreting the results. The team transforms the gathered data into meaningful information, by performing the following tasks:

- Identifying discrete pieces of information about what the user said and did.

- Recording the detailed flow of the tasks that the user performed.

- Identifying tools and pieces of information that were used.

- Identifying exceptions and alternatives that occur while the user performs the task.

- Modeling the relationship between business process, business systems, and users.

- Modeling the current environment in which the user works and any possible changes to that environment that might be required.

exam
ⓦatch
The synthesis of information is an important skill for taking the architecture exam. You will have to take the information provided and sift through the information using these steps.

The deliverable for this step includes information models and current usage scenarios. The information models include the relationship between the business process, business system and users, workflow process, and task sequence. Also included are updated user profiles, candidate requirements, and detailed use case scenarios.

Restating Requirements

The candidate requirements at this point are groups put together that are now in need of further organization. This process is the restating of requirements. Restated requirements meet the following criteria: well-defined, concise, testable, and organized in a hierarchy of related requirements. A well-defined requirement is a complete sentence and typically, uses "will," "may," "must," or "should" statements. Each requirement must address one item only. Each requirement should have specific inputs resulting in known outputs. Related items are grouped together to form feature sets. Requirements should be written in the language of the business. The following table is an example of restated requirements.

Requirement ID	Requirement
1.1	Must be able to analyze customer data
1.1.1	Must be able to analyze demographic data
1.2	Must be able to sort (descending, ascending) customers

e x a m
ⓦa t c h   *Requirement IDs are for tracking requirements from creation to implementation.*

Categorize Requirements

After restating the requirements, the next step is to categorize them into user, system, operations, and business requirements. User requirements define the non-functional aspect of the user's interaction with the solution. They help you determine the user interface and performance expectations of the solution in terms of its reliability, availability, and accessibility. A successful solution has completed all requirements and has passed user usability. Also identified in this step is the training required for users to use the solution. An example requirement would be that the user should be able to create an online resume in ten minutes. Another would be that the user should be able to complete a search with results returned within a minute.

e x a m
ⓦa t c h   *Categorizing requirements into groups allows you to focus on finding the requirements you need to focus on for the scenario questions.*

System requirements specify the transactions that have been broken down to their simplest state and their sequence in the system. This helps the project team define how the new solution will interact with the existing systems. Critical dependencies are identified and managed by the team.

An example requirement would be for the solution to not require internal users to provide additional credentials other than the logged credentials from the corporate network.

Operations requirements describe what the solution must deliver to maximize operability and improve service delivery with reduced downtime and risks. Key concepts addressed are security, availability, reliability, manageability, scalability, and supportability. An example requirement would be that the site design should include a system for managing the total system throughput and response time within the stated service levels.

Business requirements describe the organization's needs and expectations for the solution. They define what the solution must deliver in order to capitalize on a business opportunity or to meet business challenges. Requirements are identified by considering the organization as a valid entity with its own set of needs from the solution. These requirements are generally high-level requirements and provide the context in which the solution will operate. An example requirement might be that the solution must be able to interact and communicate with other business processes, applications, and data sources.

Refining Use Case Diagrams

During the envisioning state, the use case diagrams specified high-level diagrams for the organization. The purpose was to present all of the use cases available. The purpose of refining the use case diagrams is to create use cases within the scope of the solution. This is performed by the following four tasks.

First, create subordinate use cases. Each use case is revisited within the scope of the solution. Each task associated with the use case is identified and modeled as subordinate use cases. All of the actors that perform the tasks are identified, and the relationship is identified between the various tasks and actors.

Second, create usage scenarios for each subordinate use case. This takes the original usage scenario and adds detailed information to it. Added to the usage scenario are the following items: a detailed scenario narrative, specifics of the basic course, specifics for an alternative course, and a description of the preconditions and postconditions.

Third, validate each use case and usage scenario against the original artifacts and users. This step helps determine whether any steps in the process have not been documented. The features list is then developed based on the requirements. Revisions to the feature list are identified by elaborating on the use cases, and any additions are validated by the customer.

exam
Ⓦatch

Remember to validate your use cases against the requirements and user responses.

Finally, refine the requirements with the validated use cases and usage scenario information. Because the validation is an iterative process, the requirements need to be checked to make sure that they are valid or need redefining.

Selecting the Appropriate Architecture

The selection of the architecture depends on the understanding of the services that the solution must provide. A service is defined as a unit of application logic that includes methods for implementing an operation, a function, or a transformation. Services can be either simple or complex. For example, services creating, reading, updating, and deleting information are simple. More information concerning services and application architecture will be covered in Chapters 6, 7, and 8.

Creating a Conceptual Model

The final step is the optimization and creation of the conceptual model. This process is the evolving of the solution into its final form. The optimization examines looking at the future state of the solution and examines the current state scenarios. More about this and the conceptual model will be covered in Chapter 5.

CERTIFICATION OBJECTIVE 4.03

Transforming Functional Specifications into Technical Specifications

The technical specifications are a set of reference documents that in the development phase is used to determine the scope of work and define development tasks. These documents may consist of artifacts that detail the class specifications, component models, metrics, and network topologies. Also included are interface definitions, configuration files, dynamic link library (DLL) and assembly names, strong names keys, and deployment elements.

This is a living document that is completed after the conceptual, logical, and physical design phases are complete. It is updated during the development process as components are completed. The sections that would be included in the technical specifications document include items listed in Table 4-1.

During the planning phase, the following design goals should be considered: scalability, availability, reliability, performance, interoperability, and localization. These elements affect the design of the solution because some of the elements will

| TABLE 4-1 | Elements of a Technical Specifications Document |

Elements	Description
Architecture overview	Describes the architecture that will be implemented by the solution
Object model	Describes the object model of the solution
Interfaces	Contains the code and details of methods of each interface in the solution
Code flow	Describes the operation of each method in the solution
Error codes	Describes the error codes used in the solution for error handling
Error logging	Describes how various errors will be handled and logged in the solution
Configuration	Describes how the solution will be registered on the destination computer
Supporting documentation	Lists the documents that describe the solution, such as the functional specifications, and their locations
Issues	Describes any known issues with the solution

be required, and others will be based on resources available. Other considerations are based upon the available technologies, knowledge, and skills of the development and support staff.

Scalability

Scalability is defined as the capability to increase resources to produce an increase in the service capacity. This means that a solution can add resources to handle additional demands without modifying the solution itself. A scalable solution must balance between software and hardware used to implement an application. The adding of resources is supposed to create a positive benefit, but it is possible to create negative results and show no increase in capacity or even cause decreases. For example, an application that implements load balancing, which is allowing the application to balance the load between multiple servers, can have a minimal gain if lengthy datasets are generated in response to the user's request.

Approach

There are two common approaches to scalability. The first is called *scaling up*. This refers to achieving scalability by improving the user's processing hardware. This translates into adding more memory, processors or migrating to larger servers. The primary goal is to increase hardware resources. However, there can be a maximum level achieved where the capacity makes no change. Typically, you can scale up without making application changes to source code.

The second approach is called *scaling out*. This refers to the distributing of the processing load across multiple servers. The collection of computers continues to act as the original configuration. The application should be able to execute without needing information about the server where it is located. This concept is called *location transparency*. Scaling out is a way to increase the fault tolerance of the application.

Guidelines

To design for scalability, use the following guidelines:

- Design processes so that they do not wait. Processes should not wait longer than necessary. A process can be categorized as synchronous or asynchronous. A synchronous process waits for another process to complete before it continues. This is also known as a blocking call.

  A synchronous process can encounter bottlenecks for resources. These bottlenecks can affect the performance and scalability of the application. The solution to this problem is creating asynchronous processes. This is also called a non-blocking call.

  An asynchronous process spawns multiple processes that can finish at different times. Long running operations can be queued for completion later by other processes.

- Design processes so that they do not compete for resources. The biggest causes of problems involve competition for resources. This condition is also known as a race condition. The resource could be memory, processing time, bandwidth, or database connections. There are two ways to handle this problem; one is by first sequencing resource usage to the most available resources and then to the least available resources last. The second option is to acquire resources as late as possible.

- Design processes for commutability. Commutative operations are multiple processes that execute in any order and still obtain the same result. An example of this would be an operation that does not involve transactions. A busy site could create transaction tables that are updated periodically by the transaction records, allowing the database to reduce record locks. As shown in the following illustration, an example of a commutative operation would be as follows: when a product is ordered, instead of directly updating the Products table, the amount ordered is entered into the ProductTransactions table. Another process at predetermined time intervals will update the Products table with the appropriate values. This allows the application to process without having to lock the records when an update needs to be performed when a product is ordered. The locking for the transaction will happen less frequently in this scenario.

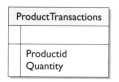

- Design components for interchangeability. An interchangeable component is designed to release its resources, move into a pool managed by a resource manager, and to be reusable by a new client. Pooling, for Open Database Connectivity (ODBC), allows a set amount of database connections to be available when needed. This eliminates the time and cost required to create and destroy these objects after every use. These types of pools are controlled by resource managers. Resource managers are the controlling mechanisms for specific types of resources. These types of components are designed to be stateless—in other words, they do not need to save information between calls to the component.

- An example of interchangeable components is a component designed for COM+ component pooling or using Open Database Connectivity (ODBC) connection pooling. With these types of object pooling, you can set the minimum and maximum pool size, and create timeout settings.

■ Partition resources and activities help prevent bottlenecks in the system. Partitioning activities can also ease the demand on resources such as processors and bandwidth. An example would be using Secure Sockets Layer (SSL) to provide a secure connection. SSL requires a high amount of overhead, and because of this you might decide to only provide SSL support for pages that require high security. This would allow you to create separate servers for handling SSL sessions. The drawback is that the system would be more complex and might require significant overhead for operating. In this situation, partitioning could be created by using many small components instead of using a few large components and by limiting the amount of cross-device communication.

Availability

Availability is a measure of how often the application is available to handle service requests as compared to the planned runtime. For some applications, high availability means that the application needs to work 24 hours a day, 7 days a week. Availability takes into account repair time because an application that is being repaired is not available for use. Advances in hardware and software have increased the quality of high-availability applications.

exam
ⓦatch
Availability does not address business continuation issues such as backups and alternative sites.

The following table shows the measurements used for calculating availability.

Name	Calculation	Definition
Mean Time Between Failure (MTBF)	Hours/failure count	Average length of time the application runs before failing
Mean Time To Recovery (MTTR)	Repair hours/failure count	Average length of time needed to repair and restore service after a failure

The formula for calculating availability is:

Availability = (MTBF / (MTBF + MTTR)) × 100

An example of this would be a 24/7 web site that has two errors a week that each require an hour to fix. The resulting calculation would look like the following, based on a year's time:

$$((8736 / 104) / ((8736 / 104) + .5)) \times 100 = 99.4\%$$

A common way to describe availability is by using 99.*. You will notice from our example the application is down for 104 hours during the year, but the percentage is still high, so these numbers can be deceiving. To determine the level of availability that is appropriate for your application, you need to answer these questions:

- Who are the customers of the application? What are their expectations from the application?

- How much downtime is acceptable?

- Do internal company processes depend on the service? An example would be to perform data maintenance during the hours of 2:00 A.M. and 4:00 A.M. because the user population is not using the application and the impact is minimized.

- What are the schedule and budget for developing the application?

Designing for availability is intended to prevent and detect errors before they happen. Availability can be ensured by providing multiple routes to application processes and data. Use only tested and proven processes that support the application throughout the solution life cycle. Some techniques used for designing for availability include:

- Reduce planned downtime by using rolling upgrades. Rolling upgrades refers to taking a specific server down in a cluster, updating the component, and bringing the server back online. A cluster consists of multiple computers that are physically networked and logically connected using cluster software. The other server during this time is taking the workload without the user experiencing any downtime. This is usually used for applications that scale out.

- Reduce unplanned downtime with clustering. Clustering is technology for creating high-availability applications. Clustering allows a multiple server web site to withstand failures with no interruption in service. This allows one of the machines in a cluster to be taken down for repairs and the other machines in the cluster will take its responsibilities. This can cause a slight delay for the customers connected. Cluster software can provide this functionality if the service and application have been designed to be cluster-aware and assigned to a cluster.

- Use network load balancing. Network load balancing (NLB) is used to distribute traffic evenly across available servers, such as in web farms. The farm has multiple web servers and NLB balances the load between the web servers, so if one is busy the next one in the list is used instead. If one of the machines needs to be taken down for maintenance, other machines can be assigned to the farm to prevent an interruption of service.

- Use a redundant array of independent disks (RAID) for data stores. RAID uses multiple hard drives to store data in multiple places. If a disk fails, the application is transferred to a mirrored image and the application continues running. The failed disk can be replaced or recovered without stopping the application, which defines RAID 0. Another type of RAID is RAID 5, which is like RAID 0 except it is striping with parity. The following illustration demonstrates how RAID 5 is stored. For high performance database systems a combination of RAID 0 and RAID1 can be used, known as RAID 10, which combines striping and mirroring.

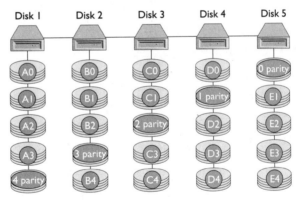

- Isolate mission-critical applications. This is an application that consumes many resources and is of vital importance to the organization. Each of the resources that the mission-critical application requests can affect the performance and availability of applications sharing the same resources. It is recommended that mission-critical applications use dedicated infrastructures and networks to prevent resource contentions between resource intensive applications.

■ Use queuing. Queuing enables your application to communicate with other applications by sending and receiving asynchronous messages. Queuing guarantees message delivery, regardless of connectivity that exists. Queuing allows an application to manage peak workloads that require a lot of hardware. More routes set up for the messages allows for successful and immediate message completion.

Reliability

Reliability of an application refers to the ability of the application to provide accurate results. Reliability and availability are very closely related. While availability measures the capacity to handle all requests, reliability measures how long the application can execute and produce expected results without failing. Unreliable systems are difficult to maintain or improve because the failure points are typically hidden throughout the system.

Reliability of the application is dependent upon the availability of individual components, because all of the systems are related. Application failures can occur for many reasons:

■ Erroneous code

■ Inadequate testing

■ Change management problems

■ Operations errors

■ Lack of ongoing monitoring and analysis

■ Lack of quality software engineering processes

■ Interaction with external services or applications

■ Changing operation conditions, such as usage level or workload changes

■ Unusual events, such as security failures and broadcast storms

■ Hardware failures, such as disk, controllers, and so on

■ Environmental problems (power, cooling, fire, flood, or natural disasters)

When considering the design for reliability of a solution, you have to examine the expected usage of the solution. Create a profile for the expected usage and design the solution from the profile. This profile should include how particular services are provided, an evaluation of failure scenarios, and designs for preferred alternatives. The profiles should consider the application's interactions with other applications, as well.

It is difficult to determine reliability problems for systems that have not been developed, but analyzing currently running applications in the organization can give clues to issues. Such analysis reveals the failure frequency and distribution, root causes and possible improvements for existing systems. This information can be used to create a reliable solution.

Creating a high-reliability application depends on the development and testing during the development and stabilization stages of the life cycle. A reliable solution ensures that the data input is correct and expected results happen consistently. The following tasks can help you create a reliable application:

- Putting reliability requirements in the specifications.
- Using a good architectural infrastructure.
- Including management information in the application.
- Using redundancy.
- Using quality development tools.
- Using reliability checks that are provided by the application.
- Implementing error handling.
- Implementing graceful degradation. Graceful degradation refers to the process of adding functionality to your application to enable compatibility with earlier technologies, mainly browsers.

Performance

Performance is defined by metrics such as transaction throughput and resource utilization. Performance is typically defined in terms of response times for users. To determine your performance goals, you should answer the following questions:

- What is the business goal? An example of this would be the solution should handle more orders each week, with an expected increase in revenue. This can then be converted into a performance goal for each functional area.

■ What is the critical functionality of the solution? Identifying critical features allows you to prioritize the system design. You might decide to degrade the performance of a low priority feature to maintain or increase the performance of a higher priority features.

■ What are the features required by different sets of users? Because of varying expectations, the performance requirements of the application can differ. You need to determine the relationship between each functional area and performance goal. For example, in a solution that uses database stores, the organization expects the solution to store valid data quickly. This converts into a performance goal of the solution that the database has fast inserts and updates to the database. Creating profiles helps in partitioning and developing accurate tests for the solution.

exam
ⓦatch   *For testing, performance goals must be expressed in a way that is measurable in your testing routines.*

Performance requirements must be defined before the team proceeds to the developing phase. Good performance requirements must identify project constraints, determine services that the application will perform, and specify the load on the application.

■ **Identifying constraints** Constraints in the project include budget, schedule, infrastructure, and the choice of development tools or technologies. You need to design an application so that it meets its performance goals within the limitations of the constraints. For example, a processor intensive application might not be able to be designed if the user's hardware cannot support the application. Instead of changing some aspects of a project to improve performance, you can modify aspects of the project to improve performance.

■ **Determining features** The features of an application correspond to use cases and usage scenarios. For each usage scenario that affects the performance of the application, specify what the user does and how the system responds. This includes how databases and other system services are accessed. This information can help create tests for measuring performance that resemble actual usage of the application as closely as possible.

■ **Specifying the load**   You can specify the load of the application as the number of clients that will use the application. In addition, examine how the load might vary over time. You can use the load to define the performance metrics of the application.

Selecting a Development Strategy

Before the development phase begins, it is important to verify the development and test environments. The test environment should ideally mirror the production environment. It is important to maintain separation between the production environment and the development and test environments to prevent occurrences in development and testing from affecting live production systems.

The development plan describes the solution development process. It identifies the tasks necessary to create and assemble the components of the solutions. This complements the functional specifications that provide the technical details of what will be developed. The plan also provides consistent guidelines and processes to the teams creating the solution. Some of the key sections of the development plan are:

■ **Development objectives**   Defines the primary drivers that were used to create the development approach and the key objectives of that approach.

■ **Overall delivery strategy**   Describes the overall approach to delivering the solution.

■ **Tradeoff approach**   Defines the approach for making design and implementation of tradeoff decisions.

■ **Key design goals**   Identifies the key design goals and the priority of each goal.

■ **Development and build environment**   Describes the development and build environment and how it will be managed.

■ **Guidelines and standards**   Lists and provides references to all standards and guidelines to be used for the project.

■ **Versioning and source control**   Describes how versioning and source control will be managed.

- **Build process**   Describes the incremental and iterative approach for developing code and for builds of hardware and software components.

- **Components**   Provides a high-level description of the set of solution components and how they will be developed.

- **Configuration and development management tools**   Identifies all the development tools the team will use during the project.

- **Design patterns**   Identifies the design patterns or templates that the team will use for this project and their sources.

- **Development team training**   Identifies the training necessary to ensure that the development team will successfully develop the solution.

- **Development team support**   Identifies the various types of support the development team will require, the sources of that support, the amount of support of each type that the team will require, and the estimated schedule for support.

The development plan includes strategies for auditing and logging, error handling, integration, globalization, localization, data storage, and state management. These priorities are included in various aspects of the sections of the development plan. The validation of the development plan is to make sure that all of the business rules for the solution are achieved.

Select Strategies for Auditing and Logging

Application monitoring is used to ensure that the application is functioning correctly and performing at an optimal level. Automated monitoring enables identification of failure conditions and potential problems. The auditing of an application is typically the responsibility of administrators within the operations team, and the operations team must establish guidelines and procedures for application monitoring. Communicating these procedures to the development team allows both teams to work together to log and monitor information that can assist problem discovery and diagnosis.

Error logging is closely related to monitoring and is a development function. The development team must communicate with the operations team to inform them of the types of error logs generated by the application. Together, both teams must decide on the appropriate logging mechanisms, then develop and monitor applications accordingly.

Understanding the use of error logging and performance monitors as an important method of collecting information.

A monitoring plan defines the processes by which the operational environment will monitor the solution. It describes what will be monitored, how it will be monitored, and how the results of monitoring will be reported and used. Once the details of the monitoring process are completed, they will be incorporated into the functional specifications and then included in the solution design. Some key sections of the monitoring plan are:

- Resource monitoring identifies scarce resources that need monitoring and determining of thresholds.

- Performance monitoring defines the metrics to be gathered for the performance evaluation of components in the solution.

- Trend analysis is the examination of the data to determine how parts of the system are used under various situations.

- Detecting failures describes how the development, operations, and maintenance teams will use the functional specifications and user acceptance criteria to detect failure incidents.

- Event logs describe how the system will capture information and how it will be reviewed.

- What tools are necessary for the teams to use to detect, diagnose, and correct errors and to improve a solution's performance.

Select Strategies for Error Handling

The reporting of errors is contained in the monitoring plan. The terms error and exception are often used interchangeably. In fact, an error, which is an event that happens during the execution of code, interrupts or disrupts the code's normal flow and creates an exception object. When an error interrupts the flow, the program tries to find an exception handler—a block of code that tells it how to react—that will help it resume the flow. In other words, an error is the event; an exception is the object that the event creates.

The level of exception handling depends on the level of monitoring required. There are several methods for handling these errors. First, a generic catchall error handling would catch all errors that occur in the solution. This could allow a centralized handler to report the error, but it would be unable to respond to the action and gracefully recover. The second option is to code the application where no exceptions are thrown outside of the class that the error resides in. The drawback with this method is that you would have to have all of your functions return some type of status and it would not allow for bubbling of event handling. The last option is a combination of these two methods. You can create a global error handler that is used for reporting purposes and acceptable graceful solution actions, while the handling of errors can be either thrown to the calling client or handled inside of the respective block of code and performing alternative actions instead.

Select Strategies for Integration

Integration is the interaction of heterogeneous applications, meaning the application needs to interact with existing applications. This can also be called interoperability. Interoperability reduces operational cost and complexity and takes advantage of existing investments. When designing for interoperability, you gain the follow advantages:

- Reduces operational cost and complexity. The customer can continue to work in mixed environments for the near future. A mixed environment is where applications are using different operating systems and platforms.

- The ability for different systems to operate in the same environment together reduces the cost of developing and supporting a heterogeneous infrastructure.

- Enables diverse deployment. A business requirement can state that the application must support external applications that exist on other platforms. An interoperable application enables the organization to continue using the diverse applications that address specific requirements.

- Uses existing investments. Typically, customers have large and diverse ranges of systems installed in their environments and move to a new platform gradually. In a typical environment, a new application must be able to interact with previous applications and might be web aware and need access from a different hosting environment such as an IBM mainframe.

- Extends the functionality of existing applications and protects the investments that the organizations have made.

To integrate heterogeneous applications, you need to consider the following types of interoperability:

- **Network interoperability** Refers to the ability of multiple vendor systems to communicate with each other without having to use common protocols. Implementing technologies or standards such as HTML, XML, or web services to make use of the Internet can make your applications independent of programming language, platform, and device.

- **Data interoperability** Refers to the ability of applications to access and use data stored in both structured and unstructured storage systems such as databases, file systems, and e-mail stores. Enterprise applications often require the sharing of data between disparate data sources and multiple applications. Published data exchange standards, such as cascading style sheets, OLE DB, and XML, allow data access to both Windows-based and non-Windows–based data sources.

exam
ⓦatch *Integration between systems is a very important concept. Most commonly integrations are accessing an existing mainframe.*

- **Applications interoperability** Refers to the infrastructure required to ensure interoperability between applications written for different platforms and languages. These new applications need to work with a wide variety of existing applications. One of the methods of enabling application interoperability is by using Common Language Specification (CLS). CLS is a standard that is currently met by more than 20 different languages, including C#, VB.NET, J++, and COBOL.

- **Management interoperability** Refers to the tasks of user account management, performance monitoring, and tuning for heterogeneous applications in the organization.

Select Strategies for Globalization

Globalization is the process of designing and developing an application that can operate in multiple cultures and locales. Culture and locale are defined by rules and data that are specific to a given language and geographical area. Globalization involves:

- Identifying the cultures and locales that must be supported
- Designing features that support those cultures and locales
- Writing code that executes property in all the supported cultures and locales

Globalization enables applications that can accept, display, and output information in different language scripts that are appropriate for various geographical areas. To globalize these functions, you use the concept of cultures and locales. These rules include information about:

- Character classification
- Data and time formatting
- Numeric, currency, weight, and measure conventions
- Sorting rules

Some of the issues that you need to consider while planning for globalization are:

- Language issues are the result of differences in how languages around the world differ in display, alphabets, grammar, and syntactical rules.
- Formatting issues are the primary source of issues when working with applications originally written for another language, culture, and locale. Developers can use the National Language Support (NLS) APIs in Microsoft Windows or the System.Globalization namespace to handle most this automatically. These factors include addresses, currency types, dates, paper sizes, telephone numbers, time formats, and units of measure.

The following best practices provide some information about globalization practices:

- Use Unicode as your character-encoding standard to represent text including all application process data, whether text or numerical. Different cultures and locales might use different data encoding techniques.

■ Unicode is a 16-bit international character-encoding standard that covers values for more than 45,000 characters that are defined out of a possible 65,535. It allows each character in all the required cultures and locales to be represented uniquely.

When implementing a multilingual user interface, you design the user interface to open in the default UI language, and offer the option to change to other languages, users who speak different languages can quickly switch to the preferred interface. This is a common practice for web applications. For .NET Windows applications, the Windows operating system can change its locale and the .NET application will automatically change, provided support for the locale has been added.

Cultural and political issues include disputes related to maps, which can induce governments to prevent distribution in specific regions. To avoid such issues:

■ Avoid slang expressions, colloquialisms, and obscure phasing in all text.

■ Avoid maps that include controversial regional or national boundaries.

Select Strategies for Localization

Localization is the process of adapting a globalized application to a specific locale, using separate resources for each culture that is to be globalized. A resource file contains culture-specific user interface items that are provided to an application as a text file, a .resx file, or a .resource file. An application prepared for localization has two conceptual blocks: the data block and the code block. The *data block* contains all user-interface string resources. The *code block* contains the application code that is applicable for all cultures and locales and accesses the correct resources file for the culture currently selected in the operating system. To create a localized version of an application, ensure that the code block is separate from the data block and the application code can read data accurately, regardless of culture and locale. Some issues to consider are:

■ **String-related issues**   Strings are the text displayed in the various elements in an application's user interface, such as menus and dialog boxes. For example, an error statement comprised of multiple concatenated strings in one language could be rearranged in a totally different order for another, making the concatenated result incorrect.

- User interface issues:

  - The length of a message might differ in different languages.

  - Menu and dialog boxes might become larger because of localization.

  - Icons and bitmaps must use symbols that are internationally accepted and convey the same meaning.

  - The keyboards used in different locales might not have the same characters and keys.

  - UI controls should not be hidden or used as parts of strings.

Some best practices to consider are:

- Examine Windows messages that indicate changes in the input language, and use that information to check spellings, select fonts, and so on.

- Detect the culture that your application uses to handle the formatting and change it to correspond to the culture that the user interface application supports.

- Store all user interface elements in resource files so they are separate from the program source code.

- Use the same resource identifiers throughout the life of the project. Changing identifiers makes it difficult to update localized resources from one version to another.

- Avoid text in bitmaps and icons. By having text in the image, the image will have to be recreated for each locale supported, instead of having a neutral image with the text located in resource files.

- Test localized applications on all language variants of the operating system.

Select Strategies for Data Storage

Data storage or data store is typically a database in which data is organized and stored. Data requirements for the solution specify how data will be structured, stored, accessed, and validated in the solution. With the requirements in mind, a technology for storing the data needs to be selected. The physical data model of a database management system (DBMS) defines the internal structure that the DBMS uses to keep track of data. The various types of physical data models that commonly exist are:

- **Flat-file** A flat-file database access stores all data in a single file as a set of rows and columns. There is no relationship between multiple flat-file databases because each database exists without knowledge of any other database. They can provide fast updates and retrieval because they support an indexing method called the indexed sequence access method (ISAM). Legacy mainframe databases, as an example, implement ISAM storage technology.

- **Hierarchical** Hierarchical databases store a wide range of information in a variety of formats. Examples of this include Microsoft Exchange and the Windows Registry. This type of storage is extensible and flexible. This option is good when the information storage requirements vary greatly.

- **Relational** In a relational model database, data is stored in multiple tables and columns. Relational databases combine the advantages of both flat-file and hierarchical databases by providing good performance and flexibility of storage. The relational model tends to be the most popular because tables can be linked together with unique values. Data integrity is maintained by applying rules and constraints.

Select Strategies for State Management

State management is the process by which information over multiple requests is maintained. State management is most commonly used in ASP.NET but does not have to exclusively be used there. ASP.NET provides multiple ways to maintain state between server round trips. Choosing among the options for state management depends on your application. Some criteria to consider include:

- How much information do you need to store?
- Does the client accept persistent or in-memory cookies?
- Do you want to store the information on the client or server?
- Is the information sensitive?
- What sorts of performance criteria do you have for your application?

.NET supports various client-side and server-side options for state management. Client-side options are the ViewState property, hidden fields, cookies, and query strings. These options are ASP.NET specific. Server-side options include application state, session state, and the database. These options are not available for WinForm applications; a WinForm application can use client-side XML files for state management.

Application state, session state, and using the database are not options for handling state for Windows forms. These are ASP.NET specific options.

Client-side state management conserves the use of server resources. These options tend to have minimal security but faster server performance because demand on server resources is minimal. There are limits on how much information can be stored using the client-side options. Table 4-2 summarizes client-side state management options and suggested uses.

Server-side options for storing page information tend to have higher security than client-side, but they require more server resources. Table 4-3 summarizes server-side state management options and when you should consider using them.

Selecting a Deployment Strategy

The deployment plan describes the factors necessary for a problem-free deployment and transition to ongoing operations. It includes the processes of preparing, installing, training, stabilizing, and transferring the solution to operations. These processes include details of installation scenarios, monitoring for stability, and verifying the soundness of the new solution. Deployment is the beginning of the realization of business value for a given solution.

TABLE 4-2	Method	Use When
Client-Side State Management Options	View state	You need to store small amounts of information for a page that will post back to itself and provide a basic level of security.
	Hidden fields	You need to store small amounts of information for a page that will post back to itself and security is not an issue.
	Cookies	You need to store small amounts of information on the client and security is not an issue.
	Query string	You are transferring small amounts of information from one page to another and security is not an issue.
	XML file	You need to store application user settings and security settings.

	Method	Use When
TABLE 4-3 Server-Side State Management Options	Application state	You are storing infrequently changed global information that is used by many users, and security is not an issue. Do not store large quantities of information in application state.
	Session state	You are storing short-lived information that is specific to an individual session, and security is an issue. Do not store large quantities of information in session state.
	Database	You are storing large amounts of information, managing transactions, or the information must survive application and session restarts.

Some key sections of the deployment plan are:

- **Deployment scope**   Describes the solution architecture and scale of deployment.

- **Seats**   Describes the magnitude of the deployment in terms of sites, number of workstations, countries, and regions.

- **Components**   Lists and describes the components to be deployed and any critical dependencies among them.

- **Architecture**   Describes the solution's architecture and how it might affect deployment.

- **Deployment schedule**   Identifies the critical dates and anticipated schedule for the deploying phase.

- **Installation**   Defines how the overall deployment will occur.

- **Deployment resources**   Identifies the workforce that will be needed to complete the deployment and the sources of the personnel.

- **Solution support**   Describes how the users will be supported during the deployment.

- **Help desk**   Describes the support provided to users and applications by the help desk team.

- **Desktop**   Describes any changes in current workstation application support that might be required during deployment.

- **Servers**   Describes any changes in current server support that might be required during deployment.

- **Telecommunications**   Describes any changes in current telecommunication support that might be required during deployment.

- **Coordination of training**   Describes how end-user and support staff training is coordinated with the deployment schedule.

- **Site installation process**   Describes the four phases of site installation: preparation, installation, training, and stabilization.

Select Strategies for Deployment, Such as Coexistence Strategies

The .NET framework provides a number of basic features that make it easier to deploy a variety of applications. These features include:

- **No-impact applications**   This feature provides application isolation and eliminates DLL conflicts. By default, components do not affect other applications.

- **Private components by default**   By default, components are deployed to the application directory and are visible only to the containing application.

- **Controlled code sharing**   Code sharing requires you to explicitly make code available for sharing rather than being the default behavior.

- **Side-by-side versioning**   Multiple versions of a component or application can coexist, you can choose which versions to use, and the Common Language Runtime enforces versioning policy. This type of versioning is only available for when the assemblies are installed into the global assembly cache.

- **XCOPY deployment and replication**   Self-described and self-contained components and applications can be deployed without registry entries or dependencies.

- **On-the-fly updates**   Administrators can use hosts, such as ASP.NET, to update program DLLs, even on remote computers.

- **Integration with the Microsoft Windows Installer**   Advertisement, publishing, repair, and install-on-demand are all available when deploying your application.

- **Enterprise deployment**   This feature provides easy software distribution, including using Active Directory.

- **Downloading and caching**   Incremental downloads keep downloads smaller, and components can be isolated for use only by the application for zero-impact deployment.

- **Partially trusted code**   Identity is based on the code rather than the user, policy is set by the administrator, and no certificate dialog boxes appear.

The deployment of a .NET application can be divided into two phases: packaging and distribution. Packaging is the creating of a manifest of required files necessary for distribution. Distribution is the actual process of moving the required files to the appropriate location(s) necessary for the solution.

The .NET framework has the following options for packaging applications. First as a single assembly, or as a collection of private assemblies, which allows the use of .dll or .exe files in their original state. Second, as cabinet (.cab) files, which are a compressed version of the required files. This option makes the distribution or download less time consuming. Lastly, as a Microsoft Windows Installer 2.0 package or in another installer format, which creates .msi files that can be used with Windows Installer.

After preparing the package, the files need to be distributed. There are three primary ways to distribute applications. The first option is the simplest, using XCOPY or FTP. Because Common Language Runtime applications do not require registry entries and are self-describing, the files can just be copied to the appropriate directory, where the application will be running from. The second is a code download, which can be accomplished by using web installers that allow the user to copy files to the client or enable automatically updating applications a location to download updates. Lastly, by using an installer application, you can install, repair, or remove .NET framework assemblies in the global assembly cache and in private directories.

There are three common deployment scenarios: the deployment of an ASP.NET application, a Windows Forms application, and a Windows Forms control by downloading the application to the client. The first, an ASP.NET application, is a package containing the application and .DLLs. These are distributed by XCOPY or FTP. The second, a Windows Forms application, is packaged into a Microsoft Windows Installer package (.msi) and distributed with Windows Installer. The last, a Windows Forms control or other code, is packaged into compressed CAB files (.cab) or compiled libraries (.dll) and the distribution is a file download from the source.

Windows Installer

One of the tools that has been mentioned as a distribution means is the Windows Installer. This is a powerful tool for the setup and distribution of assemblies. The Windows Installer packages can install assemblies to the global assembly cache or to a specific application location. The ability to isolate applications is an important part of the .NET framework. Isolating applications allows for multiple versions of components that need to be distributed.

Windows Installer has the following features that support Common Language Runtime assemblies:

- Installation, repair, or removal of assemblies in the global assembly cache (GAC). The global assembly cache allows for .NET assemblies to be shared between multiple applications.

- Installation, repair, or removal of assemblies in private locations designated for particular applications.

- Rollback of unsuccessful installations, repairs, or removals of assemblies.

- Install-on-demand of strong-named assemblies in the global assembly cache.

- Install-on-demand of assemblies in private locations designated for particular applications.

- Patching of assemblies.

- Advertisement of shortcuts that point to assemblies.

Windows Installer treats an assembly built with the Microsoft .NET framework as a single Windows Installer component. All the files that constitute an assembly must be contained by a single Windows Installer component that is listed in the component table of the Installer. When installing assemblies into the global assembly cache, the Installer does not use the same directory structure and file versioning rules that it uses to install regular Windows Installer components. Instead, assemblies are added and removed from the global assembly cache as a unit—that is, the files that constitute an assembly are always installed or removed together. With private assemblies, these files can be removed and updated individually. Windows Installer uses a two-step transactional process to install products containing assemblies, which enables the installer to roll back unsuccessful installations.

Assembly Versioning

All versioning of assemblies that use the Common Language Runtime is done at the assembly level. The specific version of an assembly and the versions of dependent assemblies are recorded in the assemblies manifest. The default policy is for the runtime to only use versions they were built and tested with. This can be overridden by creating an explicit version policy in the configuration files. These configuration files are the application configuration file, the publisher policy file, and the machine configuration file.

The runtime performs the following steps to resolve an assembly-binding request. This is where the application locates and loads dependent assemblies.

1. Checks the original assembly reference to determine the version of the assembly to be bound.

2. Checks for all applicable configuration files to apply version policy.

3. Determines the correct assembly from the original assembly reference and any redirection specified in the configuration files, and determines the version that should be bound to the calling assembly.

4. Checks the global assembly cache, codebases specified in configuration files, and then checks the application's directory and subdirectories using the probing rules.

exam
ⓦatch *Versioning is done only on assemblies with strong names.*

Each assembly has a version number. As such, two assemblies that differ by version number are considered by the runtime to be completely different assemblies. This version number is physically represented as a four-part number with the following format:

<major version>.<minor version>.<build number>.<revision>

For example, version 1.2.200.0 indicates 1 as the major version, 2 as the minor version, 200 as the build number, and 0 as the revision number.

The version number is stored in the assembly manifest along with other identity information, including the assembly name and public key, as well as information on relationships and identities of other assemblies connected with the application. When an assembly is built, the dependency information for each assembly that is referenced is stored in the assembly manifest. The runtime uses these version numbers, in conjunction with configuration information set by an administrator, an application, or a publisher, to load the proper version of a referenced assembly. The runtime distinguishes between regular and strong-named assemblies for the purposes of versioning. Version checking only occurs with strong-named assemblies. A strong-named assembly adds a public key and a digital signature to the assembly. A strong-named assembly is guaranteed to be globally unique.

EXERCISE 4-1

Creating Strong-Named Assemblies and Versioning Assemblies

In this exercise, you will examine how versioning works with .NET. The .NET framework allows applications to support multiple versions of dependent assemblies. This allows the application to determine which version of the assembly it needs to execute.

1. Start Visual Studio .NET.

2. Select File | New | Project | Visual Basic Projects | Windows Application.

3. Change the name of the project to WinVersioningApp and change the location to c:\.

4. Click More and make sure that Create Directory For Solution is checked.

5. In New Solution Name, type **Versioning** and click OK. A new project and solution is created.

6. Select File | Add Project | New Project | Visual Basic Projects | Class Library.

7. In the Name field, type **VersionLibrary** and click OK. The solution now has two projects, VersionLibrary and WinVersioningApp.

8. Modify the AssemblyVersion line of AssemblyInfo.vb in the VersionLibrary project to resemble the following example. The AssemblyInfo.vb file contains descriptive information about the assembly being built. It can contain information about who built it and why and strong-name assembly keys. The change that will be made will prevent the version number from automatically incrementing.

```
From
<Assembly: AssemblyVersion("1.0.*")>
To
<Assembly: AssemblyVersion("1.0.0.0")>
```

9. Add the following code to the Class1.vb. The code should look like the following illustration.

```
1   Public Class Class1
2
3        Public Function Version() As String
4             Return "1.0.0.0"
5        End Function
6   End Class
7
```

```
Public Function Version() as String
     Return "1.0.0.0"
End Function
```

10. To create a strong-name key for the VersionLibrary project, select Start | All Programs | Microsoft Visual Studio .NET | Visual Studio .NET tools | Visual Studio .NET Command Prompt. A command prompt window will display. This window has set up the path environment for the DOS environment for .NET.

11. Type **cd** and press ENTER.

12. Type **SN -k StrongName.snk** and press ENTER. This creates a key file for creating strong-named assemblies.

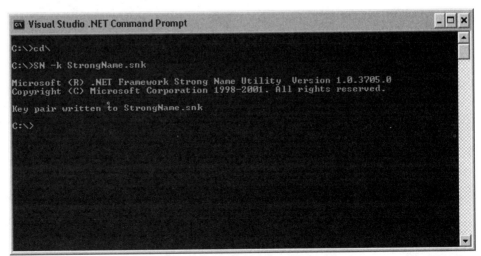

13. Copy StrongName.snk to your project directory c:\Versioning\VersionLibrary.

14. Add the following line at the end of the AssemblyInfo.vb file in VersionLibrary. This syntax indicates where the StrongName.snk file is located. After the project is built, the assembly is two levels down from the project, the signing of the assembly is performed, and the correct location of the signing key must be found.

```
<Assembly: AssemblyKeyFile("..\\..\\StrongName.snk")>
```

15. Right-click VersionLibrary project and select Build. The ClassLibrary project should build with no problems.

16. In WinVersioningApp, create a reference to VersionLibrary.

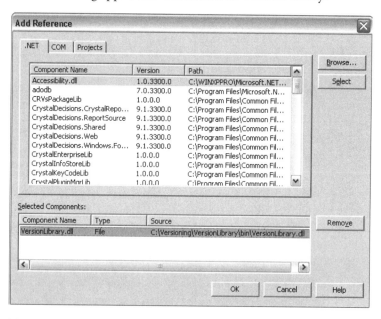

17. Add a button to Form1.vb on the WinVersioningApp project and double-click on the button in the designer.

```
Public Class Form1
    Inherits System.Windows.Forms.Form

    Windows Form Designer generated code

    Private Sub Button1_Click(ByVal sender As System.Object, ByVal e As System.EventArgs)

    End Sub
End Class
```

18. In the event handler, type the following:

```
Private Sub Button1_Click(ByVal sender As System.Object, ByVal e As
System.EventArgs) Handles Button1.Click
    Dim ox As New VersionLibrary.Class1()
    MsgBox(ox.Version)
End Sub
```

19. Build and run WinVersioningApp. Click the button on the screen (shown as Button1 in the following illustration) and a message box should appear with 1.0.0.0 as the displayed text.

20. In the .NET command prompt window, locate the path to your VersionLibrary .dll assembly and add the file to the global assembly cache. Type the following command:

```
GACUTIL /i VersionLibrary .dll
```

21. Version 1.0.0.0 is now in the global assembly cache. Change the version number in the Assemblyinfo.vb file on VersionLibrary to 2.0.0.0.

22. Change the Version function in Class1 to return "2.0.0.0" and build VersionLibrary and not the solution, by selecting the VersionLibrary project and selecting Build | Build VersionLibrary.

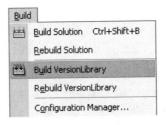

23. Close Visual Studio.NET and run WinVersioningApp again. It still displays 1.0.0.0 when the button is clicked on the form.

24. In the .NET command prompt window, execute the following command where the VersionLibrary.dll is located.

```
GACUTIL /i VersionLibrary.dll
```

25. Type the following command in the command window. This command lists all components installed into the global assembly cache that start with the name VersionLibrary.

```
GACUTIL /l VersionLibrary
```

26. A list displays the two VersionLibrary .dll that you created, each with different version numbers.

27. Select Start | All Programs | Administrative Tools | Microsoft .NET Framework Configuration. This .NET administrative tool allows for the viewing and configuring of .NET assemblies and code access security policies.

28. Select Application | Add An Application To Configure. A dialog box appears showing all .NET applications that have run on your machine.

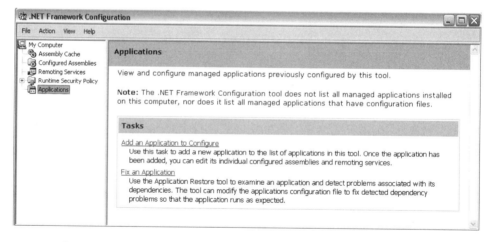

29. Select WinVersioningApp.exe | Expand Node By WindowsApplication.exe.

30. Select Configured Assemblies | Action Menu Item | Add.

31. Select Choose Assembly. In the window that opens, select the first item ("Choose an assembly from the list of assemblies this application uses"), then click Choose Assembly. Highlight VersioningLibrary and click Select. Click Finish.

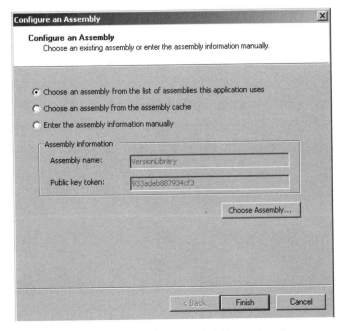

32. The VersionLibrary Properties window is displayed. Click the Binding Policy tab. Under Requested Version, enter **1.0.0.0**. Under New Version, enter **2.0.0.0**. Click OK to close the window.

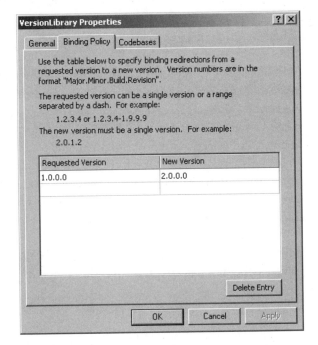

33. Run WinVersioningApp. This time, the result from the button click will be 2.0.0.0 instead of 1.0.0.0.

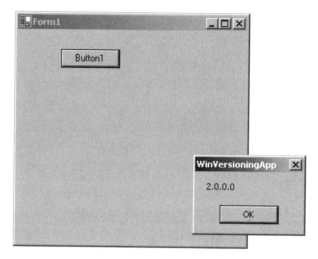

In this exercise, you created a solution with a Windows application and a class. You added assemblies into the global assembly cache and then rebinded the assembly's dependent files to other versions.

Side-by-Side Execution

Side-by-side execution is the ability to run multiple versions of the same assembly simultaneously. Components that can run side by side do not have to maintain backward compatibility. This allows applications to use newer components when necessary. For example, a component called Employee supports side-by-side executing. Between version 1.0.0.1 and 1.0.0.2 some incompatibilities were introduced. Multiple releases of the application have followed, and some releases support version 1.0.0.1 and others support 1.0.0.2. Each release can use the appropriate version needed while still having multiple versions of the Employee component installed. For side-by-side execution to occur, the necessary assemblies must be installed in the global assembly cache (GAC).

Support for side-by-side storage and execution of different versions of the same assembly is an integral part of versioning and is built into the infrastructure of the runtime. Because the assembly's version number is part of its identity, the runtime can store multiple versions of the same assembly in the global assembly cache and load those assemblies at runtime. Although the runtime provides the ability to create side-by-side applications, it is not an automatic process.

There are two types of side-by-side execution:

- **Running on the same computer**   In this type of side-by-side, multiple versions of the same application run on the same computer at the same time without interfering with each other.

- **Running in the same process**   An application running in the same process means that single applications with multiple dependencies can run multiple versions of the same component. An example of this would be web applications.

Select Strategies for Licensing

License specifications provide details for the developing and deploying phases on the number of licenses necessary for compliance. It helps to determine the purchasing requirements early in the project for both hardware and software that will be required for the solution. Purchasing specifications developed early in the process ensure that there is sufficient time for the approval process and that vendors have sufficient time to deliver hardware so the schedule will not be affected. Depending on the type of solution and number of users who will use the solution, you need to specify the number of licenses of any software that might be used.

Another area of concern is licensing of your solution. If you are developing components, your components can be licensed to ensure that only valid users can develop and use them. There are other models for licensing, such as a one-time license, subscription models for a specific time period or number of uses, or licensing based on the number of users or processors.

Select Strategies for Data Migration

Data migration is the moving of data from an existing solution to a new solution. When data from an existing solution is identified as part of the new solution, data migration becomes a critical element. A well-tested migration is necessary to prevent the introduction of risks that were never accounted for during the planning. More information about risk planning is in Chapter 1.

A document called the migration plan describes the migration from the existing systems to the new solution. Migration is typically more important in infrastructure deployments, but can be just as important in application development projects. A migration plan includes the following sections:

- **Migration strategies**   Describe how the migration process will be guided. These strategies are generally geared towards multiple software releases and preparation for each. The strategy can be organized in sections to allow for multiple software releases of solution components.

- **Tools**   Identify what will be used to support the migration strategy.

- **Migration guidelines**   Describe the constraints, validations, and order for the data migration.

- **Migration process**   Describes the preparatory activities in addition to the migration stages necessary to complete the migration process.

- **Test environment**   Describes an environment that mirrors the production environment.

- **Rollback plan**   Describes how a customer can roll back to the prior configuration if problems occur during migration.

exam
ⓦatch   *A common way to migrate data is to use Microsoft SQL Data Transformation Services (DTS) packages.*

Selecting a Security Strategy

Designing security features and policies is one of the most important aspects of an application. To be able to design a secure application, you should be familiar with the principles of security. You should consider these principles when creating security strategies. For more information on security practices, refer to Security Best Practices in MSDN. The following are some security principles:

- Whenever possible, you should rely on tested and proven security systems rather than creating your own custom solution.

- You should never trust external inputs. Validate all data that is entered by users or submitted by other systems.

- If your application receives unencrypted sensitive data from an external system, you should assume that the information is compromised.

- Service accounts should have the least permissions required. A service account refers to a user account that services on the computer use to access resources.

This account can be a local account or a network domain account for access to network resources.

- Risk will increase with the number of components and the amount of data you have made available through the application, so you should minimize the amount of public method and properties available to users.

- Do not enable services, account permissions, and technologies that you do not explicitly need. When you deploy the application on client or server computers, the default configuration should be secure. For example, if your web application needs to access network resources, the account used for IIS needs to have permission to access the minimum amount necessary.

- Encrypting data implies having keys and a proven encryption algorithm. Secure data storage will prevent access under all circumstances.

Follow the STRIDE principles. Each letter in the STRIDE acronym specifies a different category of security threat: spoofing identify, tempering, repudiation, information disclosure, denial of service, and elevation of privilege. STRIDE is used to define a security thread model to predict and evaluate potential threats to the system. Most security threats are actually a combination of types. The threat model identifies all of the possible ways a user can violate the solution and use cases are created to identify these. Testing is created later to determine if the security threats are minimized or eliminated.

SCENARIO & SOLUTION

A malicious user views and changes payroll data that travels between a web browser and the web server. List and categorize threats...	This type of action would fall into the categories of tampering and information disclosure. The user is viewing and editing restricted data.
Rank the risk of each threat...	Tampering is ranked higher than information disclosure. Both are important, but editing the restricted data is more critical.
Apply the threat model...	In applying the threat model, the site needs to encrypt data between the web browser and web server. This can be accomplished by creating public and private keys and encrypting the data. This will eliminate the risks of tampering and information disclosure.

Selecting Strategies to Ensure Data Privacy

Signing code with a strong name defines the unique identity of code and guarantees that code has not been compromised. Code signing is the process of providing a set of code with credentials that authenticate the publisher of the code. The credentials of the code can be verified prior to installing and running the code. The purpose is to ensure that users know the origin of the code and to help prevent malicious users from impersonating the identity of a publisher. It also verifies that the code has not been changed by unauthorized sources since it was published.

When encrypting data, there are two types of keys available, private and public. Private key cryptography uses a single non-public key to cipher and decipher data. This is also called symmetric cryptography. The algorithms used encrypt blocks of data at a time. Based on the type of encryption used determines the number of bytes in the block.

Public key cryptography uses a private key and a public shared key that anyone can use. The public key and the private key are keyed pairs. Data ciphered with the public key can only be deciphered with the private key, and data signed with the public key can only be verified with the public key. This is known as asymmetric cryptography—one key is used to cipher and the other is used to decipher. Public key cryptography follows a different model as far as ciphering the data. It uses a fixed buffer size instead of a variable length like private key cryptography. For example, public keys could be used to send small amounts of data between two public systems.

Cipher refers to the process of disguising data before it is sent or stored. Data that has undergone encryption is called ciphertext. Data that has not been encrypted is referred to as plaintext. Decipher is the process of decrypting ciphertext into readable plaintext. The processes of encrypting and decrypting data rely on the techniques of hashing and signing data.

Hashing is the process of matching data of any length to a fixed-length byte sequence. The fixed-length byte sequence is called a hash. A hash is obtained by applying a mathematical function, called a hashing algorithm.

Signed data is a standards-based data type. Signed data consists of any type of content plus encrypted hashes of the content for zero or more signers. The hashes are used to confirm the identity of a data signer and to confirm that the message has not been modified since it was signed.

Code Access Security

Code access security allows code to be trusted to varying degrees, depending on the code's origin, code's evidence, or strong name signature, and on other aspects of the code's identity. For example, code that is downloaded from your organization's intranet and published by your organization might be trusted to a greater degree than code downloaded from the Internet and published by an unknown entity. The .NET framework allows you to include features in your application that request a specific level of security privilege from the system.

Select Strategies to Ensure Secure Access

Role-based security relates mostly to the spoofing identity security threat by preventing unauthorized users from performing operations that they are not authorized to perform. Role-based security allows code to verify the identity and role membership of the user.

The .NET framework supports role-based security by using the principal object. This object contains the security context of the current thread. The associated identity contains at the minimum the type of security protocol and the name of the user. Security is based on the security context of the Principal object. The IPrinciple object has two classes that implement this interface, GenericPrincipal and WindowsPrincipal. Each are both used to determine the user's identity and any roles that they belong to.

Authentication   Authentication is the process of discovering and verifying the identity of a user by examining the user's credentials and then validating those credentials against some authority. Examples of commonly used authentication mechanisms include the operating system, Passport, and application-defined mechanisms like NTLM and Kerberos authentication.

The WindowsPrincipal and WindowsIdentity objects contain information about the Windows accounts. If you are using Windows NT or Windows 2000 domain for authentication, these are the objects you want to use. The following code illustrates how to get access to the WindowsPrincipal:

```
[VB.NET]
AppDomain.CurrentDomain.SetPrincipalPolicy( _
PrincipalPolicy.WindowsPrincipal)
Dim MyPrincipal as WindowsPrincipal =  __
```

```
CType(Thread.CurrentPrincipal, WindowsPrincipal)
```

```
[C#]
AppDomain.CurrentDomain.SetPrincipalPolicy( _ PrincipalPolicy.WindowsPrincipal);
WindowsPrincipal MyPrincipal = (WindowsPrincipal) Thread.CurrentPrincipal;
```

The following table lists the supporting values that can be used for setting the principal policy.

Value	Description
NoPrincipal	No principal or identity objects should be created.
UnauthenticatedPrincipal	Principal and identity objects for the unauthenticated entity.
WindowsPrincipal	Principal and identity objects that reflect the operating system token associated with the current execution thread should be created, and the associated operating system groups should be mapped into roles.

exam
ⓦatch

The WindowsPrincipal is the most common principal used. It is used for Windows Authentication, otherwise use the GenericPrincipal.

The GenericPrincipal and GenericIdentity are used for authorization independent of Windows NT and Windows 2000 domain. A classic example of this would be an application that requests user name and password for authorization, and the information is checked against a database or XML file. The following code shows how to use the GenericPrincipal is very similar to the WindowsPrincipal object.

```
[C#]
GenericIdentity MyIdentity = new GenericIdentity("MyUser");
String[] MyStringArray= {"Manager","User"};
GenericPrincipal MyPrincipal = _
    new GenericPrincipal(MyIdentity, MyStringArray};
Thread.CurrentPrincipal = MyPrincipal;
[VB.NET]
Dim MyIdentity as New GenericIdentity("MyUser")
```

```
Dim MyStringArray as String() = {"Manager","User"}
Dim MyPrincipal = new GenericPrincipal(MyIdentity,MyStringArray)
Thread.CurrentPrincipal = MyPrincipal
```

After you obtain the principal, it can be examined for validation.

Authorization   Authorization is the process of determining whether a user is allowed to perform a requested action. Authorization occurs after authentication and uses information about a user's identity and roles to determine what resources that user can access. .NET's role-based security can be used to implement authorization.

To validate where the user has permissions to perform specific actions in role-based security, is to use the PrincipalPermission object. This object determines what user and role has permission to perform the task. For example, the following code checks for the user Bob and that he is in the Manager role to perform the task. This is considered using an imperative security check.

```
[C#]
PrincipalPermission princPerm = new PrincipalPermission("Bob","Manager");
[VB.NET]
Dim princPerm As New PrincipalPermission("Bob","Manager")
```

Another way this can be done is using a declarative security check, which uses attributes for it defintion. The syntax for this method is very similar to the previous code:

```
[C#]
[PrincipalPermissionAttribute(SecurityAction.Demand, Name="Bob", Role = "Teller")]
[VB.NET]
<PrincipalPermissionAttribute(SecurityAction.Demand, Name := "Bob", Role := "Teller")>
```

If the user accessing the method did not satisfy the role or user conditions an exception would be thrown. The type of exception that is thrown is called the SecurityException.

e x a m
ⓦa t c h

There are two methods of verifying the user using role-based security, declarative (using attributes) or imperative (using code).

Authorization Strategy   To design authentication and authorization strategies for your application, you need to perform the following steps:

- Identify the resources that the application provides to the clients. An example of a resource would be web server resources such as web pages and web services.

- Select an authorization strategy. There are two authorization strategies: role-based and resource-based. Role-based has users assigned to roles and the user is verified against the authorized roles to determine if the requested operation can be performed. In a resource-based strategy, individual resources are secured by using Windows access control lists (ACLs). The application impersonates the caller prior to accessing resources, which allows the operation system to perform standard access checks. Impersonation is the act of performing an action using a different security context than the calling user's.

- Choose the identity or identities that should be used to access resources across the layers of your application. There are four types of identities that can be used:

  - **Original caller's identity**   Assumes an impersonation or delegation model in which the original caller identity can be obtained and then flowed through each layer of your system.

exam
ⓌatchWatch   *Impersonation allows a component to pass the calling user's security context to determine if the user can use network resources.*

  - **Process identity**   This is the default case. Local resources access and downstream calls are made using the current process identity.

  - **Service account**   Uses a fixed service account. For example, for database access this might be a fixed user name and password presented by the component connecting to the database. When a fixed Windows identity is required, use an Enterprise Services server application. This allows a centralized location for a component. The machine that is running the service can determine the user name and password independently.

exam
ⓌatchWatch   *Service accounts can secure parts of an application that must access network resources.*

- **Custom identity** When you do not have Windows accounts to work with, you can construct your own identities that can contain details that relate to your own specific security context.

- To support per-user authorization, auditing, and per-user data retrieval, you might need to flow the original caller's identity through various application tiers and across multiple computer boundaries.

- Selecting an authentication approach is based upon the nature of your application's user base, the types of browsers they are using, and whether they have Windows accounts, and your application's impersonation/delegation and auditing requirements.

- Decide how to flow the identity and security context at the application level or at the operating level. To flow identity at the application level, use method and stored procedure parameters, for example, adding the user name into the database queries. Operating system identity flow supports Windows auditing, SQL Server auditing, and per-user authorization based on Windows identities.

Selecting an Operations Strategy

The operations strategy deals with the daily activities to run the system. Security administration is responsible for maintaining a safe computing environment by developing, implementing, and managing security controls. System administration is responsible for the day-to-day task of keeping enterprise systems running and for assessing the impact of planned releases. Network administration is responsible for the design and maintenance of the physical components that make up the organization's networks, such as servers, routers, switches, and firewalls. Service monitoring and control observes the health of specific IT services and acts when necessary to maintain compliance. Storage management deals with on-site and off-site data storage for the purpose of data restoration and historical archiving and ensures the physical security of backups and archives.

These objectives are geared around predefined service-level agreements (SLA) negotiated by the project team and support team. A service-level agreement is defined as an agreement between the service provider and the customer that defines the responsibilities of all participating parties and that binds the service provider to provide a particular service of a specific agreed-upon quality and quantity. It constrains the demands that customers can place on the service of those limits that are defined by the agreement.

Select Strategies for Data Archiving and Data Purging

Data archiving is determining what needs to be backed up, when, and how often. The key requirements to be met for the backup process are defined by the application and the organization. Requirements to consider are described in the following categories:

- **Size requirements**   The amount of required data storage needs to be determined for each data type. Understanding whether terabytes or megabytes of data are involved has a major influence on the specific strategy.

- **Data location**   The physical and logical location of the data to be backed up must be determined. In addition to simply identifying the physical location of the data, it must be ensured that backup devices can access the data to be backed up and restored. This will help in determining the types of devices required for performing backups, the media required, and the necessary time window.

- **Backup timetable**   How often the data needs to be backed up per data type needs to be determined. For example, application data can be backed up daily, system data every week, and critical database transactions twice a day.

While defining the backup requirements for different data types, planning should also occur on how the storage media should be secured and maintained. Based on requirements some information may need to be stored off-site. The strategies that you employ can be different for each application and server. For example, SQL Server 2000 employs the use of transaction logs that can be backed up to prevent the use of full backups. There are three types of backups that you can perform:

- A full backup copies all selected files and marks each file as having been backed up, by clearing the archive attribute. For a full backup, only the most recent copy of the backup tape is required to restore all files. A full backup is usually performed the first time a backup set is created. It is a common practice to perform a full backup at regular intervals, such as every week or month. Intervals should be based on the relative dynamic nature of the data generated by the solution.

- A differential backup copies only those files that are new or have been changed since the last full or incremental backup. This kind of backup does not mark files as having been backed up. If a combination of full and differential backups is used, files or tapes from both the last full and differential backups are needed to restore files and folders.

- An incremental backup backs up only those files that are new or have changed since the last full or incremental backup. If a combination of full and incremental backups is used, the last normal backup set, as well as all incremental backup sets, is needed to restore data.

Incremental backups do not have the same behavior for SQL Server 2000.

Data purging is the elimination of unnecessary information that is not being used with the application. Over a period, solutions can generate a large amount of data. It has to be determined when it can be deleted because it is not useful anymore. The data can be removed or moved into an archive location for safekeeping. If the backup strategy is correct, the data can be removed without worry because it can be recovered if needed. There can be legal implications that require that the data be archived for long periods of time. For example, in the medical field, archived data and medical records must be preserved for various periods of time, such as seven years or longer based on the age of the client.

Select Strategies for Upgrades

It's common for errors and modifications of solutions to happen, forcing upgrades for the application after it has been rolled out to the production environment.

Typically, applications are upgraded for the following reasons:

- To apply bug fixes to remedy problems with your application
- To provide enhancements for existing features
- To provide new features or capabilities

One of the major advantages of the .NET architecture is that it provides comprehensive support for modifying or upgrading applications after they have been deployed. There are several primary methods for upgrading. First is to reinstall the application. Second is to use Windows Installer to create an update package to modify the necessary components. Windows Installer can perform the Add/Remove Program, Delete File, and Add New File functions. The deleting and adding of files to an already installed solution increases the maintenance and total cost of ownership for the solution. The third option is to create a side-by-side assembly functionality. The last option would be to have the application be able to be self-updating and download and install patches as necessary.

Create a Support Plan

Your support plan should address who will provide support, what level of support they need to provide, and how users can report problems. Determine who will support the users: will it be the project team, the help desk, or external resources? If the help desk provides the support, how will you train them? What will be the role of the project team?

Determine what service levels you can support. For example, must critical problems be resolved within a specified number of hours? During what hours must support be available to users?

Document the change management and problem management processes for the solution. Your process should address these issues:

- How are change requests submitted, approved, tested, and implemented?

- Where do users post their problems?

- Can they report problems to an existing system or do you need a new mechanism, such as a web site, where users can log their problems and questions?

- How will you review, prioritize, and fix problems?

- What escalation process will you use to notify the appropriate personnel?

Creating a Test Plan

The test plan describes the strategy used to organize, and manage the project's testing activities. It identifies testing objectives, methodologies and tools, expected results, responsibilities, and resource requirements. A test plan ensures that the testing process will be conducted in a thorough and organized manner and will enable the team to determine the stability of the solution. The test plan breaks the testing process into different elements, including unit testing, database testing, infrastructure testing, security testing, integration testing, user acceptance and usability testing, performance testing, and regression testing. These concepts are defined in Chapter 9 in more detail. All of these tests center around unit test. Each of them are at different levels and stages of the development process. Key sections of a test plan are:

- **Test approach and assumption**   Describes at a high level the approach, activities, and techniques to be followed in testing the solution.

- **Major test responsibilities** Identifies the teams and individuals who will manage and implement the testing process.

- **Features and functionality to test** Identifies at a high level all features and functionality that will be tested.

- **Expected results of tests** Describes the results that should be demonstrated by the tests.

exam
Watch

The expected results for a test can be specific results and answers or could be the visual cue of responses from the system.

- **Deliverables** Describes the materials that must be made available or created to conduct the tests and that will be developed from the test to describe test results.

- **Testing procedures and walkthrough** Describes the steps the testing team will perform to ensure quality tests.

- **Tracking and reporting status** Defines the information that test team members will communicate during the testing process.

exam
Watch

Reliable tracking of error and testing results help determine the quality of the product.

- **Bug reporting tools and methods** Describes the overall bug reporting strategy and methodology.

- **Schedules** Identifies the major test cycles, tasks, milestones, and deliverables.

The pilot plan describes how the team will move the candidate release version of the solution to a staging area and test it. The goal of the pilot is to simulate that equipment, software, and components that the solution will use when it is active. The plan also identifies how issues discovered during the pilot will be solved. The pilot helps the project team prove the feasibility of the solution approaches, experiment with different solutions, and obtain user feedback and acceptance on proposed solutions.

exam
Watch

The pilot is a very important part of testing. You can determine what processes work and do not work before going to production.

Creating a Training Plan

A training plan describes the appropriate level and type of training for all users. Training can be delivered before, during, or after installation. The training plan should follow these guidelines:

- Deliver appropriate training for each user
- Vary training based on users' background and experience
- Include a variety of media
- Train local support staff

Consider alternatives to the traditional courseware approach to training, such as coaching sessions, and a mentoring program for advanced and support users.

CERTIFICATION SUMMARY

In this chapter, we examined the functional specifications document. The functional specifications document represents what the product will be. The goals of the functional specifications are to consolidate a common understanding of the business and user requirements. This document also provides a framework for planning, scheduling, and creating the solution. This could be considered a contract between the team and the customer for what will be delivered. The functional specifications consist of the conceptual design summary, logical design summary, physical design summary, standards, and processes used by the team. The conceptual design is the process of gathering, analyzing, and prioritizing business and user perspectives on the problem and the solution, and then creating a preliminary version of the solution. The conceptual design consists of three steps: research, analysis, and optimization.

The technical specifications are a set of reference documents that usually include the artifacts of physical design, such as class specifications, component models, metrics, and network component topologies. To create this document, design considerations needed to be incorporated into the document. These design goals are scalability, availability, performance, integration, and localization.

The scalability design can be implemented two ways: scaling up or scaling out. Scaling up is the ability to add hardware components to existing server hardware, and scaling out is adding new hardware to the existing environment. Next, we discussed strategies for handling availability, which is the measure of how often an application is available for use. These are normally explained as percentages of nines. The process of designing for reliability involves reviewing the application's expected usage pattern, specifying the required reliability profile, and engineering the software architecture with the intention of meeting the profile. Performance is defined by key application metrics, such as transaction throughput and resource utilization. Integration is the ability to integrate heterogeneous applications. Localization is the process of adapting a globalized application to a particular culture and locale.

The development plan describes the solution development process used for the project. This plan includes a monitoring plan, how the data will be stored, and state management techniques to be employed by the team. Application monitoring is used to ensure that the application is functioning correctly and performing at the optimal level. The monitoring plan describes what will be monitored, how the application will be monitored, and how the results of monitoring will be reported and used.

The test plan describes the strategy and approach used to plan, organize, and manage the project's testing activities, and identifies testing objectives, methodologies and tools, expected results, responsibilities, and resource requirements.

The deployment plan describes the factors necessary for a smooth deployment and transition to ongoing operations and includes the processes of preparing, installing, training, stabilizing, and transferring the solution to operations.

 # TWO-MINUTE DRILL

Functional Specifications

❑ The functional specifications represent what the product will be.

❑ Functional specifications are a virtual repository of project and design-related artifacts.

Transforming Requirements into Functional Specifications

❑ Synthesizing of information is the process of assimilating gathered data and interpreting the results.

❑ Restating requirements involves categorizing and prioritizing the requirements.

Transforming Functional Specifications into Technical Specifications

❑ Scaling involves the designing of processes so that they don't have to wait. It also looks at the allocation of resources for processes and designing for commutability and interchangeability.

❑ Availability is the examination of the expectations of the customer of how much downtime is expected and how internal resources are available for the solution to achieve high availability.

❑ The monitoring plan determines what, how, and when results will be monitored and reported.

SELF TEST

Functional Specifications

1. The technical team has diagnosed that the web application gets very slow when more than 1,000 people are concurrently using the application. Choose the correct methods to scale the application without adding additional servers.

   A. Add more processors

   B. Add more servers

   C. Upgrade to a more powerful computer

   D. None of the options available

2. While consulting with a client to design a scalable web application, what should be considered?

   A. Design synchronous processes

   B. Design processes that do not compete for resources

   C. Design components for interchangeability

   D. Partition resources and activities

3. The solution that is being designed needs to run 24 hours a day and 7 days a week. Which of the following considerations are correct?

   A. Reduce planned downtime

   B. Reduce unplanned downtime without clustering

   C. Use network load balancing

   D. Use queuing

Transforming Requirements into Functional Specifications

4. The current application's availability is about 50 percent. The application needs to be redesigned to reduce the planned downtime. Which are the correct techniques?

   A. Promote untested code to production

   B. Take all servers off-line for updates

   C. Use clustered servers

   D. Use network load balancing

5. While identifying requirements for the new application, you want to show the customer the importance of reliability considerations. Which of these items are correct?

    A. Deploy untested code

    B. Prevent operational errors

    C. Prevent lost revenue and customers

    D. Isolate mission-critical applications

6. The client is having problems with code that consistently has errors and is designed incorrectly. What techniques can be suggested to improve the reliability of the application?

    A. Lack of requirements documents

    B. Using quality development tools

    C. Lack of quality software engineering processes

    D. Implementing error handling

7. After gathering requirements for the new solution, you are asked to identify performance requirements and techniques for the new solution. Which of these apply?

    A. Apply forms authentication

    B. The # of orders that can be created in an hour

    C. Implement performance counters in the application

    D. Use existing technology investments

8. You are writing the technical specifications document for your solution. The customer needs to understand the need for interoperability with the existing mainframe, which stores its current order data. Which of these concepts are correct?

    A. Ignore existing technologies

    B. Remove the mainframe hardware

    C. Enable optimal deployments

    D. Use existing investments

9. The new application being designed needs to support multiple languages. What must be identified in the technical specifications document on how to prepare the application for globalization?

    A. Update user documentation

    B. Design features that support those cultures and locales

    C. Write code that executes properly in all of the supported cultures and locales

    D. Performance monitoring

Transforming Functional Specifications into Technical Specifications

10. After creating the functional specifications, the customer is asking what the next step is in the process. Identify the purposes of the development plan.

   A. Determine development objectives

   B. Determine vision of project

   C. Document guidelines and standards

   D. Identify design patterns to be used

11. You are creating the technical specifications document. Identify for the support team the purpose of the test plan.

   A. Implement testing

   B. Identify methodologies

   C. Identify tools

   D. Identify versioning and source control standards

12. You are writing the deployment plan for the new application. What are the correct items that are needed to be identified in the deployment plan?

   A. Determine licensing

   B. Architecture

   C. Resource threshold monitoring

   D. Installation instructions

13. You are writing the technical specifications document. Identify the correct items about the technical specifications.

   A. Define scope of work

   B. Define configuration settings

   C. Define user training

   D. Define assembly names

14. You are writing the functional specifications document. The user is trying to understand the purpose of this document. Identify the correct items about the functional specifications document.

   A. Consolidate a common understanding of the business and user

   B. Develop an incomplete product

   C. Break down the problem and modularize the solution logically

   D. Serve as a contract between the team and the customer for what will be delivered

15. While writing the functional specifications document, identify the correct risks associated with not creating functional specifications.

    A. Developing a solution that does not completely address the customer requirements

    B. Unable to clearly define customer expectations

    C. Lower risk because it is unnecessary

    D. Unable to validate solution to customer requirements

16. You are writing the functional specifications document. The first step in conceptual design is the analysis phase. Identify the correct items about this phase.

    A. Reviewing the user and business research

    B. Documenting and modeling the context, workflow, task sequence, and environmental relationships

    C. Defining candidate requirements

    D. Validating and testing the improved business processes

17. You are in the process of restating the business requirements gathered in the initial phase of the project. Identify the common characteristics of the restated requirements.

    A. Requirements must be incomplete sentences not using will, may, must, or should.

    B. Requirements should be clear and concise.

    C. Requirements created in a testable manner.

    D. Organized in a hierarchy of related requirements

18. You are in the process of restating the business requirements gathered in the initial phase of the project. During the restatement of requirements, they are grouped into categories. Identify the main categories of requirements.

    A. User

    B. System

    C. Operations

    D. Support

19. The current application is not very secure. The new application will be used by a broader range of users and systems within the organization. You are writing the technical specifications document and need to identify security strategies for the application. Identify the correct security strategies.

    A. Trust external input

    B. Apply the principle of most privilege

C. Rely on tested and proven security systems

D. Default to secure mode

20. You are writing the functional specifications for the new application. The existing application had many security problems. Identify the correct security principles associated with STRIDE.

A. Spoofing identity

B. Repudiation

C. Information tampering

D. Degradation of privileges

LAB QUESTION

Create a C#.NET console application to copy web server log files from remote locations. The application should preprocess the log files and load them into a warehouse table. The information is then generated to rollup information from the warehouse table and populate the report structures. The source servers and file locations will be stored multiple key nodes in the config file that define: A) the web server name, B) the file location of the logs and c) the web site URL that the logs describe traffic for. All temporary files must be destroyed upon completion of processing and all system notifications, success or failure, should be written to the event log. The application config file should define a Panic E-mail key which should be used when a catastrophic failure occurs.

Refine the following requirements:

■ The application will be configured by using a configuration file that will determine the characteristics needed for the application to execute.

■ The logger application will notify the Panic E-mail Address when catastrophic errors occur. All other notifications will be sent to the event log of the running machine.

■ The parsing of the web logs will be handled on a file-by-file basis. This allows for the possibility that certain web servers are not configured correctly and for future expansion. The only files that can be parsed are files that are at least one day old.

■ Storing of resulting processed web logs.

SELF TEST ANSWERS

Functional Specifications

1. ☑ **A and B.** These options are for scaling up. Scaling up either upgrades components or replaces machines with more powerful machines.

   ☒ **C and D.** Adding more servers is incorrect because this is a scaling out option.

2. ☑ **B, C, and D.** Designing processes that do not compete for resources allows for a minimum set of hardware and increases performance. Partitioning resources and activities allows applications to minimize the shared resources needed.

   ☒ **A.** Synchronous processes are an incorrect process type for scalability; it should be asynchronous.

3. ☑ **A, C, and D.** The purpose of availability is to keep an application running continuously. This can be performed by reducing planned downtime, using network load balancing, and queuing.

   ☒ **B.** Clustering is a needed option for availability. Clustering allows applications to shut down a machine in the cluster and still maintain the services needed.

Transforming Requirements into Functional Specifications

4. ☑ **C and D.** When planning downtime, you want to minimize the time services are not available. Using rolling updates allows for the release of updates in phases. Clustering and load balancing allow machines to be taken down without loss of services.

   ☒ **A and B.** Taking all the servers off-line makes services completely unavailable and can negatively affect business. Putting untested code into production will eventually lead to downtime for fixing bugs.

5. ☑ **B and C.** Reliability is concerned with the correctness of the application. Applications that contain errors in code and in operational logic can be very costly to fix and maintain.

   ☒ **A and D.** Isolating mission-critical applications is an availablity design goal. Deploying untested code is one of the major reasons for establishing reliable code.

6. ☑ **B and D.** Implementing reliability goals for an application requires error handling, quality testing, and reuse of reliable components.

   ☒ **A and C.** Lack of quality software engineering is a cause of reliability failure.

7. ☑ **B and C.** Performance requirements are concerned with identifying critical features that need to have metrics assigned to how they perform.

   ☒ **A and D.** The use of existing technology investments is not a design goal of performance. Applying forms authentication is a security requirement.

8. ☑ **C and D.** Interoperability is the leveraging of existing hardware and software that can exist in different environments and require various protocols for communication.

   ☒ **A and B.** Ignoring existing technologies is very costly and time consuming. Removing the mainframe hardware is not an option in this situation; the goal is to preserve the hardware.

9. ☑ **B and C.** Globalization is the beginning of the process of localization. To create a world-ready application requires the preparation of resource files and identifying features that are culturally correct.

   ☒ **A and D.** Performance monitoring is clearly an incorrect globalization consideration. Updating user documentation is a factor, but is not correct for this stage of the project.

Transforming Functional Specifications into Technical Specifications

10. ☑ **A, C, and D.** The development plan is the road map for the design, standards, and features of the application.

    ☒ **B.** The vision must be clearly defined before creating the development plan and finalizing the business requirements.

11. ☑ **B and C.** The test plan identifies what will be tested, how it will be tested, and what types of results are needed.

    ☒ **A and D.** Identifying versioning and source control standards is a development plan element. Testing happens during the development stage.

12. ☑ **A, B, and D.** Deployment plans are used to determine what is needed to deliver the product to production, how this will be accomplished, and who is responsible for the deployment and support.

    ☒ **C.** Resource threshold monitoring is an important technique for performance testing and requirements.

13. ☑ **A, B, and D.** The technical specifications document identifies what work will be performed and how the environments will be set up.

    ☒ **C.** The technical specifications are not concerned with user training because this is handled by the deployment plan.

14.   ☑   **A, C, and D.** The functional specifications document is generally a contract between the project team and the customer to determine if all features are defined correctly, and is presented in business terms.
☒   **B.** Developing an incomplete product is always a danger associated with not gathering proper requirements.

15.   ☑   **A, B, and D.** By not creating the functional specifications, you run the risk of developing a solution that meets the requirements but is unusable or creating a solution then finding out too late that the business processes were incorrect.
☒   **C.** Defining candidate requirements is a step performed during the creation of the functional specifications.

16.   ☑   **A, B, and C.** The analysis of the conceptual design is the reexamination of the original requirements and creating a more detailed modeling diagram and requirements.
☒   **D.** Validation and testing the improved business process is a task performed later in the optimization of the conceptual design.

17.   ☑   **B, C, and D.** Restating business requirements is the breaking down of requirements into simpler forms and groups. These restated business requirements will be the basis for the test plan.
☒   **A.** The requirements should be complete sentences and use will, may, must, or should.

18.   ☑   **A, B, and C.** Requirements are grouped by their functionality, whether they are for the user, for the operation of the application, or for the system.
☒   **D.** Support is a subcategory that can fit under the User category.

19.   ☑   **C and D.** Security strategies are designed around the goals of protecting the data and the application. This involves applying the minimal amount of permissions and proven security methods and models.
☒   **A and B.** Trusting external input is always a problem. If the external system has information that can change data incorrectly, it would be very difficult to determine if it was authenticated to do this unless security was involved. The principle of most privilege is incorrect; the correct concept is applying security of least privilege. Give the minimal amount of permissions necessary.

20.   ☑   **A and B.** Spoofing identify and repudiation are correct STRIDE principles.
☒   **C and D.** Information tampering and degradation of privileges are incorrect STRIDE principles.

LAB ANSWER

The following is an example of how the requirements should be refined:

- **Req 1.0** The application will be configured by using a configuration file that will determine the characteristics needed for the application to execute.

User Services

- **1.1** User Services. Run application from command line and derive parameters from configuration file.

Business Services

- **1.2** Implement configuration file.
- **1.2.1** Define key for remote web server locations. Required information includes web server name, location of log files, and web site URL.
- **1.2.2** Define e-mail key for catastrophic failures.

Data Services

- **1.3** Define key for data access.
- **1.4** Define functionality for multiple keys in database to hold web server settings.

The logger application will notify the Panic E-mail Address when catastrophic errors occur. All other notifications will be sent to the event log of the running machine.

User Services

- **2.0** Verify event log entries.

Business Services

- **2.1** Create event log entries on success and failure.
- **2.2** Create e-mails when catastrophic events occur in the application.

The parsing of the web logs will be handled on a file-by-file basis. This allows for the possibility that certain web servers are not configured correctly and for future expansion. The only files that can be parsed are files that are at least one day old.

Business Services

- **3.0** Parse web logs based on configuration key information. Each web server instance will have a different name for the respective web log information directory. This information must be contained in the configuration file.

■ **3.1** Reverse lookups must be performed against the IP address to determine location. Storing of resulting processed web logs.

Business Services

■ **4.0** Store web logs based on URL information.

Part II

Designing the Solution

MCSD
MICROSOFT® CERTIFIED SOLUTION DEVELOPER

5

An Overview of Object Role Modeling

I t goes without saying that, in general, application designers and architects spend a lot of time thinking about the proper design of their systems and applications. A well-designed application will pay for itself many times over with benefits such as maintainability, scalability, and extensibility for years to come. The same benefits of good software design also hold true for the database components of two-tier and three-tier applications, which probably include the majority of enterprise applications. In the long term, a good design will save money, and a bad design will cost money—it's that simple.

For the last 25 years, *entity relationship (ER)* modeling has been the leading standard methodology for conceptual database design. ER was, and still is, a popular notation for graphically defining the structure of a database.

Object Role Modeling (ORM) is a relatively new technique for modeling database design. It is considered a successor to ER in that it fixes a number of the apparent deficiencies in the ER method. For instance, although ER models can be quite useful for documenting the design for a system, they are less useful for creating and evolving a design through a series of steps. Also, ER models do not support some of the advanced constraints that are available in the ORM method. In this chapter, we will learn more about ORM and proceed step-by-step through the process of designing a database.

exam
ⓦatch

Although the 70-300 exam may contain only a few ORM-related questions, the official Microsoft study guide devotes a full section to it.

What Is Object Role Modeling?

Object Role Modeling (ORM) is a process for developing the conceptual design for a database. ORM uses natural language to describe the conceptual elements of a system, such as objects and roles. In fact, ORM provides a step-by-step process for creating a conceptual database design known as the Conceptual Schema Design Procedure (CSDP).

Within the context of overall application design, database design might be one of the most important things to do properly. A well thought-out database design will influence application design in a positive way, while a poorly thought-out database design will have the opposite effect. Those of you who have had to design applications that run on preexisting poor designs know how hard it can be.

Three Phases of Database Design

The process of database design involves three phases: conceptual, logical, and physical. Unlike application design, database design is not a prequel to another phase. At the end of database design, you will have a database. The database may be just one small component of a larger application that still needs to be constructed, but once the database has been designed, it is ready to be used. Let's take a look at the three phases of database design.

The purpose of the *conceptual design* phase of database design is to describe the rules of a system in natural language. For instance, if we were designing the database for an online banking application, the conceptual design would establish the system's entities (such as bank, account holder, and account) and their properties. Here are some examples of account properties:

- An account has an account number.
- An account has a balance.
- An account has one or more account holders.
- Each account holder has a name.

During the conceptual design phase, the focus is on formalizing and validating the requirements of the system. It involves making an exhaustive list of these properties and checking to see if any of them need to be split or combined. Database designers often find it useful to use diagrams to help them visualize these entities. Viewing these entities and their relationships in a diagram often reveals problems with the design that could be overlooked in a textual description.

Once the most suitable conceptual design has been established, the database can be mapped to a *logical design,* which results in a schema. The logical design takes into account the type of database involved (relational, hierarchical, object-oriented, and so on) in defining tables, primary keys, foreign keys, and other constraints. Developers will often refer back to the logical design model when programming the objects and components inside the application itself because the database schema diagram provides an easy-to-read reference to the structure of the database. This is especially helpful when developing code that needs to read or update data.

on the
job

I have worked in some places where the logical design diagram was printed on large 6' × 8' pieces of paper and taped to a wall for easy reference by developers. For databases with a hundred or more tables in them, this helps make the system easier for everyone to understand.

Once the database schema has been defined in the logical design phase, it can be mapped to a *physical design*. The physical design is dependent on the actual database management system (DBMS) involved, such as SQL Server or Oracle. For relational databases, the physical design phase involves the creation of Structured Query Language (SQL) table creation statements. These SQL scripts can be run to create the database from scratch any time the database needs to be refreshed.

Benefits of Using ORM

In short, ORM is a well-developed and easy-to-understand method for modeling data at a conceptual level. ORM consists of both the process for creating this model, called Conceptual Schema Design Procedure (CSDP), and the language associated with the model, called Formal Object-Role Modeling Language (FORML).

ORM has been designed to be understandable, capable, reliable, stable, and executable. We can elaborate on how it satisfies these design objectives as follows:

- **Understandable**   Business rules are written in plain language.
- **Capable**   The graphical model supports many different advanced business rules.
- **Reliable**   Business rules are validated using real sample data.
- **Stable**   It is easy to make changes to the model.
- **Executable**   The ORM conceptual data model can be mapped directly to a fully normalized relational database schema.

Comparing ORM and ER

For years, ER modeling has been one of the most popular conceptual modeling languages for database design. ER models are still useful for documenting the conceptual design of a system but are far less useful for formulating that design or making and applying changes to it. In fact, the ORM model still includes a use for ER but only as one "view" of the conceptual data model.

ORM is a system based on *natural language* because instead of creating its own notation for describing the database of a system, it uses English. ORM is similar to another natural language design methodology called Natural Language Information Analysis Method (NIAM) and is partly based on that method.

The ability to create a conceptual design using a method such as ORM is one of the skills measured by exam 70-300.

There are other benefits to using ORM instead of ER as well. ORM allows database designers to provide more detail about the design in the diagrams and simplify the addition of constraints to the model. In short, the creator of ORM analyzed the modeling languages that came before it and created a language that overcomes many of the deficiencies of those languages while retaining their simplicity.

Creating ORM Diagrams in Visio

As we discussed in Chapter 1, Microsoft Visio for Enterprise Architects is a full-featured diagramming tool that has many applications outside of the application design arena. The tool contains hundreds of symbols and icons that can be used to create complex diagrams and graphics. Of course, because it is included with the Enterprise Architect edition of Visual Studio .NET, it contains dozens of icons and templates for designing software applications and databases as well. (Chapter 2 demonstrates how Visio could be used during the envisioning phase of the MSF to create UML state diagrams.)

The two ORM templates in Visio are located under the Database category; they are ORM Diagram and ORM Source Model. The ORM Diagram template contains over 25 ORM icons and is used when you do not want the assistance of wizards and specialized Visio plug-ins. The ORM Source Model contains only three basic icons but contains a fully integrated ORM environment (including wizards and Visio plug-ins) to help create diagrams. Using the ORM Source Model, Visio does most of the work of creating the diagrams for us.

You can see a screenshot of the Visio ORM Source Model template in Figure 5-1. I've resized several of the windows to make the Business Rules pane more prominent because that is where we will be doing most of the work.

EXERCISE 5-1

Creating a Blank ORM Diagram in Visio for Enterprise Architects

Microsoft Visio contains a number of ORM templates to help you create conceptual database design diagrams. Creating an empty ORM diagram in Visio is quite simple— the process takes only three steps. (Note that the following example requires the Visio

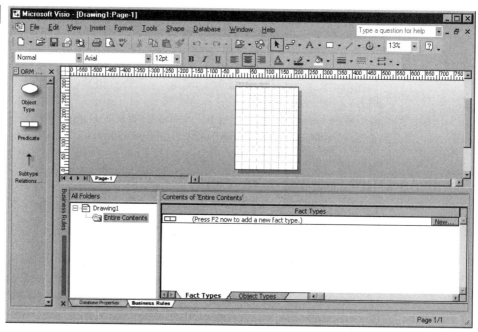

FIGURE 5-1

Visio's ORM Source Model template creates the ORM diagram for you.

for Enterprise Architects software, which comes bundled with Visual Studio .NET Enterprise Architect.)

1. Choose Start | All Programs and choose Microsoft Visio to start the application.

2. Choose File | New | Database and select ORM Diagram to create a blank UML model.

3. Choose File | Save As and assign your diagram a name. Click the Save button to save the diagram.

on the
job

Microsoft Visio also has the ability to reverse engineer an ORM model based on the physical schema in an existing database. This is done by choosing Database | Reverse Engineer from a blank ORM Source Model template. The Reverse Engineer Wizard will walk you through the steps of creating a reverse-engineered ORM diagram.

ORM Resources

Like many things in life, the best way to learn the nuances of database design is through experience. Experience will teach you things a book will have a difficult time explaining. For instance, you will sometimes need to decide between enforcing the rules of normalization and breaking those rules for the sake of performance and increased simplicity. Of course, the process of learning can be accelerated by learning new techniques from a book, reading articles, and discussing design with peers.

To learn more about ORM, I recommend a visit to the official ORM web site as a first necessary step. The official ORM web site is located at http://www.orm.net. That site contains a number of articles that discuss the process of using ORM to construct the conceptual design of databases in more detail. In particular, the article "Object Role Modeling: An Overview" is a very good primer on the topic.

Because ORM is the primary database design methodology recommended by Microsoft, the Microsoft Developer Network (MSDN) web site is also a good resource on the topic. In addition, Microsoft's ".NET Show" television show aired a two-hour episode on the topic of ORM, and Microsoft has made a copy of it available for download from http://msdn.microsoft.com/theshow/Episode025. Microsoft has also produced a five-part tutorial on creating ORM diagrams using Visio for Enterprise Architects. The first version of the tutorial is available from http://msdn.microsoft.com/library/en-us/dv_vstechart/html/vstchvseamodelingp1.asp.

For those of us who can't afford the $2,500 to purchase a single copy of Visual Studio .NET Enterprise Architect in order to get the Visio for Enterprise Architects modeling tool that comes with it, Microsoft provides another ORM modeling tool as a free download. This tool is called VisioModeler. We can't provide a direct link to VisioModeler, but we can direct you to the Microsoft Download Center at http://download.microsoft.com/. From there, you can obtain the free ORM tool by performing a keyword search and using VisioModeler as the keyword.

author's note

Visual Studio .NET for Enterprise Architects is one of the products available for download to MSDN Universal subscribers. For about the same price as a single license of Visual Studio .NET, you can receive development versions of almost all of Microsoft's enterprise software. This includes Visual Studio .NET, all current versions of Windows, productivity applications (such as Office XP), and other server software (such as SQL Server and Exchange Server). The MSDN Subscription web site is at http://msdn.microsoft.com/subscriptions.

FROM THE CLASSROOM

Understanding the Five Rules of Normalization

One of the early concepts of database development, which predates even the existence and widespread use of relational databases, is the concept of *normalization*. Normalization is the process of organizing a database according to certain rules. These rules exist to ensure that the database is unambiguous and operates as intended—efficiently and without data loss. The ORM process does a good job ensuring that ambiguity and redundancy are removed from the schema before the end of the process, so designers that follow the ORM model do not need to worry too much about normalization.

A database that follows the rules is called *normalized*, while a database that intentionally breaks one or more of the rules is called *denormalized*. There are certain circumstances where it is OK to denormalize a database for the sake of efficiency and performance. For instance, if normalizing a table would double or triple the amount of time a critical report takes to complete, you could probably justify leaving the table denormalized for performance reasons.

The five rules of normalization need to be followed in exact order; however, not all normalized databases follow all five rules, and a terminology exists to describe to what level of normalization a database complies. For instance, a database that follows only the first rule of normalization is said to be in *first normal form*, which is sometimes abbreviated 1NF. A database that follows the second rule is

in *second normal form,* or 2NF. The naming scheme continues up to *fifth normal form,* or 5NF. Oddly, most normalized databases only meet the requirements for third normal form because the fourth and fifth rules are much harder and less practical to implement.

The first rule of normalization is that there cannot be any repeating groups among the columns. For instance, let's assume we have a table named Student and we want to store the most recent three grades achieved using three columns named Score1, Score2, and Score3. In this example, the Student table does not follow 1NF, since the Score column is repeated three times. We will need to create a second table, named StudentScores, to list the most recently achieved scores as separate rows. As you can already observe, normalization tends to add more tables to a database.

The second rule of normalization is that a database must (a) be in first normal form, and (b) for tables with composite primary keys, all non-key columns must be wholly dependent on both values of the key. For instance, let's assume we have a table named StudentCourses, whose composite primary key is StudentNumber and CourseNumber. Let's also assume that table has two non-key columns, CourseGrade and TeacherID. We can see that the StudentCourses table does not follow 2NF. The reason is that the teacher of a course depends only on the course, not on the student. That is to say, the teacher specified would be teaching that course regardless of which students are actually taking that course. To make this table 2NF, we will have to create a second table named CourseTeachers to contain the teacher IDs associated with each course ID.

The third rule of normalization is that a database must (a) be in second normal form and (b) not have any columns that are not dependent on the primary key. This level of normalization goes a step further than 2NF because this applies to all tables. Let's assume you have a table named Student with a primary key of StudentNumber. Two of the columns on the Student table are StatusCode (containing either the letter *A* or *I*) and StatusCodeDescription (containing either the word "Active" or "Inactive"). This table does not follow third normal form, because the StatusCodeDescription column is not dependent on the student number but rather on the status code. The solution is to create a table of status codes and their associated descriptions. Once this is done, the Student table can refer only to a status code, and the application will be able to look up the description for that code in another table.

The fourth rule of normalization is that a database must (a) be in third normal form and (b) not have any independent, multivalued facts stored in one table. For instance, let's assume that the StudentCourses table contains StudentNumber, CourseNumber, and DegreesHeld. This table is in third normal form but not in fourth because CourseNumber and DegreesHeld are both multivalued columns—a student can enroll in more than one course, and a student can hold more than one degree. But the fourth rule says that a table cannot contain more than one multivalued column, so the StudentCourses table will have to be split into two tables.

The fifth rule of normalization is that a database must (a) be in fourth normal form and (b) be free from data redundancy that is not covered by any of the previous normal forms. An example of this rule would be an Enrollment table containing three columns—Department, CourseNumber, and StudentNumber—that cannot be split under the rules of the fourth normal form because StudentNumber and CourseNumber are related to each other (that is, we need to know what courses a student has enrolled in). Splitting the table in two would result in information being lost. But if the Enrollment table were split into three tables (DepartmentCourses, DepartmentStudents, and StudentCourses), no information would be lost. Splitting the table like this would follow 5NF.

As you can see, normalization tends to add tables to a database and create more complex dependencies, but it often makes a database smaller in total size by reducing the duplication of data. For instance, by having the StatusDescription in its own table, the database would only have to keep one copy of that string instead of having potentially thousands of copies—one for each student.

—Scott Duffy, MCSD, MCP+SB, SCJP, IBMCD-XML

CERTIFICATION OBJECTIVE 5.01

Create a Conceptual Model of Data Requirements

As we have already discussed, ORM is a process for designing the conceptual model for a database. ORM defines a step-by-step procedure for creating this model, called the CSDP. The CSDP contains seven steps, many of which involve checking the design to remove redundancies. In this way, CSDP incorporates the rules of normalization to ensure the database performs the task we expect from it without ambiguity, redundancy, or data loss.

The seven steps of CSDP are as follows:

- **Step 1**   Transform familiar information examples into elementary facts and apply quality checks.

- **Step 2**   Draw the fact types and apply a population check.

- **Step 3**   Check for entity types that should be combined and note any arithmetic derivations.

- **Step 4**   Add uniqueness constraints and check arity of fact types.

- **Step 5**   Add mandatory role constraints and check for logical derivations.

- **Step 6**   Add value, set comparison, and subtyping constraints.

- **Step 7**   Add other constraints and perform final checks.

author's
note   *Terms such as elementary facts, constraints, and arity will be defined later in the chapter.*

In the sections that follow, we will go over each of the seven steps one at a time. As we go through the steps, we will make our way through the analysis and design of a case study. By the end of the chapter, we will have a working database model for this case.

Our case study for this chapter will be the Happy Go Lucky Employment Agency (HGL). HGL is a small agency that specializes in finding talented computer professionals in order to fill either full-time or contract positions for clients. HGL currently has eight agents working on staff, although that number often changes during extremely busy and extremely slow months. Agents work from a desk within HGL's corporate offices, but they also need to be able to work from home or at a client's site.

There are two interconnected parts to the employment agency business: finding quality candidates for clients and finding jobs for candidates. Often, the agent that finds the open job is not the same agent that finds the best candidate, so agents are constantly communicating with one another. Currently, this process happens over e-mail within the company, although this system frequently results in costly communication breakdowns.

HGL has decided it needs a centralized application to assist with matching available jobs and candidates. An agent with an open position will be able to search that database for qualified candidates, and an agent with an available candidate will be able to search for jobs for which the candidate qualifies. Future versions of the software may include an entire contact management system (CMS) to log agent interactions with customers and candidates, but that enhancement does not need to be included just yet.

Step One: Creating a Conceptual Model

The first step of the CSDP is the most important step of the design process. This step involves creating a list of elementary facts about the system. In ORM, an *elementary fact* is a sentence, written in natural language, that asserts that an object has a particular property or that a relationship between two or more objects exists.

For instance, in our case study example, we could say, "Fact 1: Each candidate has a name." This fact happens to be a basic assertion about a known property of a Candidate object. The Candidate object has many more properties, to be sure, but each fact should relate to only one property or attribute.

Identifying the Elementary Facts

When designing a database using ORM, it is often helpful to use a subset of real data in order to validate facts and make it easier to work with them. For our purposes, let's review the facts using a specific candidate's data, as shown in Table 5-1.

exam
ⓦatch

Role descriptions are often reversible. For instance, the fact "An employee writes a report" can also be written as "A report is written by an employee."

Of course, the facts listed in Table 5-1 present a somewhat simplified view of a candidate. A real employment agency might need to store dozens of attributes about each candidate, including the number of years of experience for each skill, the names and addresses of previous employers, the names and addresses of educational institutions,

TABLE 5-1	Fact Number	Description
Some Basic Facts About Candidates in Our System	1	The candidate with Candidate ID 1234 has the name "John Smith."
	2	The candidate with Candidate ID 1234 lives at the address "123 Main Street, Anytown, CA."
	3	The candidate with Candidate ID 1234 has the phone number "(415) 555-1234."
	4	The candidate with Candidate ID 1234 can perform the skill "C programming" at an expert skill level.
	5	The candidate with Candidate ID 1234 can perform the skill "SQL Server" at an intermediate skill level.
	6	The candidate with Candidate ID 1234 can perform the skill "COBOL programming" at a beginner skill level.
	7	The candidate with Candidate ID 1234 is available.

and even a recent copy of the candidate's résumé. Because this is just an example, we have the benefit of not having to worry about those kinds of things.

Our case study also mentions the need for our database to track open jobs. In order to understand the range of values that can go into that field, we will need to examine a few more examples. Viewing only one row of data is often not enough to get an accurate representation of the data in a database. Table 5-2 lists the new facts we have gathered related to jobs.

From looking at Table 5-2, you can see that the fact numbers have continued in sequence from the previous list. We now have 16 facts; the first 7 facts list the candidate attributes, and the next 9 list the job attributes. We extracted these facts by looking at a couple of real-life examples of the data we need our system to capture.

One sample row of data often is not enough to capture all the potential facts of a system. Database designers need to review at least a few dozen records to check for differences within the first data row. For instance, if we looked at another candidate's record, we might find that the second candidate is not currently looking for work. In that case, fact number 7 would not apply to this new candidate, and, therefore, we would need to create a new fact to take this new data rule into account:

Fact Number	Description
17	The candidate with Candidate ID 2421 is available as of the date "05/17/2005."

TABLE 5-2	Fact Number	Description
Some Basic Facts About Jobs in Our System	8	The job with Job ID "T99" has the job title "Senior Programmer/Analyst."
	9	The job with Job ID "T99" is with the employer "Acme Health Labs."
	10	The job with Job ID "T99" has the status "unfilled."
	11	The job with Job ID "T99" has the type "full-time permanent."
	12	The job with Job ID "T99" pays an annual salary of $48,500.
	13	The job with Job ID "T99" requires the skill "VB .NET programmer" at an intermediate skill level.
	14	The job with Job ID "T99" requires the skill "SQL Server" at an intermediate skill level.
	15	The job with Job ID "T99" requires the skill "Microsoft IIS" at an intermediate skill level.
	16	The job with Job ID "T99" is located in "Downtown Anytown, CA."

exam
Ⓦatch

It is often best to review many different examples of data to validate a conceptual design.

As you may have noticed from the wording of the facts in this case study, facts in ORM are written in a specific format. *Unary facts* consist of an object and a property/role. For example, if we look at fact number 7, the two components are

- **An object**   "The candidate with Candidate ID 1234"
- **A property/role**   "is available"

Binary facts define an object and its relationship to another object or value. For example, if we look at fact number 17, the three components are

- **An object**   "The candidate with Candidate ID 2421"
- **A relationship verb/role**   "is available as of"
- **A related object or value**   "the date '05/17/2005'"

A fact can also define a relationship among three or more objects. For example, fact number 4 defines a relationship among three objects and is therefore known as a *ternary fact*.

- **An object**   "The candidate with Candidate ID 1234"
- **A relationship verb/role**   "can perform"
- **A related object or value**   "the skill 'C programming'"
- **A relationship verb/role**   "at"
- **A related object or value**   "an expert skill level"

The number of entities involved in a fact is called the *arity* of the fact. A unary fact has an arity count of 1. A binary fact has an arity count of 2. Facts can have arity counts of 3, 4, or higher, but these types of facts are rare.

Applying a Basic Quality Check

Once all the facts are identified, they should be checked to make sure all of the objects are well identified. An object in ORM is either an entity or a value. A value is either a number or a string, whereas an entity represents a real world object. For instance, "candidate" is an entity, whereas "John Smith" is a value. Each of the facts we have listed should have clear entities, values, or both.

A second quality check should be made at this stage to see if any of the facts need to be split or can be combined. For instance, in our case study, there are three facts that are nearly identical:

Fact Number	Description
4	The candidate with Candidate ID 1234 can perform the skill "C programming" at an expert skill level.
5	The candidate with Candidate ID 1234 can perform the skill "SQL Server" at an intermediate skill level.
6	The candidate with Candidate ID 1234 can perform the skill "COBOL programming" at a beginner skill level.

By stripping away the sample data we have included in each fact, we can see that all three facts state the same relationship among a candidate, a skill, and a skill level.

There is an easy way to determine if more than one fact states the same relationship, and that is to list the facts without the sample data:

Fact Number	Description
4	The candidate can perform a skill at a skill level.
5	The candidate can perform a skill at a skill level.
6	The candidate can perform a skill at a skill level.

Therefore, fact numbers 5 and 6 can be deleted from our list because they are redundant. The same can be said for some of the job facts:

Fact Number	Description
13	The job with Job ID "T99" requires the skill "VB .NET programmer" at an intermediate skill level.
14	The job with Job ID "T99" requires the skill "SQL Server" at an intermediate skill level.
15	The job with Job ID "T99" requires the skill "Microsoft IIS" at an intermediate skill level.

Fact numbers 13, 14, and 15 are also redundant. We will remove fact numbers 14 and 15 from our list as well. To avoid confusion, we will not renumber the facts because we refer to specific fact numbers later in this chapter. It is up to you to determine if you want to renumber facts for your system after removing one.

As you can see from the list of facts we have constructed, similar facts tend to repeat a lot of information. ORM defines a method for simplifying fact descriptions, called a reference scheme. A *reference scheme* is a shorthand notation that you declare at the top of your fact list, which you can use to minimize the amount of text you have to enter.

For instance, for our case study we can declare the following reference scheme:

- Candidate (Candidate ID)
- Job (Job ID)
- Skill (Skill Name)

Then, in listing our facts, we can use the string "Candidate 1234" instead of the more descriptive string "The candidate with Candidate ID 1234."

TABLE 5-3	Fact Number	Description
	1	Candidate 1234 has the name "John Smith."
A Summary of All the Facts, Using a Reference Scheme for Simplification	2	Candidate 1234 lives at the address "123 Main Street, Anytown, CA."
	3	Candidate 1234 has the phone number "(415) 555-1234."
	4	Candidate 1234 can perform the Skill "C programming" at an expert Skill Level.
	7	Candidate 1234 is available.
	8	Job "T99" has the Job Title "Senior Programmer/Analyst."
	9	Job "T99" is with the Employer "Acme Health Labs."
	10	Job "T99" has the Status "unfilled."
	11	Job "T99" has the Type "full-time permanent."
	12	Job "T99" pays an annual salary of $48,500.
	13	Job "T99" requires the Skill "VB .NET programmer" at an intermediate Skill Level.
	16	Job "T99" is located in "Downtown Anytown, CA."
	17	Candidate 2421 is available as of the date "05/17/2005."

Table 5-3 summarizes the 13 facts defined in our case study. These are the facts that exist after the end of the first CSDP step, using the preceding reference scheme.

EXERCISE 5-2

Creating a Simple ORM Diagram in Visio for Enterprise Architects

In Exercise 5-1, we created a blank ORM diagram in Visio based on the ORM Source Model template. In this exercise, we will add a basic fact to that model.

1. Choose Start | All Programs and choose Microsoft Visio to start the application.

2. Choose File | Open and navigate to the empty ORM diagram we created in the last exercise.

3. Click the Business Rules pane to give the pane focus and press the F2 key. The following dialog box will be displayed:

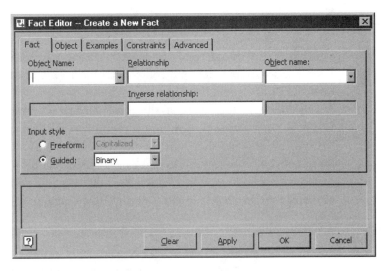

4. To enter the first elementary fact, type **Candidate** in the first Object Name field.

5. Type **has a** into the Relationship field.

6. Type **Name** into the second Object Name field.

7. Click the Apply button. We have now added the first elementary fact to our diagram: "Candidate has a Name."

8. Click the Object tab.

9. Change the type of the Name object to Value because Name is an attribute of the Candidate and not an object unto itself.

10. Click the Examples tab.

11. To add some sample data to this fact, which will help validate the fact later, type the value **1234** in the Candidate column and the value **John Smith** in the Name column.

12. Click the OK button to exit the dialog box.

13. Add each of the 12 remaining facts from the case study to the business rules list in a similar fashion.

14. Choose File | Save to save the changes to the diagram.

Step Two: Drawing a Conceptual Model

One of the cool things Visio can do with ORM models is draw an ORM diagram for you based on the facts and constraints you have entered. This will make things easier for us as we make our way through this case study.

Once we have established all the elementary facts during the first step of the CSDP, it is fairly easy to turn those facts into an ORM diagram for the second step. The process of establishing (and quality-checking) facts has actually established the list of entities contained in our database. In ORM, entities are represented by ovals, drawn with solid lines. For instance, the following illustration shows how three of our database entities will look inside an ORM diagram.

exam
ⓦatch   *Inside an ORM diagram, the << symbol is used to represent a role that is meant to be read from right to left. This is done so that objects and values can be spaced more evenly inside a diagram.*

Values, which are the text strings or numbers inside our elementary facts, are represented by dotted-line ovals. The relationship verb (or role) connects two objects on the screen, as you can see in the following illustration. This image represents a binary fact, as represented by the two boxes connecting the object and the value.

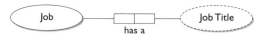

Unary facts are drawn using only the object and its role, as you can see here:

To create the ORM diagram, you simply go through each of the facts identified in step one and add them to the diagram.

EXERCISE 5-3

Autogenerating an ORM Diagram in Visio for Enterprise Architects

In Exercise 5-2, we used the Business Rules pane to add an elementary fact to an ORM diagram in Visio. Once we have added all 13 facts established in this chapter's case study, we are ready to generate a diagram. In this exercise, we will tell Visio to build an ORM diagram automatically based on the elementary facts.

1. Choose Start | All Programs and choose Microsoft Visio to start the application.

2. Choose File | Open and navigate to the ORM diagram you saved in the last exercise to open it.

3. Select all the elementary facts in the Business Rules pane by selecting the first fact using the mouse and then selecting to the last fact using the mouse while holding down the SHIFT key.

4. Drag the group of selected facts onto the blank drawing.

5. The resulting diagram, shown in the following illustration, is the ORM diagram defined by our 13 elementary facts.

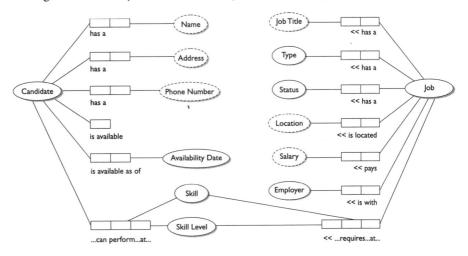

on the **job**

In Visio, the ORM diagrams that you create by dragging and dropping all the facts in one large group may not be organized on the page in the most readable manner. It is sometimes better to drag and drop each fact individually (or in smaller-sized groups) onto the page to get the diagram to look the way you would like it to look. Alternatively, you can move objects around the page manually after Visio has generated the diagram.

Step Three: Trimming the Conceptual Model

The third step of the CSDP process requires us to examine the basic entity types we have identified to see if any of them can be combined. In step three, we also need to examine the facts to see if any of them can be derived using arithmetic instead of having to be explicitly stated.

At first glance, our HGL employment agency case study does not appear to have any combinable entities. Following are the identities we have identified:

- Candidate
- Job
- Skill
- Skill Level
- Availability Date
- Type
- Status
- Employer

Two of those entities are very similar—you could potentially have the same person filling the roles of Candidate and Employer. That would occur if a person whose résumé were in your database (and presumably were not currently looking for work) also ran a small business that occasionally hired people; but since the candidate and the employer do not have very many properties in common and do not share the same relationships with other entities, it would not make sense to combine them into a single object.

For an example of when it makes sense to combine entities, let's assume that fact numbers 4 and 13 were restated as follows:

Fact Number	Description
4	Candidate 1234 can perform the **Candidate Skill** "C programming" at an expert Skill Level.
13	Job "T99" requires the **Job Skill** "VB .NET programmer" at an intermediate Skill Level.

We could make the argument, if this were the case, that the Candidate Skill and Job Skill entities could potentially be combined into a single entity named Skill. Candidate Skill and Job Skill have enough in common that combining them simplifies the model instead of making it more complex, so it appears we were correct during the first step of the CSDP to define Skill as a single entity instead of two similar entities.

The second part of this step is to see if any of the facts can be derived by arithmetic instead of being facts on their own. None of the facts in our example so far have an arithmetic component, so we're going to add an eighteenth fact in order to demonstrate this point:

Fact Number	Description
18	Employer "Acme Health Labs" has available Jobs in quantity 5.

Even though this statistic might be something that our system will have to keep track of, this value can be calculated simply by counting the number of jobs available with a particular employer. This saves us from having to store that information in the database separately. Since fact 18 can easily be derived using arithmetic, we shall safely remove it as a redundancy.

At the end of the third step, the data model for our case study has not changed from what it was at the end of step two.

Step Four: Adding Uniqueness Constraints and Checking Arity

The fourth step is to add uniqueness constraints to the diagram. Uniqueness constraints are a way to state that a particular value can occur at most once for a particular data field. You might think that certain properties can be called unique—Name, for instance—but a deeper examination would find that, in fact, it is entirely likely that two different candidates can share the same name; therefore, that field would not be considered unique. However, we could say that a candidate can have at most one name, so the candidate is unique to the name even though the name is not unique to the candidate.

The uniqueness of a particular set of values is represented in the ORM diagram as a bar across one or more roles, as in the following illustration. In this example, each Job object can have at most one Job Title value. Because a bar does not appear above the Job Title role, each Job Title can be repeated across several Jobs—that is, the title is not unique. In ER modeling, this is known as a *zero-or-one-to-many relationship*.

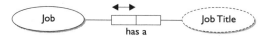

Uniqueness can occur between two unrelated entities or between an entity and an unrelated value. This is called *external uniqueness*. For instance, in our case study, we can say that in our database there is uniqueness between the candidate's name and address. That is, although multiple candidates may live at a single address, each address will contain candidates with distinct names. There will not be two John Smiths living at a single address. If there are, they will have to be made distinct somehow—for example, with the addition of a middle initial or middle name.

External uniqueness is represented on an ORM diagram by a circle with a letter *U* inside, as you can see in the following illustration. This graphic depicts the fact that the candidates must have a name unique to that address in our database.

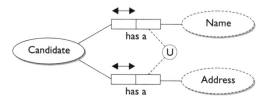

The second part of this step is checking for unnecessarily high arity counts. This step is important, particularly for ternary facts or facts with larger arity counts. Recall that a ternary fact is a fact that contains three objects. Let's assume we had included the following fact in step one as fact 19:

Fact Number	Description
19	The Candidate with Candidate ID 1234 currently has the Job Title "Programmer/Analyst" and is making an annual salary of $35,000.

In step four, we need to evaluate whether this ternary fact should be split into two binary facts, as follows:

Fact Number	Description
20	The Candidate with Candidate ID 1234 currently has the Job Title "Programmer/Analyst."
21	The Candidate with Candidate ID 1234 is making an annual salary of $35,000.

To decide if this fact needs to be split in two, we need only to ask ourselves if the Job Title and annual salary properties are dependent on each other. That is, do we lose any information by splitting the current job title and the current annual salary into two facts? In fact, we can see that we do not lose any information by splitting them into two facts, so if fact 19 were one of the facts required by our application, facts 20 and 21 would replace it.

Figure 5-2 shows how the ORM diagram from our case study looks with the uniqueness mark added.

FIGURE 5-2   The updated diagram including uniqueness constraints

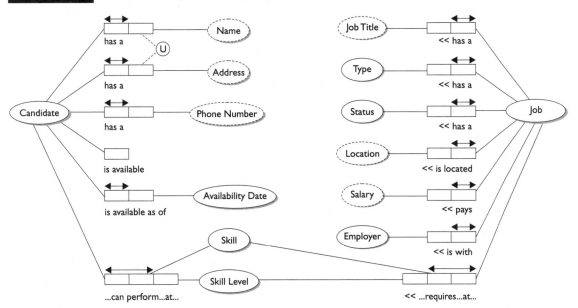

Step Five: Adding Mandatory Role Constraints and Checking for Logical Derivations

Step five of the CSDP requires that we add mandatory role constraints to our model. A mandatory role is like a mandatory field on a form. For instance, in our case study, we can say that all candidates must have a name. By stating this, we are indicating that the Name role is mandatory for the Candidate object. Likewise, we can state that a candidate may or may not have skills. Skill, therefore, would be an optional role for the Candidate object.

Mandatory roles are drawn using a dot attached to the object, as in the following example. The dot attached to the Job object in this illustration indicates that the Job Title value must be specified—it cannot be left empty or blank.

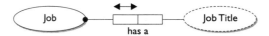

If an object must fill at least one of two or more roles, this is indicated with a dot inside a circle on the ORM diagram. For instance, in our case study example, a candidate must either be available or have an availability date on the system (as defined in facts 7 and 17).

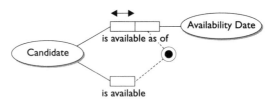

If an object plays only one role in the system, then its role is mandatory by default and no mandatory constraint needs to be added to the diagram. For example, the Skill Level entity only has one role in the system—"Candidate can perform the Skill at Skill Level"—so even though Skill Level is obviously mandatory, it does not require a dot.

The second part of step five is to check for logical derivations. We already checked for arithmetic derivations in step four—to see if any of the facts could be derived using mathematics. Now we need to check to see if any of the facts can be derived using something other than arithmetic derivations. For instance, in our case study, we could ask whether the location of a job can be derived from the company that job is with. It might be safe to assume, for instance, that if a job were with Microsoft it would be located in Redmond, Washington; but, of course, many companies (including Microsoft) have more than one office location, so we cannot safely assume the location based on the client name.

There are other ways to derive one fact from another. For instance, let's assume there were a number of years of experience associated with each candidate/skill combination, as shown here:

Fact Number	Description
21	Candidate 1234 has experience of 5 years with Skill "C programming."

If this were true, it would be worth checking to see if there were a correlation between years of experience and skill level. It might be that the beginner level has less than two years of experience, the intermediate level has between two and five years, and the expert level has five or more years of experience. If the skill level can be logically derived from the years of experience, we would be able to get rid of the fact related to skill level in this example.

Because the case study was defined after step one, no logical derivations can be found. Figure 5-3 shows how the ORM diagram from our case study looks with the mandatory role dots added.

FIGURE 5-3 The updated diagram including mandatory role constraints

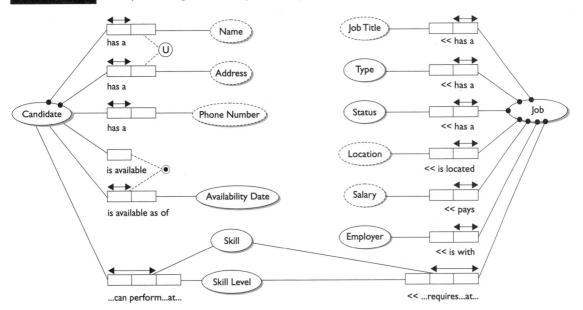

SCENARIO & SOLUTION

If a fact can be derived using mathematics, such as a count or a total,...	Follow step 3 of the CSDP to remove it from the conceptual model.
If a fact can be derived using logic or a business rule,...	Follow step 5 of the CSDP to remove it from the conceptual model.

Step Six: Adding Value, Set Comparison, and Subtyping Constraints

The sixth step of the conceptual database design is to add value, set comparison, and subtyping constraints to the ORM diagram. *Value constraints* list all the possible values for a value. For instance, the skill level can be either "beginner," "intermediate," or "expert," and the job status can be "unfilled," "pending," "filled," or "cancelled." The value constraints are added to the ORM diagram as an enumerated list of strings, enclosed in curly brackets, such as {"unfilled", "pending", "filled", "cancelled"}.

Set comparison constraints allow you to define a rule whereby in order for an object to fill one role, it must first fill another. For instance, in order for a person to be available for work, that individual must also be legally eligible to work. The set of available candidates is a subset of the set of legally eligible candidates. The set comparison is represented graphically using the ⊆ symbol, as shown in the following illustration. This diagram depicts the statement, "A candidate can't be flagged as available if that candidate is not already flagged as legally allowed to work."

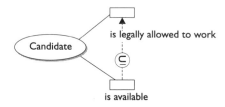

Subtyping involves inspecting each optional role to see if only a well-defined subtype of the object performs that role. For instance, only full-time jobs pay an annual salary. Contracts and part-time jobs pay an hourly wage. Therefore, we might want to create three subtypes for the Job object: FullTimeJob, PartTimeJob, and ContractJob. Additionally, we can see that part-time jobs have additional properties other jobs do not, such as number of hours per week. Contracts have their own properties as well, such as contract end date.

On ORM diagrams, subtypes are drawn with an arrow pointing from the subtype to its parent type, as shown in the following illustration.

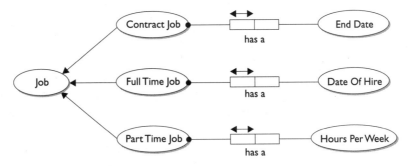

Figure 5-4 shows how the ORM diagram from our case study looks with the value constraints added.

The updated diagram including new value constraints

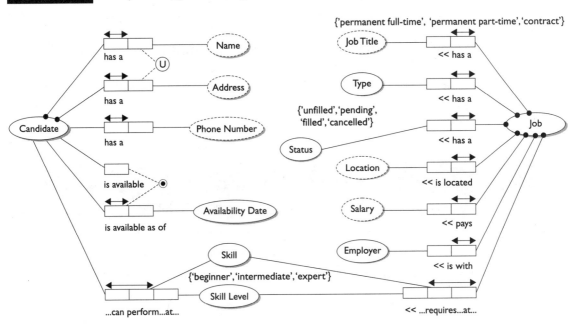

Step Seven: Adding Other Constraints and Performing Final Checks

There are a handful of other constraints that can be added to ORM diagrams. For instance, take the example of the employee who manages other employees. We can add an *irreflexive constraint* to indicate that employees cannot manage themselves; or, if an employee must have a certain number of skills, we can add a *frequency constraint* to indicate the number of times that role must exist in the database.

The CSDP process ends with some final checks to ensure that our schema is complete. Essentially, this involves checking over each of the roles in the diagram to make sure there are no redundancies and that the original intent of the database is maintained. Once we are happy with the entities, properties, roles, and constraints defined, we're done—the database schema has been defined.

Visio for Enterprise Architects does a great job of helping database designers build ORM diagrams. For those who prefer drawing these diagrams by hand, Visio also has the regular drag-and-drop template, which allows you the maximum flexibility when creating diagrams. As we said at the beginning of the chapter, these diagrams can be exported in ER format to make the transition from ER to ORM easier. If you have a large investment in ER diagrams for database documentation, that investment does not have to be thrown away.

Now that you have an understanding of designing a database schema using ORM, we can look at the entire application from the conceptual point of view. The next chapter covers the conceptual design component of designing software in Microsoft .NET. We will also discuss the types of technical architecture that can be used in our solution, as well as the various means for validating our conceptual design.

SCENARIO & SOLUTION

If a value can only occur at most one time in a data set,...	Apply a uniqueness constraint.
If a value must be present for every data record,...	Apply a mandatory constraint.
If a value must contain one of a set number of values,...	Apply a value constraint.

CERTIFICATION SUMMARY

Object Role Modeling (ORM) is a conceptual modeling language to help database designers create a proper data model. ORM is considered by many to be a successor to entity relationship (ER) modeling, although ORM diagrams can easily be expressed as ER diagrams if necessary. The main difference between ORM and ER is that ORM is designed to accommodate data models during the development stage more easily, where those models change and evolve. ER works best with data models that do not change.

ORM consists of a modeling language called Formal Object-Role Modeling Language (FORML) and a conceptual design process known as the Conceptual Schema Design Procedure (CSDP). Domain experts can use the seven steps of the CSDP in order to design a data model based on the elementary facts of a system. Once the elementary facts are defined, they are drawn on the basic ORM diagram. The rest of the process adds various constraints and performs a number of checks to ensure that the schema accurately captures the data model.

TWO-MINUTE DRILL

What Is Object Role Modeling?

❑ Object Role Modeling (ORM) helps define the conceptual design for a database.

❑ The conceptual design phase works with entities and values but not tables and fields because this phase does not include the type of underlying database (flat file, relational, object-oriented, and so on).

❑ The logical design phase converts entities and values into table names and field names and produces a database schema that is referred to throughout the development of the project.

❑ The physical design phase converts the logical schema into Structured Query Language (SQL) or other code in order to create an actual database.

❑ Visio for Enterprise Architects fully supports ORM diagrams using a helpful add-in.

Create a Conceptual Model of Data Requirements

❑ The process of defining a conceptual design in ORM is known as the Conceptual Schema Design Procedure (CSDP).

❑ Step one of the CSDP defines all the elementary facts of a system, using a natural-language syntax.

❑ Step two of the CSDP draws the elementary facts onto a basic ORM diagram that links entities with either other entities or values using roles.

❑ Step three checks for entities that should be combined and checks for values that could be derived arithmetically.

❑ Step four adds uniqueness constraints to the diagram and checks to see if any fact types need to be split based on arity.

❑ Step five adds mandatory role constraints to the diagram and checks for values that could be derived logically.

❑ Step six adds value constraints to the diagram and determines if any subtypes need to be defined for entities that fulfill complex roles.

❑ Step seven adds a few other constraints and ensures that final checks are performed.

SELF TEST

The following questions will help you measure your understanding of the material presented in this chapter. Read all the choices carefully because there might be more than one correct answer. Choose all correct answers for each question.

What Is Object Role Modeling?

1. Which two of the following methodologies, when combined, make up the Object Role Modeling (ORM) process? (Choose two answers.)

    A. ER

    B. FORML

    C. CSDP

    D. NIAM

2. What is the goal of ORM?

    A. Bug-free application design

    B. Accurate physical data model

    C. Accurate conceptual data model

    D. Identification of elementary fact types

3. Which of the following components of an application's data model is defined during the conceptual phase?

    A. The database product name, such as SQL Server or Oracle

    B. The underlying database type, such as relational or hierarchical

    C. Basic table and field names

    D. Elementary system objects

4. During which phase of database design does a formal schema get created?

    A. Conceptual

    B. Logical

    C. Physical

    D. Metaphysical

5. Which of the following are benefits that the ORM modeling methodology has over entity relationship (ER) modeling?

   A. ORM models are easier to read than ER.

   B. ORM models include actual data as a validation technique.

   C. ORM models support more complex business rules than ER.

   D. ORM models map directly to SQL statements for physical database design.

Create a Conceptual Model of Data Requirements

6. You are the database designer for a large project and have just completed the Conceptual Schema Design Procedure (CSDP) process to create your database's conceptual design. After the conceptual design is complete, what is the next step in defining your database?

   A. Normalize your tables to remove ambiguity and redundancy.

   B. Map the conceptual design to a logical database schema.

   C. Load the SQL statements into SQL Query Analyzer and execute them.

   D. Since the CSDP is iterative, go back to the first step and start again.

7. You are responsible for designing the database for a retail store. The elementary facts you have identified to date are

   ■ Item 0001 retails for the Price $15.50.

   ■ Item 0001 wholesales for the Price $6.75.

   ■ Item 0001 has the ItemName "Black T-shirt with pocket."

   ■ Item 0001 is produced by the Vendor "The T-shirt Company."

   ■ Item 0001 is in Inventory in the Quantity 5.

   Which of the following objects are entities in our Object Role Model? (Choose all that apply.)

   A. Item

   B. ItemName

   C. Price

   D. Inventory

   E. Vendor

8. Which of the following statements best describes a unary fact?

   A. A unary fact defines a relationship between two objects.

   B. A unary fact defines a property of a single object.

   C. A unary fact defines a relationship between an object and a value.

   D. A unary fact sets a uniqueness constraint for a role.

9. Which of the following statements best describes a binary fact? (Choose two answers.)

   A. A binary fact defines a relationship between two objects.

   B. A binary fact defines a relationship between two or more objects.

   C. A binary fact defines a relationship between an object and a value.

   D. A binary fact sets a uniqueness constraint for a role.

10. What is the purpose of checking an ORM model for arithmetic derivations?

   A. Arithmetic derivations should remain in the model because they reduce the amount of disk space required for a database.

   B. Arithmetic derivations check to see if any facts can be derived using business rules or logic.

   C. Arithmetic derivations should remain in the model because their values cannot be derived any other way.

   D. Arithmetic derivations can be removed from the model because they can be derived using mathematics.

11. Which of the following answers most accurately describes the business rule depicted in the following illustration?

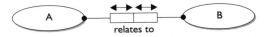

relates to

   A. An object of type A relates to zero or one objects of type B. An object of type B relates to zero or one objects of type A.

   B. An object of type A must relate to one object of type B. An object of type B must relate to one object of type A.

   C. An object of type A relates to zero or more objects of type B. An object of type B relates to zero or more objects of type A.

   D. An object of type A must relate to one object of type B. An object of type B cannot relate to any objects of type A.

12. Which of the following diagrams best depicts the statement, "An employee can have one or more offices but cannot have two offices in the same building."?

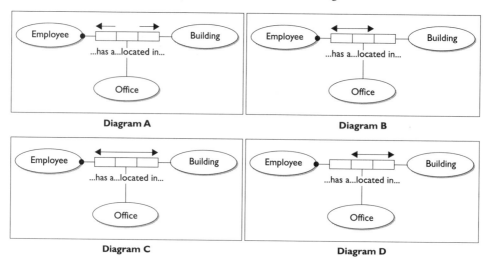

A. Diagram A

B. Diagram B

C. Diagram C

D. Diagram D

13. Which of the following diagrams best depicts the statement, "A candidate must have either a phone number or an e-mail address."?

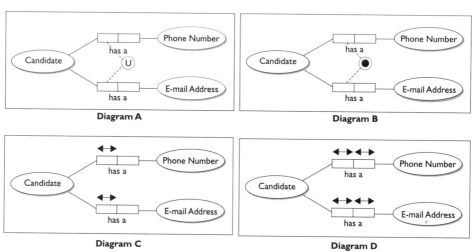

A. Diagram A

B. Diagram B

C. Diagram C

D. Diagram D

14. What is a set comparison constraint?

A. A constraint that restricts the value of a field to be less than or equal to the value of another field

B. A constraint that restricts objects from filling certain roles unless other roles are also filled

C. A constraint that restricts the value of a field to specified values

D. A constraint that restricts certain fields to be read-only

LAB QUESTION

Match the ORM artifact in the left column with its graphical symbol in the right column.

A. Entity	1. A letter *U* inside a circle
B. Value	2. A solid oval
C. External uniqueness constraint	3. A line above one or more roles
D. Internal uniqueness constraint	4. A solid dot
E. Mandatory constraint	5. A dotted oval

SELF TEST ANSWERS

What Is Object Role Modeling?

1. ☑ **B and C.** ORM is made up of two components: a language called FORML and a process called CSDP.

   ☒ **A** is incorrect because ER is a completely different notation for conceptual modeling. **D** is incorrect because, although ORM is based partly on NIAM, NIAM is not part of ORM.

2. ☑ **C.** The goal of ORM is to define an accurate conceptual database model.

   ☒ **A** is incorrect because, although bug-free application design is a benefit of proper database modeling, it is not the primary goal of ORM. **B** is incorrect because ORM deals on a conceptual level and not a physical one—the database type does not enter into consideration at this point. **D** is incorrect because, although it is a step in the ORM process, identifying fact types is not the goal of the ORM process.

3. ☑ **D.** The first step of defining an ORM model is identifying the system objects using a fact-based approach.

   ☒ **A** is incorrect because the DBMS used does not matter until the logical and physical phases of database design. **B** is incorrect because the database type does not even matter until the logical phase. **C** is incorrect because actual table and field names are not identified until the logical phase.

4. ☑ **B.** The main goal of the logical design phase is to convert the conceptual model into a proper schema.

   ☒ **A** is incorrect because the conceptual phase deals only with objects and their roles. **C** is incorrect because the physical phase manages the implementation of the schema defined in the logical phase. **D** is incorrect because there is no metaphysical design phase—at least none that we can prove exists.

5. ☑ **A, B, and C.** ORM models are written using a natural language, which makes them easier to read and understand and reduces errors. ORM models use actual data as a validation technique, which also reduces errors. In addition, there are some complex business rules that can be incorporated into an ORM diagram that ER cannot accommodate.

   ☒ **D** is incorrect because ORM models can easily be converted into a schema but not into SQL statements.

Create a Conceptual Model of Data Requirements

6. ☑ **B.** At the end of the CSDP, the resulting conceptual diagram can easily be mapped to a logical design schema, which is the next step in the database design process.

   ☒ **A** is incorrect because completed ORM diagrams are normalized—all redundancies and inaccuracies have been removed through the rigorous validation process of the CSDP. **C** is incorrect because there are no SQL statements at the end of the CSDP process. **D** is incorrect because once the process is complete, it's finished—it is not iterative.

7. ☑ **A, D, and E.** The entities of the model are Item, Vendor, and Inventory. Entities have properties of their own, while values are properties for other entities.

   ☒ **B** is incorrect because ItemName is a property of an Item and does not have properties of its own. **C** is incorrect because Price is the property of an Item and also does not have its own properties.

8. ☑ **B.** A unary fact is a property of a single object. This is generally a two-state property— "Student is enrolled." The student either *is* or *is not* enrolled.

   ☒ **A** is incorrect because only one object is involved in a unary fact. **C** is incorrect because a value is not specified. **D** is incorrect because a unary fact does not set uniqueness constraints.

9. ☑ **A and C.** Binary facts define the relationship between an object and either another object or a value.

   ☒ **B** is incorrect because binary facts do not include more than two objects. **D** is incorrect because binary facts do not set uniqueness constraints.

10. ☑ **D.** Checking for arithmetic derivations helps trim the data model of unnecessary facts. A data model that is smaller results in a smaller and more efficient database.

    ☒ **A** is incorrect because facts that can be trimmed due to arithmetic deviation should be removed from the model. **B** is incorrect because logical derivations, not arithmetic derivations, deal with trimming because of business rules. **C** is incorrect because arithmetic derivations can in fact be derived in another way—using mathematics.

11. ☑ **B.** The presence of a solid dot on both objects indicates that they are both mandatory, whereas the presence of uniqueness constraints on both roles indicates that each object can occur only once. Therefore, the relationship between A and B is a one-to-one relationship.

    ☒ **A** is incorrect because the solid dot on both objects indicates that they are both mandatory. **C** is incorrect because the presence of the lines above the roles indicates that the relationship is unique and therefore must occur at most once. **D** is incorrect because if object A relates to object B, then logically object B also has a relationship to object A.

12. ☑ **A.** Diagram A establishes that an employee and a building are unique to each other.
    ☒ **B** is incorrect because an employee is not unique to an office; that is, he can have more than one. **C** is incorrect because this diagram supports an employee having more than one office in the same building, which he is not allowed to have. **D** is incorrect because this diagram indicates that there must be only one employee to an office, which we cannot assume.

13. ☑ **B.** The external mandatory constraint is represented by a dot inside a circle and indicates that either the phone number or the e-mail address, or both, must contain a value.
    ☒ **A** is incorrect because the *U* inside a circle represents a uniqueness constraint and not a mandatory constraint. **C** is incorrect because it does not establish a mandatory relationship between a phone number and an e-mail address. **D** is incorrect because it also fails to establish a mandatory relationship between a phone number and an e-mail address.

14. ☑ **B.** A set comparison constraint restricts an object from fulfilling a role unless another role is also being filled. For instance, in ORM we can restrict Student objects from filling the "has graduated" role until the "paid tuition" role has been filled.
    ☒ **A** is incorrect because a set constraint cannot handle complex operators such as *less than or equal to.* **C** is incorrect because this is the job of value constraints. **D** is incorrect because there are no read-only constraints in ORM.

LAB ANSWER

A matches to **2.** An entity is represented by a solid oval.
B matches to **5.** A value is represented by a dotted oval.
C matches to **1.** An external uniqueness constraint is represented by a letter *U* inside a circle.
D matches to **3.** An internal uniqueness constraint is represented by a line above one or more roles.
E matches to **4.** A mandatory constraint is represented by a solid dot.

6

Conceptual
Design

I n the rush to design and develop software, conceptual design is usually one of the easiest steps to overlook. Everyone understands the importance of analyzing business and user requirements before embarking on software coding, and few people will question the wisdom of following proper database design models due to the difficulty in implementing changes later on in the process. On the contrary, convincing developers to follow a proper conceptual-logical-physical design model for software seems to be an uphill battle, but it's a battle that needs to be fought nonetheless.

The newest models in software development, such as Extreme Programming (XP) and the Rational Unified Process (RUP), have strong conceptual design elements. For instance, RUP relies on use cases and analysis models to create a conceptual design model. The conceptual model created during that process then gets transformed into a formal model for implementation.

author's note *A use case is a Unified Modeling Language (UML) document or diagram that describes all of the potential ways a user will need to interact with the system. These use cases are sometimes referred to as user stories.*

The temptation exists for many developers to jump right into coding once the business requirements are finalized. Of course, this is understandable because many developers perceive coding as the "fun" part of the software development process. This bad behavior is reinforced by some managers who place unrealistically short deadlines on projects and by the tendency for experimental prototypes to become real products without a thought given to proper design.

In Chapter 5, we saw how Object Role Modeling (ORM) could be used to create the conceptual design for databases using the Conceptual Schema Design Procedure (CSDP). In this chapter, we will move beyond the conceptual schema to create an overall conceptual design for our application. We will take into account the business, user, and operational requirements identified earlier in the design phase to create the ideal overall solution.

CERTIFICATION OBJECTIVE 6.01

Creating a Conceptual Model of Business Requirements

The goal of the conceptual design phase is to analyze the business and user requirements defined in previous design steps and to design a system that can meet all the identified needs of the user. This process of conceptual application design follows a path very similar to the path to the ORM conceptual design process that we examined in the last chapter. There are three major tasks to complete when creating the conceptual system model:

- Identify the system entities
- Establish the relationships among those system entities
- Document system flows

The conceptual schema developed during the ORM database design stage will likely contain many of the entities we will use in the conceptual application design. In addition, the conceptual schema conveniently incorporates many of the business rules governing the relationships between those entities. But when it comes to system design, in many cases the entities identified during that phase will not fully address the needs of the system. Often, there are many parts of the application that are not heavily integrated into the database model.

The first step of conceptual design is to identify the entities that comprise a system. *Identifying system entities* is a process by which the conceptual components of the system are derived from the business rules. Although these entities are usually similar to those defined during conceptual database design, often times there will be entities that are not represented in the database, such as printers, e-mail accounts, application web sites, Interactive Voice Response (IVR) telephone systems, and so on.

The second step of conceptual design is to *establish the relationships among entities* identified during the first step. This process helps us understand the system pathways over which information will flow. For instance, both the web site and the IVR system might need to connect to the database to retrieve information, but it is unlikely they would need to connect to each other. It is important to diagram both the internal and external system relationships in this step.

The third and final step of conceptual application design is to *document how information travels* through the system. This involves converting the predefined business rules into flowcharts and data flow diagrams. These diagrams each serve their own useful purposes. After all, as the old saying goes, a picture is worth a thousand words. It is a fact that humans process information visually better than in any other way, so it is well worth the effort to create these conceptual design diagrams to help us when we have to turn our system design into a logical design.

exam
ⓌatcH

It is important to understand the difference between conceptual and logical design before taking the MCSD 70-300 exam. Conceptual design *aims to document system processes as a series of steps and identify the packets of data that flow among these processes, based on the business requirements defined in an earlier design phase.* Logical design *incorporates technical considerations into the design, such as security and error handling, and builds classes and objects based on the entities defined during the conceptual phase.*

Procedure Diagrams

One of the first conceptual design diagrams that should be constructed is the procedure diagram. The *procedure diagram* serves to document a process or procedure as a series of steps. To indicate when decisions need to be made during the process, the diagram can be split into two or more paths. This type of diagram is sometimes called a *flowchart* or *workflow diagram.*

Figure 6-1 is an example of a typical procedure diagram. This example shows the procedure of a customer purchasing a book from a bookstore, from the time the customer presents the book to the cashier until the time the sale is complete.

Obviously, all of the procedures of a complex system cannot possibly be summarized in a single procedure diagram. For this reason, procedure diagrams should be clearly named according to the process they are trying to document in order to avoid confusion among multiple diagrams. It is also important to remember that many

A typical
procedure
diagram

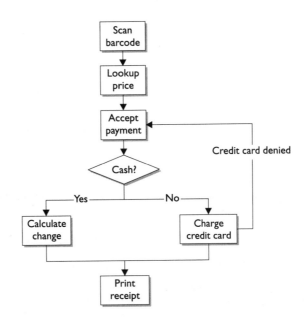

tasks integral to the success of a business are not considered system procedures. For instance, accepting a delivery of books by signing a purchase order presented by the delivery company does not belong in a procedure diagram because it is not a conceptual part of the system design. Adding those books to store inventory, however, would be included in the system conceptual design.

A Simple Procedure Modeling Methodology

As you'll recall from Chapter 3, the business requirements design and analysis part of the planning phase identified a number of core requirements the application has to fulfill in order to meet the needs of the client. These requirements are most likely stated something like this:

> "1.1 The application will allow bookstore employees to look up a book *By Title* or *By ISBN Number* to see how many copies of that book remain in inventory."

This business requirement implies a certain workflow and is very specific about the desired system functionality. Requirements will likely specify how users will employ a system and the way in which the application should respond. For instance, the preceding example business requirement can be broken down into a series of steps.

The steps involved in searching for books in inventory are as follows:

1. The system accepts some search terms from the bookstore employee.

2. If the employees are searching *By ISBN*, proceed to step 3; otherwise, proceed to step 5.

3. The system checks for any books in the book database corresponding to that ISBN.

4. Proceed to step 9.

5. If the employees are searching *By Title*, proceed to step 6; otherwise, proceed to step 8.

6. The system checks for any books in the database corresponding to that title.

7. Proceed to step 9.

8. Display invalid search message and stop.

9. If no books that match the search terms can be found, proceed to step 10; otherwise, proceed to step 11.

10. Display an out-of-stock message and stop.

11. Display the inventory count and stop.

These eleven steps can be depicted graphically using a procedure diagram. Each step in the preceding list will appear in our diagram. For instance, the first step is represented with the following symbol:

Enter search
terms

This step indicates a system or user action and is drawn graphically as a rectangle. The name of the action is written inside the rectangle so that it can be easily identified as the diagram gets more complex.

The second step in our 11-step process is not an action but a decision. Diamond shapes in the procedure diagram represent decisions that must be made by the system. The following illustration shows steps one and two, linked together by an arrow representing process flow.

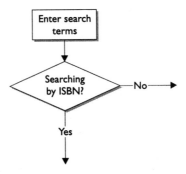

Decision diamonds usually have two or more arrows coming out of them to represent the choices the system or user has to make. For instance, our application has to distinguish between ISBN and title searches because the type of database query is different in each instance. The following illustration depicts the full procedure diagram for the task of using the application to search for a book.

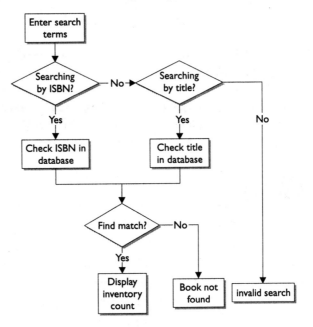

author's ⓘote *Procedure diagrams are usually drawn so that they can be read from either top to bottom or left to right. This makes them easier to read.*

Our process for the task "Search for a Book" begins with the first step, *Enter search terms.* We know this is the first step because there are no arrows leading into the action. Also, the fact that this step is at the top of the diagram is a good clue that we should start there. As we proceed through the workflow, we are presented with a number of choices, such as *Searching by ISBN?*. Our process will traverse only one of the decision arrows coming out of that diamond: either Yes or No. Eventually we make our way to the end of the process, such as the action *Display inventory count.* Once this task is complete, the process is over. We can tell that the process is over because there are no arrows leading away from this action.

We may want to number the steps in this process (as 1, 2, 3, and so on), although it sometimes makes things more confusing on a diagram such as this. One reason numbering the steps on the diagram may be confusing is that the steps are usually not executed in sequential order—some steps would be skipped depending on the decisions encountered. The most useful way to keep these diagrams effective is to keep them simple and easy to read. Don't try to put too many actions in one procedure diagram. Break up the diagram if possible.

on the
Job   *The activities contained within a procedure diagram are usually labeled on the actual diagram to make it easier for other documents to refer to them. For instance, tasks can be numbered in sequential order using point notation, such as 1.1.1, 1.1.2, 1.1.3, and so on, or sometimes the tasks are both numbered and lettered, such as A1, A2, A3, and so on. If you are going to do this, make sure the labels are unique across all procedure diagrams.*

EXERCISE 6-1

Using Visio for Enterprise Architects to Create Procedure Diagrams

Note that this exercise requires the Visio for Enterprise Architects software that comes bundled in Visual Studio .NET Enterprise Architect edition. It can be performed inside previous versions of Visio, but the steps are a bit different.

Microsoft Visio does not contain any special templates for creating procedure diagrams for conceptual design. It does, however, contain a flowchart template, which contains the appropriate symbols and connectors we need to create a procedure diagram. In this exercise, we will create a fairly simple procedure diagram using Visio.

1. Click Start | All Programs and choose Microsoft Visio to start the application.

2. Click File | New | Flowchart and select Basic Flowchart to create a blank flowchart.

3. Drag a Process rectangle from the template area on the left onto the blank page. Label the process **Create cheeseburger**.

4. Drag a Decision diamond onto the page to a spot one inch below the first Process rectangle. Label the diamond **French fries?**.

5. Drag a Dynamic Connector onto the page and connect the bottom of the Process rectangle with the top of the Decision diamond, making sure the arrow is leading away from the rectangle.

6. Drag a second Process rectangle onto the page to a spot one inch beneath the Decision diamond. Label the second process **Create French fries**.

7. Drag a Dynamic Connector onto the page and connect the bottom of the Decision diamond with the top of the second Process rectangle, making sure the arrow is leading away from the diamond. Label the arrow **Yes**.

8. Drag a third Process rectangle onto the page to a spot one inch to the right of the Decision diamond. Label the third process **Deliver meal**.

9. Drag a Dynamic Connector onto the page and connect the right side of the Decision diamond with the left side of the third Process rectangle, making sure the arrow is leading away from the diamond. Label the arrow **No**.

10. Drag a Dynamic Connector onto the page and connect the right side of the second Process rectangle ("Create French fries") with the left side of the third Process rectangle ("Deliver meal"), making sure the arrow is leading away from the second process.

11. Click File | Save As and assign your diagram a name. Click the Save button to save the diagram.

Data Flow Diagrams

Whereas a procedure diagram concentrates on the process flow of a system, a *data flow diagram (DFD)* documents the flow of data throughout that system. This type of diagram describes interactions between a system and its database so programmers can easily see what happens to data once it is read from a database and how data is collected before it gets written to a database.

Figure 6-2 shows a good example of a DFD. This diagram shows the flow of data in a simplified cash register application. We can see how data gets entered into the system using a scanner and a database of prices and how it is output from the system to a cash register display and a sales receipt, and saved to a transaction database.

In fact, a DFD really is a diagram that shows how data is processed by a system by defining the inputs and outputs. Inputs are typically entered into a keyboard, a database, an external data file, a web form, an Interactive Voice Response (IVR) telephone system, and other input devices. Output can be sent to a screen, a printer, a database, a web service, and other output devices. Data can travel through several processes on its path from input to output, or it can be used entirely in one process. For instance, a single process can read, modify and update a database without passing that data to any other process in the system.

Like procedure diagrams, DFDs can be drawn using several levels of granularity. A DFD can be fairly high level, looking at a complex system in a fairly abstract manner. For instance, a high-level DFD can display the data flow for a complex sales

FIGURE 6-2

A typical data flow diagram, which documents the data interactions of a system

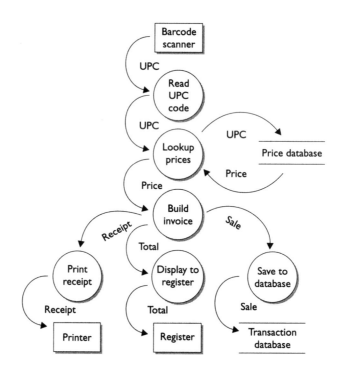

and inventory system. Within this high-level diagram, the retail sales process might be represented by a single entity. A lower-level DFD might focus on a specific process within a complex system. For instance, it is possible for a DFD to display data flow within the retail sales process only. This low-level diagram could contain a dozen or so entities, but is definitely more detailed than the high-level diagram.

Another similarity between procedure diagrams and DFDs is that it would be very difficult, and even impractical, to create a single diagram to define an entire system at a low level. It almost goes against the principals of object-oriented software design to even try. It is better to treat the system in a modularized manner, treating the retail sales process as a module unto itself. All you have to do is make sure this process can get the data it needs to succeed and that it provides other processes the data they need as well.

Two well-known notations exist for the drawing DFDs: Yourdon & Coad and Gane-Sarson. The Yourdon & Coad methodology influenced the design of UML, and Yourdon and Coad's books on software design methodologies—entitled *Object-Oriented Analysis* (Prentice Hall, 1990) and *Object-Oriented Design* (Pearson Education, 1991)—are considered key early texts on the subject. The Gane-Sarson methodology is fairly similar to Yourdon & Coad, although the symbols used are slightly different. Basically, when mapping data flows between processes in systems, you are not going to find a lot of difference between different methodologies.

Four items typically are depicted in any data flow diagram:

- Process
- Database or data store
- Data flow
- External entity

The first item represented in a DFD is a process. A *process* transforms data that flows into it (the *input*) into data that flows out of it (the *output*). In the Yourdon & Coad notation, a circle depicts a process, and the name or description of the process is placed inside the circle. Sometimes, a process is assigned a number to make it easier to refer to the process in specifications and other documentation. The following illustration gives two examples of a Yourdon & Coad process notation:

In Gane-Sarson notation, a process is depicted by a rectangle with rounded corners. The name or description of the process is placed inside the rectangle to identify the task the process performs. The following illustration gives an example of a Gane-Sarson process notation:

Process name

The second item represented in a DFD is a database, or data store. *Data stores* are repositories of data in the system. They are typically relational databases, flat files, or any other repository for storing data (other than computer memory, of course). In Yourdon & Coad notation, data stores are depicted by two parallel horizontal lines. The name or description of the data being stored is written between the lines, as follows:

Data store

In Gane-Sarson notation, a data store is depicted by an open-ended rectangle, as in this example:

Data store

The third important item in a DFD is the data flow. A *data flow* is a channel or pipeline through which packets of information flow. In both the Yourdon & Coad and Gane-Sarson notations, data flows are depicted by a line with an arrow at one end. These lines are usually labeled with a name or description of the data flow (a noun, such as Order or Invoice). The arrow points in the direction in which the data is flowing. Data flows connect processes, data stores, and external entities.

Data flow

The fourth important item in a DFD is an external entity. An *external entity* is an object, an application, or people outside this system with which the system communicates. For example, a sales cashier is an external entity. Any information that the sales cashier enters into the application is a data flow from an external entity to a process within the system. External entities are represented by rectangles, and as you'd expect, the name or description of the entity (a noun, such as Customer or Data Entry Clerk) is written inside this rectangle.

External entity

SCENARIO & SOLUTION

To add a process entity to a data flow diagram,...	Use a circle
To add a database or data store entity to a data flow diagram,...	Use a pair of parallel lines
To add data flow between two entities,...	Use an arrow
To add an external entity,...	Use a rectangle

There are a few basic rules for creating DFDs:

- Never connect two external entities to each other, because the DFD is concerned only with documenting the processes that affect the system.

- Never connect two data stores to each other, because by definition data stores have no business logic. (They only store data.)

- All processes must have at least one input and one output data flow, although some processes gather data from more than one source and provide data to more than one other entity.

If your application is fairly large and complex, there could be dozens of DFDs. Since DFDs document the flow of data through the system, every possible situation where data is read or modified must be covered.

 e x a m
ⓦa t c h

Although you will not have to draw conceptual diagrams for this exam, you may have to be able to read them.

EXERCISE 6-2

Creating Gane-Sarson Data Flow Diagrams in Visio

Note that this exercise requires the Visio for Enterprise Architects software that comes bundled in Visual Studio .NET Enterprise Architect edition.

Microsoft Visio for Enterprise Architects contains a template specifically for the Gane-Sarson DFD notation. It does not contain a template for the Yourdon & Coad notation. In this exercise, we will create a fairly simple DFD using Visio.

1. Click Start | All Programs and choose Microsoft Visio to start the application.

2. Click File | New | Software and select Data Flow Model Diagram to create a blank Gane-Sarson diagram.

3. Drag a Process from the template onto the blank page. Label the Process **Gather customer info.**

4. Drag a Data Store from the template onto the blank page. Label the data store **Customer.**

5. Drag a Data Flow Connector from the template onto the blank page, connecting the Process with the Data Store. Make sure the data flow is originating from the database and flowing into the Process, and label it **Customer Info.**

6. Click File | Save As and assign your diagram a name. Click the Save button to save the diagram.

Cross-Referencing Matrices

Once you have gone through the process of creating a conceptual data model (through ORM) and you have created high-level procedure diagrams and a hierarchy of DFDs, it is a good idea to summarize these documents in a cross-referencing matrix. A grid that has been properly cross-referenced, or even a series of grids for complex systems, will help organize all of these conceptual design artifacts into an index. These matrices serve as convenient places for looking up the conceptual design of the system.

Typically, this section of the conceptual system design document lists, in a table or matrix, all of the DFDs associated with each process, external entity, or data store. If the system you are designing has dozens of procedure and data flow diagrams, spending time creating a matrix that lists how these diagrams relate to one another is time well spent.

User Interface Conceptual Design

Many would believe that thinking about user interface design during the conceptual design stage might be a little premature; but when you think about it, user interface designers have everything they need at this stage to get started on a basic user interface design:

■ The users of the application have been defined during the user requirements stage.

- The required functionality of the application has been defined during the business requirements stage.

- An idea of the target platform and operating system (for example, if it will be a Windows application or a web application) has been defined during the solution concept stage.

Gathering User Profiles

Some applications are designed with just one group of users in mind. For instance, a data entry application may need to concern itself only with data entry clerks. If an application will have only one group of users, it makes things a bit easier when thinking about strategies for design.

exam
⍟atch

You will not be asked about conceptual user interface design on the MCSD 70-300 exam.

However, many applications have more than one category of user. A data entry application might very well need to support managers who can approve batches of records and run various reports. It may also need to support systems administrators who can create new users or archive records that are more than a few years old. Applications that need to support more than one category of user make things slightly more complex when designing a user interface to support them all.

In any event, whether you are designing an application that will be used by only one person, by one group within a company, or by every employee throughout the company, it is important to gain an understanding about the potential users, and this is done by creating user profiles.

A *user profile* is a description of the users that will be using the application and their specific characteristics. Before approaching actual graphical user interface design, it is important to understand user characteristics such as the following:

- Psychology-related characteristics (for instance, attitude and motivation)

- Experience-related characteristics (for instance, computer skills)

- Job-related characteristics (for instance, which areas of the application will likely be used the most)

- Other characteristics (for instance, fluency in English)

Having these insights into the nature of the users will help you make design decisions down the road. For example, if a good number of your potential users have never used a computer, it will have an effect on the user interface that is ultimately designed.

Building the Application Site Map

Creating a conceptual design for a user interface requires developers to think about the organization of the application from the user's perspective. The techniques for creating the conceptual model at this stage of design are remarkably similar to the techniques for other conceptual models we have created thus far. A conceptual user interface model resembles a hierarchical chart of screens, making it easy for a designer to envision how users proceed through their tasks when using the application. After all, an application is really just a tool—users will want to use that tool to perform some task reliably and without unnecessary complexity.

The conceptual user interface design typically is a diagram of boxes and arrows that connect the proposed screens of the application in order to show how the application's users will proceed through the application performing their daily tasks. Web site designers would call this a *site map,* and the metaphor can be extended to regular Windows application design. (.NET blurs the lines between web and Windows applications anyway because ASP.NET applications are constructed within the Visual Studio .NET environment alongside VB .NET and other graphical Windows applications.)

Conceptual user interface design starts by identifying the likely "top-level screens" of the application being designed. These screens become the functional categories of an application, and they can usually be derived from the business requirements documents. Following are some examples of top-level screens:

- Data entry screens
- Data review and approval screens
- Report-generation screens
- Administrator screens

This list is an example of the functional categories of a data entry application that I recently worked on. From these top-level screens, we can begin to get an

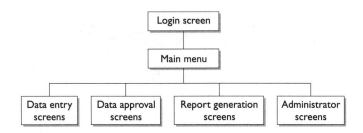

FIGURE 6-3

A hierarchical diagram of the top-level screens of a simple data entry application

idea about how the application's user interface should be organized. We can draw a simple diagram, the hierarchical chart shown in Figure 6-3, to show how users are likely to proceed through the application at this point.

Note that we haven't yet begun to think about colors, logos, navigation bars, and other graphical components of the application. These elements will certainly come into play when we begin designing and developing screens, but we are still at the boxes and arrows stage at this point.

on the Job

Programmers generally make bad user interface designers. There are many reasons why this is often true, but the one I like the most is that good user interface design requires so-called "soft skills" such as psychology, ergonomics, and the understanding of other human factors.

The user interface is one of the most subjective areas of application design. There are many ways to design an application correctly. Which design is the best can only be determined by the users themselves—after they have had a chance to see the efficiency and effectiveness of each user interface design in action.

SCENARIO & SOLUTION

To create the conceptual design of a database,…	Use Object Role Modeling (ORM)
To create a procedure diagram,…	Use flowcharts or UML activity diagrams
To create a data flow diagram,…	Use Yourdon & Coad or Gane-Sarson diagrams

CERTIFICATION OBJECTIVE 6.02

Defining the Technical Architecture of a Solution

Since we created the concept of our solution in Chapter 2, we already have a good idea of what the technical architecture of our solution will look like. For instance, we have probably already decided whether we will create a web-based solution, a wireless personal digital assistant (PDA) solution, or a regular Windows application. Technical architecture is the overall structure and technical design of an application. As many of you know, .NET applications can be designed for many target architectures, such as the following:

- Single-tier, or standalone
- Two-tier, or client/server
- Three-tier, or *n*-tier
- XML web services

author's note — *A tier is a distinct layer of an application installed on its own computer across a network. The key word is "distinct"—different computers that have identical components of a single application installed on them are considered part of the same tier.*

The best technical architecture to choose for a particular solution is usually based on many factors. In general, application designers should choose the architecture that contains the fewest number of "tiers" that will meet the clients business and technical requirements. That is, there is no point making a word processing application an *n*-tier application unless there are requirements that can only be fulfilled by introducing networks and servers into the equation. Likewise, you will probably want to investigate an *n*-tier solution for a high-performance, high-availability online transaction processing (OLTP) system because that architecture will help fulfill some of the business requirements that other architectures will have a hard time fulfilling.

exam Watch — *The MCSD 70-300 exam will test your ability to determine the best technical architecture for a particular solution.*

In this section, we will take a brief look at each of the architectures and look at the situations and scenarios where each would be used in a production environment.

SCENARIO & SOLUTION

To create an application that does not require access to a network or a server,...	Create a single-tier, or standalone, application
To create an application that requires access to a database or an application server somewhere on the network,...	Create a two-tier, or client/server, application
To create an application that distributes work between a client machine and more than one server,...	Create an *n*-tier, or distributed, application

Single-Tier Solutions

A *single-tier architecture* is the simplest form of application architecture. Single-tier applications, sometime called *standalone applications,* have everything they need to run installed locally on the client computer (also called a *client workstation*). Typically, these applications consist of a single binary executable (EXE) file, although you will find some applications that ship with their own binary libraries (DLLs), local data stores, or both. There are many examples of single-tier applications, such as word processors, spreadsheets, accounting programs, and video games.

Other than the typical productivity applications, custom-developed single-tier applications are a bit unusual in the corporate world because applications typically have to share data with other applications or a central data server. That is the nature of large corporations and governments—data is only useful if it is available in a central location. However, there are plenty of reasons you might want to develop a single-tier application:

- The application is just a tool (such as a calculator) or a game and is not required to save any information permanently.

- The application produces paper printouts, data files, or e-mail that can be sent on to other applications for processing.

- The application does save information permanently, but no other computers or people need access to that information.

- The application is easier to develop than two-tier and *n*-tier applications.

- The application is less complex than two-tier and *n*-tier applications.

There are also several reasons why you would not want to choose a single-tier application for a particular solution:

- There may be scalability concerns as the application grows in size and scope.

- It is often more difficult to back up files on a user's individual desktop than on a server.

- There may be performance issues because one computer does all the processing work in a single-tier application.

Application developers will need to analyze the business needs of their individual situation carefully in order to determine if a single-tier architecture is the proper solution.

Two-Tier Solutions

A *two-tier architecture* is only moderately more complicated than a single-tier one. Typically, a two-tier application involves an application that runs on one computer (called the *client*) connecting to a database running on another computer (called the *server*). This setup is called a *client/server architecture*.

In addition to a client/server setup, there are other ways to split the processing between the two machines in a two-tier arrangement. An application can run on a server that sits in between the client and the database to handle certain types of business processing. Because the server application and the database reside on the same computer in this case, many developers still regard this as a two-tier architecture.

Some web-based applications can be described as having a two-tier architecture. (Web applications are sometimes described as *n-tier* as well, as you'll read in the next section.) Web applications typically force the web server to do most of the processing work and require only that a web browser be installed on the client machine. That is why they are sometimes called "thin clients."

There are many good reasons why a developer may choose to split an application into two tiers:

- The server provides a way to share information between multiple clients.

- Intensive processing can be handed off to the server to perform.

- Server applications are sometimes easier to update than client applications.

- Two-tier applications can be fairly easy to develop.

- There are many ways to distribute the workload across client and server machines.

There are also a few reasons why you would not want to create a two-tier application for a particular solution:

- Two-tier applications are more complex and require more maintenance compared to single-tier solutions.

- Performance issues may arise if the client computers are relying on the server to do too much work.

- A faulty or slow network could cause application problems.

- Availability issues may arise if the server needs to be rebooted for routine tasks such as installation of operating system service packs.

Despite these considerations, the two-tier application is one of the most popular types of applications in the corporate environment. It is extremely flexible in the ways in which it can be configured, and all of the Visual Studio .NET languages (such as VB .NET and C#) easily support interacting with a database server using the ADO .NET classes.

Three-Tier and *n*-Tier Solutions

Three-tier and *n*-tier architectures are the most complex types of applications to develop. Creating systems that distribute the workload over several servers can be a complex task because it usually involves creating Component Object Model (COM) components that can run in a Microsoft Transaction Server (MTS, for Windows NT) or Component Services (for Windows 2000) transaction server environment.

The simplest type of architecture that fits this description would be an ASP.NET web application that has a database residing on another server. This three-tier architecture provides a clear distinction between the three application layers—the presentation layer, the business layer, and the data layer. The most complex application architecture would be an *n*-tier application that is divided into dozens of individual COM components installed across a dozen or more servers. These components would need to be running inside a COM+ or Distributed COM (DCOM) environment in order for all the pieces of the application to communicate with each other effectively.

In some respects, the *n*-tier architecture is the least efficient form of application configuration. Just think about the amount of effort it takes by several machines just to pass messages around in order to get something done. In fact, if you were to place a simple client/server application in a head-to-head race against a complex *n*-tier setup to process a single database transaction, the client/server application would probably win.

But the real strength of the *n*-tier setup is its scalability. If you placed the client/server and *n*-tier applications in a head-to-head race to process 10,000,000 records, the *n*-tier application would probably win. This is because in the *n*-tier configuration you have the power of several servers to process the transactions, as opposed to just one measly server in the two-tier configuration. Our *n*-tier application can even have several database servers at its disposal if the database becomes the bottleneck because there are established methods for splitting a database over many machines.

As you'd expect, there are several reasons why you would want to develop a three-tier or *n*-tier application for a particular solution:

- It is extremely scalable, which allows more transactions to be processed per hour.

- It is highly available in that servers can usually be rebooted without bringing the application down (because multiple servers perform the same task).

There are also several reasons why you would not want to choose this application type:

- It is difficult and more expensive to develop.

- It is difficult and more expensive to maintain.

- Its complex architecture means the sources of problems are not easily found.

- The costs for hardware and software licensing costs are higher than for other application types.

The *n*-tier architecture is popular for enterprise-level systems, which are designed to serve thousands of users simultaneously. This could be an e-mail system, an e-commerce web site, or some other mission-critical application that the company cannot afford to have go down for maintenance. It could also be an application that must have servers distributed geographically (around the country or around the world) to provide decent performance and reduce network risk but still needs a centralized server to consolidate the regional data. The one thing to realize about these types of systems is that they are expensive to develop and maintain.

Using Microsoft Transaction Server or Component Services

Many of the advantages of developing three-tier and *n*-tier applications are only realized when the COM objects are managed inside a transaction server environment.

In Windows NT, this environment is called Microsoft Transaction Server (MTS), and in Windows 2000 it is called Component Services or COM+.

Transaction servers provide the following benefits:

- **Object brokering** Helps applications use components, making code reuse easier

- **Transaction monitoring** Manages transactions across multiple components

- **Object caching and pooling** Allows an application client to use preloaded copies of a component for improved application performance

- **State maintenance** Allows applications to treat a component as if it had exclusive access to it, even though it doesn't

- **Data sharing between components** Uses the Shared Property Manager to allow related components to share data with one another

- **Process isolation** Protects the server from misbehaving components, so they cannot crash the server

- **Security** Manages the security settings for components

- **In-memory databases** Allows you to store frequently accessed databases in memory for performance purposes

- **Application packages** Makes it easier to place components of an application across multiple servers, called *distributed processing*

Developers who plan to use COM components in their web applications should investigate the use of MTS. You might think that this would be overkill for small applications, but MTS can have benefits even for small sites.

XML Web Services

Microsoft is positioning XML web services as one of the building blocks for applications that are distributed over the Internet. What makes a web service different from one-, two-, and three-tier applications is its interface with the outside world. Specifically, web services are accessed using XML-formatted messages instead of graphical buttons and text boxes.

The users of web services (or consumers, as they are called) are other applications, not humans. You and I are not going to sit down and format an XML message just to purchase an airline ticket over the Web—another application is needed in order to help us do that. There are two main advantages of creating web service applications:

- They work using standard protocols over the Internet.
- If the application developer allows it, anyone can write an application to interface with that service.

One analogy I use to describe why web services are important is that, in the future, you will be able to tell your mobile phone that you need to book a trip to Chicago. Your mobile phone will be smart enough to contact the airline to purchase your tickets according to your preferences, contact your favorite hotel to book a room, and contact the car rental agency to reserve an automobile. It will be able to do this by interfacing with the web services provided by these companies. It will even remind you on the morning of your trip to pack an umbrella, since the forecast is calling for rain in Chicago.

When designing a web service application, there are a few issues that will need special consideration during the physical design step of the design process. Even though this application uses standard Internet protocols such as HTTP to communicate, this does not necessarily mean it is exposed to the public at large over the Internet. For example, a company can deploy an internal document repository as a web service and ensure that the application is available only to certain employees.

Choosing a Data Storage Architecture

Another issue that must be addressed when designing applications is the data storage architecture. Almost since companies have relied on computers (since the big room-sized mainframe days of the 1960s), companies have relied on the data that computers have produced. In the old days, mainframes used to store their data to tape—big reels of magnetic tape that were stored in canisters and manually filed away for later retrieval. These days, servers are connected to massive arrays of hard drives, often arranged in striped sets such as in a Redundant Array of Independent Disks (RAID) configuration.

on the job

I'm sure there are people who still rely on tapes, because mainframes really haven't gone away, but it's been at least ten years since I have seen one.

The most common type of data storage architecture is the relational database. A few well-established and reliable relational database management systems (RDBMS) exist, such as SQL Server 2000 and Oracle 9i. These are scalable and robust applications that can support applications requiring several terabytes of data storage. These servers can typically be clustered—allowing multiple database servers to serve a single application for the most robust and reliable solution.

There is an emerging type of database called an object-oriented database management system (OODBMS). An OODBMS includes support for the modeling and creating of database objects, including complex object-oriented concepts such as classes, inheritance, and methods. Object-oriented databases are still relatively rare, and few standards exist for developers to rely on.

Another emerging type of database is the native Extensible Markup Language (XML) database. XML is a hot Internet standard for formatting data for storage and transmission. XML is a text-based format that is self-describing—elements and attributes demark the columns of data and also provide a basic definition for what each field contains. For those of you unfamiliar with XML format, the following code listing is an example of an XML document.

```
<?xml version="1.0"?>
<employees>
    <employee id="9091773">
        <name>Bob Jones</name>
        <number>123456789</number>
        <dob>07/01/1940</dob>
        <doh>01/01/2000</doh>
        <salary>52000</salary>
        <img src="BobJones.gif" />
    </employee>
</employees>
```

As you can see from the preceding code, XML can be read easily by both humans and machines. For instance, it is easy to infer that the XML element <name> gives the full name of the employee with the ID 9091773. Many of you may think that XML looks surprisingly similar to Hypertext Markup Language (HTML). That is because HTML and XML have an ancestral language in common—Standard Generalized Markup Language (SGML).

exam
⚠️atch *For the MCSD 70-300 exam, you should understand what XML is, and you should know some of the benefits of using it as a data storage format.*

There are some significant differences between HTML and XML, however, so the similarities are only superficial. XML has rules that make its format a lot stricter (and thus less flexible) than HTML. There is an XML-compatible version of HTML available called XHTML.

When a computer reads an XML document, it is said to *parse* it. One of the limitations of XML as a data storage format is that, because it is text based, XML data takes up more disk space and memory than its binary data counterparts. XML is also more difficult to sort and search on because the columns are embedded inside the XML document, and that means that all of the XML code has to be parsed in order to extract a single column of data.

author's
ⓝote
For more information on XML, HTML, or XHTML, check out the World Wide Web Consortium's web site at http://www.w3.org/.

This does not necessarily mean XML is a bad choice as a data storage format. One of XML's greatest strengths is that, as a text-based format, it can be easily shared between any set of hardware and operating system platforms in the world. An Apple Mac can easily read XML files generated by an IBM mainframe, and a PC can easily read files generated by a Palm Pilot personal digital assistant (PDA). As long as they can talk, they can share XML.

CERTIFICATION OBJECTIVE 6.03

Validating Conceptual Design

The final stage of the conceptual design process is validation. Comparing the DFDs with the conceptual database design validates conceptual application design. We must make sure all of the tables relied upon in the DFDs are represented in our database and that we have DFD diagrams for every table in the conceptual database design.

Likewise, conceptual application design diagrams have to be compared with business and user requirement specifications developed earlier on in the design process. We must ensure that every business requirement has at least one procedure diagram associated with it.

Finally, conceptual user interface design is validated with the user through a process called usability testing. In the conceptual design phase, we gathered and

FROM THE CLASSROOM

The Importance of Usability Testing

Usability is the science of designing user interfaces for effectiveness and efficiency from the user's point of view. Usability testing is a process that tests the effectiveness of a user interface using specific methodologies and metrics.

Performing usability testing is important for many applications because it focuses on how the users use the application. There are four main categories of usability issues:

- Navigation
- Screen design and layout
- Terminology
- Consistency with the user's goals

Usability experts analyze these elements of applications in order to identify those that can be improved. Improving these elements will often lead to improved user experience, which is an important goal in application user interface design.

—*Scott Duffy, MCSD, MCP+SB, SCJP, IBMCD-XML*

analyzed the user profiles and then developed an application "site map" laying out the screens of our application and the order in which users will encounter them. In order to validate this design, we need to go over it with representatives from our user community to ensure nothing was overlooked.

The process of user interface validation usually involves taking a couple of screens and developing two or three sample layouts. This is not a process of getting colors or graphics approved so much as ensuring that navigational elements and site layout are as efficient as possible. How will users know where they are within the application? How will they get from one section of the application to another? These are all important questions that need to be answered, and the answers should be discussed with the users to ensure that their concerns are addressed early on in the design process.

As you can see, conceptual design is really a process of identifying the components of a system and establishing their relationship to each other. We also must establish program flow (in terms of the user interface) and data flow (in terms of the inputs and outputs of the program).

In the next chapter, we will learn about the steps to creating logical application design. We will cover many topics, from some of the technical considerations that need to be addressed to fully designing the user interface. We will also convert the conceptual data model into a proper logical schema. The entire logical model will then need to be validated as well. Finally, we will see how a proof-of-concept can be used to further validate some of the ideas of our overall application design.

CERTIFICATION SUMMARY

The models created during conceptual application design are similar to models created during conceptual database design. Conceptual application design turns requirements identified during the business requirements phase into abstract processes and data flows. The processes of a conceptual design can be drawn using a procedure diagram. The procedure diagram is similar to a workflow diagram or a flowchart in that it attempts to capture the steps of a particular system task. You will often need many procedure diagrams in order to document all of the tasks in a business requirements document.

Data flow diagrams (DFDs) document the information or data that passes from process to process. It also captures the interaction of the system with external entities (like humans or other computer systems) and data stores. A DFD concentrates on understanding the inputs and outputs of a system—how procedures are able to get the information they need to perform their tasks and where that information flows from there.

There are several possible architectures for which an application can be designed. A single-tier (standalone) application is designed to run on its own and does not have any related outside components. A two-tier application does have one external component, although that is usually just a database running on a server. Sometimes two-tier applications have server components that are designed to handle some of the processing from the client. An *n*-tier application is designed to run across several servers in a distributed manner. Because *n*-tier applications require special server software such as Microsoft Transaction Server (MTS, for Windows NT) or Component Services (for Windows 2000) in order to communicate with one another effectively, they are the most complex to develop.

✓ TWO-MINUTE DRILL

Creating a Conceptual Model of Business Requirements

❑ Conceptual design is the process of identifying the components of the system and establishing their relationships with each other.

❑ Procedure diagrams are used to document the tasks of a system as a series of steps.

❑ Data flow diagrams (DFDs) document the flow of data through the system.

❑ Two popular DFD notations are Yourdon & Coad and Gane-Sarson.

Defining the Technical Architecture of a Solution

❑ Technical architecture is the overall structure of an application.

❑ Single-tier architecture is for applications designed to run on a single computer without connectivity to other systems or applications.

❑ Two-tier architecture, traditionally called client/server architecture, is for applications that have both client and server components.

❑ Three-tier and *n*-tier architectures distribute a single application over three or more computers.

Validating Conceptual Design

❑ Conceptual design is validated by mapping all the procedure and data flow design diagrams to the identified business requirements.

❑ Each business requirement must have one or more procedure diagrams, ensuring that each business requirement is covered in the design.

❑ The only business requirements that do not need procedure diagrams are nonfunctional requirements.

SELF TEST

The following questions will help you measure your understanding of the material presented in this chapter. Read all the choices carefully because there might be more than one correct answer. Choose all correct answers for each question.

Creating a Conceptual Model of Business Requirements

1. Which diagram notation is used to break a process down into a series of steps?

    A. Data flow diagrams (DFDs)

    B. Procedure diagrams

    C. Yourdon & Coad notation

    D. Process step notation

2. Which diagram notation is used to display how packets of information are passed between processes and other system entities? (Choose all that apply.)

    A. Data flow diagrams (DFDs)

    B. Procedure diagrams

    C. Yourdon & Coad or Gane-Sarson

    D. User interface site map

3. What is the aim of the conceptual application design phase? (Choose all that apply.)

    A. To translate business requirements into application design

    B. To design a system that meets the basic needs of the user

    C. To develop a conceptual database design

    D. To provide input to the logical design phase

4. What does a circle represent in a Yourdon & Coad data flow diagram?

    A. Data store

    B. External entity

    C. Process

    D. Data flow between processes

5. What is the purpose of conceptual user interface design? (Choose all that apply.)

    A. To develop draft versions of every screen in the application

    B. To plan and design the application based on the user requirements

    C. To document how packets of information flow through the application

    D. To construct profiles of the potential users and understand their general characteristics

6. What types of characteristics about the target users of an application are documented inside a user profile as it relates to conceptual application design? (Choose all that apply.)

    A. User names, passwords, and job titles

    B. Level of computer skills

    C. Most frequently used areas of the application

    D. Geographical location

Defining the Technical Architecture of a Solution

7. Which application architecture would most likely be used for a productivity tool, such as a simple calculator?

    A. Single-tier

    B. Two-tier

    C. Three-tier or *n*-tier

    D. XML web service

8. XYZ Corporation has a custom-designed VB .NET application that involves 11 different computers in its small corporate office. Ten of those computers are client workstations, as each employee has his or her own copy of the application. The application also requires a database server for data storage, although the application itself is not installed on that machine. What type of architecture is this application an excellent example of?

    A. Single-tier

    B. Two-tier

    C. Three-tier or *n*-tier

    D. Eleven-tier

9. XYZ Corporation is developing a complex, online ordering system for its global web site. The application must be available 24 hours per day, 7 days per week. The application designer has decided to create a distributed VB .NET application, converting .NET assemblies into COM components. These components will be running on a small cluster of Windows 2000 machines. Which Microsoft technology will enable these components to participate in transactions and object pooling?

    A. Microsoft Transaction Server (MTS)

    B. Microsoft .NET Framework and Common Language Runtime (CLR)

C. Microsoft Solutions Framework (MSF)

D. Component Services

10. Which of the following are advantages of using an *n*-tier architecture when compared with one- and two-tier architectures? (Choose all that apply.)

A. Performance is better for applications with hundreds of thousands of transactions per day.

B. Performance is better for applications with a few dozen transactions per day.

C. The application can be scaled more easily as transaction growth requires.

D. The application is cheaper to set up and maintain in the long run.

11. Which of the following are typically features of a web service application? (Choose all that apply.)

A. It cannot be used directly by users.

B. Its programming language and operating system can be different from the applications that use it.

C. A web browser is required to use it.

D. It has to be exposed to the Internet.

12. Which of the following are disadvantages of using an XML data storage solution? (Choose all that apply.)

A. Data is more difficult to search and sort.

B. All of the XML code has to be parsed in order to read one column of data.

C. XML code can be read equally well across many operating systems and platforms.

D. XML is self-describing.

Validating Conceptual Design

13. What is the best technique for validating conceptual user interface design?

A. Comparing the ORM model with business and user requirements

B. Usability testing

C. Comparing procedure and data flow diagrams with business requirements

D. Generating draft logical design documents

14. What is the best technique for validating conceptual application design?

    A. Comparing conceptual design diagrams with business and user requirements to ensure that everything is covered

    B. Creating cross-reference matrices

    C. Usability testing

    D. Comparing conceptual design diagrams with logical design diagrams to ensure that everything is covered

15. What is the most likely consequence of not validating the conceptual user interface design?

    A. The application performance is slow or degraded.

    B. Users have a difficult time accessing the features and functions they use most often.

    C. There will be a significant difference between the conceptual database design and the conceptual application design.

    D. An application that deserves to be spread over three tiers might mistakenly be developed as a two-tier application.

LAB QUESTION

Arrange the following software design tasks in proper chronological order from earliest to latest.

    A. Transforming data and business requirements into a conceptual design

    B. Developing business requirements

    C. Visualizing the design

    D. Developing an application prototype

    E. Developing functional specifications

    F. Developing a database schema

SELF TEST ANSWERS

Creating a Conceptual Model of Business Requirements

1. ☑ **B.** A procedure diagram breaks a complex system process down into a series of smaller steps. Procedure diagrams can contain a high or low level of detail.
   ☒ **A** is incorrect because DFDs display how packets of information are passed between system entities. **C** is incorrect because Yourdon & Coad is a notation for DFDs. **D** is incorrect because there is no such thing as process step notation.

2. ☑ **A and C.** A DFD is used to display how packets of information are passed between processes and other system entities. Yourdon & Coad and Gane-Sarson are two of the most popular DFD notations.
   ☒ **B** is incorrect because procedure diagrams deal only with processes and not the information passed between them. **D** is incorrect because a site map defines process flow between screens.

3. ☑ **A, B, C, and D.** All answers are correct. A conceptual design translates the business requirements identified earlier in the design phase into an application design. This design focuses on the needs of the user and does not take many system or nonuser needs into consideration. Conceptual database design is part of overall conceptual design, and the results of conceptual design are fed into the phase that follows—logical design.
   ☒ There are no incorrect answers.

4. ☑ **C.** A circle represents a process in the Yourdon & Coad DFD notation.
   ☒ **A** is incorrect because a data store is represented by two parallel lines. **B** is incorrect because an external entity is a rectangle. **D** is incorrect because data flow is drawn using a line with an arrow.

5. ☑ **B and D.** Conceptual user interface design is the process of understanding who the users are (by constructing user profiles) and conceptualizing the application from their point of view.
   ☒ **A** is incorrect because only a couple of screens are mocked up during this stage. **C** is incorrect because data flow diagrams are responsible for documenting the flow of packets of information.

6. ☑ **B, C, and D.** The user profile is used to come up with a general understanding of your users' special characteristics so that the application can be tailored to their needs. Understanding their level of computer skills is important to designing a user-friendly yet efficient application. Understanding the areas of the system they will use most frequently is important so that those areas can be streamlined. Finally, understanding general geographical locations will help determine what network, server, and other technical resources will be required.
   ☒ **A** is incorrect because user names and passwords are not important to understanding the characteristics of your users.

Defining the Technical Architecture of a Solution

7. ☑ **A.** A simple calculator most likely would be developed as a standalone, single-tier application. This is because a calculator probably would not need access to network resources such as databases and application components deployed across multiple servers.

☒ **B** and **C** are incorrect because a calculator does not need a server component. **D** is incorrect because a desktop calculator probably would not be deployed as a web service.

8. ☑ **B.** No matter how many independent client workstations are involved, the labeling of tiers usually involves counting one client plus the number of server computers that client relies on (including server computers relied on by other servers). In this case, because there is one client and one database server, this is a two-tier application.

☒ **A** is incorrect because a single-tier application does not rely on a network or on access to database servers. **C** is incorrect because this application does not have server-side components installed on multiple servers. **D** is incorrect because the number of client workstations does not affect the number of tiers.

9. ☑ **D.** Component Services is the name of the Microsoft server software that provides transaction and object pooling services in a Windows 2000 environment.

☒ **A** is incorrect because MTS only runs in a Windows NT environment. **B** is incorrect because .NET does not have native transaction services and relies on COM+. **C** is incorrect because MSF is an application design methodology and not a piece of server software.

10. ☑ **A** and **C.** Among several others, two of the advantages of an *n*-tier architecture are its ability to handle more transactions in a certain period than one- or two-tier architectures possibly can and its ability to be scaled more easily due to the fact that servers often can be added to a solution without coding changes.

☒ **B** is incorrect because *n*-tier applications have more processing overhead than single- and two-tier architectures. **D** is incorrect because *n*-tier architectures are more difficult and complex to set up and maintain and thus more expensive in the long run.

11. ☑ **A** and **B.** The users of web services are always other applications, and not users directly. Since web services are based on a set of common standards, the programming language and operating system of the client and the server are independent of each other.

☒ **C** is incorrect because any type of application, such as Windows desktop or mobile phone applications, can use web services. **D** is incorrect because web services can be used on private networks such as an intranet, without being exposed to the security concerns of the Internet.

12. ☑ **A** and **B.** The nature of XML makes it more difficult to sort and search. Because the entire XML document has to be parsed in order to extract aggregate data, filtered data, and the data from an entire column, it is many times slower than a relational database solution.

☒ C is incorrect because the cross-platform nature of XML is a definite advantage of the format. D is incorrect because XML data has embedded element and attribute names that serve to describe the data fairly well. Also, XML can point to a schema or DTD, which further describes the data.

Validating Conceptual Design

13. ☑ B. Conceptual user interface design is usually validated by some form of usability testing. Two or three sample screens are created and presented to users to solicit their feedback before a user interface design is decided on.

☒ A is incorrect because the ORM model deals with database design and not user interface design. C is incorrect because procedure and DFD diagrams deal with application component design. D is incorrect because logical design documents are not generated until conceptual design is complete.

14. ☑ A. Comparing the procedure and DFD diagrams with the business and user requirements is the best way to validate a design. Each business requirement should have one or more conceptual diagrams to ensure that everything is covered.

☒ B is incorrect because cross-reference matrices do only a partial job of validating the design. C is incorrect because usability testing is used to validate user interface design. D is incorrect because location design diagrams are not generated until after conceptual design is complete.

15. ☑ B. User interfaces that have been designed without usability testing often have unintended confusing elements. Terminology that is frequently used in the software development world may be unfamiliar to the average user, and frequently used features may be hidden in hard-to-access menus.

☒ A is incorrect because while application performance may be slower, it is not a primary consequence of skipping this step. C is incorrect because user interface design is not often affected by the differences between database and conceptual application designs. D is incorrect because a poor user interface design will not affect application architecture decisions.

LAB ANSWER

The correct order of software design tasks is as follows:

   C. Visualizing the design

   B. Developing business requirements

   E. Developing functional specifications

   A. Transforming data and business requirements into a conceptual design

   F. Developing a database schema

   D. Developing an application prototype

7

Logical Design

I n contrast to the user- and task-centric views of conceptual design, logical design in an object-oriented environment looks at an application as a series of classes and objects. During the logical design phase, application designers make high-level decisions about the application architecture. In an object-oriented programming environment, this involves creating a design based on classes, attributes, and behaviors.

We are still not ready to begin coding yet, although we are starting to think about the application more in terms of a set of related components. Whereas conceptual design was completely abstract, logical design is slightly more tangible. The logical design constructed will better resemble the architecture of the final application than the conceptual design. In this chapter, we will move away from the boxes and lines that make up conceptual diagrams to the more complex shapes that make up Unified Modeling Language (UML) class diagrams and other logical design notations.

exam
ⓦatch

Although the Unified Modeling Language (UML) provides many helpful tools for logical design and is a popular industry-standard notation for software modeling, it is not one of the certification objectives for this exam. Therefore, you should not expect any UML-related questions on the exam.

CERTIFICATION OBJECTIVE 7.01

Creating a Logical Design

There are four major steps for converting an application's conceptual design model into a logical design:

1. Identify the business objects of the application.
2. Identify the behaviors (actions) of the objects.
3. Identify the attributes (properties) of the objects.
4. Establish the logical relationships between the objects.

In addition to these steps, the other major goal of the logical design phase is to convert the conceptual data model into a logical data model. The logical data model is often called the *database schema* because it defines tables, data fields, and relationships between tables. As discussed in Chapter 5, logical database design is often used as a visual map of the database and its architecture.

The Value of a Logical Design

At the end of the logical design phase, the team will have a set of important application documents. This documentation will provide application developers with important information about the internal workings of the program. Every database table and every application object will be fully documented in such a way that application developers will not have to look at the actual code in order to learn how certain components are meant to be used.

It is important to note that specific technologies will not be discussed or considered during the logical design phase. For example, we still have not decided if preexisting .NET framework classes can be used in place of particular business objects. There are several .NET enterprise servers that provide ready-to-use components, such as Microsoft Commerce Server 2000. These components can be used in place of one or more of the business objects defined during this phase, but those components won't be investigated or considered until the physical design phase has begun.

Deriving a Logical Design from a Conceptual Design

During the conceptual design phase, we identified several potential business objects in the application. During the logical design phase, we will identify the objects that will be represented in our application.

All applications typically belong to one of the following three categories:

- **Data-oriented**   The prime objective of data-oriented systems is to collect and store data. These systems can be thought of as data entry and reporting systems. One of the key features of a system such as this is that the application is tightly integrated to a database at the back end. Almost every function of an application such as this requires the existence of a database.

- **Functional**   The prime objective of functional systems is to perform a well-defined function. For instance, the Microsoft Calculator application is a good example of a functional system, as is Microsoft Internet Explorer. Another less obvious example would be the programming logic inside a microwave oven. Functional applications can sometimes have a database component, but most do not.

■ **Behavioral** The objective of behavioral systems is to watch for, and respond to, certain events. An example of a behavioral system would be one that keeps track of inventory levels and automatically reorders more items from the appropriate supplier.

Some applications contain elements of more than one type of system. For instance, a banking application will have strong data-oriented components but may include financial calculators (functional) and automated credit-risk alerts (behavioral). In this case, the application really is made up of three interrelated applications. An application developer would probably analyze and construct each part of the application separately.

Identify Objects in a Data-Oriented System

There are several methods for identifying the objects in any system, depending on the system type. In a data-oriented system, there are four methods for initially identifying the objects in the system:

■ Locate nouns in the use case scenarios.

■ Examine the conceptual database design diagrams.

■ Consider external entities.

■ Identify events that need to be remembered.

For example, the use case document might contain the following scenario: "A data entry clerk enters orders into the application. Each order contains one or more items." The nouns in this scenario are Clerk, Orders, and Items.

At this step, we really just want to list as many objects as we can. Proceed through the rest of the user specifications to see if any other nouns can be located. One potential trap is the use of adjectives to describe the potential objects. For instance, the user specifications may specify certain details about full-time employees and other details about part-time employees. At this stage, whether an employee is full-time or part-time is really just an attribute—in both cases, we list Employee as a potential object and deal with the subclasses later.

Another source for potential objects in a data-oriented system is the database conceptual design. Back in Chapter 5, we were examining the database for an employment agency. Some of the potential objects from that database were Job,

Candidate, Skill, and SkillLevel. These all must be considered as potential objects in our application.

A third source of objects for the application would be the external entities that interact with the application, either directly or indirectly. In the employment agency application, the Agency, Client, and Candidate are all entities that the system might need to track. In an order entry application, the Customer object would likely be identified at this stage.

The fourth source of objects in any data-oriented application are the events that may need to be remembered. Identify the objects that receive the event and the objects that trigger the event. Following are some examples of some events:

- **Invoice printed**   This event increases the amount outstanding on a customer's account.

- **Payment received**   This event decreases the amount outstanding on a customer's account.

- **Online order entered**   This event triggers an e-mail to the customer account manager.

Identifying the events in a system can help you understand which application objects are important, as it makes it clear which objects need to send events and which ones should be available to accept them.

After examining these four sources for application objects, you should have a fairly complete list of all the logical entities required by the application. The list will likely need some refinement later down the line, but is a good place to start for now.

Identify Objects in a Functional System

Functional systems use slightly different sources for identifying important objects. Recall that a functional system is an application, such as the Windows Calculator, that performs a specific function but does not usually need to connect to a database or wait for an event to occur before acting. In the case of functional systems, our task is to identify the responsibilities of each of the system's components.

The first step for identifying objects in this type of system is to extract the verbs from the user requirements. (Recall that we extract the nouns for data-oriented systems.) For example, we can extract the verbs from the following user requirement: "The user will be able to calculate the monthly mortgage payment for potential new mortgages." The key verb (or action) phrase in the sentence is "calculate the monthly mortgage payment". This verb phrase is listed as a key responsibility of the system.

After the key responsibilities have been identified, the next step is to break these tasks into smaller tasks. For instance, in order to calculate the monthly mortgage payment, the system needs to do the following:

1. Enter the principal amount.

2. Enter the interest rate.

3. Enter the amortization period.

4. Calculate the monthly mortgage payment.

Subtasks should be identified for each responsibility identified in this process. It is important to keep the steps from becoming too detailed during this process. Notice, in the previous example, we did not break the fourth step (calculate the monthly mortgage payment) down into the precise formula required to do this. The subtasks identified during this process will become functions (or *methods* in object-oriented terminology) of our objects.

Another example of breaking a user requirement down into tasks is the following. The user requirements might state, "The user should be able to change their e-mail address." The key action verb in that statement is "change their e-mail address". The process of changing an e-mail address can be further refined into:

1. Retrieve user data.

2. Update database.

After completing the process of identifying all of the responsibilities of the system, you can then match the subtasks with the data they are related to. For instance:

Data	Tasks
Mortgage	Enter principal; enter interest; enter amortization; calculate monthly payment; load mortgage from database; save mortgage to database; delete mortgage.
User	Retrieve user data; update database; add new user; delete user; validate password; change password.

With a slightly larger and more complex system, a definite pattern will emerge as to what the objects in your system will be and what methods those objects will need to support. Grouping related functions and data together is known as *encapsulation* in object-oriented programming. Related data and functions are encapsulated in a *class*.

Identify Objects in a Behavioral System

Finally, behavioral systems use another set of methods to identify the objects in a system. Recall that behavioral systems are those that watch for, and process, events. These systems are typically real-time systems, such as an instant messaging (IM) client. IM clients, such as Microsoft Messenger, wait for messages to be sent to the current user from other users across the Internet, and they take some type of action (usually a pop-up dialog box in Windows) once a message is received.

As you might expect, the potential list of objects in a behavioral system is derived from the events the system acts on. An *event,* in this context, is a signal, interrupt, or message of some sort that triggers some action within the system. In our IM example, a message being received from the Internet is an event. An automated stock system that allows a stock purchase or sale to be executed automatically when the specified equity reaches a predetermined price also has elements of an event-based system in it. So does the application that monitors my laptop battery and warns me that the charge is getting too low.

Once the events are identified, we need to identify the processes that handle these events. In Chapter 6, on conceptual design, we created procedural diagrams to help us understand the processes in the application. So what process within the application triggers the event (for instance, "monitor stock ticker")? And what processes handle the event (for instance, "execute stock trade")? We need to connect events and their processes.

Finally, we need to group into logical units the processes that act on related data. For instance, the processes that access messages in an IM system can be grouped into the Message unit, or the processes that access user accounts in a stock-trading system can be grouped under the Account unit. These units become the classes in our behavioral system.

Remove Unlikely Objects

Inevitably, there may be objects that were identified during the first phase of logical design that don't serve any useful purpose and thus shouldn't be included in your application as a system object. This could happen for objects that fall far outside the scope of your application's core business purpose.

For instance, let's assume you are designing an application for employees to enter their weekly timesheets. You may have identified an OfficeBuilding object during the conceptual design phase so that your application can relate each employee to a physical location. At this stage of the design process, you should honestly try to assess the real benefit of having an OfficeBuilding object within your application. Is there any functionality within the business requirements that require the application to distinguish an employee based on his location? Could that functionality be handled easily inside the Employee object by using encapsulation to hide it? As a designer, it is your responsibility to decide which objects in your system may be so unnecessary as to be inconsequential and possibly to remove them.

Identify Object Behaviors

Once the application's system objects have been identified, you need to identify the behaviors associated with each object. For most objects, there are a core set of behaviors that need to be supported, such as the ability to create a new instance, load an existing instance, and delete an instance. Also, objects that have relationships with one another need to be able to establish and sever those ties. Finally, some system objects will need to perform other tasks in order to be useful in the context of the application.

For instance, let's assume we are developing a calendar application that allows users to add tasks and appointments. Calendars are essentially made up of dates, so the main object in this application will be the Date object. The object will need to have certain mandatory behaviors, which will then become methods, in order to do the following:

- Create a new instance of a Date.
- Load an existing instance of a Date from the database.
- Delete an existing instance of a Date from the database.
- Save changes to an existing instance of a Date.

In addition, a Date may have zero or more appointments, so the Appointment object is a child object of Date. This means that the Date object will need to have behaviors that allow it to add and remove appointments:

- Link an Appointment object to the current Date object.

■ Unlink an Appointment object from the current Date object.

Finally, this application requires the Date object to handle certain tasks, so the Date object will have the following additional behaviors:

■ Retrieve all appointments for the current Date.

■ Print the current Date to the local system printer.

Thus, we have been able to identify eight behaviors that the Date object must be able to support. These behaviors need to be documented as part of the logical design.

EXERCISE 7-1

Identifying Business Object Behaviors

If fulfilling user requirements is the ultimate goal of developing an application, defining and implementing the appropriate object behaviors is what gets you there. In this exercise, you are going to examine an object and identify appropriate object behaviors.

Let's start by looking at an example of an application that is being developed. A law firm has asked you to redesign their client billing application. From your conversations with the client, you have learned the following about lawyer's invoices:

■ Invoices must contain the name of one and only one client.

■ Invoices always have a unique invoice number.

■ Invoices always have an invoice date.

■ Invoices contain a list of one or more billable tasks.

■ Each billable task contains a descriptive text field, a lawyer name, an hourly rate, and the number of hours worked.

■ Invoices contain one subtotal, one tax line, and one grand total line.

■ The application will need to be able to create new invoices, load existing invoices, edit and update invoices, and print invoices.

From these requirements, three business objects have been identified: Client, Invoice, and BillableTask.

1. What are the core set of behaviors that the Invoice object must support? "Core behaviors" are those that support the creation and initialization of the object.

2. What are the set of behaviors that are required to support the relationship between the Invoice object and one or more BillableTask objects? When dealing with an object that is the parent to another object, you will likely need to define a method to retrieve a list of the child objects, as well as several methods to support adding and removing child objects from that list.

3. Finally, list the behaviors required to support basic application functionality, such as saving and printing.

Identify Object Attributes

The attributes of an application object that are identified at this stage will become the properties of the class that eventually gets created. For objects that were taken from the conceptual database design model, identifying the attributes may not be too difficult. The conceptual model clearly identifies the attributes of the object. However, for objects not based on an existing conceptual model, you will have to refer to business requirements or other specifications documents to identify the relevant attributes. For instance, coming back to the calendar application referred to in the last section, the Appointment object will have a number of obvious attributes:

■ The title of the appointment

■ The date when the appointment occurs

■ The time, if any, when the appointment occurs

■ The appointment's scheduled duration

■ A detailed description of the appointment

Some calendar applications may support many more details for appointments, including separate properties for the location, an array listing all of the people scheduled to attend, and the name of the originator of the appointment. The attributes identified for each object will obviously be based on what type of data each object is required to store.

Establish Logical Relationships

While you were identifying each object's behaviors, you might have already given some thought to how each object relates to other objects in order to establish methods that create and destroy relationships between objects. The final step in creating the logical design is to formalize those relationships in your logical design.

Many of the relationships between objects will be already taken into consideration in the database conceptual design diagram described in Chapter 5. There is a good reason for this—the database conceptual design aims to model the elementary facts of the system. So, for data-oriented applications, there should be many similarities between the database model and the application model. (Obviously, for functional and behavioral applications, there will not be very much similarity, if any.)

FROM THE CLASSROOM

How Does Unified Modeling Language (UML) Fit into Application Design?

UML is a popular set of modeling languages designed to standardize the way in which object-oriented applications are designed and documented. It is important to know that UML is a collection of various techniques developed independently that have evolved over the years. UML version 2.0 is currently under development by the Object Management Group (OMG). More information, including the official specifications, can be downloaded from the official UML web site, at http://www.uml.org/.

There are twelve core diagrams in the UML specification, and they are divided into three categories:

■ **Structural diagrams** Class, object, component, and deployment diagrams

■ **Behavioral diagrams** Use case, sequence, activity, collaboration, and statechart diagrams

■ **Model management diagrams** Packages, subsystems, and models

As you would expect, structural diagrams describe the structure (or architecture) of the application. The class diagram is one of the most useful diagrams during the logical design stage of development because it defines the classes that are contained inside the application. Class diagrams also contain the properties and methods of each class, as well as related connecting classes.

Behavior diagrams describe how a system is expected to behave over time. Some diagrams, such as sequence or activity diagrams, describe an order of events, while others, such as statechart diagrams, simply describe the valid states of an object.

Model management is a methodology within UML that allows complex application models to be organized into packages. This is especially helpful when more than one person is working on a large UML model. Charts of all types can be organized into hierarchies of packages, subsystems, and models. Each UML modeler can be working on the section of the application that they are an expert in without affecting other modelers working on the same model.

It is not mandatory that developers use UML models in their application designs, but being familiar with and using UML in a project will have at least four important benefits:

- UML models are self-documenting. After the application has been built, the model used to design the application can be referenced in system documentation to help future developers understand what is going on.

- UML models have a standard (and precise) notation, so models developed by one person can easily be understood by another. This reduces confusion and improves the maintainability of an application.

- Many tools exist that can turn UML models, such as class diagrams, into empty class and attribute definitions, sometimes called *skeleton code*. This can save development time and reduce errors in translating the model into an actual class.

- Some models, such as use cases, make testing the application easier. Quality assurance (QA) analysts can easily turn use cases into testing scripts instead of having to create those scripts from scratch. More accurate testing scripts usually reduce the likelihood of system errors when the application is rolled out into production.

As a .NET solution developer, it is probably in your best interest to make the effort to understand the various UML notations that exist. UML may not be used in every project, but these diagrams are easy and accurate ways to describe the design and expected behavior of an application.

—*Scott Duffy, MCSD, MCP+SB, SCJP, IBMCD-XML*

Organizing Logical Structures

Once all of the application logical classes and objects have been identified, the next step in the process is to organize them into logical structures. Most typical business applications do not perform only one task. Applications that perform only one task, such as Microsoft Calculator, are actually quite rare. Most applications end up being closer to Microsoft Outlook Express—that is, they do one key job, but can also perform a bunch of smaller jobs. Outlook Express is used mainly for sending and receiving e-mail, but it also supports an address book and newsgroups. These functions are in some ways similar but in many ways are not. The underlying Outlook Express application objects can be logically grouped as follows:

Group	Logically Related Objects
E-mail	Message, LocalFolder, MailAccount
AddressBook	Contact
Newsgroups	NewsMessage, Newsgroup, NewsAccount

Each object has its own set of encapsulated data and functionality. For instance, the Message object encapsulates data about the message (to, from, subject, and so on), and also includes functions (new message, send, and delete). But the Message object interacts with the LocalFolder object (which represents folders such as Inbox, Drafts, and Sent Items), so the functionality can be grouped. The Contact object might have some communication with the Message object (such as when double-clicking on a contact triggers a new message to be created that is addressed to that person), but the functionality required to maintain an address book is quite separate and distinct from the functionality required to compose an e-mail message.

Considerations for Auditing and Logging

To this point, the logical application design has focused on user-related functionality, and for good reason. The success or failure of the application largely (but not entirely) rests on the ability of the application to do what is expected of it. But there are some processes and procedures that are oftentimes necessary to include in an application design that do not have an effect on the user. Auditing and logging are two examples of these processes.

Auditing (sometimes called an *audit log* or an *audit trail*) is used to record system activity for the purposes of after-the-fact security. Auditing is not usually used to prevent problems from occurring, but instead to be able to answer the question, "What happened?" For example, an application that contains sensitive data might keep an audit log of all users who log in and out of the system (by recording user IDs and timestamps) or keep a log of who is making changes to the data. If it is later discovered that some data has been maliciously altered or destroyed, the audit log will contain the perpetrator's identity—as long as that log cannot be altered. In the interest of security, access to the audit log should be restricted to everyone except systems administrators.

Whereas an audit log is kept primarily for security purposes, other event logs are often needed for other purposes. The process of keeping these other event logs is called *logging*. Examples of these nonsecurity logs include:

- A record of system error messages (error logs)
- Logs required for statistical purposes (web server logs)
- Logs to assist developers with system bugs (debug logs)
- Status messages of batch processes (status logs)

It is often a good idea to segregate the processes that support application logging into a separate object. This helps with code reuse and keeps similar functionality together. Each business object in the system that needs to write information to the log can call a common logging object. This also makes it easier to change systemwide logging practices (toggle on and off, change log destinations, avoid verboseness, and so on).

There are several methods a developer can use to implement logging within the application being designed:

- Write log events to a table in the database
- Write log events to a file on the file system
- Write log events to the Windows Event Logger
- Compose and send an e-mail based on the event
- Any combination of the above

e x a m
ⓌＡＴＣＨ

Microsoft recommends developers use the Windows Event Logger, which displays operating system, security, and application events in a single interface, alongside any custom logs you have created.

Handling Errors and Exceptions

In object-oriented programming, an *exception* is an error message that is passed from one object to another. The object that first encounters the error creates an exception, and then passes it to the object that called it. If the object receiving the exception is not watching for it, which in object-oriented terminology is known as not *handing* the exception, the exception will be passed back to the preceding object in the chain, and so on. The process of continuing to pass an exception back to previous objects until it is handled is known as *bubbling*.

During the logical design phase, we need to identify the objects that can encounter either system or application errors. For example, in a database application, any objects that interact with the database could potentially encounter a database error. In a previous example, we identified a User object that had an associated method of "retrieve user profile." In the process of retrieving the user profile, a multitude of system problems could occur:

- The network could be down.

- The database server itself could be down.

- The database instance running on the server could be down.

- The database could be corrupt.

- The user authentication for connecting to the database could have failed.

- The record might not exist inside the database.

Obviously, many other problems could occur. Each of these system problems could create an exception, and so obviously any object that is relying on the "retrieve user profile" method of the User object will have to handle exceptions.

There are also application-specific exceptions that could occur. These are usually business logic errors that your application code has detected. As a programmer, you can create and send your own exceptions to indicate an error. This is known as *raising* an exception. Following are some examples of application-defined exceptions:

- The account does not have enough money in it.

■ There are not enough parts in inventory to fulfill the order.

■ The Date of Birth entry cannot be in the future.

Perhaps the most important thing to understand about exceptions at this stage of the logical design process is that they are used to report errors. This makes it crucial to document which classes and methods within the application design could raise errors and who should handle those errors.

Integrating the Solution into the Enterprise

One of the important considerations when designing a solution is how it will integrate into the existing enterprise architecture (EA). You'll recall we discussed EA back in Chapter 2. Enterprise architecture is the business, application, and technical infrastructure of an organization. How well an organization's application architecture matches its current business processes is an important factor in its operational success or failure.

Applications rarely exist in a vacuum. Oftentimes, systems will need to retrieve data from an external source—a centralized customer database, for instance—or provide data to an external system. The specific components within the logical design structure that will be responsible for interfacing with these external systems should be identified at this stage. We still are not ready to think about the specific technologies that will be implemented, but we can design generalized methods within specific objects, such as adding ExportData and ImportData methods to the Customer object, to handle these tasks.

One important suggestion to keep in mind at this stage is to try to centralize the interfacing tasks as much as possible to make it easier to make changes to those interfaces in the future. If each object in the system is required to send its data to a central reporting database each night, it might be a wise idea to create one object that does the actual transfer of data, while the individual object might only be responsible for preparing the data for transfer. For example, each object might have a "Serialize" method that will allow it to be saved to database in a retrievable fashion.

Considerations for Globalization and Localization

One of the challenges faced by application developers today is the issue of localization. *Localization*, sometimes abbreviated to l10n, is the process of designing an application that can be altered to fit the language or cultural differences of a specific locale. Many developers think that localization merely involves translating the text strings within an application into multiple languages. In fact, many considerations need to be made during the application design phase for localization:

- **Language**   Some applications need to support multiple languages such as English, French, and Spanish.

- **Dialects**   Some countries and regions have terms and phrases that would not be understood in other regions of the world.

- **Date and time considerations**   Applications that display current dates and times need to be sensitive to current time zones, observance of daylight savings time, preferred formatting of dates and times, and so on.

- **Currency and numbers**   Many countries have their own unique way of representing units of currency, the currency symbol, the thousands separator, and the decimal point.

- **National holidays**   Applications that contain embedded calendars might need to display different sets of holidays to users in different locales.

- **Other cultural differences**   Localization involves replacing examples that may be relevant in one part of the world but not relevant in another.

author's note   *The abbreviation l10n is sometimes used in place of the word "localization" because there are 10 letters between the initial letter l and the final letter n. For the same reason, the word "internationalization" is sometimes abbreviated to i18n.*

Building with Security in Mind

The word *security* can be defined as something the gives or ensures safety. You know security is working when you (and your personal property) are not at risk from attack. In real life, security is achieved using methods such as fences, locks, guards, identity cards, cameras, and metal detectors. In the world of information technology (IT), security is achieved using technologies such as firewalls, certificates, IDs, passwords, well thought-out business logic, and proper logging techniques.

It is often much more difficult to add security to an application after it has been designed and developed than if adequate consideration was given to security during the design phase in the first place. Security is, of course, an even more important concern for applications that have a network or database component.

Of course, there are various levels of security. You can have security in applications that have no user ID or password component—kiosks in a mall, for instance—just as you can have security that requires retinal eye scans or fingerprint identification. The level of security is, of course, directly related to the sensitivity of the data and the severity of the "worst-case scenario" if the application security is fully breached.

For some web sites, the worst damage that can be inflicted by outside hackers is modification (or defacement) of web pages on the site. That's embarrassing enough, and most companies will spend a reasonable effort to avoid being publicly humiliated in that way. But other types of security breaches can inflict millions of dollars in damage on a company if trade secrets are stolen, financial accounts are modified, or transaction records are deleted. These security incidents can have a lasting effect on a company, particularly if customers have lost trust in the company and sales drop as a result.

Designing security into applications always involves tradeoffs to some degree. Should you inconvenience your users by forcing them to log in every time they access the application? Should you place restrictions on what functions within an application each user can access? There are also a number of concerns relating to how a tight security system will be managed over the long term. For instance, who will decide which security restrictions to place on each user? And how easily can system privileges be granted and revoked based on an employee's changing roles within the company? After all, you do not want the process of security to seriously impede your company's ability to do business.

And therein lays the tradeoff. Security tends to be, almost by definition, a bit inconvenient for users. How much extra inconvenience would your users be willing to endure in order for their data to be completely secure? That question can only be answered on a project-by-project basis.

Security in .NET

With the flexibility and variety of the .NET framework classes, Microsoft .NET provides many ways for an application developer to implement security in a .NET application. The three most common techniques are

- Role-based security
- Web application security
- Evidence-based security

Role-based security is the concept that the various components of the application always execute under the security restrictions of the user. That is, even if an application is spread out across several back-end servers in an *n*-tier architecture, the server-side components are logged into the servers using the user's ID and password to execute their function. If the user doesn't have access to a Windows folder or SQL Server, then the application will fail. This type of security is recommended because so many of the security breaches (or "hacks," as they are commonly called) have involved a user being able to get system-level privileges. The theory is that it will be much harder for malicious users to breach security if even the back-end components run in the user's security context.

The WindowsPrincipal .NET framework class is used to handle authentication for Windows-integrated role-based security. This security model relies on each user having a user ID and password on the Microsoft Windows server or domain in which the application is running. Since many organizations already provide their employees with Windows domain-level user IDs and passwords, role-based security can be quite convenient for users. In fact, by integrating the security of an application with that of the Windows operating system, the job of managing user IDs can be centralized.

The GenericPrincipal class is used to handle authentication for applications that need to handle their own user IDs and passwords. Applications can further customize their security by implementing their own Principal classes based on implementing the IPrincipal interface.

exam
ⓦatch

It is important to understand what the WindowsPrincipal and GenericPrincipal classes do and that their respective roles are within an n-tier application security model.

Web application security is an important consideration when building ASP.NET applications. ASP.NET integrates well with the Internet Information Server (IIS) web server to support common Hypertext Transfer Protocol (HTTP) authentication schemes, such as the following:

- Basic
- Digest
- Windows NT LanMan (NTLM)
- Kerebros
- Secure Sockets Layer (SSL)/Transport Layer Security (TLS) client certificates

In addition, ASP.NET integrates into Microsoft's new Passport web-based authentication system. One of the big benefits of using Passport for your web-based application security is that Passport already has an estimated 200 million users. If your application integrates with Passport, your users will not have to create a separate user ID and password for your application.

author's note **You can learn more about Microsoft Passport at http://www.microsoft.com/net/services/passport/.**

A third technique that .NET provides for implementing security is called *evidence-based security.* This method involves placing restrictions on the type of code that can be run within the application. An example of this type of security would be a server component that does not explicitly trust the client component calling it. Some component's methods may be called freely, while others require some evidence—for instance, a client certificate, a valid digital signature from the client, or even the IP address of the machine making the request. Additionally, developers can pick and choose which methods are restricted, which need additional evidence, and which do not.

Identifying Appropriate Technologies for Physical Design

Even when we drafted the solutions concept, which was discussed in Chapter 2, we have been hinting at the technologies involved in the application design. If our application is to be a two-tiered architecture, with a Windows client that connects to a database server, there is an implied physical design. We are just now going through the process of converting the conceptual design into one that is separated into logical categories. So while it is too early to talk about specific technologies involved in the application, it is safe to begin identifying which technologies are appropriate from the design point of view.

For example, you may already have decided that the application is to be developed using Visual Basic .NET whenever custom code has to be developed. That decision does not restrict you from using third-party or off-the-shelf objects to manage certain areas of your application (messaging is a good example). One of the powerful features of .NET is the choice of application language to use (Visual Basic, C#, and C++, for instance), which is now more of a programmer choice. Whereas certain applications had to be developed in C++ in the past for performance reasons, that is less of a consideration in .NET.

Another technology decision you might have already made at this stage is which operating systems the application will have to support. If you know your users have a wide variety of Windows, Mac OS, Sun, and Linux desktops, that will restrict you from using certain technologies and may even force you into having no choice in the matter. Certain technologies are required and may even have been specified in the business or user requirements as a given—for example, "The client portion of this application will be written in HTML 4.0."

Creating the Logical Design for Data Privacy

Privacy and security are two related yet distinct topics, and it is sometimes easy to get them confused. As we discussed in a previous section, security is something that gives or assures safety. Data safety is assured by first establishing a person's identity (through authentication) and then ensuring that the person can only visit areas of the application where they have explicit permission to be.

Data privacy, on the other hand, is the notion that not all data should be shared equally. For instance, I may not mind that my local video store keeps a database with my name in it. After all, the video store and I have an ongoing relationship. But I would mind a great deal if that database also contained my social security number, my employment salary, and my medical history. There is a great deal of information about me that I wish to keep private.

A second aspect of data privacy is the handling of passwords. Applications have for years been treating password fields differently from other data fields in applications, using one-way encryption techniques to ensure that passwords are irretrievable once set. Most applications also mask password fields using a series of asterisks (such as "********") at the user interface level.

A third aspect of privacy is to protect sensitive data (such as online banking applications) from being intercepted between the bank's server and the client's PC. This is done using Secure Sockets Layer (SSL) encryption. In order to protect the privacy of the financial or other information contained on the page, most web browsers also do not cache (store on the local PC) web pages retrieved through SSL.

The proper time for application designers to give some consideration to data privacy is during the logical design phase. Security often plays a big part in ensuring privacy, but as you can see, the issue of privacy goes beyond that.

Building the Presentation Layer

The presentation layer is one of the three primary layers of traditional application design. The business and data layers are the other two. The presentation layer is represented primarily by the user interface, and we touched on that in the previous chapter (in the section titled, "User Interface Conceptual Design").

In .NET applications, the presentation layer is created using four sets of .NET Framework classes:

- Windows Forms
- Web Forms
- Console applications
- Web services

Windows Forms classes, available in the System.Windows.Forms namespace, are used to add graphical user interface controls to applications running within the .NET Framework environment.

Web Forms classes, available in the System.Web.UI namespace, are used to add graphical user interface controls to applications running remotely inside a web browser (commonly called *web applications*).

Console applications have a text-based user interface. The System.Console namespace contains classes that allow applications access to the three streams that make up the Windows console—input, output, and error. These three streams have been available to text-based applications since the early days of DOS, and it's good to see that they're still kicking around.

The user interface for web services is purely in XML text. That is because the users of web services will always be other applications and not people. Despite the lack of a direct human interface for these types of applications, web services still have nonhuman users that need to communicate with them.

Logical User Interface Design

It is during this phase of application design that you should start putting some screen shots or other UI design ideas together. You should start thinking of the application in terms of how the user will see it. Many projects actually present the UI design to the users in order to get their approval.

This does not mean, however, that the users will have a working application with which to play with. After all, we haven't even gotten into physical application design yet. We haven't decided on which underlying technologies will be used to develop the application. Logical user interface designs are often nothing more than artistic renderings of what a screen might look like once the application is developed. I have worked on projects that did the initial user interface design using a graphical image editor (such as Adobe Photoshop).

Typically, all you need at this stage is two or three representative screen shots to show overall UI concepts of how the application will look. Concentrate on colors, menus, themes, navigational guides, and other key application features. You don't even need actual content. Many preliminary user interface designs use "Blah blah blah," "Lorem ipsum dolor sit," or some other nonsense text where the written content should be. Using nonsense text actually has a beneficial purpose in some cases because it helps focus the user's attention away from the content and towards the overall UI design, where it belongs. Including actual content could distract the user into making spelling corrections, rewriting sentences and paragraphs, and so on.

Considerations for Synchronous or Asynchronous Architecture

Most applications developed today are *synchronous*. That is, when passing a task off to another component to perform, the application waits patiently for the task to complete before continuing. An example of this would be the process that occurs after a user saves a record in a data entry application. Typically, the application sends the data on to a relational database such as SQL Server and then waits for the database update to complete no matter how long that takes. Most database transactions such as this have built-in timeouts to give up after a set number of seconds or minutes have passed.

Usually, the use of this type of architecture is entirely appropriate. Most transactions, such as saving a record to a database, only take a fraction of a second and do not create a performance bottleneck for the application. Also, there are also times when the application absolutely needs to know the results of the previous task before it can move on to process the next one. In cases where tasks are heavily dependent on each other or application response time is not likely to be a concern, it is usually wise to stick with the synchronous setup.

But there are also times when you will want to do things in an *asynchronous* manner. An asynchronous application will pass a task off to another component to perform and then not wait for the task to complete before continuing. The application can then ask to be informed when the task has completed or not, depending on whether it cares about the outcome.

An example of an asynchronous process is the way printing works in Microsoft Word. You do not have to wait for the entire document to print, or even for the entire document to be sent to the printer, in order to continue working within Word. Printing a document, particularly a lengthy one, can be a time-consuming task. Before Microsoft introduced asynchronous processing into Word, users would have to wait for the document to be sent to the printer, which could take several minutes, during which time Word would not respond to user requests.

You can take advantage of asynchronous processing within your Microsoft .NET applications as well. There are times when it makes good sense to do so, such as when generating a report will likely take several minutes or a systems administration task triggered from within your application (for example, a function that updates thousands of database rows) could take hours.

The System.Threading namespace within the .NET Framework contains classes that enable asynchronous processing. Typically, an application creates a new thread for these separate system processes to run and passes in a callback function as a parameter. A *callback function* is a function in the current thread that will be called by the new thread when it is finished processing.

Creating the Logical Design for Services and Components

Designing web services and application components have their own set of unique challenges, which are slightly different from regular Windows Form or Web Form application design challenges. Services and components do not have a graphical user interface but do have an application interface. The application interface is the protocol used by clients when sending requests to and receiving responses from these server applications.

A *component* is a self-contained object that performs a specific task. It is a building block that can be combined with other components to form an application. For instance, Microsoft provides certain .NET Framework classes, such as ADO .NET, as components that applications can use to access various data sources. Developers can create their own application components, either as .NET assemblies or Component Object Model (COM) objects.

A *service*, sometimes called a *web service*, is an application that provides its functionality to other applications over a distributed network such as the Internet. Microsoft Windows has supported applications running in the background, called

Windows services, which have some traits in common with web services, but are on the whole quite different. It is important not to get Windows services confused with web services.

e x a m
W a t c h
There may be questions on services and components in .NET on the MCSD Solutions Architecture exam.

A Windows service is best described as an application that runs under Windows, which generally is always running but does not have an integrated user interface. For instance, the Microsoft IIS web server is configured to run as a service on Windows servers. Administrator access to the web server is made using a separate application, using a Microsoft Management Console (MMC) plug-in that is not part of the IIS service application.

An example of a web service would be an application that provides stock quotes. Other applications could connect to this service to request a quote, but unlike a Web Forms or Windows Forms application, users could not access the service directly themselves. Unlike Windows services, which always must be installed and running on the local PC, web services are almost always remote applications. The architecture of an application that consumes web services—web services are *consumed*, not used— is almost always two-tier or *n*-tier. Web services use widely accepted standards such as Extensible Markup Language (XML) and Simple Object Access Protocol (SOAP) to communicate with other applications.

author's
note
More information on XML can be obtained from the World Wide Web Consortium (W3C) web site, at http://www.w3c.org/XML/.

Following are some of the challenges of designing and developing components and web services:

- Since these applications are designed to be used by several users at a time, how do you deal with passing or storing session state?

- How do you upgrade or change an application that is used by hundreds or even thousands of other applications that you don't have any control over?

- With direct access to the application interface via methods and properties, how do you ensure that only authorized users gain access to certain restricted functions?

These are just some of the considerations developers have to take into account when creating application components or web services.

Creating the Logical Design for State Management

A *user session* begins when a user logs into an application that exists on a server and ends after the user has disconnected from the application. One of the biggest challenges for handling two-tier and *n*-tier applications is managing user sessions. Generally speaking, the server-side components of these applications have to be able to handle hundreds of user sessions at one time.

Session state is a snapshot of all of the data in memory for a particular user session. If you can save the state for a session somewhere (for instance, in a database, on disk, or in a browser cookie), an application will then be able to safely remove that data from its memory in order to make room for another session. Later, that server component can read the old session state information from its storage location, place all that data back into memory, and continue the session as if nothing happened.

exam
ⓦatch

The MCSD 70-300 exam requires you to understand the various ways application state may be stored in a distributed application environment, such as how application state should be stored for COM+ components.

Let's assume you are developing a web-based e-mail system. Your application will be composed of one database, one web server (running your custom-developed ASP.NET application), and potentially dozens or hundreds of client machines using your application through a web browser. To keep this example simple, let's assume that there will be only one server component available to respond to the user requests. So, if there are ten users currently using your web-based e-mail application, that single server component has to be able to receive and respond to requests from all of the ten clients at once.

Keeping the session state in memory for ten clients at once is not a big strain on resources. Assuming your e-mail application will ever need to keep only 1KB of data in memory on any particular user, ten sessions would mean 10KB of server memory used. These days, when servers regularly exceed 1GB of memory, 10KB will have no noticeable effect on server performance.

But what if user sessions take up 30KB of memory each, and your application might need to support 4,000 users at once? That would translate to over 100MB of memory in usage. That type of memory usage can have a serious negative effect on application performance. This situation is also not very scalable—any further increase in the number of concurrent users or the size of the data being kept inside the session state could cause the application significant problems.

There is another reason to support the idea of saving session state somewhere other than in memory—object pooling. *Object pooling* is the concept that a group (or pool) of identical components will provide better overall application performance than just having one component handle all the user requests by itself. For instance, if you created a pool of five identical e-mail application components running on the server to handle client requests, these requests will no longer need to line up waiting for the one component to be free. It's the same concept as that where having five open tellers at the bank is faster for customers than just having one open teller. If you get one guy who wants to open a new account, taking up ten minutes or so of the teller's time, everyone else in line suffers.

The reason why saving session state outside of memory helps with object pooling is that clients can then be serviced by any available component, instead of having to wait for one particular component to come free. If the session state data (or information on where to find it, such as a session ID) is submitted with each request, any component will have all the information it needs to resume the session right where the last component left off.

SCENARIO & SOLUTION

To store a small amount of noncritical user data in an ASP.NET application,…	Use browser cookies.
To store data that rarely changes in memory so that all sessions in an ASP.NET application can have quicker access to it,…	Use a Cache object.
To handle more than just a few concurrent users in your ASP.NET application,…	Do *not* use the Session object.
To store data that rarely changes in memory so that all applications running on the server in ASP.NET can have quicker access to it,…	Use the Application object.
To store dynamic ASP.NET web pages as static pages so that they don't have to be recreated for every call,…	Use a page output cache.
To store parts of dynamic ASP.NET web pages as static so that they don't have to be recreated for every page that uses them,…	Use a page fragment cache.

CERTIFICATION OBJECTIVE 7.02

Building a Data Model for Your Application

The quality of the database design has a direct impact on the quality of the overall application. Databases that have been designed well provide the following benefits to application designers:

- They tend to provide the best performance.

- They do not need to be overhauled for the next iteration of application changes.

- They are less susceptible to lost or corrupted data.

- The database objects have a high correlation to the business objects, which makes them easier to program for.

In this section, we will examine how a database conceptual design is turned into a logical data model.

Understanding Keys and Constraints

A *primary key* is a column (or set of columns) that uniquely identifies the contents of a table. By definition, primary keys must be unique within a table—two records cannot exist with the same primary key. Another important rule regarding primary keys is that defining one is optional, although each table can only have a maximum of one primary key. As a general rule, every table within the database should have a primary key.

There are several reasons for this policy. The first is practical: imagine you have two records in the database that are identical to each other, as in this example:

Employee Name	Position	Department
John	Programmer	IT
John	Programmer	IT

There are two guys named John working in the IT department—that's entirely possible, of course, so there is nothing wrong with the way this table is designed so far. But let's say one of the John's in IT gets promoted to the position of "Senior Programmer." How would an application be able to choose which "John" is the one who was updated? How could that application tell the database server to only update one record?

But if you had a primary key on that table, for instance, there would be no problem:

Employee ID	Name	Position	Department
1	John	Programmer	IT
2	John	Senior Programmer	IT

The other reason for having a primary key is performance. Database servers usually create some internal optimizations (called *indexes*) based on sorting by primary key. Users can define their own indexes to help with sorting and searching, but the primary key is by far the fastest type of index. For example, it is much faster to look up an employee by ID than by first name. For tables that contain a large number of records (hundreds of thousands, for instance), a primary key can make a profound difference in performance.

on the **Job** *In general, primary keys should be based on unique numeric values (such as 1, 2, and 3), instead of strings (such as "Mary," "John," and "Larry"). SQL Server has two handy data types, IDENTITY and UNIQUEIDENTIFIER, that make ideal primary keys due to their uniqueness. Although it is possible to have an employee's full name be the primary key, you run the risk of being unable to find records due to case sensitivity, extra spaces, and even spelling mistakes.*

Foreign keys establish relationships between tables. A foreign key is a column that refers to the primary key of another table for the purposes of referential integrity. *Referential integrity* is a set of rules that ensure proper order in the database. One of the rules of referential integrity is that a record whose primary key is being used as a foreign key in another table cannot be deleted. Another rule is that a record with a foreign key cannot be inserted unless that key refers to a valid value.

SCENARIO & SOLUTION	
To create a unique column in a table that other tables can use to form a relationship,…	Create a primary key constraint.
To create a column in a table that references the primary keys of another table to form a relationship,…	Create a foreign key constraint.
To make searches faster when sorting tables in an order other than by their primary key,…	Create an index.
To create a unique key on a table that is composed of more than one column,…	Create a composite key.

For instance, let's assume you have a database that contains two tables: Message and Submitter. Message has a foreign key that points to the primary key of Submitter, like so:

This means that:

- A Submitter record cannot be deleted if there are any Message records that refer to it in the database. The Message records will have to be deleted first before the related Submitter can be deleted.

- A Message record cannot be added to the database if it does not point to a valid Submitter. The Submitter referred to in the Message record must exist and cannot be empty or null.

There are other types of constraints that can be added to database table definitions during logical design. For instance, the *mandatory constraint,* sometimes called a *non-null constraint,* indicates columns that cannot be left empty. A *default constraint* can define a default value for columns that have not been assigned a value upon data entry.

EXERCISE 7-2

Converting Conceptual Database Design to Logical Design

We will turn again to the same example we used in Exercise 7-1. A law firm has asked you to redesign their client billing application. From your conversations with the client, you have learned the following about the relationship between an invoice and a billable task: "Invoices contain a list of one or more billable tasks." The following illustration depicts this elementary fact using ORM notation:

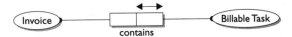

1. Using relational database terminology, describe the relationship between the Billable Task and Invoice data objects.

2. Define a basic schema for both tables, using primary and foreign keys to implement referential integrity into the data model.

Several database modeling concepts such as primary keys, foreign keys, and field-level constraints are likely to be tested on the exam.

Converting an ORM Conceptual Design to a Logical Model

Building the logical data model is remarkably simple when you're working from a well-defined ORM conceptual design model. The ORM conceptual model almost qualifies as a logical design.

Before we get into the steps required to convert such a model, we need to define a few new terms related to this context. A *simple key* can be derived from any elementary fact whose uniqueness constraint spans only one role. A *composite key* is an elementary fact whose uniqueness constraint spans more than one role. And a *compidot* (*comp*ositively *id*entified *o*bject *t*ype) is defined in the ORM specification as "either a nested object type (an objectified predicate)…, or a co-referenced object type (its primary reference scheme is based on an external uniqueness constraint)…" The most common type of compidot would be an object whose primary relationships with others are external uniqueness constraints.

There are basically four steps to convert a conceptual data model into a logical schema:

1. Initially treat the compidot as a "black box" by ignoring the external uniqueness constraint.

2. Map each composite key into its own table, creating the primary key based on the composite key.

3. Group facts with simple keys into the same table as their associated object, creating the primary key based on the object ID of this object type.

4. Unpack the compidot into its component attributes.

In order to get a better understanding of how the conceptual model can be converted, it would be helpful to look at an example.

Case Study: Creating the Logical Database Design

Most of Chapter 5 was spent working through an example of designing the ORM conceptual data model for an employment agency application. Figure 7-1 shows the final conceptual design that was created for that application.

FIGURE 7-1 A sample conceptual database design model

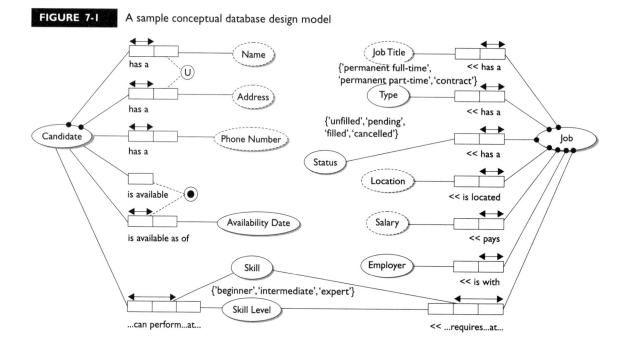

You can now work through the process of converting that data model into a logical database design, using the four steps outlined in the previous section.

The first step instructs you to temporarily ignore compidots within the application design. That is easy to do, since the conceptual model in Figure 7-1 does not have any.

The second step instructs you to move all composite keys to their own tables. Composite keys are identified on the diagram by horizontal arrows that span more than one role. There are two composite keys in Figure 7-1—the relationship between Candidate, Skill, and SkillLevel, and the relationship between Job, Skill, and SkillLevel.

So, in response to the second step, two new tables are added to the logical data model: CandidateSkill and JobSkill. The CandidateSkill and JobSkill tables each contain three fields, and they will be graphically represented in our logical database design as follows:

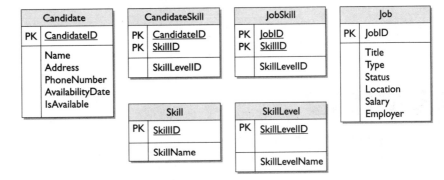

The third step is to add all single keys as attributes to their parent objects. This will add the Candidate, Job, Skill, and SkillLevel tables to our database. These four tables will inherit the attributes assigned to them in the conceptual design phase and are shown here:

You may notice that we actually added a couple of attributes (assigning a Name property to the Skill and SkillLevel objects) that were not present in the original conceptual design. It is not too late to make these types of changes at this stage if you discover one or two columns that should probably be there.

Once the conceptual data model has been mapped to a logical design (or schema), all database changes should first be made to the conceptual model and then to the logical one. The conceptual model does not get discarded once we have created the database schema.

The fourth step is to unpack the compidot into its component attributes, if any. Again, we don't have to worry about this step. But if we did, the basic procedure would be to get rid of the object that only has external uniqueness facts and roll it into another object.

We need to map down many of the other ORM conceptual constraints, such as the value constraints and mandatory constraints, to ensure they do not get forgotten. We also need to map any existing table relationships, such as the relationship between Candidate, Skill, and SkillLevel. The following illustration represents the final database diagram for this model:

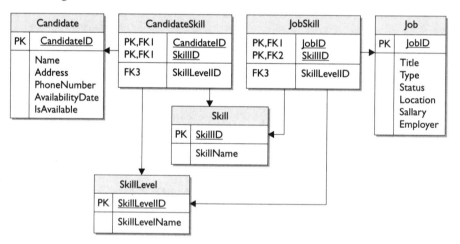

EXERCISE 7-3

Creating Logical Design Diagrams Using Microsoft Visio for Enterprise Architects

Note that this exercise assumes you have access to the Microsoft Visio for Enterprise Architects (VEA) software that ships with Visual Studio .NET Enterprise Edition.

In this exercise, we will be creating a logical database design diagram using Microsoft Visio.

1. Click Start | All Programs and choose Microsoft Visio to start the application.

2. Click File | New | Database and select Database Model Diagram to create a blank database model.

3. Drag the Entity icon from the left panel onto the blank page.

4. Using the Database Properties tab at the bottom of the screen, enter a name for this table.

5. Select the Columns category from the Database Properties tab. Enter the names and data types of the columns of the database.

6. Indicate the mandatory columns as well as the primary keys on this screen as well.

7. Click File | Save As and assign your diagram a name. Click the Save button to save the diagram.

Validating the Proposed Logical Design

Once the application and database logical designs have been developed, you can proceed to the final stage of logical design—validation. The validation step is important because it is "one final check" before the application moves into physical design.

The main goal of validation is to ensure that nothing has been overlooked during the logical design process. The task of validating the design need not take a lot of time or effort, and the potential costs of missing out on an important application requirement until late in the development process can be high. For example, imagine not realizing that an application had to have the same user interface look and feel as an existing application until the user acceptance stage of development. The amount of work required in redesign and redevelopment could have been saved had someone just spent a few hours validating the design.

There are two main techniques for validating the logical design, both of which we will discuss in this section:

■ Compare the proposed logical design to the known business requirements.

■ Validate the proposed logical design against usage scenarios.

Reviewing the Effectiveness of the Proposed Logical Design in Meeting Business Requirements

The easiest and best way to validate a logical design is to reexamine carefully the business and user requirement documents. By extracting each requirement from those documents and comparing them with the logical design, you should quickly be able to verify if an application will do all the tasks the user wants it to.

When comparing the logical design and business requirements in this way, there are eight important considerations to keep in mind:

■ What types of performance problems are likely to occur with this architecture?

■ What types of scalability problems are likely to occur with this architecture?

■ Is the application extensible, in that it will be able to easily accommodate new requirements in the future?

■ Will application availability be a factor?

■ How easy will the application be to maintain in the long run?

■ How easy will the application be to deploy into the production environment?

■ What are the major security risks?

■ Have all of the user's accessibility needs been taken into consideration in the user interface design?

These eight considerations are important, to be sure, as they look beyond the business requirements at the operational requirements of the application. But the most important consideration still remains the comparison against the business requirements. Does the application do what it is supposed to do? If not, either the application or the user requirements have to be corrected so that those two pieces are in alignment at the end of this phase.

Validating the Proposed Logical Design Against Usage Scenarios

Another technique for validating the proposed logical design is to run through the predefined use cases. (If you recall, use cases were discussed in Chapter 3.) Of course, since we do not have a functioning application at this point, "running through" a use case is mainly a matter of comparing the application-related requirements of that case to the logical design.

Start by choosing a use case from the collection of cases developed during the business requirements phase. For instance, assume you will be going through the "Add a New Appointment" use case.

The logical design should be able to support every task requested of it in the case. For instance, if the first step of the "Add a New Appointment" case is for the application to create an empty appointment for the user to work in, the Appointment object should support creating an empty appointment.

Likewise, if the use case mentions certain fields that get updated, the object should support modification of those fields. If the object is called upon to perform a task, such as to save to the database, the logical design should include an appropriate behavior for that object.

Creating a Proof of Concept for the Proposed Logical Design

A proof-of-concept (POC) is perhaps the first actual bit of coding that gets done for an application. The purpose of the POC is to test out some of the most difficult technical requirements in order to prove their viability. The POC is not a sample application or a working prototype. In fact, the POC usually bares no visible resemblance to the final application.

For example, let's say the design of your application called for the application to save and retrieve all its data from the database in XML format. There is some concern, for good reason, that this might cause some performance problems for a heavily used application. To prove this concept, you develop a sample application that replicates the architecture of your production application and attempts to save and load thousands of records in XML format. This is a reasonable test because if the performance is not good enough, you may have to change your plan.

Another example of a POC would be an application to test the performance gains that could be made by creating a multithreaded (asynchronous) application instead of a single-threaded one. A POC application could have a user interface switch that allowed testing various scenarios under both synchronous and asynchronous conditions.

Not all applications need proof-of-concepts. They are only usually required when you are trying to test something that has never been done before to see how it works. Code developed for POCs can often be reused. For instance, when you have the asynchronous components working as a proof-of-concept, that code can be copied into the production application when the time comes for development.

The main problem with POCs is that they are sometimes used as the foundation for the production application. POCs are designed mainly to be quick tests and do not have many of the important architectural traits of production-quality applications. Try to avoid using the POC as the basis of the production application design. Instead, just incorporate some of the ideas and code from the POC into the final application.

In the next chapter, we will examine the application physical design. Physical design results in the actual technical specifications that can be used to develop the application. Many of the concepts that were introduced during the logical design phase get formalized during the physical design.

CERTIFICATION SUMMARY

The logical design of an application is based largely on identifying the business objects that will later be turned into classes within your application. Depending on the type of application—data-oriented, functional, or behavioral—there are different techniques for determining likely candidates.

Data-oriented systems, which usually have heavy data entry and retrieval components, contain objects based on the nouns within use case scenarios, conceptual database design, external entities, and events that need to be remembered. Functional systems, which are focused on performing a well-defined task, tend to revolve around the verbs in user requirements. The business objects defined in behavioral systems, which monitor and act on events, are usually based on the events themselves.

For all three systems, once the business objects have been identified, developers should go through the list to weed out any unlikely candidates. Unlikely candidates are usually those who are very loosely related to the actual purpose of the application and serve little or no useful purpose. You will often find that these objects can be encapsulated inside other, related objects with no loss in functionality and no decrease in maintainability.

The logical database design can be constructed straight from the ORM conceptual model. In order to create a proper logical model (called a *database schema*), you need to decide which type of database your application will be using. In most cases, this will be a relational database; but depending on the application and your unique circumstances, you can choose to use a purely object-oriented database or even a flat-file database. Database schemas usually contain the relevant details regarding the table and field names, data types, and keys within a database. This is the last step before a database actually gets physically created.

The final step of logical design is validation. The overall logical design needs to be examined with a critical eye to ensure that all business requirements are being met. At this stage, we are usually able to identify the components of the application that will require special attention by the developer. For instance, if a single component will need to respond quickly to the requests of hundreds of users, performance might be an issue; or if a component will be relied upon by hundreds of scattered tools and components, some thought should be given during physical design to future maintainability. The purpose of this stage of logical design is simply to make sure the logical design makes sense.

TWO-MINUTE DRILL

Creating a Logical Design

❑ The first step of logical design is to identify the business objects of the application.

❑ There are three types of applications: data-oriented, functional, and behavioral.

❑ Data-oriented applications usually revolve around data entry and reporting. Business objects usually come from nouns within the user requirements, conceptual database design, external entities, and events that need to be remembered.

❑ Functional applications usually need to perform a well-defined task reliably. Objects usually come from verbs within the user requirements.

❑ Behavioral applications usually monitor a real-time system watching for certain events and intelligently acting on them. Objects usually come from the events that are being monitored.

❑ The second step of logical application design is to identify the behaviors (actions) of the business objects.

❑ The third step of logical application design is to identify the attributes (properties) of the business objects.

❑ The fourth step of logical application design is to establish the logical relationships between the business objects.

❑ *Auditing* is used to record system activity for after-the-fact security.

❑ *Logging* is generally not used for security. It is used to record other system events, such as errors or statistical events.

❑ The Microsoft Event Logger is a logging tool built into Windows that can be used to handle all application, system, and security events in one place.

❑ Within .NET applications, errors should be handled by using *exceptions*.

❑ When an exception occurs, Windows attempts to find an object to *handle* that exception.

❑ Exception handling is done through a technique called *bubbling,* where the exception is passed back to the previous object until it is finally handled.

❑ *Localization* is the process of designing an application to accommodate the different needs of other languages and cultures around the world.

❑ Application security should be included during the logical design phase because attempting to include it later could result in a lot more time and effort.

❑ Security in .NET can be role based, web application, or evidence based.

❑ Role-based security can be integrated into the Windows security model using the WindowsPrincipal class.

❑ The GenericPrincipal class allows applications to handle their own security, or custom security classes can be developed.

❑ Many forms of web application security are integrated into ASP.NET. These security techniques are designed to work over an HTTP connection such as the Internet.

❑ ASP.NET can even integrate into the Microsoft Passport security model.

❑ Evidence-based security allows components to decide which components can and cannot be trusted, based on developer-designed rules. It is code-specific security.

❑ Data privacy is a basic human right and is the notion that user's personal information should be kept private, unless the user explicitly authorizes it to be shared.

❑ The Windows Forms classes, located in the System.Windows.Forms namespace, provide graphical user controls, such as buttons and text boxes, for .NET applications.

❑ The Web Forms classes, located in the System.Web.UI namespace, provide graphical controls, such as buttons and text boxes, for ASP.NET web-based applications.

❑ Console applications have a text-based user interface provided by the System.Console namespace.

❑ Web services have a user interface as well, although it is purely in XML format.

❏ Logical user interface design involves designing an overall look for the user interface, and usually involves creating a small number of screen shots as examples for the users to approve.

❏ *Synchronous* applications always wait for a task to finish before the application continues on with other work. This could be a potential application performance bottleneck for tasks that take more than a few seconds to complete.

❏ *Asynchronous* applications create separate threads for tasks to execute. The application can then go on and process other work, and the thread will notify the application when it is complete.

❏ A *component* is a self-contained object that performs a specific task.

❏ Components are building blocks that are combined with other code to form applications.

❏ A *service* is an application that provides its functionality to other applications over a distributed network such as the Internet.

❏ Web services use widely accepted standards such as XML and SOAP to communicate with other applications.

❏ Session state is a snapshot of all the data in memory for a particular user session. Server-side applications are able to save and restore this state information, which allows them to be much more scalable.

Building a Data Model for Your Application

❏ The Object Role Modeling (ORM) conceptual design model can easily be turned into a logical database model.

❏ In ORM, a *simple key* is a fact type whose uniqueness constraint spans only one role. In the ORM diagram, this is represented by an arrow spanning only one role box.

❏ Likewise, a *composite key* is a fact type whose uniqueness constraint spans more than one role.

❏ Simple keys become the attributes (or columns) of a table, while composite keys become their own tables.

❏ A *primary key* is a column (or set of columns) that uniquely identifies the contents of a table. By definition, primary keys must be unique within a table.

❑ A *foreign key* is a column that refers to the primary key of another table for the purposes of referential integrity.

Validating the Proposed Logical Design

❑ Logical design is validated primarily by comparing it with the business requirements document.

❑ Another useful technique is to run through each of the use cases to ensure that the business objects support the required functionality.

❑ A proof-of-concept (POC) is a small application developed solely to test out risky technical requirements.

SELF TEST

The following questions will help you measure your understanding of the material presented in this chapter. Read all the choices carefully because there might be more than one correct answer. Choose all correct answers for each question.

Creating a Logical Design

1. Which of the following types of applications best describes a type of application that is focused on performing a specific, well-defined task?

   A.   Data-oriented applications

   B.   Behavioral applications

   C.   Functional applications

   D.   Microsoft Windows Calculator

2. Which of the following are useful techniques for identifying the business objects in a data-oriented system? (Choose all that apply.)

   A.   Locating the nouns in the user requirements

   B.   Locating the verbs in the user requirements

   C.   Considering external entities that interact with the system

   D.   Identifying events to be remembered

3. Which of the following events would likely trigger an entry in an audit log?

   A.   The system calendar changing to a new day

   B.   An asynchronous thread completing a task

   C.   The database encountering a serious error

   D.   A user deleting a data record

4. What is the name of the system process that passes unhandled exceptions back to previous objects?

   A.   Exception passing

   B.   Exception bubbling

   C.   Error handling

   D.   Exception raising

5. What is the process of ensuring that an application can be altered easily for other languages and cultures?

    A. Translation

    B. Culturization

    C. Localization

    D. Personalization

6. Which of the following should be taken into consideration when developing an application that will need to support users in different countries? (Choose all that apply.)

    A. Translation

    B. Formatting of dates, times, and numbers

    C. Maintaining a different code set for each country

    D. Replacing examples that may not be relevant to each culture

7. Which of the following is almost always a tradeoff that has to be made in order to achieve tight security?

    A. User friendliness

    B. Data privacy

    C. The ability for the application to work over the Internet

    D. User convenience

8. Which of the following .NET security models require the application to run entirely in the user's Windows security context?

    A. Role-based security

    B. Web application security

    C. Implementing the IPrincipal interface

    D. Evidence-based security

9. Which of the following .NET security models is most likely to use Secure Sockets Layer (SSL) over a Hypertext Transfer Protocol (HTTP) connection?

    A. Role-based security

    B. Web application security

    C. Implementing the IPrincipal interface

    D. Evidence-based security

10. Which statement best describes data privacy?

    A. Applications that support data privacy always implement a strict Windows-based security model.

    B. Applications that support data privacy do not require a user's permission before sharing their personal information with others.

    C. Applications that support data privacy never share a user's information with others under any circumstances.

    D. Data privacy requires the proper treatment of sensitive personal information and user passwords, and reasonably protects sensitive data from being intercepted during transmission.

11. Which .NET Framework namespaces contain the classes needed to create a user interface? (Choose all that apply.)

    A. System.Windows.UserInterface

    B. System.Web.Forms

    C. System.Windows.Forms

    D. System.Web.UI

12. What type of user interfaces do web services provide?

    A. HTML web forms

    B. Either web forms or Windows forms based on the type of client

    C. XML

    D. None of the above

Building a Data Model for Your Application

13. Which of the following best describes the concept of a simple key in ORM relational mapping?

    A. A primary key

    B. A uniqueness constraint spanning exactly one role

    C. A uniqueness constraint spanning multiple roles

    D. A mandatory constraint

14. Assume the conceptual data model contains three objects: Candidate, Skill, and SkillLevel. These three objects are linked together using a single role, such that they form a composite key. Using the ORM relational mapping methodology, which of the following best reflects the tables required by this application?

    A. Candidate and Skill

    B. Candidate, Skill, and SkillLevel

    C. Candidate, Skill, and CandidateSkill

    D. Candidate, Skill, CandidateSkill, and SkillLevel

15. Which of the following relational database features is used primarily to enforce referential integrity?

    A. Table indexes

    B. Primary keys

    C. Foreign keys

    D. Database triggers

Validating the Proposed Logical Design

16. What is the best way to validate a proposed logical design?

    A. Compare the logical design with the business and user requirements to ensure everything is covered.

    B. Compare the logical design with the database schema to ensure consistency.

    C. Develop a fully-working proof-of-concept of the application.

    D. Send the system design documents to the users for approval.

LAB QUESTION

Acme Corporation is a manufacturing company that creates and distributes over 300 products to hundreds of clients around the world. It is currently using a Microsoft Excel spreadsheet to manually manage the catalog of products it carries. Acme would like to create a small catalog application that will allow users to browse the catalog of items in stock. The company's business requirements are fairly simple:

- A database will exist that will contain a detailed listing of all of the products in the catalog, sorted by ID.

- Each of the products must belong to one and only one product category.

- The product category assigned to each product will be one of a predefined list of twelve categories.

- Users should be able to browse the catalog with the products sorted by category.

- Choosing any item from the catalog will cause a full-page window to display, showing a picture of the product and all of the relevant details.

Based on the preceding list of business requirements, what business objects will this catalog application need to support?

SELF TEST ANSWERS

Creating a Logical Design

1. ☑ C. Functional applications center on the performance of a well-defined task, such as Microsoft Windows Calculator.

☒ A is incorrect because data-oriented applications center on a database. B is incorrect because behavioral applications tend to monitor the events of a system and react accordingly. D is incorrect because, although Windows Calculator is an example of a functional application, it is not one of the three application types defined earlier in this chapter.

2. ☑ A, C, and D. These three tasks all help identify objects in a data-oriented system.

☒ B is incorrect because verbs are used to identify objects in a functional application and not a data-oriented one.

3. ☑ D. The goal of auditing is to track the changes to key database tables as a means of after-the-fact security. This identifies the changes specific users made to the database.

☒ A is incorrect because the changing of the calendar day is not something that needs to be audited, although you may want to include that event in some type of log. B is incorrect because routine application events do not get audited, although they, too, might end up in a log. C is incorrect because system errors should be saved to an error log.

4. ☑ B. Exception bubbling is the system process that passes unhandled exceptions back to previous objects.

☒ A is incorrect because exception passing is not the correct term. B is incorrect because error handling is the process of handling errors. D is incorrect because exception raising is the process of creating exceptions.

5. ☑ C. Localization is the process of ensuring that an application can be altered for different locales.

☒ A is incorrect because localization involves more than just translation. B is incorrect because there is no such term as culturization. D is incorrect because personalization describes the process of creating different views of an application based on the user.

6. ☑ A, B, and D. Localizing an application involves translation, properly formatting dates and numbers, and ensuring that the content is still relevant to each culture.

☒ C is incorrect because, ideally, only the presentation layer should change for different countries while the vast bulk of the code should remain unchanged.

7. ☑ **D.** The most common tradeoff made to achieve tight security is user convenience.
   ☒ **A** is incorrect because an application can still be friendly while having tight security. **B** is incorrect because data privacy is usually enhanced, not lost, with tighter security. **C** is incorrect because properly designed and configured applications can be very secure and still operate over the Internet.

8. ☑ **A.** Role-based security forces application components to run in the user's security context.
   ☒ **B** is incorrect because web applications are made secure using protocols better suited to the openness of the Internet. **C** is incorrect because using the IPrincipal interface allows you to handle your own security model, which can be handled any way you wish. **D** is incorrect because the evidence-based model deals with the ability of applications to run specific code and doesn't deal with the security context of the components themselves.

9. ☑ **B.** SSL over HTTP is an ideal method for encrypting the connection between a web browser and a web server.
   ☒ **A** is incorrect because SSL over HTTP is not part of the role-based security model. **C** is incorrect because implementing IPrincipal is not the best way to implement SSL over HTTP. **D** is incorrect because as SSL over HTTP protects the connection, it does not assure privileges that the evidence-based model requires.

10. ☑ **D.** Data privacy aims to protect sensitive user information from being shared without the user's knowledge.
    ☒ **A** is incorrect because data privacy can be achieved with any type of security model and with no security model. **B** is incorrect because applications that support data privacy have an obligation to keep a user's sensitive data private. **C** is incorrect because data privacy does not preclude an application from sharing a user's data with others, as long as the user is aware of what is being shared.

11. ☑ **C** and **D.** System.Windows.Forms and System.Web.UI are two of the namespaces that provide user interface support in .NET.
    ☒ **A** and **B** are incorrect because these namespaces do not exist in .NET.

12. ☑ **C.** Web services provide interfaces to other applications using XML.
    ☒ **A** is incorrect because, although an HTML application may ultimately use a web service, the HTML web form is not the web service's interface. **B** is incorrect because, although a Windows form or web form application may ultimately use a web service, such an application would not be the web service's interface. **D** is incorrect because C is correct and therefore the answer cannot be "none of the above."

Building a Data Model for Your Application

13. ☑ **B.** A simple key is any uniqueness constraint in the ORM conceptual model that spans exactly one role.
     ☒ **A** is incorrect because a table can have only one primary key, while it can have any number of ORM simply keys. **C** is incorrect because uniqueness constraints that span multiple roles are moved to separate tables. **D** is incorrect because mandatory constraints do not become keys.

14. ☑ **D.** Because the ternary fact that links the three tables together has uniqueness that spans two roles, a new table will have to be created to map Candidates and Skills, called CandidateSkill. The other objects exist as their own tables.
     ☒ **A** is incorrect because the SkillLevel table is missing. **B** is incorrect because a fourth table is required to map Candidates to Skills. **C** is incorrect because the SkillLevel table is missing.

15. ☑ **C.** Foreign keys are primarily used to enforce referential integrity.
     ☒ **A** is incorrect because table indexes cannot be used in referential integrity. **B** is incorrect because, although referential integrity relies on the existence of primary keys in the table being referenced, the primary key does not enforce that integrity. **D** is incorrect because, although complex database triggers can be written to enforce referential integrity, they are primarily used to enforce other business rules. Triggers are also slower and less efficient than foreign keys, making them less useful for that purpose.

Validating the Proposed Logical Design

16. ☑ **A.** The best way to validate a logical design is to compare it to the business and user requirements identified during an earlier phase to ensure that all requirements are being handled.
     ☒ **B** is incorrect because objects from the conceptual data model were used to identify the business objects, making that model less useful for validating the end design. **C** is incorrect because, although you may want to develop a limited proof-of-concept to vet certain ideas, by definition a proof-of-concept cannot be a fully working version of the application. **D** is incorrect because users are not likely to understand the logical system design. Although they might have some role in the process, the job of validating system design lies squarely with the development team.

LAB ANSWER

The catalog application will likely contain the following business objects. Also included is the list of object behaviors (methods) for each object, divided by security role.

Object Name	End User Service	Administrator Service
Catalog	List product categories.	Add/remove product categories to the catalog; create/edit catalog details.
Product Category	List products.	Add/remove products to a category; create/edit product category details.
Product	Retrieve product details.	Create/edit product details.

8

Physical Design

Following the conceptual and logical design stages, the third and final stage of the application design process is physical design. The purpose of physical design is to apply technical constraints and decisions on the logical components created during logical design. Physical design also usually involves designing internal data structures, record formats, and a data dictionary.

Whereas the conceptual and logical stages were approached from the perspective of the underlying business (making sure every business requirement was fulfilled), the physical design stage should be approached from the perspective of the developer (fulfilling the technical requirements). At the end of this stage, we will have created a technical specification or blueprint that will lead us right into the development phase. The technical specification will contain details regarding the target platform or set of technologies—any technical issues will be resolved by the end of this phase.

The physical design stage can be broken down into five smaller tasks:

- Deriving the physical design from the logical design
- Developing an appropriate deployment model
- Creating the physical design for maintenance
- Creating the physical data model
- Validating the physical design

This chapter discusses these five steps in greater detail.

CERTIFICATION OBJECTIVE 8.01

Deriving a Physical Design for the Solution

The first step in creating the physical application design is to derive that design from the logical model (which was developed in the last chapter). The logical design model lists the business objects of the application, along with the methods and properties they support. The physical design model will take into consideration the technical factors, such as:

- Auditing and logging
- Error handling

- Integration with other applications
- Application security
- Data privacy strategies
- User interface design
- Managing application state

In this section, we will examine these issues a bit closer, and see how they impact the design of a solution.

Creating Specifications for Auditing and Logging

During the logical design phase, you gave consideration to the need for auditing and logging in your application from the business perspective. An *audit log* is a transaction log that records system activity for the purposes of after-the-fact security. For example, if you want to see the history of data changes for a particular record, you can examine the audit log. During the physical design phase, you should also consider whether additional logging is required for technical purposes, such as debugging.

There are many other purposes for application logging. These include:

- Keeping a record of all application error messages (error logs)
- Keeping a record of activity for statistical purposes (web server logs)
- Keeping a record of application processing to track system bugs (debug logs)
- Keeping a record of status messages from batch processes (status logs)

During the physical design stage, you will need to create a technical specification for the application's approach to logging. The extent to which this part of the application needs to be designed at this stage depends largely on the importance you place on creating and maintaining logs within your application. If the application needs to be extremely secure (for instance, an online banking application) or will contain sensitive data (for instance, patient medical records at a doctor's office), you should spend some time thinking about the design approach for this important part of the application.

Unless your application does not need much in the way of logging, we suggest you create a separate .NET component to handle this task. This is the most flexible approach, as it allows you to easily adjust the method and type of logging without having to modify the rest of the application. Whenever an event occurs within your application that needs to be logged, your application simply passes a message to your logging component to handle. This makes things easier all around.

There are two key decisions that need to be made with respect to this component. The first is the method by which other components within your application pass the event details to the logging component. Essentially, you need to decide what types of information need to be recorded for a particular event. Typically, log events contain information such as:

- Date and time the event occurred

- The name of the application component that encountered the event

- The user ID that triggered the event

- A numerical error code or message ID, to make it easier to act on specific events

- A descriptive string containing the error message text or event details

When dealing with audit logs, the details of the changes being made to the database are what are important. That is, if you are auditing the changes to the account balance table of a banking application, the audit log will also usually contain before and after values for the data being changed.

The second key decision that needs to be made at this stage is the output location of the log. The location chosen should be one that:

- Doesn't impede application performance

- Will be easy for administrators to access

- Will be easy to manage, such as backing up or deleting logs after a period of time

When designing applications for a Windows environment, developers have many choices for where to store system logs, such as:

- Write log events to a database table

- Write log events to a file on the file system

- Write log events to a Windows event log

- Compose and send an e-mail based on the event

- Any combination of the above

Of course, the location (or locations) you choose to store your logs will be based on the circumstances of your application. Some applications store logs in multiple locations, writing messages out to a file and storing them in a Windows event log at the same time.

e x a m

ⓦa t c h

It is important to understand what a Windows event log is, and the three default categories of events it can record: System, Security, and Application.

Microsoft provides a component in the .NET Framework called EventLog to help you manage your application's interactions with the Windows event log. This component exists in the System.Diagnostics namespace. By default, there are three separate event logs in Windows:

- **System**   A place for errors generated by the Windows operating system
- **Security**   A place for errors generated by the Windows security system
- **Application**   A place for errors generated by registered applications

The EventLog component allows you to connect to event logs on both local and remote computers. It also allows you to create new event logs for your messages, instead of using one of the default logs. It is important to remember that access to certain event logs depends on the security settings associated with the application. Obviously, for security reasons, you don't want an unauthorized application to be clearing an event log.

author's

ⓝote

In Windows XP and 2000, the Windows event log can be reviewed using the Event Viewer application. Event Viewer can be found by navigating to Start | Control Panel | Administrative Tools | Event Viewer.

Windows provides an application called the Windows Event Viewer to help developers and system administrators diagnose errors that are occurring inside a system or application. Figure 8-1 shows how the Windows Event Viewer looks. Double-clicking on an event inside the Event Viewer will allow you to see all of the details of a particular event as you can see in Figure 8-2.

FIGURE 8-1

The Windows
Event Viewer in
Windows XP

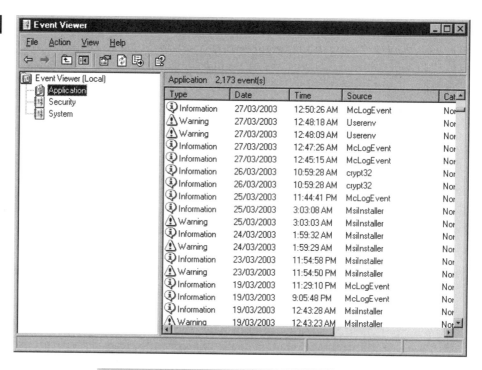

FIGURE 8-2

Details of one
event inside the
Event Viewer

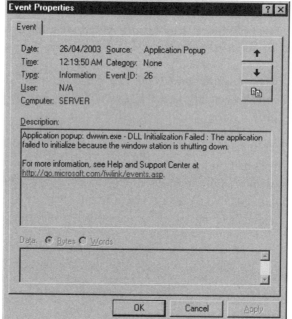

Each event that is placed in the event log has a severity associated with it. There are five types of event severities, and each type has its own icon in the Event Viewer.

Information   **Warning**   **Error**   **Success Audit**   **Failure Audit**

- **Information**   An infrequent but successful operation
- **Warning**   A problem that is not immediately significant
- **Error**   A significant problem
- **Success Audit**   A successful audited security event
- **Failure Audit**   A failed audited security event

If the application writing an event to the log does not specify a severity, events are assigned the Information severity by default.

Creating Specifications for Error Handling

Error handling is an ability developers give to applications that allows them to intelligently react when problems occur. It is important to think about what types of errors can occur within your application, and how each individual component of an application will react.

There are two categories of errors that can occur within an application: application errors and system errors. An *application error* is a custom-designed error within your application. For instance, in a bank loan approval application, the application might

SCENARIO & SOLUTION	
To add error logging capabilities to your .NET application…	Use the EventLog component in the System.Diagnostics namespace.
To add system process monitoring capabilities to your .NET application…	Use the Process component in the System.Diagnostics namespace.
To add system performance monitoring capabilities to your .NET application…	Use the PerformanceCounter component in the System.Diagnostics namespace.

trigger an error if an applicant's income does not reach a predefined level. That is, the component that analyzes the credit risk of a particular applicant may wish to create an error (known as *raising* an error) as soon as it discovers the applicant doesn't meet the income test. A *system error* is an error triggered by the operating system, such as when the application tries to use a service for which it does not have the appropriate permissions.

There are two key decisions that need to be made when creating the error handling specification for your application. The first key decision is analyzing the type of errors your application is likely to encounter. For instance, if your application has heavy reliance on a database, you will need to check for errors each and every time a connection is made to the database. If certain components within your application will be returning errors (for instance, the bank loan approval component), other components will need to check for those errors. For every component in your application that could potentially cause an error, another component will need to watch for (or handle) those errors.

The second key decision that needs to be made is how to handle each error that could occur. For instance, when an application cannot connect to its database, what should it do? There is a wide range of possible reactions that can legitimately occur:

- The application can completely ignore the error and attempt to continue

- The application can report the error to the user in the form of a message box

- The application can report the error to the user, and ask the user to decide the next step

- The application can stop running

- The application can store the details of the problem in an error log

- The application can analyze the type of error (using an error code, for instance), and choose between many different alternatives based on the type

- The application can wait for a few seconds and retry the same task that failed, hoping for a successful result

- Any combination of the above

As you can see, there are many different methods of handling errors. The choice of which method to use depends on several factors, such as the type of application, the sophistication of your users, the severity of errors, and so on. For example, if your users will all be highly technical system administrators, you might want the details of the error to be displayed to the user to enable them to try and correct the problem. Or if your users will be technical neophytes with little technical expertise, you may want to shield them from seeing the error as much as possible.

In any event, your technical documentation needs to be very specific about the types of errors that can occur, and how they should be handled. If your application does not provide any error handling, Windows will be forced to handle the errors itself, which will likely mean your application will be forcibly closed by the system. In addition, your users will receive a strange message about the error, so in most cases it is best to have the application handle the error. Figure 8-3 shows how a system-handled error message could look.

It is important to have one coherent strategy for this, especially when multiple developers will be working on different parts of the application. We have seen applications that attempted to have one central error handling component (similar to the central logging component described in the last section), but that is a very difficult undertaking. It is often better to have each component handle its errors itself, perhaps relying on an outside component only for logging.

Creating Specifications for Physical Integration

In corporate environments, applications often need to work alongside other applications on the user's PC. Even in applications that are being developed for a home user or for a single-tier architecture, there is usually a set of standards that

FIGURE 8-3

An example of an unhandled error message

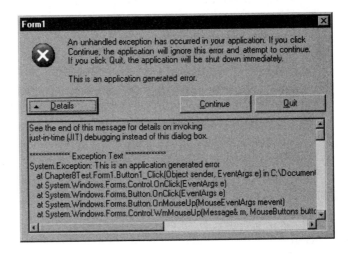

need to be adhered to. When applications need to communicate with other applications by exchanging data, the integration issues become even more prominent.

Depending on the nature of the application being designed, the method by which an application will integrate with the surrounding environment needs to be accounted for in the technical design.

author's note *Of course, Microsoft has an excellent product to help with enterprise application integration (EAI) called BizTalk Server. You can find out more information on BizTalk from their website at http://www.microsoft.com/biztalk/.*

To understand the possibilities of application integration, you only have to look at some of the marketing materials for .NET. Microsoft has been airing a series of commercials to introduce the concepts of .NET to the general public. One ad features a customer choosing the color of his automobile from the dealership, while robots in the manufacturing facility wait for him to make up his mind. Once he has chosen a color, the robots get to work painting a car for him. This may never happen in real life, but the purpose of the ad is to demonstrate application integration. The salesman's order entry system is integrated with the back-end production system so that the manufacturing department has up-to-the-second information on current orders. Integration like that does not just happen—it needs to be planned.

Considerations for Application Integration

When planning for application integration in your design, several factors need to be taken into consideration:

- Need for real-time access to information
- Network considerations
- Application availability
- Handling data changes

In an integrated application, there are two types of data accesses with external applications: reading data from other sources, and being a source of data. For instance, in a typical order entry application, the program is required to provide data (the orders) to other systems for processing. But this application can also require information from others. For example, an order entry application frequently requires customer profiles, order statuses, and product lists.

You'll remember that the data exchanged between the application being designed and external entities (other applications) is documented in the data flow diagrams created during the logical design phase. Every instance of an external entity on that diagram is an integration point for your application.

For each integration point, you will need to determine how frequently the data needs to be updated. For instance, let's assume your application needs to acquire product lists from the sales and marketing system. But how frequently does that data change? Can you just import that information once a week, or does it change by the hour? It would certainly be faster to have a local copy of data such as a product list, even though your application would treat the table as read-only, just for the sake of application performance. However, any time you keep a local copy of data that is maintained by other systems requires you to have a strategy for regularly updating it.

Another consideration for each integration point would be the nature of the network between the two systems. If the two applications are on the same high-speed network, and the size of the data exchange is relatively small, the network may not be much of an issue. But if your application needs to send hundreds of megabytes a day to an application that is located across the country, the network may be a problem.

The two major issues when dealing with networks across long distances are performance and availability. Networks are notoriously slow and unreliable across long distances. If your application is relying on the availability of an application that is on the other end of a slow network, you will need to have proper error handling when dealing with that connection. It might be a good idea to have a recent local copy of the data ready (a local cache) in case the network is unavailable. Or be able to queue requests until the network is back up.

The performance and availability of external applications you are integrating with should also be taken into account. The more integrated your application is with others, the more difficult it is to schedule maintenance on the related applications. For instance, if ten applications within your company have heavy reliance on a central customer database, it becomes very difficult to take the customer database down for maintenance. Once again, applications should be able to automatically detect when the resources they rely on are unavailable and take intelligent action.

Finally, there are less obvious (business-related) implications to application integration. Once data has been transmitted from an application to others, it loses control of it. For example, let's assume orders are transmitted immediately from an order entry system, once the user saves a record, to several back-end systems. What if the user realizes a few minutes later that they made a mistake entering the order?

Ordinarily, it would be a simple task to allow them to update a record from the database. But since the order has been sent to several other systems, our application has to inform them of the change. These other systems have to recognize this as a change and not a new order, and correct their own data. If those systems have already sent the order on to other systems, the amount of effort required to change a simple typographical error becomes a massive endeavor.

FROM THE CLASSROOM

The Challenge of Availability

It is fair to say that, for most applications, availability is an important criterion. Not all applications need to be scalable—for instance, single-tier applications that are designed to support only one user at a time. And not all applications are designed to be extensible—for instance, the developers of Microsoft Calculator will not be adding any new mathematical operations into their product. But in most applications, from single-tier to *n*-tier, availability usually ranks high in importance. Users expect their application to be available for use when they attempt to use it.

In software engineering, *availability* is the ratio between the number of hours per year the system is actually accessible to users and the number of hours per year they expect it to be accessible. For instance, if an application that is expected to run 24 hours per day needs to be 99 percent available, that means that the system must be available for 8,672 out of the 8,760 hours in an average year—no more than

88 hours of system downtime. Availability is usually expressed as a percentage.

Achieving 99 percent availability sounds impressive, but it means that your application can be inaccessible for up to 88 hours per year. Many applications strive for 99.5 percent availability (40 hours per year of downtime), or even up to 99.9 percent availability (8 hours of downtime per year).

Applications that strive to be more than 95 percent accessible are known as *high availability* systems. Applications that strive for more than 99.5 percent are called *very high availability* systems. Keep in mind that hardware costs often increase dramatically for each fraction of a percentage increase in availability. For instance, hardware that costs $10,000 for 98.5 percent availability will probably cost $35,000 for 99.5 percent availability.

Be careful when promising very high availability to your users. If you think about the factors that could affect the availability of a two-tier or *n*-tier system over the course of its life, many of them are difficult to mitigate:

- Necessary operating system security patches and upgrades (that often require a reboot)
- Network problems
- Power outages
- Application version upgrades
- Hardware failures (such as hard drives that can and do crash)
- Accidents (Murphy's law—if anything can go wrong, it will)

If you can convince your users to accept a 98 or 99 percent availability rate instead of 100, you are giving yourself two or three hours a week to handle the planned and unplanned maintenance issues that inevitably will occur. If you do find yourself having to design an application that requires 99.9 percent availability, there are several things that can be done:

- Multiple application and database servers
- Redundant networks and Internet service providers (ISPs)
- Intelligent client-side code that can switch to a backup server when a primary server is unavailable
- Servers located in different cities to handle localized events such as storms and long-term power outages
- Emergency backup power supplies

The key to creating very high availability systems is redundancy. The failure of a single server or component should not affect the application in any way. High and very high availability systems need to be planned, so that contingencies have already been developed for most scenarios that can occur. It is worth the time to develop and implement disaster recovery plans and backup strategies in case of emergencies. Don't forget to expect the unexpected.

—*Scott Duffy, MCSD, MCP+SB, SCJP, IBMCD-XML*

Creating Specifications for Security

The security of computer systems has become a very high priority in many organizations in recent years. Along with the rapid increase of interconnected computer systems during the last decade, the opportunity for hackers to attempt to gain unauthorized access into sensitive systems has risen proportionately as well.

Of course, not all applications need to worry about security. The programmers of Microsoft's Windows Calculator probably did not have to give more than a passing thought to the issue, since the impact of even the most serious security breach would be almost negligible. The importance of security in application design really does depend on the type of application being developed.

Security Considerations

When designing applications, there are a number of issues that should be taken into consideration, such as:

- **Security goals**   Know what it is you want to be kept secure.
- **Security risks**   Understand your application's vulnerabilities, and the likelihood/severity of an attack.
- **Authentication**   Choose a method of validating the user's identity.
- **Authorization**   Choose a method of determining which resources a user has access to.
- **Securing data transmission**   Encrypt sensitive data that will move across public networks.
- **Impersonation**   Server components should run in the context of the current user's permissions.
- **Operating system security**   Establish Access Control Lists (ACLs) to restrict access to the application to prevent intruders.
- **Securing physical access**   Ensure the server computer is placed in a secure room. All the security controls in the world can't stop a hacker if he has physical access to the machine.
- **Code access security**   Understand that in two-tier or *n*-tier architectures, the server shouldn't always naively trust the client application.

In this section, we will examine some of the application security factors that need to be taken into consideration when developing applications in .NET.

Establishing Security Goals

It would be overly simplistic to think that every application has the same security needs as every other application. Some applications are extremely sensitive in nature (such as banking systems) and security is a paramount concern. Other applications are more like electronic tools (such as word processors) and security is less of a concern. As a developer, your job is to understand how secure your particular application needs to be.

If the security requirements have not yet been included in the business requirements document, they should be added now. In order to establish these goals, you should establish:

- Does your application require users to log in before it can be used?
- Which screens/areas of the application require security and why?
- Is there more than one security role, or will all users have equal privileges?

This part of the security documentation may be fairly straightforward for most applications.

Authentication in .NET

Programmers most commonly think of authentication when they think of security. Authentication is the process of verifying a user's identity before granting them certain privileges. The most common form of authentication is the user ID and password, although other forms exist, such as:

- **Digital certificates**   Requires the user to have a special digital token.
- **Smart cards**   Requires the user to be in possession of something unique, such as a magnetic card.
- **Biometrics**   Uses unique human characteristics, such as a fingerprint or retinal eye scan, to authenticate a user.

The .NET Framework provides a set of classes in the Windows.Security.Principal namespace to help applications enable security. The basis of .NET security is the security principal—an object that represents the identity and role of the user, and acts on the user's behalf. The three main types of principal objects in .NET are:

- WindowsPrincipal
- GenericPrincipal
- Custom principal

The *WindowsPrincipal* class allows your application code to check the built-in Microsoft Windows security model for permissions and groups. Using this technique, you can actually integrate the security of your application with the security already built into Windows XP and Windows 2000. If a user has successfully logged into Windows, that same account can be used to authenticate the user in your application. Your application would assign roles to certain users depending on the level of access to an application. For instance, let's assume a user belongs to the YourAppDataEntry role inside the Windows security system. Your application would then know the user is a data entry clerk, and can provide the user appropriate access based on that information. If the user belonged to the YourAppAdministrator role, they could have expanded permissions within your application. It's important to note that granting your own custom roles to a user in Windows does not grant them additional access to Windows itself.

The *GenericPrincipal* class is used when your application intends to handle security itself. Assuming you have user IDs and passwords stored in a database, you could have the login component of your application set up this principal object to define which roles the user belongs to. Other parts of the application can check this principal component for authorization purposes.

Finally, if either the WindowsPrincipal or GenericPrincipal object cannot adequately service your application, you can always develop your own principal component. This is known as a *custom principal* object. For example, you may want a component that contains more information than just the user's identity and which roles he or she belongs to. Custom principals are the most flexible method. However, they obviously require the most work to code and configure.

Protecting Code in .NET

Protecting the code and infrastructure from malicious attack is also an aspect of application security these days. More and more systems and applications come under various types of attacks these days, such as denial of service (DOS) and buffer overflow attacks. Hackers have many different motives for these attacks—sometimes it's just for fun and sometimes it's for profit—but from a programmer's perspective, the motives shouldn't matter. Application security needs to be in place to protect against these events.

There is no one solution to preventing malicious attacks against an application. A combination of hardware, operating system, user training, and application techniques must be applied. Understanding the hardware and operating system prevention methods is outside the scope of this book, except to say that a secure network almost always includes routers and firewalls as frontline defense forces. Just having them, of course, provides very little protection unless they are properly configured.

One significant weakness in any security policy is the human element. You can devise the most secure computer application in the world, but if a user divulges their user ID and password to the wrong person, a security violation can occur. In the past, many hackers have just called up novice users, told them they were calling from "IT" and needed their ID and password, and received the information. The importance of keeping this information confidential should be addressed in user training.

Within the application, there are several methods a developer could implement to help protect the application from attack. The most basic technique is to implement auditing and logging. Auditing was covered earlier in this chapter, in the section entitled, "Creating Specifications for Auditing and Logging." Recording as much information as possible about users who log in (the date and time and the user's IP address, for instance) can be handy when attempting to track down a security problem after it occurs.

Another important technique is to perform field-level validation on every data field before using the data for the first time. This is not only to ensure against data corruption, but also to ensure malicious code is not being transmitted within the data. This type of an attack is sometimes known as a *buffer overflow attack*, which is a common way for hackers to try to break into secure applications.

In the past, it was quite common for the server-side components of *n*-tier applications to have full control over the environment. The application would take care to ensure that users could only perform limited tasks, but the application itself could perform any task. This led to a number of security issues, as hackers have exploited bugs in the application to perform tasks they aren't authorized for. That type of security configuration is no longer recommended for Microsoft applications. Now components should run in the same security context as the users. That is, whatever the user is authorized to do, the component is authorized to do—and no more. With this security configuration, even if hackers attempted to get the component to run an unauthorized task, the operating system would stop the component from doing so.

The .NET Framework provides a security mechanism known as code access security to help enforce access restrictions on code. Code access security is quite powerful, since it can be configured for many different types of security restrictions. Specifically, it allows you to:

- Restrict a component's ability to access system resources

- Assign components into code groups, and grant permissions to those groups instead of the individual components

- Define the mandatory and optional security permissions a code will need in advance (called a *permissions request*)

- Require users have specific permissions before they can access specific components

- Require users have a digital certificate before they can access specific components

Another way .NET enforces security is through type-safe code. Managed code in .NET is checked before being loaded into memory for the first time (during Just-In-Time compiling, or JIT) to ensure it only accesses the memory locations it is authorized to access. This way, .NET assemblies can be isolated from each other, ensuring that poorly written code does not affect any applications other than itself. For example, before they are executed for the first time, assemblies are checked to ensure they do not attempt to access the private data members of other objects.

The only way to bypass the type-safety validation step in .NET is to assign the SkipVerification security permission to the component. Skipping this step will make starting a component a tiny bit faster, however, you can potentially introduce application instability in the process. SkipVerification is not recommended under normal conditions, and should only be used with extreme deliberation.

Privacy in .NET

Privacy is often overlooked when dealing with application security. Privacy is the aspect of security that ensures sensitive information is protected from everyone except authorized individuals. This includes techniques such as data encryption.

The .NET Framework includes a new set of framework classes for cryptography, including:

- Encryption
- Digital signatures
- Hashing
- Random number generation

All of the framework classes relating to cryptography exist in the System.Security .Cryptography namespace. Most of these classes are managed-code wrappers to the Microsoft CryptoAPI security functions that ship with Windows.

author's note *Recent enhancements to .NET allow XML web services SOAP messages to be encrypted or digitally signed as well. These enhancements can be downloaded from the Microsoft MSDN web site at http://msdn.microsoft.com/webservices/building/wse/default.aspx.*

Including Constraints in the Physical Design

Constraints are added to the physical design at this stage in order to support business rules. A business rule is a specific business use of data. Some examples of business rules are

- Product orders over $50 receive free shipping.
- Customers that have purchased $1,000 worth of product within the past six months get an automatic 10 percent discount applied to their order.

SCENARIO & SOLUTION	
If your application has a user interface...	Make sure you validate all the data fields, checking specifically for field length and malicious data contents.
If your application is designed to run in ASP.NET...	Make sure you use Secure Sockets Layer (SSL) to encrypt sensitive data between the client and the server.
If your application needs to be security aware...	Make sure you program permission requests into each of the components, to ensure your code only receives only the permissions it actually needs.

Constraints relating to business rules are incorporated during the physical design phase, instead of the logical design phase, since the rules are often unique to a particular circumstance. For instance, if you examine the two business rules previously stated, you'll see that they appear to be sales incentives. These incentives are likely to change over time, and different businesses will likely have different sets of incentives.

Another example of a business rule would be:

- When the user enters this screen for the first time, the received date field will default to yesterday's date.
- The value for received date must be prior to the value for processed date.

Once again, these are rules that will typically be found in a business requirements document, but are not included during the conceptual or logical designs. The goal of including these constraints during this phase is to identify which components will be responsible for enforcing them.

Designing the Presentation Layer

During the conceptual and logical design phases, only a small amount of consideration was given to the presentation layer. During those phases, you started thinking about the screens in only a general way, drawing up a couple of examples for user review. You also made some decisions regarding on-screen elements such as application menus, user navigation, and other metaphors. Now that your application has reached the physical design phase, you will complete the design of the user interface.

Different types of applications will have different needs for the presentation layer. Windows services applications have the simplest presentation layer of all—they have no user interface. Console applications have a text-based presentation layer, and design is usually quite simple. Web services simply communicate with the outside world using XML format, so designing the presentation layer for these applications involves defining the XML format by creating a schema. And finally, Windows and web applications have graphical presentation layers. Graphical user interfaces (GUIs) require more upfront design planning in order for them to be effective.

At this stage in the design process, decisions regarding application type have already been made. As a developer, you will now have to make important presentation layer technology decisions such as:

- For web applications, which browser versions and Internet standards will you have to support?
- For Windows applications, what is the lowest user display configuration (color depth, screen resolution, graphic card memory, and so on) that you will have to support?

Designing Services and Components

Broadly speaking, a component is a stand-alone piece of code that provides a service to other code. Technically speaking, a component is not an application in that it cannot be started on its own and doesn't act independently. It simply sits there, waiting for another application to ask it to perform a task.

Microsoft provides application developers thousands of built-in components for use within their applications. These components are organized into logical hierarchies called namespaces, and packaged in a convenient form known as the .NET Framework. Classes within the .NET Framework do not run on their own—they wait for an application to invoke them, and perform specific tasks as requested.

There are two types of service applications within .NET. A Windows service is an application that runs in the background on a Windows-based personal computer, regularly performing a task of some sort. For instance, some anti-virus software is available as a Windows service. It typically runs in the background the entire time a computer is running, diligently checking for viruses.

The other type of service that can be created within the .NET environment is a web service. This service resembles a component in many ways, although it uses an Internet standards-based interface (such as HTTP, XML, and SOAP) to communicate with the applications that call it. This makes it much better suited for working in a diverse platform environment such as the Internet. It is very difficult (if not impossible) to get the old component model for Windows, COM, to work over such long distances.

The challenge when designing components and services is to define the Application Programming Interface, or API. The API is the set of functions and methods that are exposed to other applications. It is important to have a consistent API—one that is not going to change radically if you need to add a new feature to the component.

Another challenge when designing APIs is backward compatibility. Since components are stand-alone pieces of code, it is relatively easy to upgrade them when a new version comes out. In an unmanaged programming model, new components are simply registered with the Windows Registry. In the new .NET model, components can be deployed using a command-line tool as simple as XCOPY.

In order to make it easier to manage components, .NET comes with two important new features that will make life easier for application developers:

- **Side-by-side execution** .NET has the ability to let multiple versions of a component exist on a computer, and intelligently decide which is the correct one to call when an application invokes a function within that component. Registering a new component no longer overrides an older one.

- **Private components** Applications can install their components in their own private directory structure, and request that components used be called from there.

The downside to this approach is that, over time, multiple versions of each component will accumulate on a machine taking up more disk space and memory. As well, the process of updating a component (when significant bugs have been fixed, for instance) is more difficult, as it becomes harder to track when it is acceptable to overwrite a component and when it needs to be installed side by side.

Designing State Management

The interaction between a component and a client application is similar to the interaction between a restaurant waiter and a customer. The customer calls the waiter over to her table and orders a drink. In response, the waiter fetches it and serves it to her. Some time later, the customer orders an appetizer. Again, the waiter fetches it and serves it to her. This process continues through dinner, dessert, and the bill.

From the waiter's point of view, this interaction is fairly easy to manage. All he has to do is remember what the customer orders, in order to be able to bill her at the end of the meal. In this scenario, the waiter might just be able to recall the order history by memory.

But when the waiter is serving five tables at once, it becomes harder to accurately recall what each table ordered. On top of that, each customer is at a different stage of his or her dinner. Some are just ordering the appetizer while others are asking for the bill. Imagine what will happen if the waiter attempts to serve 25 tables at once.

As far as the waiter is concerned, the order history of each individual customer is all he needs to remember. In programming terms, the amount of time that elapses between when the customer first sits down until when they leave can be called the *user session.* Likewise, the information that the waiter needs to remember for each session in order to be able to do his job effectively can be called the *session state.*

Coming back to applications and components, managing session state can be a tricky task. Imagine we had a hypothetical component that needed to remember 1 MB of data about each session that was in progress, and then consider what would happen if our component had to manage 1,000 sessions at one time. There will be approximately 1 GB of user data that will have to be temporarily stored somewhere, and you just can't tuck that kind of data under your hat.

Another issue to consider with session state is the scenario where there are ten identical components set up to manage user requests—a configuration called *object pooling.* An application can make a request to one component at one moment in time, and then make another request to a completely different instance of the same component the next. This is done for performance reasons, so that one long-running user request doesn't slow down requests from other applications unnecessarily. Components sometimes need to share user state data between them.

This issue is most prevalent in ASP.NET web applications, where multi-user processing is a must. There are several reasons why session state needs to be stored primarily on the server side of the application, as opposed to the web browser client side. The two biggest reasons are the relatively slow network that makes transferring large amounts of data back and forth unpractical, and the wide diversity of web browsers (some almost ten years old) in use.

There are several methods for storing session state within .NET and ASP.NET applications:

- The Application object
- The Session object
- Browser cookies
- Hidden form fields
- HTTP query string
- The Cache object
- The Context object
- The ViewState object
- Web.config and Machine.config files

Three of these objects deserve to be looked at in greater detail. The first two are the Session and Application objects. The third is the Cache object.

The Session and Application Objects

In ASP.NET, there are two built-in system objects that help you maintain session state information. One is the Session object, and the other is the Application object. The Session object is used to store application data relating to the current session segregated from other sessions. The Application object allows data to be shared between objects and sessions, allowing for object pooling.

Both of these objects provide developers with a collection data type, inside which user data can be stored. But there are downsides to this approach. Most importantly, when run in in-process mode, user data is simply stored in memory on the web server. This approach does not scale very well, and application performance suffers after only a few dozen concurrent users.

ASP.NET applications can also be configured to use the Session object in State Server mode. This state server can be used in conjunction with a database such as SQL Server in order to have the session state stored external to the application.

ASP.NET applications that require scalability in order to handle more than a few dozen simultaneous users should avoid the ASP Session object. The ASP Application object is a good place to store global data, however, the Cache object should be used for maximum flexibility.

The Cache Object

The .NET Cache object is an extremely powerful and flexible tool for storing session state data. Cache is a .NET Framework component that resides in the System.Web.Caching namespace. Data stored in Cache can be specific to a particular session, shared with certain other sessions, or available to all sessions. Data can be set to expire after a period of time, which makes managing sessions much easier for component developers.

When developing high-performance, distributed, scalable ASP.NET web applications, caching is vital. ASP.NET allows developers to cache entire pages, or parts of pages (called fragments) using the @OutputCache directive. Embedding this directive into the ASP.NET web page allows you to set the duration and location of the cache, plus other settings.

SCENARIO & SOLUTION

To have cached data expire after a set time period has elapsed since it was created…	Set the absoluteExpiration property of the Cache.Add() method.
To have cached data expire after a set time period has elapsed since it was last accessed…	Set the slidingExpiration property of the Cache.Add() method.
To define a delegate that gets called when data in the cache is about to expire…	Set the onRemoveCallBack property of the Cache.Add() method.
To insert an object in the cache that may already exist…	Use the Cache.Insert() method.

For ASP.NET applications, Cache is the recommended technique for storing user session data. Since this object is new with .NET, this option is not available to developers of old ASP applications—they are stuck using Session and Application.

The Cache object also comes with the unique ability to be able to call a function within your application once data is about to expire. You can then create some code that deals with the situation of when a session expires for increased security.

CERTIFICATION OBJECTIVE 8.02

Developing an Appropriate Deployment Model

Deployment is the process of moving an application from the development environment into the production environment. Depending on the application, the process of deployment can take anywhere from a few minutes to several months. A deployment model is a strategy that ensures a successful deployment.

When designing a model that ensures a successful deployment, the following issues should be taken into consideration:

- Deployment specifications
- Licensing specifications
- Data migration specifications
- Upgrade path

In this section, you will learn how these issues affect deployment.

author's
Ⓝote   *Microsoft TechNet contains an excellent deployment guide to help you design a deployment model at http://www.microsoft.com/technet/itsolutions/net/deploy/netdgv2.asp.*

Creating Deployment Specifications

There are five main methods for deploying Microsoft .NET applications:

- XCOPY
- Windows Installer
- MSI database utilities
- Microsoft Application Center 2000
- Microsoft Systems Management Server (SMS)

XCOPY is a command-line utility that can be used to copy files and directories en masse. .NET assemblies can, in most cases, simply be copied to the desired location on the target computer. The need for registering components or placing them in a specific directory such as C:\WINDOWS\SYSTEM has also been eliminated, making this type of deployment easier. The drawback to using XCOPY deployment is that the application will not get added to the Windows Start menu, will not be listed in Add/Remove Programs in the Control Panel, and a desktop shortcut icon will not be created.

Windows Installer replaces the Windows Cabinet (.CAB) deployment model in older versions of Windows. Windows Installer files end in the extension .MSI, and provide a flexible method of installation.

The *MSI database utilities*, contained in the msidb.exe tool, can be used to export and import Windows Installer databases, merge .MSI files, and apply certain transformations to these databases.

Microsoft Application Center 2000 provides tools for deploying .NET applications in a web server farm or load balanced environment. The servers in a multi-server environment can be treated as a single server, making things much easier to administer. Application Center can also be scripted using an API it exposes.

Microsoft Systems Management Server (SMS) is a software management tool that allows system administrators to manage hundreds or thousands of Windows computers remotely. It allows administrators to install new software to some or all of the desktops in an environment, monitor everything that is installed on each machine, and track the hardware/software configurations from one central location. SMS has been around for many years and is an established method of software deployment in many organizations.

Creating Licensing Specifications

It's important to understand what the licensing issues surrounding deployment are before development begins on an application. If you decide to use a third-party component in your application, you need to understand how much it will cost you to license use of that component and how to go about obtaining that license in case you discover too late that a component cannot be licensed due to cost or other factors.

There are usually two main issues surrounding licensing in a commercial application environment:

- Cost
- Usage restrictions

The issue with cost is fairly easy to understand: if you want to include software that is copyrighted or patented by someone else, you generally have to purchase or acquire a license for it. For instance, if you decided to develop a video player that includes support for the MPEG-4 video compression format, you will probably have to pay royalties to the Moving Picture Experts Group Licensing Administrator (MPEG LA) to gain the right to do so.

Other licensing costs relating to application development are for third-party applications that your application relies on. For instance, if your application creates Excel spreadsheet files, you will have to consider what the cost of providing everyone with a copy of Microsoft Office would be.

The second issue related to licensing is usage restrictions. Some software is licensed to all at no charge. The open-source and free software covered by the GNU Public License (GPL) comes to mind. But that license includes terms that restrict how the software can be used within other applications, sometimes including the requirement that any developers using the software must also release their source code under the GPL.

Creating Data Migration Specifications

As we stated in Chapter 5, a well thought-out database design will influence application design in a positive way, while a poorly thought-out database will have the opposite effect. One consideration that generally does not impact the database design process until this point is the nature and format of the existing data. *Data migration* is the process of transforming data from one format into another.

Data migration can sometimes be an irreversible process, such as when data is being modified "in place." That is, the data inside existing tables is simply being updated, not copied. It is a good idea to perform a database backup before performing the migration in case something goes wrong.

If your data currently exists as a stack of file folders sitting in large metal filing cabinets, you need to give some serious thought as to how you're going to get all that data into your application. Even if your data already exists in some electronic format, it is a wise idea to think about the logistics of transforming that data into the new format required by your application.

Some of the considerations that a data migration specification will have to take into consideration are

- What format is the data currently in?
- Will this be a one-time migration, or will you have to perform this task again several times in the future?
- Are there any other applications that rely on the data in the old format or location? Will data have to be maintained in two places?
- What tools can be developed or are already available to make this task easier?

The purpose of data migration specification is twofold. First, this specification needs to define the column mappings from the old data format to the new. For columns that did not exist in the old format, what defaults will they acquire?

The second purpose is to identify the logistical challenges (such as timing) with the data migration, and define how they will be overcome. For instance, if the database is extremely large, data migration could take hours. It is best to identify these potential issues early, before encountering them during the deployment process. If you schedule a deployment to take 2 hours, and then realize database conversion alone will take 18 hours, it will be too late to do anything to mitigate that.

One important point to remember when designing a data migration plan is that it is a good idea to include the use of a log file in your data migration script. After the data migration is complete, you should examine the log to determine what error messages were encountered along the way. This will allow you to fix the cause of the errors before running the script again.

on the

Job

In my experience, data migration is not usually a one-time event. You will likely want to test your data migration scripts out several times before running them in the production environment. You will also want to pre-populate the development and quality assurance (QA) databases for testing purposes. There will be times when the database gets into a state where it needs to be refreshed. Be prepared to run the data migration scripts several times, which is a good thing since it will help you find bugs in the scripts.

Designing the Upgrade Path

Deploying the first version of an application is usually quite straightforward—you just install the application. Not that the process of deployment is always easy, we just mean that you do not have to deal with the complexities of existing files, folders, applications, and settings.

When dealing with subsequent releases of your application, you always have to give some thought to the upgrade path. The upgrade path is the process of moving your users from the older version of the application to the new one, with as little hassle as possible. Some of the issues you may encounter when deploying an upgrade are

- Stopping the existing application if it is running
- Overwriting existing files and folders with newer versions
- Deleting application files that are no longer needed
- Retaining user settings and preferences

Alternatively, some applications choose to ignore the fact that a previous version existed and simply overwrite the older version as if it were a new installation. Other applications even require users to manually uninstall older versions of an application before the installation of the newer version can proceed. Neither of these alternate approaches is user friendly or necessary. A properly designed application will make it the upgrade path easier for users. Steps will usually be taken during the design stage to separate user settings into a separate file, and to standardize on file names and locations, to make it easier to upgrade the application in the future. The .NET Framework even allows applications to be upgraded while they are running.

CERTIFICATION OBJECTIVE 8.03

Creating the Physical Design for Maintenance

Ensuring that the application can be maintained once it is deployed is another important consideration for application design. As an application designer, you should try to answer several questions about the maintainability of your application before proceeding past the physical design phase, such as:

- Will application support staff have easy access to the application code in production to find and fix problems? Or is the production environment off limits to developers?

- What design changes can you make now to make it easier on yourself to debug problems after deployment? What additional auditing and logging should be implemented to support maintenance?

- How easy will it be for other developers to maintain your code after the application has been implemented? What types of documentation should be created during the development process to support maintenance?

It is sometimes hard to be thinking about what happens after implementation when coding hasn't even begun on the application. But you will discover that changes to the design that occur at this stage in design are much easier to implement than those that happen during or after implementation.

The ability for application developers to support an application during the maintenance phase is impacted by the type of application architecture chosen, for instance:

- **Single-tier architectures** The simplicity of the application design makes problems easier to find, fix, and test, but the stand-alone nature of the application makes it harder to deploy fixes. The same challenges in deploying the entire application will be faced for each bug fix or enhancement to be made.

- **Two-tier architectures** There will be bugs and enhancements that can be implemented by simply changing the server-side component of this application, but changes to the client will still be a hassle to deploy. Application bugs are a bit more difficult to find and fix because the application is broken into two components, either of which could be the problem.

- **Three-tier and *n*-tier architectures** Three-tier and *n*-tier applications are generally easier to maintain, because the amount of server-side code is more significant. However, finding bugs can be problematic because of all the components involved.

- **High and very-high availability** This is not technically an application architecture, although it deserves special mention. Applications that require 100 percent (or close) availability can also be difficult to maintain. This is because changes have to be coordinated between several clients and/or servers, and might have to be done without any system downtime. The seamlessness of the transition makes maintainability so difficult.

Designing Application Monitoring

When designing the deployment strategy for mission-critical applications, it is often important that there be some way to monitor their status after rollout. This can be accomplished in a variety of ways:

- A developer or support analyst performs a series of manual tests against the production application daily.

- An automated script is developed to regularly check the status of the application, server and database.

- A full-blown application monitoring tool is purchased or developed to check the status in real-time.

- The application itself can have some features that monitor its own performance, such as refusing new connections once CPU and/or memory usage reaches critical levels.

The responses of these monitoring tools to perceived problems can be varied as well. Some tools can be programmed to send an e-mail to key support personnel, or even dial a pager or mobile phone. More advanced tools can automatically reconfigure servers to bypass the potential problem until a support person can examine the issue. Some monitoring tools come with complex reporting features, providing support staff with accurate performance and availability benchmarks, which can help warn of potential problems before they occur.

CERTIFICATION OBJECTIVE 8.04

Creating the Physical Design for the Data Model

For relational databases, transforming the logical database design into a physical model is often not that difficult. The logical model does a good job of identifying the tables, their fields, the primary key or keys, and the relationships with other tables.

In order to convert a logical design into a physical one, three key properties must be added to the data model:

- Assign a system data type to each of the fields
- Define the physical file structure of the database, including file names and locations
- Identify frequently searched fields that need additional indexes for performance reasons

e x a m
ᗯatch

The MCSD 70-300 does not contain specific SQL syntax questions, although you have to understand how databases are modeled.

In this section, we will examine the issues related to designing the physical database design model.

Creating an Indexing Specification

In relational databases, an index is a special database construct that makes searching for data faster on a particular column or columns within a data table. There is a slight additional overhead for maintaining each index, so it is important not to index every column on every table. However, if there is a particular column that will frequently be used as one of the criteria in a search or a join operation, you should consider creating an index for that field.

Application developers do not need to specify particular indexes in their searches. The database server will intelligently make use of appropriate indexes when executing search or join operations by creating an *execution plan.* One of the important tools for database developers when tuning their applications for performance is to examine the execution plans for all the application queries, to see if adding more indexes could improve performance.

One important thing to remember when designing an indexing strategy is that primary keys do not need to be indexed. Primary keys are, by definition, already indexes. Databases already do their best to make searches against a primary key one of the most efficient database operations imaginable. On the other hand, foreign keys are not automatically indexes. Foreign keys are the most likely candidates to become indexes, because they are usually involved in join operations.

Generally speaking, there are two types of indexes: clustered and unclustered. A clustered index simply means that the data table is actually physically sorted according to the index itself. Any table can have at most one clustered index— usually the primary key. Unclustered indexes do not affect the order in which data is sorted on the physical disk drive. The database keeps a separate record of the sort order of the index, and can quickly link them to the existing sort order.

Certain columns make better indexes than others. Here are a few general guidelines for when to create indexes:

- Columns that are frequently sorted on using the ORDER BY clause should be indexed.

- Columns that participate in joins should always be indexed.

- The column that stores the primary key of the table is frequently made a clustered index, especially if it is used in join operations. There can only be one clustered index per table.

- A column that is often searched for in ranges of values could potentially be made a clustered index.

- Take the nature of your application into account. If the nature of your application is to frequently write to the database (such as an online transaction processing, or OLTP, application), then indexes can slow down your application. However, if the nature of your application is to frequently read from the database (such as an online analytical processing, or OLAP, application), then indexes will often speed up your application considerably.

Creating new indexes is often a task that happens near the end of the developing phase. A database administrator (DBA), working with members of the development team, can analyze the performance bottlenecks of all of the application's queries and reports.

Partitioning Data

In SQL Server, you can create a database table that is stored on two or more database servers. One way to do this is to split the data into *horizontal partitions*. A horizontal partition is a database table that only stores a subset of the total data. For example, look at the Sales table in Table 8-1.

A horizontally partitioned database table splits the database table based on the value in one of the columns. Looking at the example from Table 8-1, and assuming this Sales table consists of millions of data rows similar to those examples shown, we can split this table between the two sales offices: office number 32 and office number 13. We can set up and install two SQL Server machines, one in each of the offices, to handle the primary database workload. The tables are separate from each other, as each machine only handles search requests for the data in the tables it manages. But behind the scenes the two databases are linked, as you could easily run a search request against all the rows in the Sales database, and the results would return matches from both offices.

One of the biggest drawbacks to using partitioned tables is that you use the ability to manage unique keys between the two servers. Therefore, you must partition the tables based on a column that is unique to each one, such as the Office ID. Even though Sales ID would normally server on its own as a primary key, because the tables are partitioned the Office ID becomes part of the key as well.

TABLE 8-1	Office ID	Sales ID	Customer ID	Product ID	Quantity
The Sales Table Data for All Offices	32	0000121	1236	020165783X	5
	32	0000122	1298	1861000871	4
	13	0000363	2213	020165783X	6
	13	0000364	2213	1861000871	4

CERTIFICATION OBJECTIVE 8.05

Validating the Physical Design

The final step of the physical design phase is to validate the design. Like conceptual and logical designs, physical designs are validated against the business and user requirements to ensure that the system meets the needs of the user. Since the physical design phase has approached the design from a technical view, the following eight items in particular should be taken into consideration during the validation:

- Performance
- Maintainability
- Extensibility
- Scalability
- Availability
- Deployability
- Security
- Accessibility

In this section, we will review the effectiveness of the proposed design against those fundamental technical requirements.

Reviewing the Effectiveness of the Proposed Physical Design

The effectiveness of application *performance* is a bit difficult to judge when you are still in the design phase of application development. Certainly the best conclusion that you can come to about application performance is that all of the potential bottlenecks in the system have been identified, and efforts have been made to mitigate those problems. If you realize that the wide area network (WAN) will be the slowest part of the system for your users, and then ensure servers are being physically placed as close to users' office locations as possible, one can conclude that adequate thought has been given to performance.

We talked a bit about *maintainability* earlier in this chapter. Basically, the application should be easy to support over a period of many months and years. This includes the ability to find and fix bugs, and implement some minor new features every once in a while.

Extensibility is the ease with which an application can have new features added to it. Obviously, an application's design should not unnecessarily limit what features get added to an application over time.

Scalability is the ability for an application to handle increased load. This is not to say that an application needs to support 1 million concurrent users on its 32 MB Pentium 333 MHz computer. But could an application support 1 million users were there a powerful server farm for it to run on? You should at least understand the upper limit to how many users or transactions your application will be able to support, to ensure it meets the current and future needs of the business.

Availability is the requirement that an application be available for use during certain periods of time. Availability is usually expressed as a percentage, where 100 percent availability implies absolutely no downtime allowed during defined periods of time. For 24 hours-per-day, 7 days-a-week systems, 100 percent availability is very difficult (and very expensive) to achieve.

Deployability, which was discussed earlier in this chapter in the section entitled "Developing an Appropriate Deployment Model", is the ability of an application to be deployed. Some application architectures, such as ASP.NET web sites, are easier to deploy—deployment can literally be done in a second by copying an updated .ASPX file to a specific location. However, other applications require significant planning and effort to deploy, such as distributed, highly available *n*-tier applications.

You should validate the application design to ensure that it meets the user and business requirements in terms of *security* as well. Will the application be able to properly identify users using authentication? And will it be able to block out unauthorized users using authorization?

And finally, *accessibility* is a measurement of how easily your application can be used by people with disabilities, especially the various forms of blindness. Does it rely too much on colors to differentiate between items, thereby making it harder to use for people with color blindness? Does your web-based application follow the W3C's Web Accessibility Initiative (WAI) standards? These standards can be read at http://www.w3.org/WAI/.

author's note *Visual disabilities are only one of the disability categories accessibility tries to address. Other disabilities that need to be considered include hearing, mobility, and cognitive.*

At this point, the physical application design is complete. There is only one step in the application design process remaining, before coding can begin on the application, and that is incorporating standards into the design. This will be the topic of the next chapter.

CERTIFICATION SUMMARY

The physical design phase applies technical constraints to the application logical design. Whereas the conceptual and logical design phases were approached from the point of view of the business, physical design is approached from the developer's point of view. At the end of the physical design phase, you should have detailed enough technical specifications to begin development.

Many technical constraints need to be added to the application, including auditing and logging, error handling, security and privacy, designing the presentation layer, and managing user session states. The Microsoft .NET Framework provides many components to help application developers handle these tasks programming-wise.

The physical design model also takes into consideration deployment issues such as deployment specifications, licensing, data migration, and upgrading applications. Although application development has not started, you may be able to make a few changes to application design at this stage to help with the potential issues with deployment.

Application maintenance is also an issue that really doesn't come up until after deployment. But once again, application designers have an opportunity during the design stage to make the application easier to support in the future. This can be anything from having the application log more information to setting up full-blown application monitoring servers.

The physical data model design happens during this stage of development as well. Physical database design involves assigning data types to columns, deciding what type of indexes need to be created, and finding and configuring database servers. Developers can employ a technique called horizontal partitioning to split a database table into sets of rows that are divided between several servers. Applications can search these partitioned tables just as if they were hosted on a single server.

Physical design model validation, like that of conceptual and logical design model, centers on a comparison of the application design to the user and business design documents. Does the application fill the needs of the business? There are also some key technical benchmarks for application technical design, such as performance, maintainability, deployability, security, availability, accessibility, scalability, and extensibility.

✓ TWO-MINUTE DRILL

Deriving a Physical Design for the Solution

- ❏ Physical application design is a process that applies technical constraints to the logical design model.

- ❏ Physical design also involves defining data structures, Application Programming Interfaces (APIs), and a data dictionary.

- ❏ An *application log* records specific events that you want to record, such as application errors. An *audit log* records system activity for the purpose of after-the-fact application security.

- ❏ During the logical design phase, logging was added to support business purposes. During the physical design phase, the purpose is technical, such as usage monitoring.

- ❏ Windows has a built-in logging facility, and comes with three default logs: System, Security and Application. These logs can be accessed using the Windows Event Viewer.

- ❏ .NET applications access the Windows event logs using the EventLog component that lives in the System.Diagnostics namespace.

- ❏ Error handling is the ability for an application to detect and intelligently respond to errors that occur within the application, instead of just crashing.

- ❏ BizTalk Server is a Microsoft server product that makes application integration easier among different diverse platforms and applications.

- ❏ Microsoft .NET provides a complete set of security classes under the System.Security.Cryptography namespace of the .NET Framework. Many of these classes are managed-code wrappers to the Microsoft CryptoAPI cryptography functions built into Windows.

- ❏ Role-based security is highly recommended, as it restricts application components to running in the security context of users. Thus, even successful attacks such as buffer overflows will not give hackers system-level access to an application.

- ❏ There are two classes in .NET that provide an authentication mechanism within your applications: *WindowsPrincipal* and *GenericPrincipal*. The WindowsPrincipal class integrates into the security model built into

Windows, while the GenericPrincipal allows application to implement their own security model. Developers can create their own custom principal class if they wish to extend these features at all.

❏ A *component* is a piece of code that provides a service to other components within the environment, but is not an application itself.

❏ *Session state* is the data an application has to remember in order to be able to come back and restart a session from where it left off.

❏ The built-in Session and Application objects allow ASP.NET developers to store data for use later in the current session, or for use by other objects within the application. This, however, is an old way of storing user data.

❏ The Cache object is the new recommended technique for storing user data on the server. It is highly configurable, and can even be configured to call a function, as user data is about to expire.

Developing an Appropriate Deployment Model

❏ There are five main methods for deploying applications in .NET: XCOPY, Windows Installer, MSI database utilities, Microsoft Application Center, and Systems Management Server.

❏ A license is a legal right granted to a user by the license owner to use a piece of intellectual property. Licenses often cost money, and some have severe restrictions as to what you can do with the code.

❏ Data migration is the process of converting data from one format to another. This generally involves converting data from a legacy file format into Microsoft SQL Server.

❏ When designing the second and subsequent releases of an application, special consideration has to be given to retaining the user's setting and preferences when they upgrade to the new version of the application.

Creating the Physical Design for Maintenance

❏ It is important to include a plan for maintenance in system design since you may be able to include features in the application that will make it easier to support once it has been deployed.

❑ It is generally easier to support a server-based application, since a faulty server-based component can usually be fixed and implemented without difficulty. Implementing changes to client-side applications and components is often more difficult.

❑ Depending on the nature of your application, you may want to include some support for application monitoring. Monitoring an application will help you to respond to problems faster, and address issues before they become problems.

Creating the Physical Design for the Data Model

❑ The first goal of physical database design is finishing off the data model, by adding data types and indexes to the model.

❑ The next goal is to prepare the database management system for application development. This involves choosing development, testing, and production servers to host the application and designing the physical file structure of the database.

❑ Indexes can improve database performance significantly by pre-sorting frequently searched columns.

❑ There is a certain amount of additional overhead maintaining an index, so you probably do not want to index every column.

❑ The database server will intelligently make use of appropriate indexes when executing search operations by creating an *execution plan.*

❑ Data tables can be *horizontally partitioned,* so that sets of data rows in the table can be stored on separate SQL Server machines.

Validating the Physical Design

❑ Physical designs are validated against the business and user requirements to ensure the design meets the needs of the end user.

❑ Designs need to be analyzed from a technical point of view to ensure that they meet the organizational standards in terms of performance, maintainability, extensibility, scalability, availability, deployability, security, and accessibility.

❑ Analyze the potential performance bottlenecks of the application and see if any changes need to be made to the design.

SELF TEST

The following questions will help you measure your understanding of the material presented in this chapter. Read all the choices carefully because there might be more than one correct answer. Choose all correct answers for each question.

Deriving a Physical Design for the Solution

1. Which of the following statements best describes the purpose of the physical design model?

    A. To choose the architecture model of the application.

    B. To determine the schedule of application design, and provide cost estimates for the solution.

    C. To apply technical constraints to the logical design.

    D. To turn Visio class diagrams into actual .NET skeleton code.

2. Which of the following considerations will be taken into account during the physical design process? (Choose all that apply.)

    A. Security

    B. Error handling

    C. Identify business objects

    D. User interface design

3. Which Windows application would you use to access the log records generated by the Windows security system?

    A. Event Viewer

    B. Event Logger

    C. Log Viewer

    D. Internet Explorer

4. Which .NET Framework component must you include in your application in order to write to the application log?

    A. System.Log.EventViewer

    B. System.Diagnostics.Log

    C. System.Log.Events

    D. System.Diagnostics.EventLog

5. Which of the following are event severities that can be found in an event log? (Choose all that apply.)

    A. Error

    B. Success Audit

    C. Security

    D. Serious

6. Jand'l is an intermediate developer at one of the country's largest banks. He has developed a small financial calculator component in VB .NET that will calculate the monthly principal and interest payments required for mortgages and loans. This component is used by several applications within the organization, mostly without problems. Whenever the component encounters a situation it can't handle, it raises an exception to pass a message back to the calling application. Which of the following statements best describes how the .NET runtime handles exceptions generated by components of an application, if the calling application itself does not catch them?

    A. If the calling application does not handle the exception, the .NET runtime will ignore it.

    B. This cannot occur, since .NET compilers make sure that all components within an application have their exceptions handled.

    C. The exception will be passed back to other applications and components, until one of them handles the exception. If the exception remains unhandled when it reaches the .NET runtime level, an error message will be displayed to the user.

    D. The exception will be passed back to other applications and components, until one of them handles the exception. An error message will be displayed to the user regardless if the exception is handled or not.

7. Which Microsoft server product supports hundreds of adapters to make enterprise application integration (EAI) easier?

    A. Content Management Server (CMS)

    B. Systems Management Server (SMS)

    C. Exchange Server

    D. BizTalk Server

8. Trevor is a junior programmer at a large, multi-national human resources consulting firm. Trevor has been asked to recommend a security model for the .NET-based application his project team is working on. The application's user IDs and passwords will be stored inside a SQL Server database. Which .NET Framework component can be used to enable an application to use its own user ID and password authentication system?

   A. ApplicationPrincipal

   B. WindowsPrincipal

   C. GenericPrincipal

   D. WindowsSecurity

9. Which of the following statements best describes the primary benefit of object pooling?

   A. Allows business objects to be installed on multiple servers, thereby improving overall application performance.

   B. Instantiates multiple identical objects to serve application requests, thereby ensuring a single, long-running transaction does not affect application performance for other users.

   C. Establishes a set of open database connections available for use within the application, which removes the need for objects to initialize those connections, thereby improving application performance.

   D. Allows data objects to share their resources with one another, thereby improving overall resource usage.

Developing an Appropriate Deployment Model

10. My nephew Jarryle just received a laptop for his birthday, and the first thing he wanted to do with it was develop a web-based card trading application. This ASP.NET application will allow him to list some of the trading cards he no longer needs, and see if any of his friends in the neighborhood have cards he would like to get. Jarryle is almost finished with the application physical design, when he begins to worry about deployment. Which of the following deployment techniques is best suited for ASP.NET applications to remote clients?

    A. XCOPY deployment

    B. Microsoft Windows Installer

    C. Microsoft Systems Management Server (SMS)

    D. None of the above

11. Besides cost, which of the following is the other major issue that needs to be taken into consideration when it comes to licensing third-party software and components to be used in your application?

   A. Application support

   B. Usage restrictions

   C. Deployment

   D. Copyrights and patents

Creating the Physical Design for Maintenance

12. Aaron has recently given up his career as a musician to become a professional application developer at a major security firm. His first task is to design and develop a software application that will be used to track security card usage in large office towers. Once he has developed his application, it will be rolled out to each of the hundreds of office towers his security firm protects. Although the application is two-tier, each office tower will have its own client and server machines independent of the head office. There is no central network connecting the office towers. Aaron is aware that architecture has certain flaws. Which of the following statements best describes this application's biggest maintenance problem?

   A. This application will be difficult to maintain and support because there is no central network connecting the machines.

   B. This application will be difficult to support and maintain because it uses a two-tier architecture instead of a one-tier architecture.

   C. Once the application is deployed, it will be impossible to upgrade the application to fix any bugs.

   D. Once the application is developed, it will be impossible to deploy the application for the first time due to the number of office towers.

13. Michael works for a large, multi-national corporation that has offices in 20 countries across 3 continents. He is part of a team that is developing a distributed, *n*-tier application for customer and client management. The application servers will be placed in several key offices around the world, to improve application responsiveness in those regions. One of Michael's concerns is monitoring server performance from his office in Manila, Philippines. The application will probably employ some external monitoring application, but Michael would like to include the ability within his application for servers to report their own performance to a central database

for statistical purposes. Which two components in the .NET Framework allow applications access to the process and performance monitoring capabilities built into Windows 2000 servers?

A. The APP2UI and APP4UI components in System.Performance

B. The ServerProcess and ServerPerformance components in System.Diagnostics

C. The CPU and Memory components in System.Process

D. The Process and Performance components in System.Diagnostics

Creating the Physical Design for the Data Model

14. Which of the following statements best describes how unclustered indexes improve the performance of data-oriented applications?

A. Unclustered indexes often significantly improve the performance of referential integrity checks by foreign keys. Referential integrity involves a lot of data searching, and since indexes improve the performance of searching in general, they improve referential integrity checks as well.

B. Unclustered indexes can significantly improve the performance of data inserts into the database. Every time a record is inserted into the database, the server first searches the unclustered indexes to ensure there are no duplicate keys.

C. Unclustered indexes change the physical sort order of the records on the hard disk, making it much quicker to search for a specific value. Since the database server can stop searching when it finds a value, it often significantly decreases the number of records that the server will have to search through in the data table.

D. Unclustered indexes do not change the physical sort order of the records on the disk, but keep their own sorted lists, apart from the data. When the database server can search an index first, it often significantly decreases the number of records that the server will have to search through in the data table.

15. What is the term used to describe a data table whose rows have been split across multiple and often distributed SQL Server instances?

A. Table splitting

B. Horizontal partition

C. Distributed computing

D. Normalization

Validating the Physical Design

16. Leander has been asked to ensure that his application "scales." To which feature of sound technical design does the term "scalability" refer?

A. Scalability refers to the ability of a mission-critical application to stay up and running a long time without service interruption.

B. Applications that can easily accommodate a new feature or module without application architecture redesign are said to "scale" well.

C. Applications that can handle increasing user load without application redesign are said to "scale" well.

D. Scalability refers to the ability of vision-impaired users to be able to hear the web page read out to them.

LAB QUESTION

Match the following error log severities in the left column with the corresponding descriptions in the right column.

Severity	Description
A. Information	1. An audited event has succeeded.
B. Warning	2. An infrequent but successful operation.
C. Error	3. A problem that is not immediately significant.
D. SuccessAudit	4. An audited event has failed.
E. FailureAudit	5. A significant problem.

SELF TEST ANSWERS

Deriving a Physical Design for the Solution

1. ☑ C. The purpose of physical design is to apply technical constraints to the logical design.
   ☒ A is incorrect because the architecture model of the application was determined during the solutions concept stage of envisioning. B is incorrect because estimates and costing are part of envisioning, and do not enter into application design. D is incorrect because actual .NET code does not get created until the developing phase.

2. ☑ A, B, and D. Security, error handling, and user interface design are all issues that get addressed during the physical design process.
   ☒ C is incorrect because business objects should have been identified during the conceptual and logical design stages.

3. ☑ A. The Event Viewer application lets users examine the records in the Windows event logs.
   ☒ B is incorrect because there is no Windows application called Event Logger. C is incorrect because there is no Windows application called Log Viewer. D is incorrect because Internet Explorer cannot be used to view the event logs.

4. ☑ D. The System.Diagnostics namespace contains a component called EventLog that allows applications to write to the event log.
   ☒ A is incorrect because there is no System.Log namespace. B is incorrect because there is no class called Log in the System.Diagnostics. C is incorrect because there is no System.Log namespace.

5. ☑ A and B. Error and success audit are two of the five event severities that can be found in Windows event logs.
   ☒ C is incorrect because Security is one of the default logs, not a severity. D is incorrect because Serious is not a severity in the event logs.

6. ☑ C. Other code along the chain of function calls will be first given a chance to handle the exception, and only if the exception remains unhandled will the runtime handle it by displaying an error message.
   ☒ A is incorrect because unhandled exceptions are not ignored. B is incorrect because applications can use components without handling all (or any) of their exceptions. D is incorrect because, once an exception is handled, it will stop being passed.

7. ☑ **D.** BizTalk Server is the Microsoft server whose job it is to coordinate communications between disparate servers.

☒ **A** is incorrect because Content Management Server deals primarily with web site management. **B** is incorrect because Systems Management Server deals primarily with application deployment. **C** is incorrect because Exchange Server deals mainly with e-mail and office communications.

8. ☑ **C.** The GenericPrincipal component allows .NET applications to handle their own security.

☒ **A** is incorrect because there is no such component as an ApplicationPrincipal. **B** is incorrect because the WindowsPrincipal helps applications with Windows-managed security. **D** is incorrect because there is no component called WindowsSecurity.

9. ☑ **B.** Object pooling allows several identical objects to serve multiple clients at once, thus ensuring one long-running request does not hold up other clients. This is just like having multiple checkout lines open at the grocery. The person who needs a price check does not have to hold up everyone behind, because there are other cashiers available.

☒ **A** is incorrect because object pooling is not related to distributed application setup. **C** is incorrect because this answer describes database pooling. **D** is incorrect because data objects use other techniques for data sharing, such as the Application object.

Developing an Appropriate Deployment Model

10. ☑ **D.** ASP.NET applications can be installed entirely on a web server, thus avoiding the deployment issue altogether. The application is accessed using a web browser.

☒ **A** is incorrect because ASP.NET applications are not deployed to client machines. **B** is incorrect because there are no components that need to be installed using Windows Installer. **C** is incorrect because Microsoft Systems Management Server is too complex for an eight-year-old to install and configure. And besides, SMS is used for desktop applications, not web-based applications.

11. ☑ **B.** Software licensing often places usage restrictions on the circumstances under which software can be used. It can also obligate the organization to certain responsibilities, such as posting a link to the developer's web site or releasing the modified code out to everyone.

☒ **A** is incorrect because applications need to be supported in largely the same manner as they would without the licensed component. Not having source code might be an issue for some, but not many. **C** is incorrect because licensed components are deployed in much the same way as regular components. **D** is incorrect because you do not have to worry about copyrights and patents when using a licensed component.

Creating the Physical Design for Maintenance

12. ☑ **A.** Having to support hundreds of unconnected offices will present the most maintenance challenges to this project.
☒ **B** is incorrect because having a one-tier or two-tier architecture makes very little difference from a maintenance perspective in this example. **C** is incorrect because the application's bug fixes and product enhancements can be deployed using CD-ROM and by other means, so it is not impossible to maintain. **D** is incorrect because the application itself can be deployed using CD-ROM and by other means, so it is not impossible to deploy.

13. ☑ **D.** The Process and Performance components provide server monitor capabilities to .NET applications.
☒ **A** is incorrect because there is no namespace called System.Performance. **B** is incorrect because there are no components named ServerProcess or ServerPerformance. **C** is incorrect because there is no namespace named System.Process.

Creating the Physical Design for the Data Model

14. ☑ **D.** The database server often saves itself a lot of time by looking up certain fields first in the related index, which narrows down the number of data records that need to be searched in the main database table.
☒ **A** is incorrect because foreign keys rely on the primary keys of other tables, and primary keys are indexes, usually clustered, by default. **B** is incorrect because indexes make insert operations take longer, since the index needs to be updated as well after every insert operation. **C** is incorrect because unclustered indexes do not change the sort order on disk.

15. ☑ **B.** Dividing the rows of a data table across multiple servers is called horizontal splitting.
☒ **A** is incorrect because table splitting is not an official term. **C** is incorrect because distributed computing refers to distributed applications and components, not databases. **D** is incorrect because normalization has a different meaning.

Validating the Physical Design

16. ☑   C. Scalability is the ability of an application to handle an increased load without application redesign.

    ☒   A is incorrect because this description refers to availability. **B** is incorrect because extensibility refers to the ability to add new features to an application. **D** is incorrect because the ability for people of differing abilities to use an application is called accessibility.

LAB ANSWER

The answer is:

A. 2

B. 3

C. 5

D. 1

E. 4

9

Developing Standards for Your Solution

I n this chapter, we will look at establishing standards, processes, and quality and performance metrics. Standards are an effective way for your project staff to have a common set of criteria to follow when designing and developing your solution. This extends to user, code, and project documents, allowing for a consistent look and feel for those documents. By establishing standards for what types of documents to generate, the team can focus on gathering the appropriate information.

These standards can extend into coding practices, such as source code formatting and naming conventions. There are also user interface standards for Windows and web applications. Although these application types each have different needs, we will analyze some of their common characteristics. Finally, there are testing standards, which determine how much or how little testing you need to perform. Testing standards also define how testing should be configured and implemented.

An important part of the development lifecycle is code and document review. Code reviews help to enforce standards in the development process. This examination helps ensure that the team agrees on how to solve the problem and develop the solution. Microsoft Visual SourceSafe is a common tool for maintaining code and configuration information. Visual SourceSafe has advanced features for handling single and multiple checkouts and can handle deployments and maintenance of code releases.

The testing and deployment phase helps to focus on the transition from building features to focusing on quality. Quality and performance metrics make predictions about the release date, bug quantity or severity, the bug resolution progress, and the quality of the solution. Accurate predictions result from applying effective techniques such as assuming a fixed ship date mindset and using bug convergence and zero bug bounce as stabilizing indicators.

CERTIFICATION OBJECTIVE 9.01

Establishing Standards

In this section, we will begin by discussing documentation standards ranging from standards for initial requirements documents to those for final support documentation and end user documentation. The examination will cover the types of documents used in a project and their purpose. Next, we will discuss user interface standards. The effective application of proper user interface design is an essential task for the developer because the user interface is the only part of the application most users will see, and all opinions will be formulated based on that small portion of the application. Last, we will examine standards for testing, which determine if the project requirements have been met and are correct.

Documentation Standards

Solutions documents come in many forms. There is user documentation, project documentation, and developer documentation. The development of documentation standards is important for providing a consistent look and feel for developers, users, and others in the organization.

Fundamentally, the creation of documentation is a business decision, not really a technical one. Although it may sound strange, documentation takes time and resources. To the stakeholders, that time and those resources are money that could be spent in other ways. Therefore, the stakeholders decide the types of documentation that will satisfy their needs, and those types can be determined using an adopted business methodology or can be custom defined.

Documentation is a communication tool. When working with groups of people, face-to-face discussions are not always possible. For this reason, documentation is a great support mechanism for communicating with users and stakeholders. However, without verbal communication, documents can be misleading because in order to understand them fully requires interpretation.

exam
ⓌatcH

Documentation is not a replacement for face-to-face discussions.

Another purpose of documentation is to help verify that you understand the information. Basically, you are creating a written expression of your understanding of the problem or solution. Because writing it down requires you to think through logical steps and solutions, it can help you discover issues that were not previously considered. For example, creating code comments before coding helps you think about what you are trying to achieve and to determine if the approach you are taking is the correct way to achieve it.

exam
ⓌatcH

Creating documentation is a process for thinking about how to solve a solution or problem.

User Documentation

User documentation explains how the solution works. You can gather much of the information needed for this explanation from the use cases defined for the project and from the user interface. The goal is to provide the information in a way that assists the user in performing specific tasks. For example, if a user is looking for help on how to create a user account, the documentation should provide a path that details how to perform that task. Further, user documentation usually includes common elements such as a table of contents, a glossary, and a quick index.

You can produce user documentation in different formats. Hypertext Markup Language (HTML) is one option, and a number of third-party tools are available to create documentation in HTML format. HTML documentation can be a great tool for users who are in different locations because it is easy to deploy. It can be time-consuming to generate and maintain, however, so you should take into consideration the available resources for those tasks.

Another option is to create external Help files. Windows forms support this type of help by using the HelpProvider component. HelpProvider is a .NET native object that resides in the System.Forms.HelpProvider namespace. Identified in the following table are key properties and methods of the HelpProvider component.

Property or Method	Description
HelpNamespace property	Specifies the name of the Help file
SetHelpKeyword method	Provides the key information, from the Help file specified by HelpNamespace, for retrieving the help associated with this control
SetHelpString method	Specifies the Help string associated with the specified control

HTML Help Workshop (Hhw.exe) is a Help authoring tool with an easy-to-use graphical interface for creating Help project files, HTML topic files, contents files, index files, and everything else you need to put together a Help system or Help web site. This tool supports creating a resource .DLL file for language-specific information. This option is more difficult to deploy because it requires more developer interaction and therefore is not a standalone solution.

The last type of format for user documentation is a traditional manual document. In a manual document, screen shots are incorporated and instructions are contained within some type of binder. Manual documents share some common characteristics with the other documentation methods described here, such as a table of contents, a glossary, and a quick index. This option requires no developer interaction but can be difficult to distribute due to the labor and time required to copy, bind, and mail each copy. There are ways to make this easier, however, such as by creating electronic copies of the manual and distributing them via company e-mail.

You can use distribution methods other than the web and Help files. For example, using e-mail to distribute help documentation.

Project Documentation

Project documentation provides a high-level analysis of the business and solution. Project documents describe each phase of the project from inception to completion. One example of a project document is the vision/scope document, which defines the system at a high level with defined boundaries. Also in this document are cost estimates, a risk analysis, staffing requirements, and the project milestones. A typical project also contains other types of project documents that detail project tasks, requirements, high-level use cases, and testing procedures. The project team creates project documents during various phases.

Requirements Documents   Requirements documents are one of the first sets of documents created when starting a project. These types of documents detail what the solution is required to accomplish. Documents such as use cases, UML, and data flow diagrams, on the other hand, are considered architecture documents. Architecture documents detail how the solution, in technical terms, is going to be solved.

Functional Specifications   The functional specification is the basis for building the master project plan and schedule. It is maintained as a detailed description, as viewed from the user perspective, of what the solution will look like and how it will behave. Note that a functional specification can be changed only with customer approval.

Interface Documents   An interface document details how different systems interact. This information should contain sample data because it helps with the creation of testing and support documentation for determining if the system is working properly. An interface document may be a simple document or a very complex one, depending on the systems involved. For example, when working with web services, you need to provide documentation to the developer that explains the methods available from the web service. For some systems, there is an interchange between different types of data files. By having examples, the developer and support personnel have an idea of how to create code to accommodate the interface.

Support Documents   Support documents range from administrator user documents to deployment scripts. The purpose of support documents is to give other types of users, such as technical support personnel, network administrators, and security administrators, information on how to use the solution. Each type of user has different perspectives on roles and responsibilities as far as a solution is concerned.

Technical support personnel care about how the application functions for users but also need a more detailed view about how the processes work and how to fix users' problems. This type of documentation may also include specialized tools for support personnel or details about how to execute specific scripts to fix problems. For example, the solution could need some customized security maintenance tools to be created for support.

- **Deployment Documents**   Network administrators are concerned about how to install and deploy the application. Deployment documents detail how to deploy the solution into the testing and production environments, which in a typical company is not done by developers. Network administrators or testing personnel set up and deploy to the testing and production environments for the solution. This separation of environments is necessary to allow the testing of the deployment process before going to the production environment.

- **Security Documents**   Security administrators want to know how to manage the security of the solution. Security documentation is similar to user documentation except that it details only administrative tasks, such as how to add new users. Security documents detail the security functionality within the application and explain how to implement it. The project team and users define security roles and permissions to determine who needs access to all or various parts of the solution.

Developer Documentation

Developer documentation is created specifically for developers, to provide them details on how to create the solution, and it can come in several forms: physical documents, electronic documents or diagrams, and code comments. These documents cover the whole spectrum of the development process, ranging from the approval of the solution concept to project deployment. They include functional specification documents, use cases, system and component diagrams (UML and/or data flow diagrams), system operational documents, and source code.

Developer Response Documents

Another type of developer-specific document is one that takes the project tasks and turns them into developer language. This document is called a *response document*. From this type of document, developers can be assigned tasks and responsibilities. The purpose of a response document is to take the tasks defined from a project point of view and turn them into developer-sensible types of tasks, which is also a useful way to determine overlaps in task responsibilities and components. The general structure of a response document is as follows:

Section	Description
Task name	This usually includes a unique identifier associated with the requirement being solved, along with the requirement name.
Task description	This generally is a short summary of the requirement being solved. This description can be technical or nontechnical.
Dependencies	These identify other tasks and external systems that are required to complete the task.
Steps required	This section lists the steps required to complete this development task, including steps for SQL, steps for other non-code dependencies, and programming steps.

Code Comments   Code comments should be self-documenting, meaning that they should make clear the purpose of the code. Comments should make the code understandable for other developers. Here are some key commenting techniques recommended by Microsoft:

- Keep comments up-to-date when modifying code.
- Put boilerplate comments before the start of each method. For example:

```
/*
Developer: [Developer]
Date: [Date]
Method Name:
Purpose: Example of Sample Formatted Boilerplate Template
*/
```

- Avoid adding comments at the end of a line of code; however, end-of-line comments are appropriate for variable declarations. For example:

```
int iCounter = 0; //This is an acceptable place for a comment.
versus
if ( sStatus == "Employee ReHire" ) // This is a bad place for a comment.
```

- Avoid using lines of asterisks in your code comments because it can be very cluttering. Use white space instead.

- Before development, clean up comments to avoid confusion during future maintenance.

- Use comments to detail complex sections of code.

- Use complete sentences when writing comments.

- Avoid extraneous comments.

- Use comments to explain the intent of the code.

- When bugs are found, comment them and note what caused the bug as well as the fix for it.

- Use a uniformed style in commenting code; that is, the code should have the same look and feel throughout.

- Use white space to separate comments from comment delimiters. For example:

```
//This is a sample comment (incorrect).
// This is a sample comment (correct; notice the use of white space).
```

XML Documentation   C# has additional documentation features that allow for the creation of XML documentation files. The C# compiler option to generate the XML comments is /doc. The standard C# comments begin with // for inline comments or /* ... */ for code blocks. In the source code, the comments start with /// instead of the standard C# comments. To use the generated .xml file for use with the VS.NET IntelliSense feature, the filename of the .xml file should be the same as the assembly you want to support and the .xml file should be in the same directory as the assembly.

If you were compiling the assembly from the command line, you would use the following syntax for C#:

```
csc XMLsample.cs /doc:XMLsample.xml
```

or this syntax for VB:

```
vbc XMLsample.vb /doc:XMLsample.xml
```

This can also be accomplished in the Visual Studio environment by following these steps:

1. Open the project's Property Pages dialog box.
2. Click the Configuration Properties folder.
3. Click the Build property page.
4. Modify the XML Documentation File property.

We will perform these steps later in the XML documentation example. A feature to be aware of in the environment setup is incremental builds. Incremental builds allow the assembly to be built more quickly by examining only the changes since the last build and compiling those items. Because the entire project is not being rebuilt, the XML documentation file property is ignored.

exam
Watch

The /doc switch will be ignored in a compilation that uses /incremental; use /incremental- to ensure that the XML documentation file is up-to-date.

The following table lists the XML documentation tags most commonly used in user documentation. The compiler will process any tags that are valid XML. The documentation tags require delimiters to indicate where the documentation comments begin and end.

<c>	<para>	<see>
<code>	<param>	<seealso>
<example>	<paramref>	<summary>
<exception>	<permission>	<value>
<include>	<remarks>	
<list>	<returns>	

The default /// delimiter format can be seen in documented examples in the Microsoft Developer Network (MSDN) and in the C# project templates. A feature of the Visual Studio integrated development environment (IDE) for the automatic insertion of the <summary> and </summary> tags is called *smart comment editing*. This feature is activated after typing /// at the appropriate location in the code. The common syntax for block comments is /* … */.

Following are the tags for the XML documentation, including an example of each tag:

- The <summary> tag is one of the main tags. This tag is used to describe members, and it is the primary source of information about the type in IntelliSense. This information is also displayed in the Object Browser and Code Comment Web Report.

  Syntax: <summary>*description*</summary>

  Example:

  ```
  /// <summary> My Method is a method in the class.
  /// <para>This creates a second paragraph.
  /// See cref="System.Console.WriteLine"/> for information.
  /// </para>
  /// <seealso cref="MyClass.Main"/>
  /// </summary>
  ```

- The <value> tag describes a property.

  Syntax: <value>*property-description*</value>

  Example:

  ```
  /// <value> Name accesses the value of the name data member.</value>
  public string Name
  ```

exam
Watch *When using the Visual Studio .NET development environment, it will add a <summary> tag for the new property, so you will need to add the <value> tag.*

- The <c> tag indicates that text within a description should be marked as code.

  Syntax: <c>*text*</c>

Example:

```
/// <summary><c>MyMethod</c> is a method in the <c>MyClass</c> class.
/// </summary>
```

■ The <code> tag indicates multiple lines as code.

Syntax: <code>*content*</code>

Example:

```
<code>
int x = 1;
int y = 5;
</code>
```

■ The <example> tag lets you specify how to use a method or other members.
This tag is commonly used with the <code> tag.

Syntax: <example>*description*</example>

Example:

```
/// <summary>
/// Summary Text
/// </summary>
/// <example>
/// <code>
/// class MyClass
/// {
///    public static int Main()
///    {
///        return GetZero();
///    }
/// }
/// </code>
/// </example>
```

■ The <exception> tag lets you specify which exceptions can be thrown. This
tag is generally applied to a method definition.

Syntax: <exception cref="*member*">*description*</exception>

The compiler checks that the given exception exists, translates it into
a member in the XML, and must be in double quotation marks.

Example:

```
/// <exception cref="System.Exception">Thrown when …</exception>
```

- The <include> tag lets you use an external comment file to describe the types and members in your source code. This is an alternative to placing documentation comments directly in your source code file. The <include> tag uses the XML XPath syntax.

   Syntax: <include file='filename' path='tagpath[@*name*="*id*"]' />

- *Filename* is the name of the file containing the documentation. The filename is enclosed in single quotation marks. The path can be included with the filename.

- *Tagpath* is the path of the tags in the filename that leads to the specific tag name. The filename is enclosed in single quotation marks.

- *Name* is the name specifier in the tag that precedes the comments; if the name is specified, the *id* is also used.

- *Id* identifies the tag that precedes the comments. The *id* is enclosed in double quotation marks.

   Example:

   ```
   ///<include file='xml_include_tag.doc'path='root/node[@name="test"]/*'/>
   ```

- The <list> tag allows the creation of multiple types of lists to appear in the XML. The list can create a bullet, a number, or a table type.

   Syntax:

   ```
   <list type = "bullet" | "number" | "table" >
     <listheader>
       <term>term</term>
       <description>description</description>
     </listheader>
     <item>
       <term>term</term>
       <description>description</description>
     </item>
   </list>
   ```

The <listheader> block is used to define the heading row of either a table or a definition list. When defining a table, the <term> element is the only one that needs to be used. Each item in the list is specified with a <list> block. When creating a definition list, you need to use both *<term>* and *<description>*.

Example:

```
/// <remarks> A sample bulleted list
/// <list type="bullet">
/// <item>
/// <description>Item 1.</description>
/// </item>
/// <item>
/// <description>Item 2.</description>
/// </item>
/// </list>
/// </remarks>
```

■ The <para> tag is used inside another tag such as <summary, <remarks>, or <return> to add structure to the text. This is necessary because all of the text will run together regardless of how the comments are presented in the code.

Syntax: <para>*content*</para>

Example:

```
<summary>
<para>
This is an example of a paragraph of Text
</para>
<para>
This is an another paragraph of text. These will be separated.
</para>
</summary>
```

■ The <param> tag specifies parameters used in a method declaration. The text for the <param> tag is used in Visual Studio IntelliSense, in the Object Browser, and in the Code Comments Web Report.

Syntax: <param name="*name*">*description*</param>

Example:

```
///<param name="Int1"> Used to indicate status.</param>
public static void MyMethod(int Int1)
```

■ The <paramref> tag provides a way to specify that a word is a parameter. The name of the parameter in the syntax is enclosed in double quotation marks.

Syntax: <paramref name="*name*"/>

Example:

```
/// <remarks> MyMethod is a method.
/// The <paramref name="Int1"/> parameter takes a number.
/// </remarks>
```

■ The <permission> tag allows the documentation of the access of a member. The **System.Security.PermissionSet** lets you specify access to a member.

Syntax: <permission cref="*member*">*description*</permission>

Example:

```
/// <permission cref="System.Security.PermissionSet">
Everyone can access this method. </permission>
```

■ The <remarks> tag is used to add additional information within a <summary> tag or alone. This information is displayed in the Object Browser and in the Code Comments Web Report.

Syntax: <remarks>*description*</remarks>

Example:

```
/// <summary>
///  Primary Information
/// </summary>
/// <remarks>
///  Some Additional Information
/// </remarks>
```

■ The <returns> tag is used to identify the return value from a method declaration.

Syntax: <returns>*description*</returns>

Example:

```
/// <returns>Returns Zero.</returns>
public static int GetZero()
```

■ The <see> tag specifies a link within text. The *member* in the syntax must appear within double quotation marks.

Syntax: <see cref="*member*"/>.

Example:

```
<see cref="GetZero()"/>
```

■ The <seealso> tag specifies text that can appear in the See Also section.

Syntax: <seealso cref="*member*"/>

Example:

```
<seealso cref="GetZero()"/>
```

You may notice that the default XML documentation has much functionality built into it. In the next exercise, we will practice creating an XML document and view how to create a Web Comments Code Report.

EXERCISE 9-1

Create XML Documentation and Comment Web Pages

1. Create a new project by selecting File | New. The New Project dialog box appears.

2. From the New Project dialog box, select Visual C# Projects from the Project Types pane, and select Class Library from the Templates Pane.

3. In the Name field, give the project the name **XMLDocumentation**.

4. Within the Solution Explorer, right-click Class1.cs and rename it to Employee.cs.

5. Modify the code to match the following lines:

```
using System;
using System.Text;
namespace XmlDocumentation
{
    /// <summary>
    /// Summary description for Class1.
    /// </summary>
    public class Employee
    {
        private string _FirstName;
```

```csharp
private string _LastName;
private DateTime _HireDate;
public Employee ()
{
      FirstName = "Hello";
      LastName = "World";
      HireDate = DateTime.Now;
}
public string FirstName
{
      get { return _FirstName;}
      set { _FirstName = value;}
}
public string LastName
{
      get { return _LastName; }
      set { _LastName = value; }
}
public DateTime HireDate
{
      get { return _HireDate; }
      set { _HireDate = value; }
}
public bool FireEmployee()
{
      return true;
}
public void SomeMethod()
{
      this.ToString();
      FireEmployee();
}
public override string ToString()
{
      StringBuilder sb = new StringBuilder();
      sb.Append("Name:");
      sb.Append(LastName);
      sb.Append(", ");
      sb.Append(FirstName);
      sb.Append("\n");
      sb.Append("Hire Date:");
      sb.Append(HireDate);
      return sb.ToString();
```

```
                        }
                }
        }
```

6. Compile the code to make sure everything runs properly.

7. When you hover your mouse over the methods in **SomeMethod( )** and **ToString( )**, they should look like the following two illustrations. The properties in the **ToString( )** method have the same characteristics, they will display IntelliSence help.

```
FireEmployee();
```
bool Employee.FireEmployee ()

```
this.ToString();
FireEmploy string Employee.ToString () (+ 1 overloads)
```

8. To start getting more interaction with IntelliSence, we need to start adding XML documentation comments. Let's start with the class, modifying the code description to look like the following above the class declaration:

```
/// <summary>
/// Summary description for EmployeeFinish.
/// </summary>
```

9. Add the following code description above the **_FirstName** variable.

```
/// <summary>
/// Instance variable to hold the FirstName
/// </summary>
private string _FirstName;
```

10. Add the following code description above the **_LastName** variable.

```
/// <summary>
/// Instance variable to hold the LastName
/// </summary>
private string _LastName;
```

11. Add the following code description above the **_HireDate** variable

```
/// <summary>
/// Instance variable to hold the HireDate
/// </summary>
private DateTime _HireDate;
```

12. Add the following description above the **Employee** constructor declaration.

```
/// <summary>
/// Constructor for the Class
/// </summary>
/// <remarks>
/// The FirstName, LastName, and HireDate are set to
/// initial values.
/// </remarks>
/// <example>private EmployeeFinish e = new EmployeeFinish()</example>
```

13. Add the following description above the **FirstName**, **LastName**, and **HireDate** properties and replace <Property Name> with the appropriate bolded property name being described.

```
/// <summary>
/// <Property Name> Property Construction
/// </summary>
/// <value>Value tag to display the <Property Name> </value>
```

14. Add the following code description above the **FireEmployee( )** method.

```
/// <summary>
/// Function to Fire the Employee and reset
/// Values
/// </summary>
/// <returns>If the FireAction was performed successfully.</returns>
```

15. Add the following above the **SomeMethod( )** method.

```
/// <summary>
/// Test Method
/// <seealso cref="EmployeeFinish.ToString()"/>
/// </summary>
```

16. Add the following code description above the **ToString( )** method.

```
/// <summary>
/// Override the String.ToString functionality to return
/// a custom set of information.
/// </summary>
/// <remarks>
/// <list type="bullet">
/// <term>List Term  1</term>
/// <description>ListItem 1</description>
```

```
/// </list>
///</remarks>
/// <returns>Returns a formatted string of values</returns>
```

17. We have finished adding code comments.

18. Next we want to create code comments Web Reports that can be distributed to give information to other developers.

19. Set up the project properties as shown in the following illustration. By having the XML documentation filename mirror the project file, the created assembly and the XML documentation file will move to other projects when a reference is created. IntelliSence will use the XML documentation file for the descriptions of the accessible properties and methods.

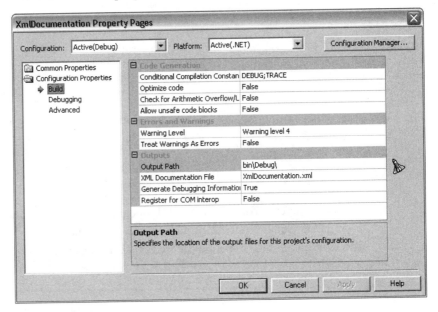

20. Press OK to save the settings.

21. Press Tools | Build Comment Web Pages. The Build Comment Web Pages dialog box appears.

22. Point the destination for the output to your project directory by clicking the Browse button. Then click OK to start the build process.

23. The documentation automatically shows up in your browser. It shows the solution structure and shows the comments that were added to the properties and methods. The following illustration shows an example of the finished output from the web report.

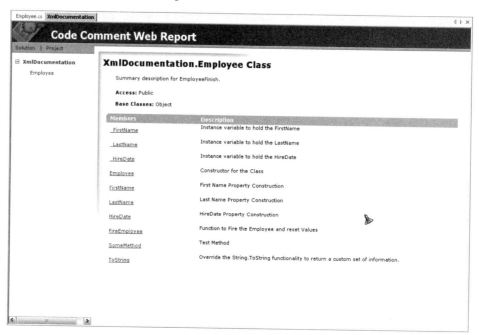

In this exercise, you saw how XML documentation works and viewed the Web Comments Code Report. Although the main tag that you used in this example was the <summary> tag, you should note that there are other options not used in the exercise.

Coding Standards

This section looks at some common developer coding principles necessary for you to succeed. Each organization has its own variation of some type of standard that it has either developed or discovered. Many problems with the development and maintenance of an application come from following behind another developer and making modifications. Some of these problems can be addressed by applying generic standards for naming and formatting of code, and by applying some best practices.

Naming Conventions

The readability of source code has a direct impact on how well a developer comprehends the solution. The code maintainability affects the ease with which other developers can make changes to existing software. By using solid coding techniques and practices, the quality of the code is improved. Here are some suggestions for naming conventions:

- Begin each name with an alphabetical character, a digit, or an underscore. This is required by Microsoft.

- Begin each separate word in a name with a capital letter, such as searchLastName.

- Begin function and method names with a verb, such as hideShowPanel.

- Begin class and property names with a name, such as EmployeeLastName.

- Begin interface names with the prefix I, followed by a noun or a noun phrase, such as IComponent, or by describing a behavior. Do not use underscores, and use abbreviations sparingly. Underscores are usually used for internal variables, and abbreviations can make variables difficult to understand.

- Begin event handler names with a noun describing the type of event followed by EventHandler, such as MouseEventHandler.

- Include the "EventArgs" suffix in names of event arguments classes, such as DragEventArgs.

- Use a prefix in present or past tense, such as ListAdd or ListAdded, if an event refers to an action carried out before or after something else.

- Avoid using names in an inner scope that are the same as names in an outer scope. For instance, if you create a variable name Date, it would conflict with using the Date function alone and you would have to call the date function by calling System.Date.

- Use Pascal casing for routine names and camel casing for variables. *Pascal casing* is when the first letter of each word is capitalized. *Camel casing* is the same as Pascal casing except that the first word is lowercase. Examples are shown here:

```
Pascal casing example: CalculateSummaryTotal
Camel casing example: calculateSummaryTotal
```

exam
watch

Pay attention to the conventions required for naming variables and methods.

Routine Conventions Some guidelines for creating method and function names are as follows:

- Avoid elusive names that make it difficult to determine the purpose of the method or function. It is redundant to include class names in the name of a class property, such as Employee.EmployeeLastName. Use Employee.LastName instead. In .NET, since we can do function overloading, the overloaded functions should perform similar tasks.

- For routine conventions, use a verb-noun method, such as **EmployeeUpdate( )**, when naming routines that perform operations on a given object.

Variable Conventions General guidelines for creating variable names include the following:

- Append computation qualifiers (Avg, Sum, Min, and Max), when appropriate, to the end of variable names.
- Use "Is" in Boolean variables, which implies a True/False value.
- Avoid using terms such as Flag when naming status variables. For example, instead of documentFlag, use a more descriptive name such as documentFileFormat.
- Give meaningful names even to short-lived variables.
- Use single-letter variable names such as **x** and **y** for short-loop indexes only.

Use constants in place of literal numbers and strings for ease of maintenance and understanding.

Tables Conventions When naming tables, the following conventions are useful:

- Express the name in singular form. For example, use Customer instead of Customers.

- Avoid using the table name in column name fields. For example, instead of CustomerFirstName, use FirstName.

- Make column names data-type neutral. By not having the data type as part of the name, if the data type changes in the future, the column will not have to be renamed.

Avoid making field names too long, because you will have to type them and because you lose the uniqueness of names when they are too long.

SQL Server   Microsoft SQL Server has some conventions to make Transact Structured Query Language (TSQL) easier to understand. Some those are listed here:

- Avoid prefixing stored procedures with **sp**. This prefix is reserved for identifying system-stored procedures.

- Do not use **fn_** as a prefix. This prefix is reserved for identifying built-in functions.

- Avoid using **xp_** as a prefix. It is reserved for identifying system-extended stored procedures.

- When writing SQL statements, use uppercase for keywords and mixed case for tables, columns, and views.

- Put each major SQL clause on a separate line to make the statements easier to read and edit.

Formatting Conventions

The purpose of formatting of code is to make it logical and understandable. If you take the time to format your code properly, you and other developers will be able to maintain and decipher your code easily. When using opening and closing braces, there are two styles you can follow: block and slanted. Block style is when you align braces vertically, as shown here:

```
for ( i = 0; i < 100; i++ )
{
. . .
}
```

Slanted style is when the opening brace appears at the end of the line and the closing brace appears at the beginning of the line, as shown here:

```
for ( i = 0; i < 100; i++ ) {
    . . .
}
```

This style is most commonly seen in C++ and Java. The style you choose should be based on your preference, but you must use that same style throughout your source code.

One of the first techniques of formatting is to establish a standard amount for the indention of your code and follow this standard for all of your code. The indenting of code makes it easier to follow. For example, the following code lines:

```
If … Then
If … Then
…
Else
End If
Else
…
End If
```

are better formatted like this:

```
If … Then
    If … Then
    …
    Else
    …
    End If
Else
…
End If
```

The second part of this code listing is much easier to read than the first one.

The aforementioned formatting techniques can be automated by properly setting up the Visual Studio IDE. In the IDE environment, under Tools | Options, the Text Editor shows options that allow the formatting of your code based on the type of source code or all source code. The following illustration shows the formatting options available for Text Editor, All Languages.

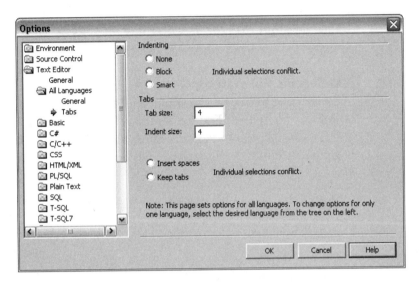

This screen allows the setting of default options for the Text Editor. You might see the message "Individual selections conflict" displayed next to the Indenting or Tabs options. This indicates that one or more individual languages have indenting or tab selection types that differ from the other languages. For example, the message displays if Visual Basic has Smart indenting selected while Visual C++ has Block indenting selected. This message alerts you that selecting a particular indenting or tab type in this dialog box affects all languages and sets their indenting or tab types to whatever you select here.

There are three indenting settings: None, Block, and Smart. When None is selected, no automatic indention occurs when you press ENTER to move to a new line of text. The cursor starts in the first column of the next line. The Block setting automatically indents to the same tab stop on the next line when ENTER is pressed. The Smart setting creates new lines of text based on the formatting rules established for the respective language. For example, if you were writing a loop in VB, the new line after the loop statement would indent to the right one tab stop.

The tab settings specify the tab size and indent size. These indicate the number of spaces entered when indenting is necessary and when the TAB key is pressed. The Insert Spaces option, if selected, inserts space characters instead of tab characters when the TAB key or indent button is pressed. If Keep Tabs is selected, tab characters are inserted instead of spaces when possible. Tab characters are not possible if the Tab Size and Indent Size settings are not the same. If the indent size is not an even multiple of the tab size, space characters will fill the remaining space.

exam
ⓦatch

Remember that with the Tab Size and Indent Size settings, the number of characters used depends on the indent style selected.

VB-Specific Formatting Options   Under Text Editor I Basic I VB Specific, there are three additional formatting options for Visual Basic.NET. The first is Automatic Insertion of End Constructs, when you type the first line of a procedure declaration and press ENTER; the editor adds the matching End Sub, Function line. If a property is used, it will automatically create the appropriate **get** and **set** statements. For example, if you enter:

```
Public Property LastName As String
```

the Code Editor will reformat the code and add the following:

```
        Public Property LastName() As String
            Get
            End Get
            Set(ByVal Value As String)
            End Set
        End Property
```

The Pretty Listing (Reformatting) Of Code option allows the text editor to align your code on the correct tab location. The Enter Outlining Mode When Files Open option allows you to view the document in outlining mode. For more information about outlining code, view the MSDN documentation under Outlining Code. The following illustration displays the Visual Basic–specific formatting options.

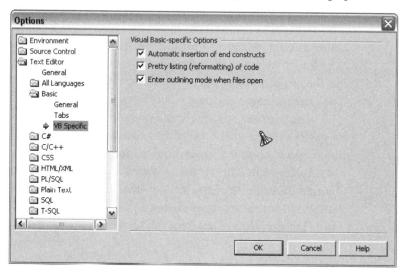

C#-Specific Formatting Options   The C#-specific options provide additional C#-specific indentation and outlining features. The Leave Open Braces On Same Line As Construct option determines the brace style as either block or slanted style, which was demonstrated earlier. The Indent Case Labels option indents **case** statements for a **switch** statement. (By default the **case** statements are aligned with the first character in the **switch** statement.) The Automatically Format Completed Constructs And Pasted Source option will format typed code constructs automatically. As the constructs are closed, the inner content is formatted. This option will also format automatically any code pasted into the editor. The Smart Comment Editing option allows you to activate the XML documentation tags when /// is typed. The following illustration shows the C#-specific formatting options.

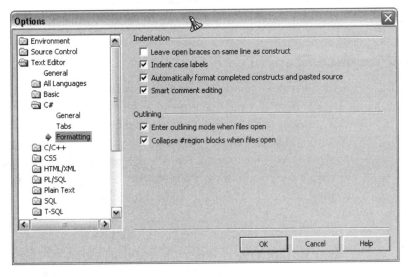

e x a m
ⓦa t c h

Remember that /// starts smart comment editing in C#.

General Recommendations   Here are some recommended formatting techniques that you should follow regardless of the language you're using:

- Use a monotype font when publishing hardcopy versions of source code.

- Establish a maximum line length for comment and code to avoid having to scroll to the right on the source code editor and to allow for clean presentation of hardcopy.

- Use spaces before and after most operators. An example of an operator that cannot have spaces is a += operator. Spacing would create a compiler syntax error.

- Use white space to provide organizational clues to source code. This creates paragraphs of code, which aid others in comprehending it.

- When having to break a line of code over several lines, make continuation obvious by placing the concatenation operator at the end of the line.

- Avoid placing more than one statement per line. One example of an exception to this is a C# **for** loop, as shown here:

```
for ( i = 0; i < 100; i++)
```

As you see in this section, there are many formatting standards that you can apply to make your code more readable and maintainable for other developers. These techniques and conventions take time and practice. However, by using the environment properly you can save many hours in the commenting and formatting of your code.

User Interface Standards

User interface standards help define and promote consistency within the user experience. The *user experience* is the end-to-end relationship that the user has with your application. This extends to the type of help provided and controls, layout styles, and colors used. You should be able to view a section of an application, and it should have a consistent look and feel so you cannot tell who created that section of the application. Good interface design adheres to the following design principles: the user should feel in control, and the interface should be direct, consistent, forgiving, aesthetic, and simple, as well as provide feedback.

User in Control

The user should always feel in control *of,* rather than being controlled *by,* the software. In this model, the user plays an active role instead of being reactive. For example, users should be able to choose or control automated tasks and be able to personalize aspects of the interface based on their skill and preferences. This could be user preferences for colors, fonts, and other options. The software should be as interactive and responsive as possible. For these reasons, the developer should avoid using modes when possible. A *mode* is a state that excludes general interaction. Sometimes a mode is the best or only design alterative. In these instances, make sure the mode is obvious, is visible, is the result of an explicit user choice, and is easy to cancel. Some examples of this design goal in action would be to create modeless secondary windows in which the user can perform actions while long-running processes execute in the background.

The user interface should allow users to make decisions about what they want to perform.

Directness

Directness is when the design of the software allows users to change indicators that have special meaning and see how their actions affect the objects on the screen. Graphic information and choices reduce the mental workload of the user. An example of this would be to use, or allow the user to assign, custom icons to simulate status for a given action that has meaning to them. Familiar metaphors provide a direct and intuitive interface for user tasks. Metaphors support user recognition rather than recollection. Users remember a meaning associated with a familiar object more easily than they remember the name of a particular command. An example of a metaphor would be a magnifying glass being used to represent the ability to search for a specific item.

Use visual clues that the user will understand.

Consistency

Consistency allows users to transfer existing knowledge to new tasks, learn new things more quickly, and focus more attention on tasks. When different elements of the interface are presented in a similar format, the user does not have to spend time trying to figure out the differences. This promotes a sense of a familiar and predictable interface. Consistency is applied to the whole interface, like names of commands, visual presentation, operational behavior, and placement of elements. Following are two tips for implementing consistent graphical interface items:

- Present command functions using a consistent set of commands and interfaces. For example, avoid implementing a Copy command that immediately carries out an operation in one situation but in another situation displays a dialog box requiring user interaction to set a destination.

- Use graphics that are consistent with what their metaphors imply so it is easy for the user to associate the correct behaviors with the objects. For example, a wastebasket icon is more intuitive than an incinerator icon to represent a repository that allows you to recover the objects placed in it.

Find someone that is graphically oriented to design a common color scheme or allow users to change colors externally in the solution.

Forgiveness

Forgiveness refers to the ability to learn by trial and error. An effective interface allows for interactive discovery. It provides an appropriate set of choices and warns users about potential situations where they could damage the system or data. Users very commonly make mistakes, so an effective design avoids situations that are likely to result in errors. An effective design also accommodates potential user error by making it easy for the user to recover from incorrect choices.

Users will always make mistakes, so design interfaces that allow them to recover.

Aesthetics

The graphical interface design is an important part of an application's interface. The interface should not have too many visual elements on the screen because everything on the screen is competing for the user's attention. The interface should provide a coherent environment that clearly facilitates the user's understanding.

Simplicity

Interfaces should be easy for the user to learn. An effective interface balances maximizing functionality and maintaining simplicity. One way to provide simplicity is to reduce the amount of information in the presentation. Use simple and direct description and phrases. By building on the user's existing knowledge and experiences, things that are familiar often seem simpler than things that are not. You can help users manage visual complexity by using progressive disclosure. Progressive disclosure is when, with the use of careful organization, you present information only at the appropriate time. Instead of displaying a very large screen full of information, successive groups of information are added gradually as the user steps through the process.

It is much easier to add information to the screen gradually than give the user a screen full of information and expect them to understand.

Feedback

Effective feedback helps confirm that the software is responding to input and communicates details that distinguish the nature of the action; it is timely in that it is presented as close to the point of the user's interaction as possible. Even when the application is processing a particular task, it should provide the user with information about the state of the process. If it is an option, it should show the user how to cancel the process. Feedback allows the user to feel confident that the application is running while a process is executing.

exam
ⓦatch

Provide users with visual clues during long processes so they know that the application is still running.

Checklist for a Good Client Interface

The following checklist applies the user interface principles discussed above. By applying these user interface principles, the user will determine whether the solution is a success or a failure.

■ Your application installs easily in a minimum number of steps.

■ Your application installation does not require the system to restart.

■ Users do not have to read a Readme file before using your application.

■ User-generated data files are stored by default in the My Documents folder.

■ Your application avoids cryptic file names that are visible to users.

■ Your application does not create folders outside of the Program Files folder.

■ Your application does not write files to the root of the hard disk.

■ If your application uses a disk cache, it also registers itself with the Disk Cleanup utility.

■ Your application does not include entries to its Help, Readme, and Uninstall files on the Start menu.

■ Your application does not install icons to the Windows desktop without the user's permission.

■ If your application is run at startup, it loads without displaying splash screens and dialog boxes.

- Your application does not use the taskbar notification area for status, launching applications or utilities, or querying properties. It uses the notification area only to alert the user of an important change.

- Your application appropriately applies the color choices the user selected in Display Properties in Control Panel.

- Your application is accessible from the keyboard.

- Your application works correctly if the user increases the size of the default font.

- Your application supports the standard set of keyboard shortcuts, where applicable.

- Your application's uninstall process leaves no remaining files or registry entries other than files created by the user.

- Your application does not use jargon in its user interface text. It uses industry-specific or technical terms only if they are clearly understood by the user.

- Your application adjusts appropriately when the user changes the display resolution or configures the display for multiple monitors.

Web Standards

Web standards use the above user interface concepts in the design of web sites. In addition, web sites require some specific content. For example, every page should include the name and e-mail address of a responsible person or entity (for example, support@myweb.com) or a link to a support page. To ensure that users can navigate back to the beginning, include a graphical or text link. Some design standards require the inclusion of a link to the home or parent page on all pages.

The use of style guides or templates help to provide visual consistency across pages. Use logical tags as they are intended rather than as graphical devices; for example, use the <H1> tag to create a true heading and not just to just accomplish bold text. The best way to divide the presentation into parts is to use Cascading Style Sheets (CSS). Avoid using too many graphics that may slow down your site. For a consistent look and feel, add navigational aids for users, such as "Table of Contents," "Return to Top," and "Next/Previous Page" for the individual pages, as appropriate. When writing text, be sparing in the use of bold, italics, and so on.

Some other suggested content is as follows:

- Include a copyright statement.
- Use a warning statement if a link will lead to a large document or image.
- Include a "What's New" section or link on the home page.

exam
Watch

Including footers containing contact links on every page is important so the user can contact you if there is a problem.

exam
Watch

Names of action button should be consistent so the meanings are apparent.

Testing Standards

Testing is the process of checking an application to ensure that it fulfills the requirements for the solution. This is also a way to ensure that the application meets the appropriate customer expectations. The purpose of testing is to reduce the cost of developing the application. Finding mistakes early can result in a considerable financial savings later, because it can cost 40 to 100 times more to resolve design mistakes later in the development process than correcting them during development. Ensuring that the application works the way the user expects it to work helps reduce the unpredictability of the application. Further, the user will require fewer hours of training and less support if the application tested properly. The primary goal of testing is to gain the customer's loyalty and word-of-mouth market share.

Requirements-based testing provides the basis for all testing on the solution. The purpose is to identify the bugs that create or cause inappropriate behavior in the application. While creating requirements for testing, it helps to follow these simple rules:

- All requirements should be unambiguous and interpretable only one way.
- Requirements must be testable in a way that ensures that the application compiles.
- Requirements should be binding because those requirements are things the customers needs.

Unit Testing

Unit testing is the process of taking the smallest pieces of an application and testing their individual functionality. Unit testing has proven its value by catching a large percentage of bugs. The basic concept is to test the units separately before integrating them into other modules and then testing among modules.

A known tool for performing unit testing is NUnit.

A common way to use unit testing is to create testing fixtures (or *harnesses*) and testing stubs. The *fixture* simulates the calling of an assembly, which could be a DLL or an EXE file. The *stub* simulates the execution of individual functionality of the called assembly. The fixture and stub together are considered a *unit*. The unit is built around a single class or file. The creation of fixtures and stubs requires an investment of time, but the advantage is that together they automate the testing process. This process is the execution of tests against the code to determine the quality of the application, as well as the meeting of the stated requirements. By automating the testing process, you can discover errors when integrating components and errors in complex parts of the application. This type of testing allows for the retesting of code later on, after a large amount of code has been added. This is very helpful when there are multiple developers working on a solution. If there are components that are shared between parts of the application, the automated testing can determine if code has been broken in the process of integrating functionality.

Integration Testing

After the unit test for the components has been created and run, integration testing begins. In its most basic form, an integration test consists of two units that have been tested individually already and then are combined together to perform a task. This intercommunication is the integration that needs to be tested. Eventually all of the modules making up a task or process are tested together. The goal is to identify problems that occur when units are combined. Integration testing can be done in a variety of ways, but here are the three most common strategies:

■ The *top-down* approach requires that the highest-level modules be tested and integrated first. This allows high-level logic and data flow to be tested early in the process, and it tends to minimize the need for creating testing fixtures. However, the need for stubs can create problems when utilities are tested late in the development cycle. Later in the process, stubs are harder to create to test specific functionality if the utility being tested was designed incorrectly. Another disadvantage of this approach is that it provides poor support for early releases of limited functionality.

- The *bottom-up* approach requires the lowest-level units to be tested and integrated first. These units are frequently referred to as *common utility modules* (or *components*). By using this approach, these modules are tested early in the development process and the need for stubs is minimized. This approach, like the top-down approach, provides poor support for early releases of limited functionality.

- The *umbrella* approach requires that functional data and control-flow paths are tested and integrated first. The inputs are tested at the lowest level, as in the bottom-up approach. The outputs are then integrated in the top-down manner. This approach supports the early release of limited functionality. This approach minimizes the need for creating testing fixtures and stubs. The drawback of this approach is that it requires more regression testing because it is less systematic.

exam
ⓦatch

Integration testing causes more applications to fail than when it is not used, because the details involved can be very complex.

Regression Testing

When modifying an existing implementation of an application, you will want to perform regression testing. This is the rerunning of a test against the modified code to determine whether everything works as planned. Providing adequate coverage without wasting time should be a primary consideration when conducting regression tests. Some strategies and factors to consider during this process include the following:

- Test fixed bugs promptly. The programmer might have handled the symptoms but not have gotten to the underlying cause.

- Watch for side effects of fixes. The bug itself might be fixed, but the fix might have created other bugs.

- Write a regression test for each fixed bug.

- If two or more tests are similar, determine which test is less effective and get rid of it.

- Identify tests that the program consistently passes and archive them.

■ Focus on functional issues, not on those related to design.

■ Make changes (small and large) to data and find any resulting corruption.

■ Trace the effects of the changes on program memory.

The most effective approach to regression testing is to develop a library of tests made up of a standard battery of test cases that can be run every time you build a new version of the program. Automated tests, as well as test cases involving boundary conditions and timing, almost definitely belong in your library. Periodically review the regression test library to eliminate redundant or unnecessary tests. Duplication is quite common when more than one person is writing test code. An example of this duplication is the concentration of tests that often develop when a bug or its variants are particularly persistent and are present across many cycles of testing. Numerous tests are sometimes written by different developers and added to the regression test library. These multiple tests are useful for fixing the bug, but when all traces of the bug and its variants are eliminated from the program, select the best of the tests associated with the bug and remove the rest from the library.

There are many types of tools available to handle this type of testing. The tools and tests you use depend on whether you are testing web or Windows client applications.

Standards help to create a consistent environment, as well as rules and the knowledge of what to expect. When new developers are added to the team, it is much easier to work from a practical set of standards that are clearly defined than to try to do a cold assessment of how the processes, documents, and user interface should be integrated.

exam
ⓦatch

Standards are a tremendous help when working with new developers or multiple teams of developers.

CERTIFICATION OBJECTIVE 9.02

Establishing Processes

The section of the chapter examines the development of processes for performing code reviews; builds; testing; bug tracking; source code, change, and release management; and maintenance tasks. These processes can be used throughout the development lifecycle. The goal is to simplify the development phases as much as possible.

Reviewing Development Documentation

The viewing of development documentation and code is called a *design review.* This is an industry best practice for detecting design flaws and determining the validity of the solution. The other purpose for a design review is to create an awareness of how other developers solve specific problems. The peer review is performed after the design review and coding is completed. The elements of a peer review, whether it is formal or informal, consist of a structured review process, a standards checklist, and defined roles for participants and reporting of the results. Peer reviews happen during three phases: specification and design, development, and testing. These are integral during the project lifecycle.

Design reviews are performed with your peers and then possibly with your customer.

There are two types of reviews used in the design review process. The first is the architecture review, sometimes called the *software walkthrough,* and the second is peer review. The *architecture review* is generally necessary in order to generate artifacts to solve a problem or to get feedback on a particular strategy. The purpose is to get group consensus between the code reviewers and coders of the reviewing code. The author initiates the session. The goal is to determine open issues and action items that need to be taken to get consensus.

The software inspection, or code review, is structured to serve the needs of quality management. It ensures that the application or component follows the appropriate rules for completeness, correctness, style, standards, and user needs. The code review is led by a moderator, a recorder, and one or more reviewers. The moderator determines if the code is ready for the review and keeps the flow of the code review going during the review. The recorder creates a written archive of the meeting that identifies the changes and action items left to complete. The reviewer performs the review. The structured review process is organized around the following activities: planning, preparation, entry criteria, conduct, exit criteria, reporting, and follow-up.

Planning the Code Review

Planning of the architecture review starts early in the project planning process, while requirements are being gathered and refined to create a functional specifications document. The architecture review is performed and recorded into project documents. The information gathered from the architecture review is then used in creating the testing and software assurance plans.

The moderator determines the product's volatility status to determine when the code review is appropriate. He or she then briefs the reviewers, the recorder, and the reader on their roles, along with artifacts for the review.

Before the start of the code review, the moderator checks exit criteria. The moderator determines if the scheduled code review is to proceed by answering the following questions:

- Has the development activity been concluded for the reviewed item?
- Are there any changes to the baseline?
- Are review participants in place and briefed?
- Have all participants received all the review materials and the checklist?
- How many minutes of preparation did each participant perform?

The moderator, not the author(s), reviewers, recorder, or reader, directs the code review session. This allows the review to be done in an objective and unbiased way. Each component is inspected using the predefined checklist. As each issue is raised, the producer may wish to obtain clarification on why the issue is raised. The producer may choose not to defend or clarify but will have an opportunity to resolve issues during the follow-up. To complete the review, the following questions should be answered:

- Are there any completeness issues?
- Are there correctness issues?
- Are there any style issues?
- Are there any rules of construction issues or standards issues?
- Are there any customer needs issues?

The moderator checks exit criteria at the close of the code review and verifies that all of the components have been inspected. The recorder verifies that all of the metrics have been reviewed. The recorder should also have a list of defects containing the following information: the defect type, category, and severity, and why the issue was raised. The examination of why each issue was raised should identify resolutions from the reviewing group or detail the standard that was broken.

The Reporting Phase

During the reporting phase, the moderator, with the help of the recorder, reports the findings of the code review in the appropriate format. This report provides a review summary, the preparation time, the type of defects, and recommended solutions.

The author performs the follow-up rework on the application. The associated tasks that need to be completed are entered into the project action plan. As each additional action is completed, it is marked off, and the application reflects the change in status. Tracking issues can be used as an indicator of the readiness of the software for production.

System of Checklists

Checklists are the heart of code reviews. They are the result of your defined standards and can be used as guides to make the review process smoother. A design and code checklist might contain the following sections: Completeness, Correctness, Style, Rules of Construction, and Multiple Views. Following are explanations of each of these sections, along with questions they might contain:

Completeness   The Completeness section indicates whether or not there is traceability among product artifacts such as requirements, specifications, designs, and code:

- Has traceability been assessed?
- Have all predecessor requirements been accounted for?
- Were any product fragments revealed not to have traceability to the predecessor requirements?

Correctness   The Correctness section indicates whether or not the correct assumptions were made about the solution:

- Is the function commentary satisfied?
- Are programs limited to single entry and single exit?
- Is the loop initialized and terminated properly?
- Have legal values for inputs been used?
- Is there systematic exception handling for illegal values?

Style   The Style section indicates whether or not project-specified style guidelines were followed:

- Were naming conventions followed?

- Were style conventions for commentary followed?

- Are the semantics of the application component traceable to the requirements?

- Have templates been used for repeating patterns?

Rules of Construction   The Rules of Construction section indicates whether or not code writing rules, templates, and conventions defined by the organization were followed:

- Were guidelines for unit construction followed?

- Were data representation conventions followed?

- Was the interprocess communication protocol followed?

- Was the system standard time defined and followed?

- Have encapsulation, localization, and component layering been used to achieve object orientation?

- Has scalability been achieved through nonparameterization and portability?

Multiple Views   The Multiple Views section indicates whether or not the various perspectives and viewpoints required of the software product by the different users were assessed:

- Has the logical view of user interface and object orientation consideration been assessed?

- Has the static view of packaging consideration, including program generation and deployment processes, been assessed?

- Has the dynamic view of operational considerations, including communication concurrency, synchronization, and failure recovery, been assessed?

All together, this process allows for team cooperation and pooling of ideas to make sure that the code follows the prescribed standards of the team and the organization. Whether you use a formal or informal process, each piece of code should have this type of review to ensure completeness and accuracy.

Creating Builds

There are two types of builds: debug builds and release builds. While you are testing, the debug build is the preferred method because it allows debugging in the development environment. The process of creating a build accomplishes two goals: the first is to check the syntax of code, misspelling of words, and type mismatches. The second is to correct logic and runtime errors detected by using the debugger. After debugging and testing the solution, a release build is deployed into production. The difference between the two builds are shown in the following table:

Debug Build	Release Build
The result is a DLL or EXE file and a DBG debug file that stores the debugging symbols for each project.	The result is a DLL or EXE file for each project.
The DBG file is typically two to three times the size of the compiled project DLL or EXE file.	No debug file is created.
There is no execution optimization. The debug version carries so much extra information that the execution is slower than the release version.	The build is optimized to be small and execute faster.
	Various optimization options are available, such as checking for numeric bounds. If checking for numeric bounds is turned off, it is possible to have collisions in memory usage because the numeric values could spill in into unwanted memory locations.

exam
ᗯatch

There is a large difference in execution times between debug and release versions of assemblies.

Builds are the periodic assembly of all solution elements that are sufficiently complete to be included in the build. Builds are created to confirm the viability of solutions in a simulated environment and are the basis for iterative development. Builds include code components, directory structures, and documentation and deployment scripts. This could be few or many components depending on the stage of the development process. Builds are should have a build number for tracking purposes and be placed under version control. A typical development process consists of internal release cycles developed over the course of several "daily" builds. After stabilizing the solution, external builds can be created for testing purposes, such as release candidate builds and deployment builds. After approval, the solution can be released to the users, and subsequent external builds are generated to include enhancements or to create completely new versions.

The "daily" build process has three steps: development, testing, and validation. The goal of daily builds is to avoid long periods where the actual state of development cannot be verified. This does not mean that you have to perform these builds on a daily basis; the frequency is based on the needs of the project, but these builds should be performed frequently enough to establish the progress of the project. The development phase allows you to work on the feature schedules for the upcoming release milestone. The testing phase uses the project test plan, which could include manual or automated scripts, or both. The validation is the recording of the results according to quality criteria.

Build Configurations

Build configurations provide a way to select the components you will build, exclude those you will not build, and determine the order of how the projects will build within the solution. There are two levels of build configurations: project configurations and solution build configurations.

A solution build configuration determines how the projects contained within the build are built and deployed. A solution can contain many projects. Each project contains a configuration that determines what will be built for that specific project and other settings. The default build configurations are Build, Release, and All Configurations. Each entry in the build configuration includes a project name, the configuration, the platform, a Build check box, and, if enabled, Deploy check boxes for selecting those projects that will be built. Each project can select the debug/release or custom configuration that it will use when building, and you can determine which project(s) of the solution you want to build.

With Visual Studio.NET, there are multiple options for handling and managing builds. Following are some common procedures.

To build or rebuild an entire solution:

1. From the Build menu, choose Build or Rebuild All.

To build or rebuild a project:

1. Select or edit the project you wish to build.
2. From the Build menu, choose Build [Project Name] or Rebuild [Project Name].

To batch-build multiple project configurations:

1. From the Build menu, choose Batch Build.
2. Select the check boxes for the project configurations you wish to build.
3. Click Build or Rebuild.

To make one project dependent on another:

1. Add at least two projects to your solution.
2. In Solution Explorer, select a project.
3. From the Project menu, choose Project Dependencies. The Project Dependencies dialog box opens.
4. Change the project in the Project list if you want to establish the dependencies of a different project.
5. In the Depends On field, select the check box of another project that must be built before this project.
6. To see the resulting order in which projects will build, click the Build Order tab.

To set the order in which projects build:

1. Open the Project Dependencies dialog box and choose Dependencies.
2. From the Project menu, select the project you want to build last.

3. In the Depends On field, select the project you want to build next to last.

4. Select the check boxes beside the other projects you want to build before the one you selected in step 3.

5. Return to the Project menu and select a project you want to build next to last.

6. In the Depends On field, select the project you want to build before the one you want to build next to last.

7. Select the check boxes beside all projects you want to build before the project you selected in step 5.

8. Continue this process until the only projects remaining are those without project dependencies.

9. Select Build Order in the Project Dependencies dialog box to view the order in which your project will build.

Tracking Issues

Tracking of issues is a common way to follow bug changes. You can use a commercial software package or something as basic as a spreadsheet to track information. Some of the more common information to capture includes issues names, the module where the bug was found, the date entered, the resolution date, comments, the developer the bug was assigned to, and so on. The goal is to gather enough information so that the assigned developer or team can decipher the problem and determine the solution. Tracking the issues keeps you from losing track of bugs that need to be fixed. Tracking can also be used to single out issues to be enhanced in the future, because tracking frequently highlights issues that have room for improvement.

Managing Source Code, Changes, and Releases

Microsoft Visual SourceSafe is an excellent way to manage source control for code, documents, changes, and deployments. Visual SourceSafe manages the work of multiple developers working on the same code and projects.

When developing a process for a web project, you must choose one working method from each of the following categories: local host vs. remote host, web access methods, and shared checkouts, and collaborative development models.

Local Host vs. Remote Host

When determining whether to use the local host or the remote host for the location at which to save web project files, it is important to consider the differences between the two methods. Web projects whose working location starts with http://localhost are referred to as *local host projects*. Projects that have a nonlocal host location are referred to as *remote host projects*.

exam
ⓦatch

When using remote host projects, the debug process locks the shared web server and prevents other users from working on the server until the debugging session is over.

Local host projects are executed and debugged locally. The address http://localhost is the default and recommended host for web projects. On the other hand, remotely located projects are debugged on the remote machine.

There are two main reasons for using remotely located solutions: when your computer cannot be used as an IIS web server and when you want to perform predeployment testing and debugging on a production server.

Web Access Methods

Web access methods specify how Visual Studio obtains write access to web project files on a network. Visual Studio uses two web access methods: File Share and FrontPage. File Share is the default and recommended method for Visual Studio. A File Share web application maintains itself at a shared network location. The address that is used is the HTTP address, but it resolves the address to a universal naming convention (UNC) share. All access to the project will use the resolved UNC share. Visual Studio creates a working copy of the project's source-controlled master copy in your working folder. A working folder is located on a web server. The File Share method allows multiple developers to work in isolation, so developers can work in parallel. File Share web access is the preferable method for the following reasons:

- It supports shared checkouts.
- It supports source control commands, such as branch, merge, pin, and label.
- It allows for isolation, meaning that team members can edit shared files and then merge them.

FrontPage server extensions are the second method of accessing the files. The FrontPage extension is integrated with Visual SourceSafe. With this method, there is only one working copy, it is contained on the web server, and it is considered the master Web. This environment is suitable for only one developer at a time.

You cannot use Visual Studio to add a project to source control through the FrontPage server extensions. Projects have to be added on the web server manually.

Shared Checkouts

SourceSafe has two forms of checkout: exclusive checkout mode and shared checkout mode. *Exclusive checkout mode* allows only one user at a time to check out a file. *Shared checkout mode* allows multiple users to check out and modify files. This allows developers to make changes to different parts of the file that are checked out at the same time. It is important to note that the shared checkout mode sometimes results in *merged conflicts*—overlapping changes that cannot be automatically resolved. This is not something that happens often, but Visual SourceSafe provides an interface that allows for the side-by-side comparison of the changes.

Merged conflicts manage multiple checkouts when there are conflicts.

Collaborative Development Models

Web applications have three development models: the isolated model, which is the recommended model, the semi-isolated model, and the nonisolated model. Each model determines how the environment is configured and how web access methods are used.

Isolated Model In the isolated model, editing, debugging, and execution are completely separate on your workstation using the http://localhost. Source control is maintained in Visual SourceSafe using the File Access method. The isolated model has the following advantages and disadvantages.

Advantages:

■ Two or more developers can work on the project and debug at the same time.

- It supports shared (multiple) checkouts, and the merge, branch, pin, and label commands.

- Web references are easier to create and maintain than in other environments. The creation of web references creates a directory that moves with the solution to point to the web references.

Disadvantages:

- Testing is not realistic as it is in the production environment; for example, you can't test the effects of web farms.

- Each developer must maintain his or her IIS settings to a common standard. This is a disadvantage because you might have to spend time maintaining your machine to keep it in the same configuration when things change, as opposed to the changes being maintained in a single location.

- All developers must have access to the same network LAN.

Semi-Isolated   Using the semi-isolated model, a developer creates a web project on a remote server and then adds it to source control. The first time project contributors open the project from source control, they save their working copy to the same remote web server using a different project name and a different save location. In this model, the master copy is maintained on the shared web server, and working copies are maintained in developer-created shared folders.

Advantages:

- Teams can have a network administrator who specializes in the management of shared developmental resources.

- It does not require access to http://localhost. IIS need not be installed on every developer's computer.

- It supports source control functionality, such as shared (multiple) checkouts, and the merge, branch, pin, and label commands.

Disadvantages:

- When any one user is debugging, the debug process locks the shared web server, preventing other users from working on projects on the same server.

- Web references are not automatically shareable.

- All developers must have access to the same local area network (LAN) or virtual private network (VPN).

Nonisolated   This model uses the FrontPage extensions as its primary access method. All work is done against the master Web. Work cannot be done in parallel and is not isolated from other developers. A FrontPage web project cannot be added to source control in the IDE. Rather, its version control status must be changed in IIS. Both IIS version-control options, Built In and Use External, enforce exclusive checkouts, limiting write access to a file to only one developer at a time. The difference between these version-control options is that Built In does not send the latest version to source control on check in, but Use External does. For FrontPage web projects, the Use External option is recommended.

e x a m
Ⓦ a t c h   *Projects must be saved on an NTFS partition.*

Maintenance Tasks

Maintenance tasks are actions performed to maintain the application. This could range from configuration changes to data updates. These tasks are designed to support the existing solution. They could be as simple as executing simple SQL statements for updating values for a new user interface option or as complex as creating external applications to handle the complex update and maintenance of transactional data. Another common example is reporting, because reporting can require time-consuming processes and resources. Maintenance tasks are normally scheduled as an evening batch process, thus allowing the application to be maintained with updated information on a regular basis.

Enterprise Templates

Enterprise templates allow software architects to provide guidance to development teams about how to work within the architecture by eliminating many decisions such as what files to add to the project, how to format controls, and what Visual Studio options to make available. These decisions can affect the integrated development environment (IDE) features in Visual Studio. The enterprise templates can provide starting blocks for applications or for different parts of solutions. Enterprise templates are composed of three primary items: a prototype file, a policy file, and custom help topics. The *prototype file* is the structure of the project and source to be in the template. The *policy file* defines rules about how the environment interacts with the template. *Custom help topics* can be created so that they activate and provide additional help for users of the templates. The use of enterprise templates has three primary goals:

- They define the initial structure of a distributed application. This allows a solution to create a directory structure and the appropriate starting files.

- They reduce complexity to a more manageable state. This allows for control of the development environment and provides defaults for the developer.

- They provide architectural and technological guidance. This allows the IDE to display guidance through the Task List items and provide reusable templates. Items and hints about different sections of the templates can have preset tasks associated with them in the Task List to help the user find information.

The enterprise application consists of many separate projects contributing components, interfaces and services. The enterprise template is comprised of three items: the initial project structure, custom help topics, and the policy file. Creating a new project from an enterprise template allows the creation of predefined templates for the needed solution. Table 9-1 details Visual Studio IDE features managed by the enterprise template's policy file and their effects.

TABLE 9-1   Features Managed by Policies

IDE Feature	Description of Effect
Solution Explorer	Determines what connections are available and settings
Add Project dialog box	Determines what types of projects can be added to the current solution
Add New Item dialog box	Determines what new items can be added to the project
Properties	Determines the range of values for properties and preset values for components when added to the appropriate solution file
Toolbox	Determines a list of items to populate in the Toolbox or hides unnecessary components
Menus	Turns menu options on and off

EXERCISE 9-2

Apply Constraints in an Enterprise Template Policy File

In this exercise, you are going to apply an enterprise template policy file to a project and apply constraints that effect the development environment.

1. Start Microsoft Visual Studio .NET. Create a new Windows application project. In this example, the project name is WindowsApplication1.

2. In the exercise folder, a file named MyPolicy.TDL is the template policy file that you will be modifying. Please save this file in the directory as **WindowApplication1**.

author's
⓪ote   *Make sure that the file is not marked as Read Only.*

3. To add the policy to the project, in the Project Properties list, select the ellipsis button at the end of the Policy File property, as shown in the following illustration. A dialog box will appear in which you can select the MyPolicy.TDL file in the WindowsApplication1 project location.

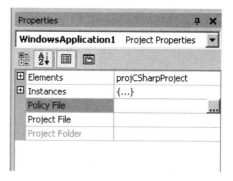

4. After selecting the policy, a warning is shown that will state that the project will be reloaded. When the project is reloaded, the policy file is then validated and any constraints are applied to the environment.

5. To see an example of a menu constraint, click on the WindowApplication1 project in the Solution Explorer. In the following illustration, you will notice on the Project menu that the New Folder option is enabled.

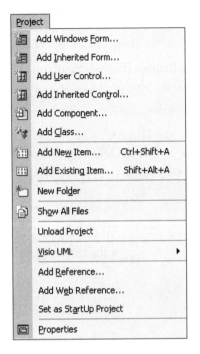

6. Close the solution.

7. Open the MyPolicy.TDL file and add the following CONSTRAINTS nodes indicated in bold below the DEFAULTSETTINGS section of the policy file.

```
<DEFAULTSETTINGS>
        <DEFAULTACTION>INCLUDE</DEFAULTACTION>
        <ORDER>EXCLUDEINCLUDE</ORDER>
        <POLICYMODE>RESTRICTIVE</POLICYMODE>
        <CONSTRAINTS>
                <MENUCONSTRAINTS>
                        <MENUCONSTRAINT>
                                <ID>menuProject.NewFolder</ID>
                                <ENABLED>0</ENABLED>
                        </MENUCONSTRAINT>
                </MENUCONSTRAINTS>
        </CONSTRAINTS>
</DEFAULTSETTINGS>
```

8. Save the changes and close the policy file.

9. Reopen the WindowsApplication1 project. Select the Project menu, and you will notice that New Folder option is disabled.

10. To disable a Toolbox item, open Form1 in design mode. View the Data tab and note that SQLConnection is enabled.

11. Close the solution.

12. Edit the DEFAULTSETTINGS node in MyPolicy.TDL to include a TOOLBOXCONSTRAINT to disable the tboxDataSQLConnection. An example is shown in bold in the following listing:

```
<DEFAULTSETTINGS>
        <DEFAULTACTION>INCLUDE</DEFAULTACTION>
        <ORDER>EXCLUDEINCLUDE</ORDER>
        <POLICYMODE>RESTRICTIVE</POLICYMODE>
        <CONSTRAINTS>
                                <TOOLBOXCONSTRAINTS>
                <TOOLBOXCONSTRAINT>
                        <ID>tboxDataSQLConnection</ID>
                        <ENABLED>0</ENABLED>
                </TOOLBOXCONSTRAINT>
                </TOOLBOXCONSTRAINTS>
        </CONSTRAINTS>
</DEFAULTSETTINGS>
```

13. Save the changes to the policy file.

14. Reopen the WindowsApplication1 project, view the Toolbox again, and notice that SQLConnection is disabled.

15. To set up property constraints, you are going to set up default settings for the SQLConnection object. Close the solution.

16. Open MyPolicy.TDL and add the following code in the policy file. Search for codeDataSQLConnection to find the correct location. Add the content in bold.

```
<ELEMENT>
<ID>codeDataSQLConnection</ID>
                <IDENTIFIERS>
                        <IDENTIFIER>
                                <TYPE>CODEVARIABLE</TYPE>
                                <IDENTIFIERDATA>
                                        <NAME>TYPENAME</NAME>

        <VALUE>System.Data.SqlClient.SqlConnection</VALUE>
                                </IDENTIFIERDATA>
                        </IDENTIFIER>
```

```
                                </IDENTIFIERS>
                                <FEATURELINKS>
                                        <TOOLBOXLINKS>
<TOOLBOXLINK>
tboxDataSQLConnection
</TOOLBOXLINK>
                                        </TOOLBOXLINKS>
                                </FEATURELINKS>
                                <CONSTRAINTS>
                                        <PROPERTYCONSTRAINTS>
                                                <PROPERTYCONSTRAINT>
                                                        <NAME>ConnectionString</NAME>
                                                        <DEFAULT>data source=localhost;
                        initial catalog=pubs;persist security
info=false;
   Integrated Security=SSPI;
   </DEFAULT>
                                                        <READONLY>0</READONLY>
                                                </PROPERTYCONSTRAINT>
                                        </PROPERTYCONSTRAINTS>
                                </CONSTRAINTS>
                        </ELEMENT>
```

17. Save your changes to the policy file.

18. Reopen the WindowsApplication1 project. Open Form1 in design mode and drag a SQLConnection object to the form. You will notice in the properties window for the newly created control that the ConnectionString property is filled in and is Read Only.

19. Save your solution, and you are finished.

In this exercise, you have seen how to add a policy file to a project and modify constraints for your environment.

These processes are guidelines to help with your development processes. If each developer understands these processes, it will help create a quality product and streamline your development. Processes are not just for the coding process. They involve the reviewing of code, design, and bug tracking. You probably do many of these processes already, but maybe you don't realize it.

Establishing Quality and Performance Metrics

Quality and performance metrics help to measure whether the application meets the planned expectations. Quality metrics is the examination of the quality of the code and the application. The goal of software quality is to reduce the time spent reworking code, either from requirements changes, design changes, or debugging errors. These metrics are the summary of the correct collection of requirements the correctness of the program logic and testing. Fixed date mindset is one method to enforce quality in an application. Bug convergence and zero bug bounce are two techniques for measuring the quality state of the solution and predicting the release date. Along with testing, managing the project effectively and determining organization performance goals also help with the quality of the product. The return on investment is the examination of how well the project went and how existing resources were utilized.

Fixed Ship Date Mindset

Having a fixed ship date mindset means having an attitude about schedules that helps the team meet due dates and establish the date the software will release to commercial users. It views a project's projected ship date as both realistic and unchangeable. The concept of a fixed ship date does not mean the date cannot change, but it does mean any variation from the planned schedule needs to be justified. The idea is to prevent *scope creep*—the tendency to add additional features over the course of development. Using a fixed ship date establishes a high-level goal for the development team to achieve, and it forces justification for additional features or design changes, which can cause the date to slip.

Bug Convergence

Bug convergence is the point where the rate of bugs resolved exceeds the rate of bugs found. This helps to provide an indicator to customers and key stakeholders of whether the project is on track. Typically, many bugs are found early in the testing process, and the rate of bugs found exceeds the number of bugs the team is able to resolve each day. Over time, however, fewer bugs are found on average every day, forming a downward trend line. If bug convergence actually occurs significantly later than the targeted bug convergence milestone date, then the team knows that the release date is at risk. Figure 9-1 is an example of bug convergence; and it details three things on the left side: days, number of new bugs found, and number of bugs resolved. Looking at the graph, you can see that the two different-colored lines will meet at day 8, showing when bug convergence happened.

FIGURE 9-1   Bug convergence

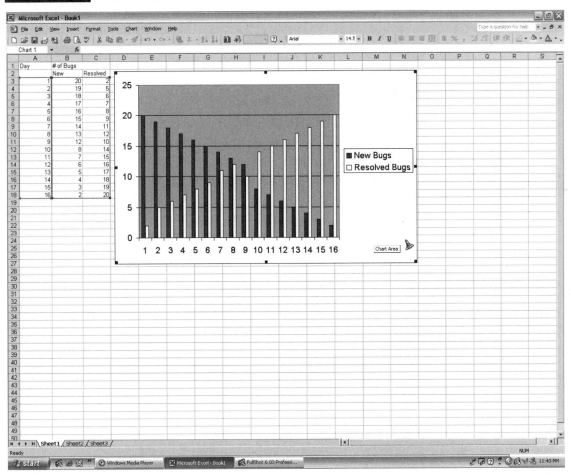

Note that if reported and fixed bug counts are not converging over a period of time, this is a warning sign that something serious is wrong with the project. Convergence fails to occur when as many new bugs are being reported as are being fixed. There are various explanations of what could be causing this, but the team must troubleshoot this as a serious issue.

Zero Bug Bounce

Zero bug bounce is when there are no active bugs, usually followed by a "bounce" in the number of active bugs. A "bounce" occurs when the product has finished testing a build cycle. This cycle could take place daily or on some other time interval. Zero bug bounce is a positive indicator for a project, indicating that development has caught up with the backlog of active bugs needing resolution. It is a sign that the quality of the builds are improving.

Evaluating Project Control

The evaluation of project control is the examination of the cost based on budget, project progress, and team performance. Many of these tasks can be performed by using traditional project management technologies and methods. The goal is to determine if the team knows what it is building, which goes back to planning the project. Effective planning reduces risks in such areas as defects, project costs, timing, and overall project quality. It sets up the project for success by providing more predictability, which in turn gives the team more control over outcomes. Effective project controls help to detect bugs early on, and costs can be controlled by examining what resources will be needed, when they will be needed, and how they will be utilized.

Evaluating Organizational Performance

Performance management includes activities to ensure that goals are met in an effective and efficient manner. It can focus on performance of the organization or department, or on the effectiveness of processes to build a solution. This is the examination of organizational members and processes. Just because a process has been used for years does not necessarily mean it should be used; it should be used only if it contributes directly to the preferred results of the organization. Performance management reminds us that being busy is not the same as producing results.

It reminds us that training, strong commitment, and lots of hard work alone are not results. Further, evaluation performance should not end with the completion of the project. After the project has been completed, it is a good practice to review and discuss how the organization can work better together and what processes worked as they should.

Identifying Return on Investment

Identifying the return on investment is analyzing the current situation and determining whether making the software changes saves money or increases revenue. The savings can be in the form of reduced maintenance costs, fewer employees, or less hardware. When looking at these areas, it helps to ask the following questions:

- Does the solution automate current manual tasks, and how much time does it save?
- Does the solution consolidate or remove outdated hardware or software?
- Can you get rid of unnecessary maintenance contracts?
- Does the solution require fewer developers or support staff to maintain than before?
- Does the solution create new revenue?

These are some examples of what to look for, but many other areas of possible savings can be included in calculating the return on investment.

CERTIFICATION SUMMARY

In this chapter, we examined standards and processes, which represent some guidelines for best practices. We started by examining standards, including coding, user interface, documentation, and testing standards. Coding standards look at rules and conventions for formatting code. There are great features in Visual Studio .NET to help with this process. The formatting options can be configured for all or specific languages. Without using the VS.NET environment, many of these options would be unavailable for you during development. The proper use of coding conventions helps other developers to understand your code. User interface standards help define a common look and feel with the use of common industry standards. An example would be the Microsoft user interface standards for XP, which detail appropriate user-interface standards for windows, menus, and other visual elements. Documentation standards help with the common communication of the team. Each team member understands the flow of information and what needs to be documented. Each team member can set up a level of expectation for common understanding. Testing standards help to improve customer confidence and software quality by putting in place policies and procedures for testing and by doing unit testing.

Processes discussed were design review, code review, creating builds, tracking issues, management of source code, changes and release management using Visual SourceSafe, and establishing maintenance tasks. Standardizing processes are the next evolution of the standards process. After defining what you want to record and keep track of, a process needs to follow to sequence the events. A design review helps you to determine if you know what you are going to build. It looks at a group collaboration of the ideas of different individuals who look at solutions in different ways. This helps the team to understand how the solution will be solved and helps other developers who could be dependent on your code to start evolving their process. Code review is the examination of completed code to make sure existing standards are followed and complex tasks are explained. The creation of builds is the heart of the iterative development process. These cycles include the compiling of code, deployment, and testing. They allow the team to determine the progress of the project. Visual SourceSafe is integrated with the Microsoft Visual Studio environment to help with the source code and deployment processes. Visual SourceSafe includes multiple configurations for handling this integration. This integration depends on your environment configuration.

Quality and performance metrics help to determine whether the team met the agreed upon goals and objectives. Project control metrics help to control both the nondevelopment and development processes. Some concepts used in this process include the fixed ship date mindset, bug convergence, and zero bug bounce. These concepts help establish the quality of the project and software. Organizational performance is evaluated by examining how well the team works together. This helps determine efficient process and employee practices. Finally, the identification of return on investment is the determination of the financial value of the solution.

✓ TWO-MINUTE DRILL

Establishing Standards

- ❑ Documentation standards define a collection of artifacts that help define information for multiple stages of a project.

- ❑ Coding principles help a developer with the formatting of source code and formatting conventions.

- ❑ User interface standards help define the look and feel of the user experience.

- ❑ Testing standards define what methods are used to provide unit testing and test configurations.

Establishing Processes

- ❑ Reviewing development documentation is the examination of the design of a solution or pieces of a solution.

- ❑ Reviewing code is a process for ensuring that developers follow the approved coding standards and conventions. This process helps other developers learn techniques to apply.

- ❑ Tracking issues is the identification and following of bugs and critical tasks that affect the development of the solution.

- ❑ Managing source code, changes, and releases can be performed using Microsoft Visual SourceSafe. This allows for the sharing of documents among developers and team members.

- ❑ Establishing maintenance tasks is the identification of supporting tasks and applications needed for the solution.

Establishing Quality and Performance Metrics

- ❑ Evaluating project control is the determination of the project schedule and the control of costs.

- ❑ Evaluating organizational performance is the analysis of processes and employees to determine what techniques are effective for the organization and the project.

- ❑ Identifying return on investment is determining the financial value of the solution for the business.

SELF TEST

Establishing Standards

1. You are writing the technical specifications document. The application is a web application. The requirement is to provide documentation in a physical form to the user and provide an online form of the documentation for the web application. Identify the correct user documentation types to meet the requirements. (Choose all that apply.)

   A. User manual

   B. HTML Help file

   C. Requirements documents

   D. CHM Help file

2. You are taking over the project midway through and you need to examine the high-level documents for the project. Choose the correct project documents. (Choose all that apply.)

   A. Requirements document

   B. Use case

   C. Response document

   D. Functional specifications

3. You are writing the developer standards document for coding. Identify which of the following statements is incorrect.

   A. _FirstName

   B. %FirstName

   C. firstName

   D. first_name

4. You are writing the testing plan. Identify which stage of testing is the most critical.

   A. Integration testing

   B. Regression testing

   C. Unit testing

   D. None of the above

5. You are writing support documentation. Identify the correct support documents for the solution. (Choose all that apply.)

   A. Security documents

   B. User manual

   C. Vision statement

   D. Deployment documents

6. You are writing developer coding standards. The previous application did not have good comments. Identify the correct statements for code comments. (Choose all that apply.)

   A. Avoid extraneous comments.

   B. Comments should explain the intent of the code.

   C. When bugs are found, comment them, note what caused the bugs, and note the fix for them.

   D. The use of asterisks (*) is a great way to comment code.

7. When performing a code review and using the naming conventions adopted from Microsoft; which of the following options correctly identify the naming of an interface?

   A. iEmployee

   B. Employee

   C. _Employee

   D. IEmployee

8. While creating coding standards for the application, identify the correct naming convention for a Boolean variable.

   A. TrueFlag

   B. IsEmployeeCreated

   C. CreateFlag

   D. Done

9. You are writing the technical specifications. Using the SQL standards, identify the prefixes not to use with stored procedures. (Choose all that apply.)

   A. xp_

   B. fn_

   C. sp_

   D. ep_

10. While creating standards for the development staff, it is necessary to identify development environment standards on environment settings. Identify the correct behavior if the tab size is not the same as the indent size and the Keep Tab option is selected to be included in the document.

    A. If the indent size is not a multiple of the tab size, space characters fill the remaining space.

    B. If the indent size is not an even multiple of the tab size, space characters fill the remaining space.

    C. If the indent size is not an even multiple of the tab size, space characters fill the remaining tab characters.

    D. If the indent size is not an even multiple of the tab size, all space characters fill the line.

11. You are creating the standards document. Identify the examples of good user interface to include in the document. (Choose all that apply.)

    A. Users can cancel out of transactions.

    B. The system does not display feedback at any time.

    C. To cancel an action, the action is named Cancel on some screens and Return on others.

    D. Consistent color schemes are used on each screen.

Establishing Processes

12. You are creating the testing plan. Identify the correct term for the following statement: "The rate of bugs resolved exceeds the rate of bugs found."

    A. Zero bug bounce

    B. Fixed ship date mindset

    C. Bug convergence

    D. Project control

13. You are creating the testing plan. Identify the correct term for indicating when there are no active bugs, usually followed by a "bounce" in the number of active bugs.

    A. Zero bug bounce

    B. Fixed ship date mindset

    C. Bug convergence

    D. Project control

14. You are creating the testing plan. Identify the correct term for describing the intention to release the software to commercial users on a certain date.

    A. Zero bug bounce

    B. Fixed ship date mindset

    C. Bug convergence

    D. Project control

15. You are creating the testing plan. Identify the correct term for describing the examination of the cost based on budget, project progress, and team performance.

    A. Zero bug bounce

    B. Fixed ship date mindset

    C. Bug convergence

    D. Project control

16. The development environment is to be established by creating isolated builds. Which of the following statements is correct for describing isolated builds? (Choose all that apply.)

    A. They do not require access to http://localhost. IIS does not need to be installed on every developer's computer.

    B. Visual SourceSafe supports shared (multiple) checkouts and the merge, branch, pin, and label commands.

    C. When any one user is debugging, the debug process locks the shared web server, preventing other users from working on projects on the same server.

    D. Each developer must maintain his or her IIS settings to a common standard.

17. The development environment is to be established by creating semi-isolated builds. Which of the following statements are correct for describing semi-isolated builds? (Choose all that apply.)

    A. Does not require access to http://localhost. IIS does not need to be installed on every developer's computer.

    B. It supports shared (multiple) checkouts and the merge, branch, pin, and label commands.

    C. When any one user is debugging, the debug process locks the shared web server, preventing other users from debugging projects on the same server.

    D. Each developer must maintain his or her IIS settings to a common standard.

18. The development environment is to be established by creating nonisolated builds. Which of the following statements are correct for nonisolated builds? (Choose all that apply.)

    A. It does not require access to http://localhost. IIS does not need to be installed on every developer's computer.

    B. It supports shared (multiple) checkouts and the merge, branch, pin, and label commands.

    C. When any one user is debugging, the debug process locks the shared web server, preventing other users from working on projects on the same server.

    D. File access is used.

19. You are creating the development standards. Identify the types of issues to be examined by the code reviews. (Choose all that apply.)

    A. Code syntax

    B. Standards

    C. Design

    D. Proof-of-concept

Establishing Quality and Performance Metrics

20. While examining the management of the solution, you want to keep an eye on items that can effect the return on investment (ROI) of the solution. Identify the positive ROI situations. (Choose all that apply.)

    A. Greater number of support personnel

    B. Reduction of staff

    C. Reduction of old hardware

    D. Increased support calls

LAB QUESTION

Create a C#.NET console application to copy web server log files from remote locations, preprocess them, and load them into a warehouse table. Then generate rollup information from the warehouse table and populate the report structures. The source servers and file locations will be stored on multiple key nodes in the config file that define a) the web server name, b) the file location of the logs, and c) the web site URL for which the logs describe traffic. All temporary files must be destroyed upon completion of processing, and all system notifications, successes, or failures should be written to the event log. The application config file should define a Panic Email key that should be used when a catastrophic failure occurs.

Identify the types of documents necessary to be created for this solution.

SELF TEST ANSWERS

Establishing Standards

1. ☑ **A, B, and D.** A user manual, HTML help, and .CHM files would allow the application to provide online and offline help.

    ☒ **C.** Requirements documents are considered project documentation.

2. ☑ **A, B, and D.** Requirements documents, functional specifications, and use cases are types of project documents.

    ☒ **C.** A response document is considered a developer document.

3. ☑ **B.** %FirstName is the correct answer. The percent symbol (%) is a special character and cannot start variable names.

    ☒ **A, C, and D** are incorrect because _FirstName, firstName, and first_name have the correct format for creating a variable.

4. ☑ **A.** Integration testing is the correct answer because you are combining solutions together, and integration of the application takes the most time and effort.

    ☒ **B, C, and D.** Regression testing and unit testing are important but the risk to these processes can be controlled.

5. ☑ **A and D.** Support documents contain details about how to secure and maintain the applications.

    ☒ **B and C.** The vision statement is a project document, and a user manual is a use document.

6. ☑ **A, B, and C.** Avoiding extra comments, explaining difficult sections of code, and commenting where bugs are found help to have readable code and are true statements about comments.

    ☒ **D.** The minimizing of asterisks help the readability of the resulting code.

7. ☑ **D.** The naming convention for interfaces is to start with a capital I.

    ☒ **A, B, and C.** These options are in the incorrect format for the interface syntax naming convention.

8. ☑ **B.** A Boolean field starts with an I and is descriptive.

    ☒ **A, C, and D.** TrueFlag and CreateFlag are incorrect because you do not want to use the work flag in the definition, and Done is incorrect because it is not descriptive and does not start with an I.

9. ☑ **A, B, and C.** The prefix xp_ is used as an extension for extended stored procedures. The prefix fn_ is used for system-defined functions, and sp_ is used for system-defined stored procedures.
☒ **D.** The ep_ prefix is valid and is not used by SQL as a system prefix.

10. ☑ **B.** The correct behavior for the indent size and the Keep Tab option is to fill in with space characters for the remainder if the indent size is not an even multiple of the tab size.
☒ **A, C, and D.** These are incorrect definitions for the behavior when the tab size is not the same as the indent size and the Keep Tab option is selected.

11. ☑ **A and D.** Examples of good user interface design are allowing the user to cancel out of transactions and using consistent color schemes. This gives the user the ability to correct mistakes and applys a consistent look and feel.
☒ **B and C.** Not displaying feedback and having inconsistent user interface elements creates a nonstandard application that will potentially confuse the user and increase the need for application support.

Establishing Processes

12. ☑ **C.** Bug convergence is where the rate of bugs resolved exceeds the rate of bugs found. This marks a milestone in the development. This date helps determine the release date schedule.
☒ **A, B, and D.** Zero bug bounce is a measure of the number of bugs found after testing has started. Project control is concerned with whether or not the project is on schedule and how much the project costs. A fixed ship date mindset allows the developers and team to help prevent scope creep.

13. ☑ **A.** Zero bug bounce is where there are no active bugs, but a new list of active bugs is found after testing.
☒ **B, C, and D.** A fixed ship date mindset allows the developers and team to help prevent scope creep. Bug convergence is the tracking of when the number of bugs resolved is lower than the number of bugs found. Project control is concerned with whether or not the project is on schedule and how much the project costs.

14. ☑ **B.** Fixed ship date mindset is having a projected release date of the software. This gives the team and the customer a way to determine if changes are necessary instead of waiting for the next release.
☒ **A, C, and D.** Zero bug bounce is a measure that tracks the number of bugs found after testing has started. Bug convergence is the tracking of when the number of bugs resolved is

lower than the number of bugs found. Project control is concerned with whether or not the project is on schedule and how much the project costs.

15. ☑ **D.** Project control is the examination of the cost, the progress, and the team performance on a project.
    ☒ **A** is incorrect because zero bug bounce is a measure that tracks the number of bugs found after testing has started. **B** is incorrect because a fixed ship date mindset helps the developers and the team prevent scope creep. **C** is incorrect because bug convergence tracks when the number of bugs resolved is lower then the number of bugs found.

16. ☑ **B and D.** With isolated builds, an IIS instance is required locally and multiple checkout is available.
    ☒ **A** is incorrect because isolated builds do require IIS to be on the developer's machine. **C** is incorrect because debugging is performed locally and is not shared, so there is no interference with other developers.

17. ☑ **A and C.** Semi-isolated builds do not require a local IIS, and because debugging is done against a shared instance, the developer debugging locks other developers from debugging against the server.
    ☒ **B** is incorrect because multiple checkouts, merge, and additional features are not supported on nonisolated builds. **D** is incorrect because each developer will not be maintaining IIS in this environment.

18. ☑ **A, C, and D.** Nonisolated builds do not require the developer to maintain a local IIS because multiple checkout is unavailable and file access is used.
    ☒ **B** is incorrect because you would not support multiple checkouts during nonisolated builds.

19. ☑ **A and B.** Code reviews look at the syntax of the code and where standards have been followed.
    ☒ **C and D** are incorrect because the design and proof-of-concept are determined before code is written; therefore, you would not perform these during a code review.

Establishing Quality and Performance Metrics

20. ☑ **B and C.** Reduction of staff and old hardware affect the return of investment by allowing the application to be more stable and have reduced support costs.
    ☒ **A and D** are incorrect because adding support personnel and increasing support calls and complaints affects the ROI by making the application one that will have constant maintenance and fixes. They also increase the support cost of the application.

LAB ANSWER

The console application would need project documents as follows: a functional specifications document to lay out the requirements necessary for the solution and to determine if the project team and the customer understand the needs of the solution. This document typically provides a high-level overview of the solution and the timelines for completion. The next document would be the technical specifications document. This document would detail the different layers of the application, such as that the user services would be the actual console application and that the data layer would be in SQL and in the file system. It is also necessary to keep key information for the solution in an app.config file that will also be defined in the document. The last document would be the deployment document. This document would detail how to create the SQL databases and tables necessary for the solution. It would also detail the specific environment variables for the different deployment environments and how to move the application into each environment.

MCSD
MICROSOFT® CERTIFIED SOLUTION DEVELOPER

Part III

Appendixes

APPENDIXES

A

About the
CD-ROM

The CD-ROM included with this book comes complete with MasterExam and an electronic version of the book. The software is easy to install on any Windows 98/NT/2000/XP computer, and must be installed to access the MasterExam feature. You may, however, browse the electronic book directly from the CD-ROM without installation. To register for the second bonus MasterExam, simply click the link on the Main Page and follow the directions to the free online registration.

System Requirements

Software requires Windows 98 or higher and Internet Explorer 5.0 or above and 20MB of hard disk space for full installation. The electronic book requires Adobe Acrobat Reader.

Installing and Running MasterExam

If your computer CD-ROM drive is configured to auto run, the CD-ROM will automatically start up upon inserting the disc. From the opening screen you may install MasterExam by pressing the MasterExam button. This will begin the installation process and create a program group named "LearnKey." To run MasterExam, use Start | Programs | LearnKey. If the auto run feature did not launch your CD-ROM, browse to the CD-ROM and click on the "RunInstall" icon.

MasterExam

MasterExam provides you with a simulation of the actual exam. The number of questions, type of questions, and the time allowed are intended to be an accurate representation of the exam environment. You have the option to take an open-book exam, including hints, references, and answers; a closed book exam; or the timed MasterExam simulation.

When you launch the MasterExam simulation, a digital clock will appear in the top-center of your screen. The clock will continue to count down to zero unless you choose to end the exam before the time expires.

Electronic Book

The entire contents of the Study Guide are provided in PDF. Adobe's Acrobat Reader has been included on the CD-ROM.

Help

A help file is provided through the help button on the main page in the lower left-hand corner. Individual help features are also available through MasterExam.

Removing Installation(s)

MasterExam is installed to your hard drive. For best results for removal of programs, use the Start | Programs | LearnKey | Uninstall options to remove MasterExam.

If you desire to remove the Real Player use the Add/Remove Programs Icon from your Control Panel. You may also remove the LearnKey training program from this location.

Technical Support

For questions regarding the technical content of the electronic book or MasterExam, please visit www.osborne.com or e-mail customer.service@mcgraw-hill.com. For customers outside the United States, e-mail: international_cs@mcgraw-hill.com.

LearnKey Technical Support

For technical problems with the software (installation, operation, removing installations), please visit www.learnkey.com or e-mail techsupport@learnkey.com.

B

Exam 70-300
Objective
Mapping
Document

T he following table is designed to help focus your exam preparation. Each exam objective is listed in the left column, with the corresponding chapter where that objective is addressed in the right column. These objectives were current on the Microsoft site at the time of the creation of this table. Because Microsoft reserves the right to change objectives without notice, you should check the exam site prior to finalizing your exam preparation.

Exam 70-300: Analyzing Requirements and Defining Microsoft .NET Solution Architectures	
Microsoft Exam Objective	Located in Chapter
Envisioning the Solution	
Develop a solution concept	2
Analyze the feasibility of the solution	2
Analyze the business feasibility of the solution	2
Analyze the technical feasibility of the solution	2
Analyze available organizational skills and resources	2
Analyze and refine the scope of the solution project	2
Identify the key risks	2
Gathering and Analyzing Business Requirements	
Gather and analyze business requirements	
Analyze the current business state	3
Analyze business processes	3
Analyze the organizational structure, both current and projected	3
Analyze vertical market position and industry position	3
Analyze personnel and training needs	3
Analyze the organizational political climate	3
Analyze business reach or scope	3

Exam 70-300: Analyzing Requirements and Defining Microsoft .NET Solution Architectures	
Microsoft Exam Objective	Located in Chapter
Analyze current and future regulatory requirements	3
Analyze business requirements for the solution	
Identify business requirements	3
Identify dependencies, both inside and outside the company	3
Identify features of the solution	3
Define design goals, such as extensibility requirements	3
Define data requirements, types, and flows	3
Create data flow diagrams	
Gather and analyze user requirements	
Identify use cases	3
Identify usage scenarios for each use case	
Identify globalization requirements	3
Identify localization requirements	3
Identify accessibility requirements	3
Gather and analyze operational requirements	3
Identify maintainability requirements	3
Identify scalability requirements	3
Identify availability requirements	3
Identify reliability requirements	
Identify deployment requirements	3
Identify security requirements	3
Gather and analyze requirements for hardware, software and network infrastructure	
Identify integration requirements	3
Analyze the IT environment, including current and projected applications, and current and projected hardware, software, and network infrastructure	3
Analyze the impact of the solution on the IT environment	3

Exam 70-300: Analyzing Requirements and Defining Microsoft .NET Solution Architectures	
Microsoft Exam Objective	Located in Chapter
Developing Specifications	
Transform requirements into functional specifications. Considerations include performance, maintainability, extensibility, scalability, availability, deployability, security, and accessibility	4
Transform functional specifications into technical specifications. Considerations include performance, maintainability, extensibility, scalability, availability, deployability, security, and accessibility	4
Select a development strategy	4
Select strategies for auditing and logging	4
Select strategies for error handling	4
Select strategies for integration	4
Select strategies for globalization	4
Select strategies for localization	4
Select strategies for data storage	4
Select strategies for state management	4
Include constraints in the development plan to support business rules. Constraints include data validation	4
Select a deployment strategy	4
Select strategies for deployment, such as coexistence strategies	4
Select strategies for licensing	4
Select strategies for data migration	4
Select a security strategy	4
Select strategies to ensure data privacy, such as encryption, signing, and sealing	4
Select strategies to ensure secure access	4
Select an operations strategy	
Select strategies for data archiving and data purging	
Select strategies for upgrades	
Create a support plan	

Exam 70-300: Analyzing Requirements and Defining Microsoft .NET Solution Architectures	
Microsoft Exam Objective	Located in Chapter
Create a test plan	4
Create a user education plan	4
Creating the Conceptual Design	6
Create a conceptual model of business requirements or data requirements. Methods include Object Role Modeling (ORM)	6
Transform external information into elementary facts	6
Apply a population check to fact types	6
Identify primitive entity types in the conceptual model	6
Apply uniqueness constraints to the conceptual model	6
Apply mandatory role constraints to the conceptual model	6
Add value constraints, set comparison constraints, and subtype constraints to the conceptual model	6
Add ring constraints to the conceptual model	6
Validate the conceptual design	6
Creating the Logical Design	7
Create the logical design for the solution	7
Create the logical design for auditing and logging	7
Create the logical design for error handling	7
Create the logical design for exception handling	7
Create the logical design for integration	7
Create the logical design for globalization	7
Create the logical design for localization	7
Create the logical design for security	7

Exam 70-300: Analyzing Requirements and Defining Microsoft .NET Solution Architectures	
Microsoft Exam Objective	**Located in Chapter**
Create the logical design for data privacy. Options include encryption, signing, and sealing.	7
Include constraints in the logical design to support business rules	7
Create the logical design for the presentation layer, including the user interface (UI)	7
Create the logical design for services and components	7
Create the logical design for state management	7
Create the logical design for synchronous or asynchronous architecture	7
Create the logical data model	7
Define tables and columns	7
Normalize tables	7
Define relationships	7
Define primary and foreign keys	7
Define XML schema	7
Validate the proposed logical design	7
Review the effectiveness of the proposed logical design in meeting business requirements. Business requirements include performance, maintainability, extensibility, scalability, and accessibility	7
Validate the proposed logical design against usage scenarios	7
Create a proof of concept for the proposed logical design	7
Creating the Physical Design	
Select the appropriate technologies for the physical design of the solution	
Create the physical design for the solution	
Create specifications for auditing and logging	8
Create specifications for error handling	8

Exam 70-300: Analyzing Requirements and Defining Microsoft .NET Solution Architectures	
Microsoft Exam Objective	Located in Chapter
Create specifications for physical integration	8
Create specifications for security	8
Specifications can apply to strategies for physical data privacy, such as encryption, signing, and sealing	8
Include constraints in the physical design to support business roles	8
Design the presentation layer, including the UI and online user assistance	8
Design services and components	8
Design the data flow between services	8
Design state management	8
Define the look-up data and the configuration data used by the application	8
Create the physical design for deployment	
Create deployment specifications, which can include coexistence and distribution	8
Create licensing specifications	8
Create data migration specifications	8
Design the upgrade path	8
Create the physical design for maintenance	8
Design application monitoring	8
Create the physical design for the data model	8
Create an indexing specification	8
Partition Data	8
Denormalize tables	8
Validate the physical design	8

Exam 70-300: Analyzing Requirements and Defining Microsoft .NET Solution Architectures	
Microsoft Exam Objective	Located in Chapter
Review the effectiveness of the proposed physical design in meeting the business requirements. Business requirements include performance, maintainability, extensibility, scalability, availability, deployability, security, and accessibility	8
Validate use cases, scenario walkthroughs, and sequence diagrams	8
Create a proof of concept for the proposed physical design	8
Creating Standards and Processes	
Establish standards. Standards can apply to development, documentation, coding, code review, UI, and testing	9
Establish processes. Processes include reviewing development documentation, reviewing code, creating builds, tracking issues, managing source code, managing change, managing release, and establishing maintenance tasks. Methods include Microsoft Visual Studio .NET Enterprise Templates	9
Establish quality and performance metrics to evaluate project control, organizational performance, and return on investment	9

INDEX

C

F

H

Q

R

S

T

X

INTERNATIONAL CONTACT INFORMATION

AUSTRALIA
McGraw-Hill Book Company Australia Pty. Ltd.
TEL +61-2-9900-1800
FAX +61-2-9878-8881
http://www.mcgraw-hill.com.au
books-it_sydney@mcgraw-hill.com

CANADA
McGraw-Hill Ryerson Ltd.
TEL +905-430-5000
FAX +905-430-5020
http://www.mcgraw-hill.ca

GREECE, MIDDLE EAST, & AFRICA
(Excluding South Africa)
McGraw-Hill Hellas
TEL +30-210-6560-990
TEL +30-210-6560-993
TEL +30-210-6560-994
FAX +30-210-6545-525

MEXICO (Also serving Latin America)
McGraw-Hill Interamericana Editores S.A. de C.V.
TEL +525-117-1583
FAX +525-117-1589
http://www.mcgraw-hill.com.mx
fernando_castellanos@mcgraw-hill.com

SINGAPORE (Serving Asia)
McGraw-Hill Book Company
TEL +65-6863-1580
FAX +65-6862-3354
http://www.mcgraw-hill.com.sg
mghasia@mcgraw-hill.com

SOUTH AFRICA
McGraw-Hill South Africa
TEL +27-11-622-7512
FAX +27-11-622-9045
robyn_swanepoel@mcgraw-hill.com

SPAIN
McGraw-Hill/Interamericana de España, S.A.U.
TEL +34-91-180-3000
FAX +34-91-372-8513
http://www.mcgraw-hill.es
professional@mcgraw-hill.es

UNITED KINGDOM, NORTHERN,
EASTERN, & CENTRAL EUROPE
McGraw-Hill Education Europe
TEL +44-1-628-502500
FAX +44-1-628-770224
http://www.mcgraw-hill.co.uk
computing_europe@mcgraw-hill.com

ALL OTHER INQUIRIES Contact:
McGraw-Hill/Osborne
TEL +1-510-420-7700
FAX +1-510-420-7703
http://www.osborne.com
omg_international@mcgraw-hill.com